# Praise for Church Privacy 101

I recommend *Church Privacy 101*. Every church leader and church member needs to avoid violating privacy and intruding on certain private matters. Privacy is important. In my 23 years as an associate minister, my privacy has been violated on different occasions by fellow leaders and members. I didn't like it, but I also didn't confront the individuals who made my private information public. Truthfully, I've gone against my own privacy needs at times by sharing when I knew I didn't desire to do so. *Church Privacy 101* empowers people to recognize their privacy needs to not share all their business with everyone in church and outside, and to protect what they share. I'm very cautious with certain private information about myself for many reasons, not limited to safety. The older I get, the more private I am.

Roxanne Zeigler, Paralegal, Retired Nurse, and Minister

This is the book everyone wishes they wrote, but they were too scared to do it. Grace is a fearless slayer. She killed it, period!

Peyton Moses, Churchgoer

My, my, my! Grace is the most exciting and engaging global privacy expert ever! I connected with her right away. I totally feel her passion. This book is a huge gift to humanity, not just churchgoers! Grace has helped me rethink some wrongly held beliefs about privacy. I dove into this book thinking about one or two privacy issues, but by the time I finished, I lost count. This is wisdom I need for myself and to pass on to our church, friends, my children, and their children. Everyone needs to read this book!

Lynn Williams, Care Minister and Counselor

Life-changing! Perfect for a book club just for my family and friends. We need to respect each other's privacy more and stop hurting ourselves.

Erline Brooks, Church Usher and Event Planner

Masterfully written and right on time! In the age of social media, influencers, and most recently, artificial intelligence, there is a renewed need to understand the importance of privacy and the effects of disregarding it. Let's get "real" about how we do our Father's business and how we do church if we are to have the impact on society and in the lives of believers that we hope to. I often hear that churches are the hospital for the sick and sinners—where we go to learn about and how to live for the One who provides wholeness and restoration. And if churches are the hospitals for sinners, then their number one priority is to protect the privacy of their patients. Grace does an amazing job providing relevant and relatable stories that show readers the impact of privacy in every aspect of society and how relationships, organizations, nations, and even churches are destroyed when privacy is not taken seriously.

Elizabeth A. Hannah, Churchgoer

# CHURCH PRIVACY 101

Church Privacy 101

Copyright © 2024 by Grace Buckler.

First Edition: Published in Washington DC by NAD Publishing, Washington DC, 20044
www.NadPublishing.com.
Request for information should be sent to info@nadpublishing.com.

All rights reserved. No part of this book may be reproduced, amended, stored in a retrieval system, used, distributed, sold, or transmitted in any form or by any means—digital, electronic, mechanical, recordings, photocopy, or other—except quotations in printed reviews or articles, without prior written permission of the author or publisher.

All Scripture quotations, unless otherwise stated are taken from the Holy Bible, New International Version® NIV®. Copyright © 1973, 1978, 1984, 2011 by Biblica Inc.™ Used by permission of Zondervan. All rights reserved worldwide. www.zondervan.com. The "NIV" And "New International Version" are trademarks registered in the United States Patent and Trademark office by Biblica, Inc.™

Scripture quotations marked (NLT) are taken from the *Holy Bible, New Living Translation*, copyright © 1996, 2004, 2007, 2013 by Tyndale House Foundation. Used by permission of Tyndale House Publishers, Inc., Carol Stream, Illinois 60188. All rights reserved.

Scripture quotations marked (ESV) are taken from The Holy Bible, English Standard Version® (ESV®), copyright © 2001 by Crossway, a publishing ministry of Good News Publishers. Used by permission. All rights reserved.

Scripture quotations marked (NKJV) are taken from the New King James Version®. Copyright © 1982 by Thomas Nelson. Used by permission. All rights reserved.

Scripture quotations marked (KJV) are from the King James Version of the Bible.

Illustration by Anna Trubina
Author's Photo by Teron James

**Publisher's Cataloging-in-Publication Data**

Names: Buckler, Grace, author.
Title: Church privacy 101: how to protect your privacy in and out of church / Grace Buckler.
Description: Includes bibliographical references. | Washington, D.C.: NAD Publishing, 2024.
Identifiers: LCCN: 2023952586 | ISBN: 978-1-7369478-7-6 (hardcover) | 978-1-7369478-0-7 (paperback) | 978-1-7369478-4-5 (ebook)
Subjects: LCSH Privacy, Right of. | Privacy--Moral and ethical aspects. | United States--Religious life and customs. | Confidential communications--Clergy. | Data privacy--United States. | Christian life. | BISAC SELF-HELP / Safety & Security / General | RELIGION / Christian Living / General | FAMILY & RELATIONSHIPS / General
Classification: LCC JC596 .B83 2024 | DDC 323.44/8--dc23

Library of Congress Control Number: 2023952586

Printed in the United States of America

# CHURCH PRIVACY 101

## HOW TO PROTECT YOUR PRIVACY IN AND OUT OF CHURCH

## GRACE BUCKLER

# Resources By Grace Buckler

*Church Privacy 101*

*Church Privacy Team*

*Church Privacy: Who Cares? You!*

# Motivate and Inspire Others!

## Share These Books

### Special Quantity or Bulk Orders

Buy 10 or more books for a 30–40% discount.

To place an order, visit NADPublishing.com.

Scan the QR code for discounts.

NAD Publishing titles may be purchased in bulk at a discount for educational, business, fundraising, event, or promotional use. Custom imprinting or excepting is available to fit special event or branding needs. For general information, please reach us at NADPublishing.com.

# LEGAL NOTICE AND DISCLAIMER

Please note that the information in this book offers a broad application of privacy best practices, implementation, and goals. You are responsible for your own choices and actions either directly or indirectly. Your results will be highly dependent on your efforts, the scope of your data collection activities, and your legal and regulatory obligations. Individual church environments and applicable laws are different and require consultation with a licensed professional for assessment and insights. You acknowledge that the information contained within this book is for educational and awareness purposes only. Please consult a licensed professional for more customized guidance and advice that is tailored to your specific church and your needs. All effort has been made to present general, accurate, reliable, up-to-date, and relevant information. No warranties of any kind are declared or implied. Note that the author is not engaging in the rendering of legal, financial, medical, IT, security, or professional advice. Therefore, the reader acknowledges that under no circumstances is the author or publisher responsible for any direct or indirect losses incurred as a result of the use of the information contained within this book, including (but not limited to) errors, omissions, or inaccuracies.

Any company information, products, website addresses, phone numbers, or links referenced in this book are offered as resources and for illustration purposes. They are not intended in any way to be or to imply endorsements.

Details and names in some anecdotes and stories have been changed to protect the privacy or identities of the persons involved.

To my mom, Annah,
and to my grandmothers, Lydia and Gracè.

To everyone who could use a little privacy and to
those who don't judge them.

*So whatever you wish that others would do to you, do also to them, for this is the Law and the Prophets.*
(Matthew 7:12 ESV)

# SUMMARY OF CONTENTS

| | |
|---|---|
| Acknowledgements | 1 |
| Introduction | 3 |
| 1. A Church Lady Gets Sued Over Privacy | 21 |
| 2. What Is Privacy? | 44 |
| 3. Five Things the Bible Says to Hush About | 76 |
| 4. Managing Your Circle | 99 |
| 5. Finding Confidants in Church | 122 |
| 6. Confession Privacy Sacred Confidence | 140 |
| 7. Financial Privacy: Money Matters | 162 |
| 8. Personal Privacy: Emotional and Physical Well-Being | 181 |
| 9. Mental Health Privacy: The Illusion of Perfection | 200 |
| 10. Medical Privacy: Your Body Is the Temple | 219 |
| 11. Privacy in Marriage and Courtship | 244 |
| 12. Parenting and Privacy at Home | 271 |
| 13. Family Privacy and Safety | 288 |
| 14. Privacy in Your Relationships | 317 |
| 15. Keep Your Private Life Private | 331 |
| 16. Privacy in the Workplace | 366 |
| 17. Privacy in the Afterlife | 389 |
| 18. People Who Leave the Church | 411 |
| Conclusion | 428 |
| Church Privacy Team: Introduction | 439 |
| Further Reading | 453 |
| Connect with Grace beyond the Page | 454 |
| About Grace | 457 |
| Ways You Can Engage with Grace throughout the Year | 459 |
| Available Anywhere Books and E-books Are Sold | 462 |
| Special FREE Bonus Gift for You | 464 |
| Additional Training Resources | 465 |
| Church Privacy Team: Introduction Notes | 468 |
| Notes | 470 |

# Contents

ACKNOWLEDGEMENTS ... 1

INTRODUCTION ... 3

    How Privacy Violations Led to the Holocaust ... 7

    A New Perspective on Privacy ... 9

    Empowering People ... 12

    Great Relationships Are Golden ... 17

    How and Why ... 19

## 1. A CHURCH LADY GETS SUED OVER PRIVACY ... 21

    Privacy Goes Public ... 21

        Who was Sister Bodil Lindqvist? What was her crime? ... 23

        Globally, how did the church react? ... 25

        What did Mrs. Lindqvist say in her defense? ... 26

        Well, did she commit the crime she was accused of? ... 26

        How did the court come to their decision and why? ... 26

        What exactly was the content of the web pages she got sued over? ... 27

        Although she deleted them immediately, it was still too late? ... 27

 If she had the photo in her photo album or on her device, would it have been okay? ...... 28

 What was her punishment for this crime? ...... 28

It's Not Just about Technology ...... 30

What Is Personal Information? ...... 33

Privacy Q &A and Principles ...... 34

Privacy Principles ...... 40

Privacy Is Essential and Lawful ...... 41

## 2. WHAT IS PRIVACY? ...... 44

The Unknown Need ...... 44

 Privacy has many definitions and uses. ...... 45

 Is there another word for privacy? ...... 46

 Does the Bible have another word for privacy? ...... 47

 Does the meaning of privacy depend on who you ask? ...... 47

 There is a private cost to being a public figure. ...... 49

 There's no privacy in the public eye. ...... 49

 There is sanctity in solitude. ...... 51

 There is relief in emotional release. ...... 52

 Privacy is good medicine. ...... 53

 Privacy is about having choices. ...... 54

 The drama of life is at play. ...... 55

Familiarity breeds contempt. ........................................................ 58

Privacy affects our close and intimate relationships. .......... 59

Enjoy a day of rest. ..................................................................... 61

Privacy provides focus. ............................................................. 62

Is sharing or disclosing personal stuff healthy? ................... 64

Dealing with organizations regarding your privacy
is important. ................................................................................. 66

**Protect Your Privacy** ...................................................................... 69

What types of personal information should your
church protect? ............................................................................ 73

Privacy doesn't mean only one thing. ..................................... 74

# 3. FIVE THINGS THE BIBLE SAYS TO HUSH ABOUT ........ 76

Does the Bible Value Privacy? ..................................................... 76

Your Prayers .................................................................................... 77

Your Fasts ........................................................................................ 80

Your Offering .................................................................................. 81

Your Body ........................................................................................ 83

Even when you're not strutting your stuff,
you may be watched. ................................................................. 84

Sexual Intimacy .............................................................................. 86

Situational Privacy ........................................................................ 86

Church Privacy Myths ... 91

    Be intentional and discreet. ... 97

## 4. MANAGING YOUR CIRCLE ... 99

Making Onion Rings ... 99

    Preparation is key. ... 100

Plan for Change ... 104

    What happens next? ... 104

    The wise men understood that a privacy breach could get a baby killed. ... 104

    Queen Esther's privacy prevented discrimination and distraction. ... 105

    Check your heart before you share people's private business. ... 107

The Gossip Detection Test ... 108

Privacy and Betrayal ... 110

    Privacy invasions and betrayals occur in your church. ... 112

    When admiration turns to envy, privacy is at stake. ... 113

    The trials of Joash were originally privacy battles. ... 114

    Moses escaped death. ... 115

    Personal information is in the hands of malicious former friends. ... 116

    Samson shared his password. ... 117

Does God have privacy? Does he protect it? ... 119

Does God violate privacy? ... 120

## 5. FINDING CONFIDANTS IN CHURCH ... 122

### Partners in Privacy ... 122

### Be the Friend You Want to Have ... 124

People add value. ... 126

What are the benefits of a church support network? ... 128

Is everyone in church trustworthy? ... 128

Can you have a trusted confidant without a close relationship? ... 130

Read between the lines to uncover their trustworthiness. ... 131

How does God make friends? ... 131

Should you trust all good friends and confidants equally? ... 132

Can privacy needs stop you from enjoying fellowship in church? ... 134

There's a privacy rock star in you. ... 135

Should you forgive someone who has violated your privacy? ... 137

How do you create fellowship? ... 137

Should I share when I fellowship? ... 138

## 6. CONFESSION PRIVACY SACRED CONFIDENCE ... 140

### Between You and God Alone ... 140

The Race of Your Life ... 144

Do your homework. ... 147

DIY confession is flexible and gives you privacy control. ... 148

### Can Your Private Confessions in Church Go Public? ... 150

Prophesied confessions are public but have a benefit. ... 153

There are risks to keeping secrets in church. ... 155

Watch out for the confession culture. ... 156

Even on Sundays, confessors need privacy protection no matter when, where, and with whom they confess. ... 157

### Helping to Heal ... 159

A court order can require an investigation and the release of church records. ... 160

## 7. FINANCIAL PRIVACY: MONEY MATTERS ... 162

### Lack of Discernment Will Cost You ... 162

Harold's story ... 163

Etta's story ... 164

Keep your financial business quiet. ... 165

Don't give with expectations. ... 166

Privacy is peace. ...................................................................167

Helen's story ...........................................................................168

Kelly's story .............................................................................169

Allison's story .........................................................................170

Avoid judgment without knowledge. ...............................170

These Houston, Texas, church stories are about privacy, not just cash. ...........................................................................171

Lending to friends comes with its own privacy complexities. .............................................................175

Don't let your giving turn into an enabling gesture. ....175

Lending and borrowing require trust. ..............................177

Save your friendship. .............................................................178

## 8. PERSONAL PRIVACY: EMOTIONAL AND PHYSICAL WELL-BEING ...............................................181

### Health Privacy .....................................................................181

### Emotional Health and Wellness ....................................186

Don't let domestic violence and abuse become your secret. ................................................................................189

Identify dangerous people and situations. .....................190

Impotence is private, but healing begins when you talk—to the right person. ..........................................192

Knowledge is power. ..............................................................195

    Keep your onion small. ...... 196

    Dangerous Decisions ...... 197

## 9. MENTAL HEALTH PRIVACY: THE ILLUSION OF PERFECTION ...... 200

    Don't Judge a Book by Its Cover ...... 200

        How depression creeps in is unreckonable. ...... 202

        Offer support and guidance to someone who needs it. ...... 203

        Doing God's work also means accepting responsibility for preserving privacy. ...... 206

        Honor privacy choices even when private information about a person is known. ...... 207

    Dealing with Loss ...... 209

        The loss of a loved one can lead to decisions one shouldn't have to explain. ...... 211

        Till death do us part? ...... 212

        The loss of a job is a delicate matter and seldom makes sense. ...... 214

        Listen intently to others. ...... 216

## 10. MEDICAL PRIVACY: YOUR BODY IS THE TEMPLE ...... 219

    Family and Heritage ...... 219

        Be careful with your DNA. ...... 221

**Privacy and Hospitalization** ........................................................... 223

    Be a good hospital patient. .................................................... 225

    Be a good hospital visitor. ..................................................... 226

    Bring good cheer and laughter. ............................................. 228

    Be sure to protect personal health information. ..................... 229

    Out of the mouths of babes privacy can be violated. ............. 230

    Selfies and photos are private even if patients say yes
    to taking them. ....................................................................... 231

    Praying is almost always appreciated, but sharing
    without consent is a different matter. .................................... 232

    Is there conflict or tension? ................................................... 233

**Health Tests and Privacy** ................................................................ 234

    Mrs. Lacks was a modern miracle who
    changed history. ..................................................................... 234

    Genetic information abuse is a critical privacy concern. ....... 235

    Are you signing your privacy away? ....................................... 237

    John Moore's story .................................................................. 239

**11. PRIVACY IN MARRIAGE AND COURTSHIP** ................. 244

    **A More Perfect Union** ......................................................... 244

        When should you start asking questions, and
        what should you ask? ......................................................... 245

        Make smart moves. ............................................................ 245

Premarital counseling rarely goes in depth on critical privacy matters. ... 248

Know who you're marrying. ... 250

**Discussion Points** ... 251

To each his own? ... 257

Dealing with trust issues can be tricky. ... 257

Is social media driving up divorce rates? ... 259

The devil is in the details. ... 260

Don't succumb to temptation. ... 262

Revenge porn is not always about payback. ... 263

Just because you can doesn't mean you should. ... 269

## 12. PARENTING AND PRIVACY AT HOME ... 271

### Protecting Your Children and Their Privacy ... 271

Children, teens, and young adults are often denied privacy. ... 272

When parental intrusion is important. ... 275

Balancing privacy and parenting is a must. ... 279

Pay it forward. ... 281

### Home Privacy ... 283

Home sweet home is where privacy lives—until relatives arrive. ... 284

## 13. FAMILY PRIVACY AND SAFETY ... 288

### Airing Our Dirty Laundry ... 288

Photos and recordings can help expose and clean up some laundry. ... 291

Recording conversations is a privacy issue. ... 292

Suicide is the silent killer. ... 295

Protecting your children from privacy invasions starts the day they're born. ... 297

Adults justify the inside job of ruining children's futures. ... 299

Parental wisdom is not old-school. ... 300

Don't invite strangers into your bedroom. ... 301

The sins of the fathers hunt the children. ... 304

Is there a Decker in your family? ... 306

Reforming the likes of Decker in church is a privacy issue. ... 306

Teach your youth online discretion. ... 312

There's no such thing as free. ... 313

There's always a price to pay. ... 313

## 14. PRIVACY IN YOUR RELATIONSHIPS ... 317

### Creating Authentic Relationships ... 317

The bond of friendship is held together when there's trust and privacy. ... 319

When the Bond of Friendship Breaks ... 323

Be a Good Neighbor ... 327

Random acts of privacy kindness is neighborly. ... 327

## 15. KEEP YOUR PRIVATE LIFE PRIVATE ... 331

Manage Your Inner Circle ... 331

Who to tell and what you share should be grouped. ... 333

When singles become a couple, privacy must be transparent. ... 339

Wedding bells are ringing. ... 340

What if you're not invited to the wedding? ... 341

Invasive Questions ... 345

Do we need to justify our choices? ... 346

How do you answer privacy-invading questions? ... 349

Invaders shouldn't say everything they think. ... 351

Setting Privacy Boundaries ... 353

Be held accountable. ... 356

Our Confidants ... 359

Transparency is a choice. ... 361

Needing space is okay. ... 363

## 16. PRIVACY IN THE WORKPLACE .......... 366

### The Best of Both Worlds .......... 366

Working for God means caring for needs and obeying authority. .......... 367

### Consistency Inside and Outside of the Church .......... 375

Strive for excellence. .......... 377

Do unto others . . . .......... 379

Be an influencer. .......... 380

Ignorance is not bliss. .......... 381

What could possibly go wrong? .......... 381

Who will the law make an example of next? .......... 382

Litigation awaits church workers who steal. .......... 384

The peril of payback is that you end up losing more. .......... 385

Be a catalyst for change. .......... 387

## 17. PRIVACY IN THE AFTERLIFE .......... 389

### Privacy Is for the Living .......... 389

The pain of the past controls the present. .......... 390

Honoring the dearly departed means being in the moment. .......... 390

Family feuds can be avoided. .......... 391

Take a stand for privacy and peace. .......... 393

    Do not disturb. ................................................................................ 394

    Choose who should deliver the sad news. ....................... 396

**Death of Privacy—Wills and Probate** ................................... 397

    Who gets the kids? ......................................................................... 403

    What if death is not quick? ....................................................... 404

**The Cost of Saying Goodbye** ........................................................ 405

    Beneficiaries—who's getting what? ...................................... 405

    Protect your progress. ................................................................... 405

    Online forms and templates can help, but protect your privacy. .......................................................................................... 406

    Exclude people, but don't announce it. ............................. 407

    Don't get ghosted. .......................................................................... 408

## 18. PEOPLE WHO LEAVE THE CHURCH ........................ 411

**God Is Calling Me Elsewhere** ..................................................... 411

    Truth is exposed, not discovered. ......................................... 413

    Jana's story ............................................................................................ 415

    Be careful of your reaction. ...................................................... 417

    Louann's story ................................................................................... 418

    Pam's story ........................................................................................... 421

The Point ... 423

    Pray for your friends and move forward. ... 424

    Privacy is not paranoia. ... 425

    Privacy Conflict Resolution in the Church ... 425

CONCLUSION ... 428

    Our Privacy Journey ... 428

    The Evolution of Privacy Laws ... 433

Church Privacy Team: Introduction ... 439

Further Reading ... 453

Connect with Grace beyond the Page ... 454

About Grace ... 457

Ways You Can Engage with Grace throughout the Year ... 459

Available Anywhere Books and E-books Are Sold ... 462

Special FREE Bonus Gift for You ... 464

Additional Training Resources ... 465

Church Privacy Team: Introduction Notes ... 468

Notes ... 470

# Acknowledgements

I'm so glad God created readers! I thank God for my calling and for giving me the foresight and direction for this book. And I thank God for you, reader! Thanks for encouraging me to finish this book as well as my other books, *Church Privacy: Who Cares? You!* and *Church Privacy Team*. Thanks for allowing me to refurbish and share some of your personal privacy stories and hurts to help other churchgoers and faith leaders for the good of the greater church. In many ways, you've helped me gain insight into my own life. I pray that your personal privacy habits and the privacy practices and traditions in your church improve for your sake and for those you care about!

To my phenomenal editorial team, Callie, Pam, Carol, Lady Rhoda, Stephanie, Alex, Josh, and Gabrielle, thanks for staying committed through thick and thin. Your talents amaze me! Thanks for making this series a success and a critical resource for churches all over the globe.

I thank the many churchgoers, nonchurchgoers, and faith leaders I've met along the way, some of whom have already contacted me about how the books in this series have impacted their lives. I truly enjoy connecting and bonding with you even outside of my own local community.

To my family (Kiss Kiss), friends, professional circles, leadership circles, privacy students, awesome church and Sunday school family, and NAD Publishing, I love you! Let me say that again. I love you! Your prayers and encouragement mean so much to me.

You all deserve a spa treatment!

*Whatever you have learned or received or heard from me, or seen in me—put it into practice. And the God of peace will be with you.*

(Philippians 4:9)

# Introduction

"I can't believe John is now in this category of people in my life. Who would have thought?" Frustrated, Elias jammed his key into the rental car's ignition and dropped his head onto the steering wheel.

"Help me, Lord! Just help me!"

He gathered himself together and drove out of the driveway as George looked on from his front porch.

Elias had been going through a rough patch in his marriage. He decided to confide in John, a friend who was a minister at another church he sometimes visited. John usually asked if he had any prayer requests. Elias never had anything specific, but on that day, he decided to open up to John and share that he was going through marital problems and that he and his wife were living separately. John told Elias he would pray on it.

A week later, Elias visited John's dad, George, to bring him a few essentials. George was getting on in years, and it wasn't always easy for him to get around. Elias wasn't the only one who stopped by to see him that day. A few relatives were visiting. As everyone milled around, George asked Elias why his wife had left him. Elias was surprised and too embarrassed to answer as George asked even more personal questions about his marriage. Elias was still hopeful things would work out with his wife and never would have confided in George. Although he respected him, he knew George was a talker. What made it even worse was that George asked him extremely personal questions in the presence of others, who were now waiting expectantly for answers. Flustered and embarrassed, Elias hurriedly said his goodbyes and left.

Not long after, Elias expressed his concerns to John about what he'd done. John seemed taken aback that he was upset.

"We all care about you," John retorted. "When I visit my family, we pray together, and I asked my dad to pray for you. What harm can he possibly do? Besides, it's not a life-or-death situation."

An apology and empathy would have soothed Elias' hurt. But John was unapologetic about disclosing his friend's personal affairs, which he had been told in confidence. An apology was far from John's mind. So was compassion. He didn't even admit he'd violated Elias' privacy. Instead, he expressed disappointment that Elias, of all people, was acting paranoid. He not only invalidated Elias' concerns, but also disregarded his feelings. Elias didn't share anything else with John, even when he called weeks later and asked how things were going. For Elias, their sacred trust was forever broken. He no longer trusted John—and was careful about what he shared with him. He didn't visit John's church as often as he used to.

Years ago, I worked as a junior consultant for a global firm in Vienna, Virginia. After a meeting with the CEO, I discovered that Andrew, the new hire who'd just joined our team, was not really new. The CEO explained how Andrew had previously worked for the company for more than four years. He was an overachiever and fully committed. Then one day, he quit. This wasn't strange to me. After all, employees leave companies for what they believe are better opportunities, which is what the CEO also thought. However, Andrew hadn't left because he'd gotten a better offer. In fact, he had loved his job. He had left because his new supervisor and team members had trivialized his concerns about some work practices, which had made Andrew complicit. As a result, he had lost trust in his team. He had felt like a fraud, and it had become unbearable for him to do his job unethically. But he hadn't wanted to seem like a troublemaker, so he had left quietly.

The CEO found this out when he ran into Andrew years later at a function, and Andrew opened up about why he had left. He loved the company and wanted to keep growing there, but he could not work under that super-

# Introduction

visor and team. It became clear Andrew had quit his team, *not* the company. The CEO made him an offer and rehired him. Andrew's story was told on many occasions. The firm used this insight to teach employees about transparency—open discussions about negative experiences—for the purpose of making changes to protect everyone.

This way of thinking should be adopted by churches. Your church. Churchgoers don't normally quit churches. They quit the people. They quit members, ministry leaders, preachers who violate their privacy, and those who react with inhumanity when privacy is violated. And if a member withdraws because their trust is violated, the church should take notice, make every effort to extend the person a delicate response, and come up with a thoughtful remedy. As a member, would your church or ministry leaders care if you left because of the devastation of a privacy violation? As a ministry leader, would you prefer to have an unbiased conversation and help correct the emotional damage in a safe environment to help a wounded member whose confidence was crushed? Or would you rather condemn them after they've taken their grievance elsewhere? And hopefully not to court. Elias didn't quit the church he really enjoyed visiting; he quit the minister. As a result, he also lost the great relationship he'd had with that church community.

When Donna Williams reported catching a fellow church member going into her phone and reading her text exchanges, her pastor's response was, "I'm not called for these types of issues." He even berated her for mentioning it. "You and your husband are one of the most respected families in this church. You have nothing to hide. Or *do you?*" She certainly didn't feel comforted or even heard. In addition to having her privacy violated and her trust in the church member destroyed, she couldn't believe her pastor wasn't taking the matter seriously, even implying that she might be in the wrong. Does expecting privacy make her an immature or paranoid Christian? Could her preacher be wrong, and should she file a police report? She found herself in a terrible dilemma.

Who do you think was right? The preacher or Mrs. Williams?

You may be thinking of privacy in only one way. Privacy is not only the need to be alone and in private or the absence of negative people, activities, or things. Privacy is also your personal need for freedom from invasion and intrusion by things—technology or people—regardless of whether they are good or bad. It's your need, right, and choice to set certain limits to block access to your things, behavior, activities, information, preferences, beliefs, and choices—and not to be secretly monitored, watched, or observed. These are necessary boundaries that change or adjust to your needs in different circumstances and relationships. Limits set for your significant other, relatives, coworkers, church community, or neighbors will vary. Privacy is also about what you choose to disclose to people and how you expect them to handle that information.

Privacy is the reason doors, windows, keys, locks, walls, rooms, fences, and passwords exist. It is why websites encrypt your payment information and why you keep important personal documents in a safe and secure place. Privacy is the reason financial transactions at your bank are undisclosed, even to your loved ones, unless authorized, and why your doctor shuts the door before asking personal questions. Privacy is the reason closing the divider in a hospital room makes you feel more relaxed and at ease. Privacy is why you whisper when sharing your opinion with the person sitting next to you in church, at a wedding, in a meeting, or on a train. Wanting privacy does not make us selfish, self-centered, immature, or paranoid. It does not mean we are scheming or up to no good.

Privacy dates back to when the first humans hid themselves among the trees in the Garden of Eden (Genesis 3:8). When God called out to Adam

Introduction

to show himself, Adam said, "God, wait a sec. We're not dressed." It's not an exact quote, but you get the point. The rest of the story is history.

Fast-forward to 1791, when the US constitutional amendments, the Bill of Rights, went into effect to protect your beliefs (First Amendment), your home from the government mandating that it be used to host soldiers (Third Amendment), your person from unreasonable searches and seizures by law enforcement agents (Fourth Amendment), and, among other things, protect you from yourself so you don't shake in your boots and spill personal information that will incriminate you in a court of law—also known as *the right to remain silent* (Fifth Amendment). You need privacy.

## How Privacy Violations Led to the Holocaust

About seventy-nine years ago, Adolph Hitler killed millions of innocent people. Before the genocide, he secretly gathered citizens' personal records and analyzed them. Using that information, he was able to find out who voted for him and supported his ideals and who did not. He then sought out and detained people based on their religious or philosophical beliefs. If you were not a supporter, you were isolated, discriminated against, and torn from your family. Your property and assets were seized. If you weren't killed outright, you were denied health care, shamed, imprisoned, tortured, starved, stripped, gassed, and eventually killed.

Hitler raided churches, synagogues, and religious associations and seized membership records. He combed national registers. He searched for anything that tied a person to a religion or ideology he didn't fancy. And over the next four years, six million Jews and other minority groups were murdered. Hitler's abuse of personal information records originally kept for social good was a horrifying invasion and violation of privacy that induced the Holocaust.

That's how much power your unguarded privacy can wield, how dangerous it can be, and how much damage it can lead to in the wrong hands.

After this atrocity, the United Nations gathered its representatives from fifty-eight countries and drafted the Universal Declaration of Human Rights (UDHR). The bottom line is that every human being has the right to be treated with respect, fairness, and dignity and to peacefully and freely live where they want. It sums up the basic notion that everyone has the right not to be subject to cruelty or stripped of their privacy and freedom. The UDHR affirms that basic human rights are to be protected regardless of differences in political, philosophical, or religious beliefs and views. Have you ever heard of Human Rights Day? UDHR is celebrated internationally every December 10, on the day it was adopted in 1948.

Of course, the UDHR didn't say a word about the Internet or email communication. It certainly didn't mention Facebook censorship. We didn't have today's cutting-edge technology then, but those things were implied. UDHR's vision and proclamation all those years ago have relevance and application today. (I've seen maybe one article hinting at amendments to UDHR in 2020, but I don't see any official amendment yet unless I'm missing it.) This is why human rights laws have mushroomed around the globe. After the declaration avowed human rights, different governments carried out the idea. That's basically what privacy laws are—a subset of human rights laws. They protect God-given rights, dignities, liberties, constitutional rights, civil rights, legal rights, and freedoms by preserving personal information, no matter who the person is or what they believe. Today, some of us are concerned about the damaging consequences of not properly protecting privacy in its physical form, on the Internet, and in church. Rightfully so.

This is why privacy laws are necessary and why they exist today—and extend to your church. They borrow the same principles you'll find in the UN's Universal Declaration of Human Rights. Privacy laws then and today are no

Introduction

different from traffic or road safety laws. Recklessness on the road claims innocent lives. Privacy laws save lives in many ways, be it spiritually, emotionally, physically, or mentally. They save you from others and from yourself—even in church. Privacy laws exist because folks are often wounded or killed, and relationships are ruined by reckless violations of privacy. Hitler was no doubt reckless. It makes sense to want to protect your privacy from all manner of people who might be up to no good: dictators, narcissists, abusers, fraudsters, scam artists, hackers, colleagues, nosy churchgoers, or identity thieves who want to steal, defraud, or discriminate against you. Discrimination, profiling, tracking, or being singled out as a result of your private information being used against you is a privacy issue. It makes sense to obey privacy laws that protect people from discrimination in many contexts.

## A New Perspective on Privacy

God's people need protection from intentional and unintentional privacy recklessness. In *Church Privacy 101*, I'll not only show you what to do to protect your privacy, but I'll also help you understand why you should care about privacy and why it matters in your personal and spiritual life. In the upcoming chapters, we'll look at the privacy hurdles in your private life and church community. This will include the privacy of your relationship with God, how to share information of a personal nature with your clergy, and how your personal information should be handled by church staff. Your privacy should be protected against many of life's Hitlers, hackers, and folks who habitually misuse, abuse, and mishandle your personal information in church. Get ready, I want to give you a new perspective on privacy.

It can be tough to get people to change their thinking, especially when many are missing the point about privacy. You may be one of them. Privacy often gets a bad rap. If you only think about secrets when you think about privacy, you're missing the point. If you don't understand the damage that an invasion of privacy can inflict on people, you're in danger of committing these offenses, and being punished for them, or being violated by someone else.

Elias' and Mrs. Williams' stories are not out of the ordinary. Privacy violations are all *too* common in church. But there's more to privacy violations, invasions, and risks than insensitive preachers and church members. There's technology. Undeniably, modern technological conveniences have made our lives and chores easier. And these days, with so many technological advances and ways to store our data and track our movements—through digital storage, facial recognition, and digital chips in our credit cards, driver's licenses, cell phones, and vehicles—our privacy is at a premium.

As our online presence increases, more personal and interconnected information is being collected from our cell phones, doorbells, credit cards, web browsers, text messages, and even through our social media interactions and habits and from the ads, groups, and people we engage with. Have you noticed that when you click on a website or a product online, you almost immediately start seeing ads for that site or product as you surf the Internet? That's because your browser is helping track you and taking note of how you interact on the Web. Just how much does your technology use impact the church?

Well, 49 percent of church donations are made by credit card. This is a sharp contrast to past trends. In the US in 2021, people donated a record high of nearly $485 billion. The largest share of those donations (27 percent) went to religion. Education followed at 14 percent, while human services and foundations were the other popular causes with 13 percent each. About 67 percent of all donations came from individuals, and 9 percent were from will bequests. Foundations and corporations contributed only 19 percent and

# Introduction

4 percent respectively.¹ Since the pandemic, live-streaming church services have increased online attendance, which has increased online tithing by 70 percent.² Most church event attendees register online, and most church activities have an online alternative—all the more reason your church should use better payment and personal information collection processes and constantly maintain them to protect your privacy. Yet, even as more personal data is being collected and stored, a survey from Lifeway Research shows that a large percentage of churchgoers do not trust church leaders. "Almost 7 in 10 U.S. adults (69%) say religious leaders act unethically at least some of the time, with 10% saying they do so most of the time."³ Could this be mostly about privacy concerns?

For twelve years, between 1992 and 2004, over one thousand churches were surveyed and tracked on Churchleadership.org. The results are quite eye-opening: "Sixty-one percent of people (2,039) left their last church because of a conflict with another member resulting from gossip or strife that would not stop, was not true, or was not properly dealt with. They also marked a lack of hospitality and a lack of Bible teaching second or third, making this category 91 percent of significance."⁴

Have you ever left a church because of a fight?

The data shows that privacy awareness is an area that lacks teaching in the church. Gossip results from privacy violations. Churches will fail if members lack discretion and an understanding as to what privacy is and what a privacy violation involves. This falls to the leadership in the church, but it's also every member's responsibility. But, as the data illustrates, privacy leadership is lacking.

## Empowering People

As a privacy instructor and trainer for corporations, I empower people to take ownership of their privacy and to respect privacy in their intimate circles. I also help them understand the importance of good privacy practices at home, at church, at work, and in general. I nurture people. I wrangle many of life's privacy issues to empower people and nurture relationships. Although I'm the founder of a leading global privacy consulting firm, have consulted for the United States Secret Service, was vice-chair of the advisory board for the largest global privacy association, and studied many privacy laws and regulations, this book is food for thought, not legal advice.

I wrote *Church Privacy 101* to give you a new awareness and understanding of privacy, which is long overdue. Privacy is a physical, spiritual, mental, and emotional need. It is power over your private matters and that of others. When you understand what privacy is, what it does, and why, that understanding will protect you and those around you. You'll also learn how to anticipate your privacy needs, the needs of others, and the needs of your church community so that you can build better and more lasting relationships.

God motivated me to write this book. And he sent me Mrs. Bodil Lindqvist, whose story you'll read about in Chapter 1. Sister Bodil (I address women in the church as *Sister*) was sued by fellow churchgoers because of a privacy invasion. She posted their personal information online. Globally, her case remains one of the most shocking privacy enforcement actions. Her case was decided long before Facebook was conceived. She was sued the same year Google was officially launched, and back then, "the Internet had 188 million users, little more than a 20th of its present size."[5] Bodil Lindqvist is not a household name, but when tech giants like Google face legal battles over violating privacy, her name and her case crop up. As part of a group of students in a privacy law course hearing about Mrs. Lindqvist for the first

# Introduction

time, we all wanted to argue that she was innocent of any crime. But it's about the law.

You or someone you know could end up in court, like Sister Bodil. Maybe you'll sue someone for violating your privacy. Or maybe you're afraid to ask for privacy because you don't want to hurt anyone's feelings. Whoever you are, whatever your privacy needs are, and whatever your understanding of privacy is, this book will give you a deeper and broader understanding of its importance in all areas of your life and the lives of those you love. These days, any churchgoer can become a criminal in a matter of minutes simply because they lack an understanding of what privacy is and what privacy invasions actually are.

Here are three things you'll learn about privacy:

1. How to protect yourself

2. How to protect others

3. How to protect the church and its mission

*How to protect yourself* means recognizing your privacy needs. Privacy is a human need and right; it is not a sin. And you're not paranoid for wanting to protect it. It's totally healthy to want privacy—to give it and to expect it. Your need for privacy is a natural, built-in feature. It came with you; it is not a thing you created—it's part of the organic package that makes up who you are. Be intentional about your privacy, give it thought, and plan for it. Understand that an invasion of your private life and private information has far-reaching mental, emotional, physical, and financial consequences. I kid you not. Privacy protects you from yourself. You can cut down on the harm you can cause yourself and others if you know how to handle privacy. Tactlessness with your privacy or someone else's can hurt or ruin you the same way indiscretion with sex and can. As long as people are in your life, you'll face privacy issues. It's best to be proactive and become more intentional about understanding and managing privacy.

*How to protect others* means respecting other people's privacy the same way you'd like them to respect yours. Even if you don't care about your own privacy, do it anyway. Or if you think it's the last thing you'd do for someone because they don't deserve it, do it anyway. When you violate another person's privacy or private life, "I'm sorry" is not enough. Depending on the situation, if they escalate it to the authorities, you might have to pay state fines, go to jail, or both. You can avoid this if you know what to do or, better yet, what *not* to do. Did you know that being a social and friendly person can get you charged in court for violating a friend's privacy? Being intentional about privacy sets healthy expectations and boundaries. You get to keep your relationships longer and stay out of legal battles. Wouldn't that be great? Before I knew better, I would make close friends feel guilty for not disclosing what I wanted to know. But now I know better. As Maya Angelou said, "Do the best you can until you know better. Then, when you know better, do better."[6]

Privacy is also about timing: when someone is comfortable sharing information with you, they will. You shouldn't force them. It's invasive, disrespectful, and insensitive.

*How to protect the church and its mission* means contributing to making your church community a better custodian of people's personal information and private lives. Church business is like any business, and people quit people, not churches. You don't want to be the reason someone quits. Trust me, people do leave churches when their privacy is violated. They just don't say that's the reason. I think it's partly because they don't even know privacy has been violated—that what's distressing them is a violation of privacy. They just know it hurts. Others don't see privacy violations as a significant enough issue to raise in church, so citing other reasons for leaving the church sounds more justified. Leaving doesn't necessarily solve the problem. They'll

# Introduction

end up at another church and deal with people who might be as ignorant of privacy violations as folks in their old congregation. We forget that the church is a body of people. The grass is not greener in any church. Like with any organization, the church has strengths and weaknesses in managing certain aspects of business. But negligence and poor management have consequences—the same consequences that for-profit businesses face. No church or business has privacy all figured out. But they need to start somewhere. You can be the catalyst for the change needed in your church community.

The Internal Revenue Service doesn't play with compliance. Just as the IRS doesn't feel sorry for churches for dropping the ball on taxes or breaking tax laws, the state won't go easy on you or your church if you break privacy laws. Realize also that members won't stay with churches that show irresponsible privacy management—exposing their members' private affairs, phone number, email, home address, date of birth, photos, and other identifying information to the public or to criminals. Members expect their valuable personal information to be protected. They expect the church to be diligent and responsible. You can help your church avoid consequences if you know how to safeguard private information. This is the world we live in today. Our personal information is valuable and potentially dangerous if it falls into the wrong hands. Every role you play in church as a volunteer, employee, or worker is a privacy role. Your ignorance, carelessness, or negligence affects everyone.

Online privacy is not what this book is primarily about, but it is equally important for you personally and for church business. COVID-19 has made the church rely heavily on technology and access to digital information to carry out its mission. *Cyber hygiene* has always been important to workers and employees of any organization. If a church employee working from home grabs personal and confidential information stored in the church network so she can get her job done, it's dangerous for that information to travel over the Internet without protection. While certain network technology can help church employees secure remote communication with the church network, the best protection is good privacy awareness and training. Privacy errors boil down to what people do or fail to do that makes personal information and confidential information accessible to unauthorized users.

You'd never see the driver of an armored vehicle walking on the street carrying from the bank in a see-through plastic bag. That would tempt people to stare and invite thieves to attack them. When the is tucked inside a canvas bag and then an armored vehicle, a thief needs to work much harder to gain access.

Your church may be as vulnerable as that see-through plastic bag—with members' very personal information in it. That's why this book has a companion book, *Church Privacy Team,* to give you specifics about the vulnerable digital and physical areas of church and show you how to better protect them according to the laws of your state.

You may think, *Grace, we've got our cybersecurity down at church. We don't need to worry about privacy.* This thought is very telling of the church's understanding of the difference between cybersecurity and privacy. The two have an important distinction. Cybersecurity is the cousin of privacy. They are often confused.

Privacy issues arise in areas that are not always about physical, Internet, or cyberspace activities. They can sometimes arise from communication that's not written or in digital form. It could be an annoying neighbor of the opposite sex whom you've tried to avoid because they're stalking you. Then one day they're knocking on your door to let you know they have your underwear—the ones you "forgot" in the apartment building's laundry room. You want to thank them, but you can't help thinking, *Couldn't they just leave it alone?* This is a privacy issue, but it's not cyber-related. Cybersecurity *only* focuses on issues—privacy or otherwise—related to the Internet and cyberspace.

And there's another cousin, information security, which is the protection of digital and physical information and resources from unauthorized access. Although information security intersects with, or is a component of, information privacy, it is significantly different. People use them interchangeably, but they're not the same. They mean two very different things, just like when I tell someone my name is Grace, and the next minute they call me Joy. It's all good. But I'm not Joy.

Usually the technology, apps, and platforms used by your church are not wholly owned, operated, and controlled by your church—for example, social media, Christian radio stations, Hillsong's website, The Potter's House, or *Vatican News*, just to name a few church resources. It's not always what the ministry does with your personal information that is concerning. It's often what third parties or tech firms do with the information. Trust me, Pope Francis isn't tracking you or studying your online behavior. Someone else is.

I cover this and more in the companion guide to this book, *Church Privacy Team*, which discusses how church and ministry leadership should handle privacy organizationally as it relates to employees, volunteers, technology, business processes, compliance, and risk management. There's an excerpt from it at the end of this book.

## Great Relationships Are Golden

In the upcoming chapters, you'll read stories about real people and real privacy needs, issues, and implications in everyday life. Some involve church situations and members I've met along the way. Great relationships are golden, and I want to see relationships in church communities and outside of them last. So, with God's help, I offer you the knowledge, insight, tools, and techniques to protect your privacy and that of the people you love and work with and whose personal data you handle or manage.

Not all issues in this book specifically happen to people in the church, but they happen *around* people in the church, which is just as serious. Sometimes relatives or friends of people in the church violate privacy. We don't call them church issues because they're personal in nature. However, when a member of the church is dealing with a problem, it automatically becomes a church problem. The church is not immune to issues because they're happening to its members privately. For example, the church does not ignore nutrition, fitness, adoption, finances, parenting, marriage, education, mental health, illegal behavior, addiction, or job skills. I've heard just about every sermon around the globe on these topics. These and more fall under the purview of personal matters. Carelessness in any of these private areas can negatively impact the member and the "one body" of the church. We need sermons on privacy.

During the pandemic, if you were unable to see God answer any prayer, please see this one. God has been answering the Jabez prayer of 1 Chronicles 4:10 like I've never heard or seen. Churches are getting the answer to their prayers for God to expand their territories wide and far. The COVID-19 lockdown converted every church into a global church. Because of live streaming, attendance at worship services and Bible studies has increased astronomically. But with this blessing comes the responsibility of your church to meet the requirements of privacy laws and regulations. To access certain live-streaming platforms, people have to register with their personal information. This information is then stored on the church platform and, if not protected, can be seen and potentially accessed by an unauthorized church volunteer, employee, app manufacturer, or hacker.

# Introduction

On November 3, 2020, California was number one on the chart with the strictest privacy laws in the world. In 2018, it was number two, with European Union privacy law leading as number one.[7] In 2021, the state of Virginia made the list. With America leading with some of the most stringent privacy laws, you can only benefit yourself, your loved ones, and your church family if you understand what privacy is and how to manage it so privacy needs are not disregarded or violated.

## How and Why

As you read, you'll see sections titled "Reflect" and "The Point." These offer you questions to mull over. "The Point" sections summarize the *why* of the topic or chapter. Throughout, you'll see additional resources and information.

There are different ways to use *Church Privacy 101* to get the many benefits it has to offer. One option is to read the book from beginning to end chronologically. The other option is to browse the Table of Contents for topics most relevant to you and read those first, then come back to the others. If you choose that option, I suggest you first read Chapter 2: What Is Privacy? to understand what privacy is and its relevance to you, your significant other, your family, your congregation, and your coworkers. If you're counseling or advising someone who you think will greatly benefit from a particular topic or chapter, by all means, point them to the relevant section. This is also a great book to use to facilitate informal discussions in small gatherings and a great icebreaker for difficult privacy conversations one-on-one.

With my extensive background in privacy advisory and data protection strategy, why am I writing about privacy in the church? Privacy is spiritual, among other things. This is not new to me. I have a long history with the church, not only because my parents were missionaries and church planters.

I love helping churches. It's been this way for many years. Privacy is the intersection of my calling and career, where I can marry both of my passions: privacy and my faith. I know firsthand how privacy violations can wreck lives and bring down organizations. I have seen churchgoers get hurt countless times. I advocate for my brothers and sisters in the church and give insight that is not only helpful to the flock but also to save marriages, friendships, relationships, and businesses. I empower people and strengthen church communities and leadership while doing this.

# 1
# A Church Lady Gets Sued Over Privacy

*Do not be anxious about how you should defend yourself or what you should say, for the Holy Spirit will teach you in that very hour what you ought to say.*

(Luke 12:11–12 ESV)

## Privacy Goes Public

The irony of a church lady getting sued by her fellow churchgoers over an invasion of privacy was that it was so unnervingly *public*. As in the Court of Justice of the European Union kind of public. Yep, it went *all* the way there. First, it was news in twenty-eight countries. Then it was global news. Privacy has strict codes and rules, and this church lady fell way short of them.

It was 1998, and Mrs. Bodil Lindqvist's case was such a milestone case that, afterward, her name went into the annals of every university curriculum, textbook, training manual, and public register. She is the most well-known church lady in privacy law and practice discussions and in law schools—especially if your specialization, like mine, is privacy or data protection. The court referenced Lindqvist in other cases (involving international transfers of personal data), including *Google Spain* in 2014—but that's a story for another time. Mrs. Lindqvist caught a lot of flak and was dragged into a legal battle of epic proportions that not only gained international attention but also created a global privacy buzz.

Her offense?

She posted a group photo of church volunteers and tagged people in the photos. It seems pretty trivial, right? That's what most people do. It's common. We all get away with it, right? Yes. If that shocks you, wait until I get into revenge porn in Chapter 11.

Let's go back to discussing Mrs. Bodil's case. So why did her innocent post cause such a stir? Was it on social media? No. Facebook, Twitter, and Instagram didn't exist in 1998.

Read on.

Life was good for Mrs. Bodil Lindqvist. She was comfortable and blessed to have a fantastic and supportive church family with whom she could be a warm influence in the church community. She was celebrated for the positive person that she was. But Sister Bodil's world came crashing down when she received a shocking court summons alleging that she had violated the privacy of fellow church volunteers. The date of her trial was fixed, and she needed a lawyer. The nightmare had begun. Have you ever been sued? Have you ever been sued by a fellow church member? That's a churchgoer's worst nightmare.

Poor Sister Bodil. Imagine for a moment you're in her shoes. You volunteer with these folks at church. You look forward to this amazing fellowship and friendship. Everyone is cool and has never had a problem with each other, and all of a sudden, you're being sued. How could this be happening to you? In *church?* Worse, you weren't even given a chance to apologize or correct your mistake before it went public. Whatever happened to Matthew 18:15, if your brethren sin against you, go to them in private? Or 1 Corinthians 6:7?

## A Church Lady Gets Sued Over Privacy

After all, posting a photo couldn't be that serious. Confused? If you were Sister Bodil, you might even question why God didn't stop you from accidentally breaking the law or stop your fellow church volunteers from taking things too far. What good could possibly come from having your name and possibly your career and reputation ruined? What are you going to do? Journalists are clamoring around your church, and you're pushing yourself through a sea of curious bystanders crowding the front of your place. You may know lawyers, but how many *privacy* lawyers do you know?

Sister Bodil did what you and I would have done. She surged to her computer, removed the identifying information about the volunteers from the photo on her website, took off the tagging, and then deleted the photo and other related private information.

I'm sure the church was split between differing opinions. Has your church community ever been divided or taken sides? Or expressed different opinions on all kinds of issues? Worse, did these things cause close relationships in the church to break up? That's when you find out who people really are. If you've ever been in a church where two people broke up—as in a broken engagement or divorce—you know what I mean. I bet this was the perfect storm for division. Sister Bodil didn't only have to worry about herself but also about the church community.

> *For we all stumble in many ways. And if anyone does not stumble in what he says, he is a perfect man.*
> (James 3:2 ESV)

### Who was Sister Bodil Lindqvist? What was her crime?

Bodil Lindqvist was a catechist at her church. That's church-speak for a church worker. That could mean a number of roles, depending on the church and denomination. In some churches, seasoned catechists can fill in as teachers for priests or preachers if they are unavailable.[1] It's possible she assisted clergy during special ceremonial events such as Communion and baptism. Or she may have worked with church volunteers to carry out her duties.

Court records show that Sister Bodil used her personal website as a resource to give church attendees very useful information about when ceremonies were scheduled. She used her personal site to update baptism candidates with what was required or expected.[2] It's similar to what I volunteer to do in church on Sundays, except I don't have a personal website that I use to disseminate or post church information. If you volunteer at church, you probably know someone like Sister Bodil: someone who is helpful and resourceful, with a wide range of skills. In my church, Sister Kathy is like Sister Bodil. She does it all—setting up Communion trays, sewing, washing church baptism laundry, ironing, helping in the nursery and Sunday school, altering bridal party dresses, you name it.

I don't know the number of businesses that had websites back in the mid-90s or in 1998. There weren't that many. But this church lady took a coding course and then created and kept up her own personal website.[3] Now, that's impressive sister power! Remember, back then, Wix didn't exist. Nor did YouTube to show us how to make a delicious chickpea stew, let alone how to code our own websites. Could this crime have been committed without her posting the information online? It's hard to predict if it would have resulted in the same outcome in court. She could have posted the information on a bulletin board in church that the public could access and still gotten into trouble with the law, depending on the elements of personal information she included. Although a bulletin board is limited to folks who come inside the church, it would still be sharing someone's personal information without their consent. But on a website, anyone could see it.

Every church needs a few Sister Bodils—resourceful women and men who passionately go above and beyond and are willing to take courses to

# A Church Lady Gets Sued Over Privacy

help them support people better. Unfortunately, most churches don't have courses on how to lawfully treat other people's personal information or how to properly share, post, distribute, use, store, or handle that information.

## *Globally, how did the church react?*

Was the next Sunday's sermon in every church titled "Respect Privacy: It's Your Righteous Duty"? Were women's conferences around the globe themed "Relentless Privacy Protection"? Did the church slow down on processing people's personal information? And did they pick up their old habits when the dust settled? It's like when we slow down when we see the cops stopping another driver who is speeding. Half a mile after the cop is out of sight, we're right back to speeding. That's what churches did, judging from my keen observation. No privacy sermons. No privacy-themed conferences. There were no privacy courses or workshops. Just business as usual. As if Sister Bodil was never prosecuted.

We underestimate the importance of privacy. We snub the laws surrounding it, especially as most activities and new members of local churches now span global territories via the Internet. Church privacy awareness is even more essential with church activities and processes being carried out online—prayer requests, testimonies, counseling, and small group meetings, for instance. These activities mean more potential disclosure of personal and sensitive information to the wrong person, even to those who are authorized to use it for church purposes but instead abuse it. Today, Sister Bodil's story may be out of sight and out of mind in churches, but it is not in law schools, courts, laws, and regulations around the globe. The church (not only Sister Bodil and churchgoers) is under the law—more so now that an example has been made of Sister Bodil.

# Church Privacy 101

At the time Sister Bodil was being charged with a crime, privacy laws weren't new, but the medium of communication was—the Internet was brand new. Also, the law was not nearly as strict as the privacy laws we have today in California, Virginia, New York, Maryland, the European Union, and across the globe. What does this tell you?

### *What did Mrs. Lindqvist say in her defense?*

- She stated that her website was just for her own personal use, meaning the entire world wasn't intended to be her audience.

- She erased the personal information her church members complained about when she found out their privacy was violated.

- She didn't intend to harm anyone.

### *Well, did she commit the crime she was accused of?*

It's a difficult question to answer. But technically, yes. The court reached that decision on November 6, 2003.[4] Should this be a crime? That's another argument and another book entirely. Critics of the law and the case say the court's decision "appears draconian and abusive."[5]

### *How did the court come to their decision and why?*

The court found her guilty of these transgressions:

1. On her post, which contained a group photo of volunteers and other information, she drew attention to or referred to one of the volunteers as having a "foot injury resulting in part-time sick leave."[6] This went against personal health information rules—by law, health information is considered *sensitive* personal information.

A Church Lady Gets Sued Over Privacy

2. She used their personal information online without first notifying those volunteers and getting permission—by law, she needed *consent*. The eighteen volunteers she posted information about didn't even know her web pages existed or that she would post their photos.

3. Even if she didn't physically or intentionally transfer personal information across country borders, technically it was possible for people outside her jurisdiction to view the web pages. Personal information disclosure *across borders* is prohibited in the EU. This means making another person's personal business available online or across borders must be according to government-approved standards, rules, laws, and practices. Long story short, Lindqvist failed.

### *What exactly was the content of the web pages she got sued over?*

Court documents say that in addition to photos, her website "contained information about Mrs. Lindqvist and 18 colleagues in the parish, sometimes including their full names and in other cases only their first names. Mrs. Lindqvist also described, in a mildly humorous manner, the jobs held by her colleagues and their hobbies. In many cases family circumstances and telephone numbers and other matters were mentioned. She also stated that one colleague had injured her foot and was on half-time on medical grounds."[7]

### *Although she deleted them immediately, it was still too late?*

Yes. According to the law, anything you do with somebody else's personal information is deemed "processing."[8] It doesn't matter if you're an individual like Sister Bodil, a business, a nonprofit organization, or a church—you must follow the rules for processing. This is why data protection regulations and privacy laws exist. The court told Sister Bodil that she was processing other people's personal information. How? According to the judge, "That provision gives several examples of such operations, including disclosure by transmission, dissemination or otherwise making data available. It follows that the operation of loading personal data on an Internet page must be considered to be such processing."[9] As soon as you take personal information from someone (on the phone, through a form, a photo, or documents, or in any form), you're processing it. Anything you do to or with that personal information after you create or obtain it is also processing—editing, texting, posting, storing, analyzing, marketing, tagging, you name it. You need consent from the person the information is about.

### *If she had the photo in her photo album or on her device, would it have been okay?*

Personal use is fine. It would've been fine if she hadn't shared and tagged the photos. Posting it on her website meant someone else could potentially find and view the information. Again, she also discussed the interests and hobbies of the people in the photos and the health situation of one person in the photo. Those identifiers violated the law, especially the health information piece, which is considered sensitive information and should not be publicly disclosed without consent. Sister Bodil accepted the court's verdict. But she, like most people, didn't see how this made her a criminal. She insisted she wasn't guilty of a crime.

### *What was her punishment for this crime?*

She was fined by the district court but appealed the sentence. The court went on to fine her the equivalent of forty times her salary and required her to donate to the government to support crime victims.[10]

## Reflect

- Have you ever taken photos during fellowship? Where are those photos?

- Have you ever tagged or mentioned people's names in your posts? Do you know how they felt about it? Did you ask?

- Have you ever included their full names and the photos they appeared in?

## The Point

You might be thinking, *But everyone does those things.* Everyone behaving a certain way doesn't make it right or legal. The cops can't pull over twenty cars speeding in the same lane at the same time. They only catch one—to make an example of them. And I hope it's not you, friend.

The way privacy laws work is similar to traffic laws. If you violate privacy laws, just like traffic violations, penalties and fines will follow. Bad decisions will cost you.

*Can the church stop this?* Yes! The church is capable of educating its members on how to take privacy seriously, adhere to privacy laws, and manage personal information. Also, church leaders should stop believing privacy is an IT problem—no, it's personal.

*You can't control what people will do.* Don't count on 1 Corinthians 6:1–8. When the government grants privacy rights to people, expect them to exercise their rights and meet their personal privacy needs, whatever those needs are. You can't control who can or will exercise their right to sue you as an individual or when they will take legal action against the entire church.

*According to the law, a wrong is a wrong.* Just because you text and drive undetected in a state where it's unlawful doesn't make it right. It may seem like posting photos without consent is no big deal; however, according to privacy laws, it is.

*Privacy existed before Internet technology.* The significance of privacy extends beyond the Internet and encompasses how personal information is processed and used. I haven't mentioned any specific software or other technology issue in this story—neither did the court. This was regarding the decisions Sister Bodil made or failed to make. You're responsible for protecting personal information you obtain from others and also for obtaining express consent *before* sharing it.

## It's Not Just about Technology

Again, Sister Bodil's crime wasn't about technology; it was about privacy. You need permission to publicly share someone's photos. Forget the law for a minute. Let's talk about why not getting permission is a disservice and disrespectful. When you put a church member's photo and name on your post and share sensitive details about them that they entrusted to you, is it fair to them? For instance, just because you and your best friend are enjoying a vacation and capturing photos together doesn't mean you want your photos posted on social media. You may not like how your hair, tummy, smile, or eyes look in the photos. You may be uncomfortable with how a particular outfit you wore looked. Or you're altogether uncomfortable with your photos on Facebook or Instagram. You may not want certain people to see them. Would it be fair to you if your friend posted those photos and tagged you without your knowledge or consent?

No, it's unfair, and according to the law, it's also illegal. Your friend needs your permission. That's privacy—the need of one person and the responsibility of the other person to meet the need.

## A Church Lady Gets Sued Over Privacy

Someone agreeing to be in a photo doesn't mean they automatically agree to you posting or sharing it. The group of volunteers may have posed for a photo, but they didn't give their consent to have it shared—and tagged with additional personal information. Sister Bodil should have mentioned how she intended to use the photos and gotten permission to post them. Posting on the Internet is not illegal. But posting personal information about others without their consent is.

Put yourself in the shoes of those fellow churchgoers who sued her. Now your fellow churchgoers think you're awful, immature, evil, and heartless for suing Sister Bodil. You're on the brink of breaking down. Holding back tears, you want a chance to explain your side of the story. You've not only been tagged in a photo, but your contact information, your hobbies, your likes and dislikes, and your medical issues have been disclosed without your knowledge or consent. Would you feel betrayed and uncomfortable? The people in the photo Sister Bodil posted on her website felt this way.

Consider the very real consequences of Sister Bodil's innocent post. Has an insurance company ever denied or tried to deny your coverage—for your car, apartment, house, or health? The church member in the photo with the foot cast could have potentially lost their health insurance coverage or employment. Insurance companies scrape the Internet all the time for evidence of fraud and can misconstrue a photo of someone who's on medical leave. They'll cut off their medical leave, declare them fit to work, and have the employer order them to return to their job—when, in reality, they're not ready to return to work.

How about stalking, harassment, tracking, unwanted marketing, or ID theft? What if someone in that church was under a protective or restraining order or hiding from an abusive ex, and Sister Bodil posted her phone number and address? Do you see the serious ramifications? Let's not forget that the church comes under the authority of the law, just as a church building has to follow codes and rules. Privacy has codes and rules to protect people from these negative impacts.

## Reflect

- Do you sometimes find it inconvenient to ask people for permission to use their personal information or photos? I used to.

- Do you sometimes feel that people who express the need for privacy are paranoid or making a mountain out of a molehill? Would you tell a judge they are paranoid?

- Has anyone ever asked you not to post a photo of them online or share it with others? Were you glad they spoke up?

- Do you get upset when someone asks for privacy because you don't ask others for privacy?

- Are you genuine and understanding about honoring their privacy wishes? Or do you think, *You know what? That's the last time I'm dealing with you.*

## The Point

*Your church can't save you.* You can't hide behind your church—even if your church is worth billions of dollars. If you neglect to protect personal information, the law will call you a privacy offender.

*Don't assume anything.* Don't presume that being friends or friendly with someone exempts you from getting permission. Don't be afraid of the answer. Asking before using information is better than making amends later. Be comfortable accepting no from people you care about.

*Ask and get permission.* Consent requires clear communication. You must ask and *only* proceed after getting permission. Thinking, *I know he won't mind,* is not consent.

*Be flexible.* If they're not sure, don't use their personal information. If they agree but later change their mind, remove the information or photo immediately.

*Stop comparing yourself.* Don't use the modest or large size of your church as an excuse to behave irresponsibly. All it takes is for one person to exercise their rights and expose you.

*You can't count on your good intentions.* Sister Bodil didn't intend to hurt anyone. I believe her. But that was not enough to avoid charges. Good intentions are not a substitute for negligence or the illegal handling of personal information.

*Help your church.* Protect yourself, your church, and others. If you notice your church privacy practices appear deceptive, unfair, risky, inadequate, unmanaged, or lax, let someone in leadership know and help resolve them right away.

## What Is Personal Information?

In the next few chapters, I will go deeper into the rules and principles that could have kept Sister Bodil out of this mess. Below is a Q&A of privacy questions I'm often asked, as well as a few guiding golden rules you should be aware of when handling or posting personal information—yours or someone else's. Anyone working or volunteering for the church should pay close attention to how their own personal information is handled by the church and how they use, store, protect, and share other people's personal information.

Church Privacy 101

## Privacy Q &A and Principles

1. What information is really personal?

Any information about a person. Below are general examples of information deemed personal:

- identifiers or identifiable information: photos, profile names, passwords, and ID cards (including badges, driver's licenses, and passports), Social Security numbers or national identification numbers, financial accounts, and contact information, which can include home address, email address, and phone number

- physical space: information about what's happening inside your private space, home, apartment, dorm room, documents, office desk, or anywhere you'd expect privacy

- bodily privacy and personal characteristics: your body, nakedness, health, treatments, genetics, DNA, and biometrics—fingerprint, voice, facial recognition

- communication and the Internet: personal information or thoughts you say, write, or share about you or others on paper, online, on your phone, via postal mail or email, and by other means and devices as well as profiling information—your behavior, preferences, location, and products and services you purchase that are tracked when you're online

- education records: any information in a school related to you as a student, with some exceptions

- employment information: any information related to employment—not limited to salary, employee file, retirement plan, health insurance, background checks, or substance tests

## A Church Lady Gets Sued Over Privacy

And there's more. I will cover other personal information throughout this book.

2. How do laws define personal information?

Great question. Personal information is *any* information that identifies a person or is about a person who's identifiable. Laws often copy one another. Lately, almost every law under the sun uses the word *any* to broadly describe what personal information is. Simply put, in legal and regulatory jargon, it is *personally identifiable information*. That's any information that relates to you or identifies you as who you are—by name, physical attributes (tattoos, eye and hair color, race, gender), ethnicity, religion, sexual orientation, age, political affiliation, photo or video of you, contact information, location, and online behavior. The law says these and more are personal. If it can identify you or can be used in combination with other personal information to identify you, it's personal. Now you see how Sister Bodil was playing with fire and didn't even realize it until she got burned. I empathize.

3. How do courts define personal information?

It depends on the situation. Many factors play out in the context, so the court interprets and defines personal information accordingly. For instance, if you're a medical worker, you have more factors to consider in the definition of personal information. As I mentioned earlier, health information is considered a sensitive class of personal information. If you're a doctor and you take a patient's personal information, such as their full name, address, and phone number, out of the patient's file for unauthorized or unconsented uses, it is a violation of health privacy, even if that same information is public elsewhere. The source of information matters, even though the information might not be personal health information. You could have gotten it from the public domain, such as the Internet. But I'm not encouraging you to do that either. It's safer to request to *friend* someone (from your personal Facebook account) who's not your patient than one who is. It's never a good idea to repurpose information for unauthorized purposes. Even if you're not in the medical field, the law treats how you use or share health information with more stringency, and the court considers many factors. The definition of personal information and privacy violations varies based on the situation or context. Laws, courts, and cases differ, and so do the outcomes.

4. Who really defines privacy anyway?

Every continent, country, state, and industry sector has its own definition of privacy. Societal values play a role in how people see privacy. The UN, to which 189 nations in the world belong (and are held accountable), defines what privacy is. It does that to set expectations for member countries. The Universal Declaration of Human Rights details how people should be treated with respect and dignity. Member countries get dinged if they drop the ball. Now, more than ever before, the definitions of *privacy* and *personal* have indeed become universal. Laws, constitutions, policies, and treaties define privacy. But long before they defined privacy, God defined privacy.

5. What if the privacy laws in my state or country are not that strict?

They might be more strict than you realize or think. Sister Bodil didn't see trouble coming. She didn't realize how strict the law was—and how it would be interpreted in her specific situation. Not only that, but more than one privacy law can apply to you at the same time, not just the one in your state. Think beyond the borders. Even if the privacy laws in your state or country appear toothless, you should always err on the side of caution.

## A Church Lady Gets Sued Over Privacy

6. Why do people get so upset over a privacy violation?

Has someone ever put you in an embarrassing situation or betrayed you? You probably got upset because it hurt. It burned inside. That's a privacy violation. It creates this terrible feeling: a loss of control—of your personal information, dignity, space, or moment, depending on the situation. When your privacy has been violated, you feel betrayed, disappointed, disrespected, and very uneasy. Not having an opportunity to consent to how your personal information is handled or used is upsetting. If you violate someone's privacy, for example, by disclosing or misusing their personal information, even innocently, they might go to the authorities without ever saying anything to you first (partly because they don't think you quite understand the emotional impact of what you did). And before you know it, like Sister Bodil, you end up in court. A church community is where people come to worship, build relationships, help others, and do God's work—to be disciples and make disciples by saving souls. When a privacy violation happens in church, it's even more hurtful and distressing because, for most people, this is a sacred place where they trust unreservedly. The church is the only safe space they have. And to have that trust violated feels almost unforgivable. It hurts more.

7. Why are privacy laws so strict?

Privacy laws are strict because a privacy violation has real and serious social, physical, mental, emotional, and philosophical impacts on a person. There are so many negative impacts. Some people can discriminate against an individual based on personal information they have about them. They can also isolate the person. Not protecting privacy can get someone killed or shamed or cause the loss of credibility, opportunities, individuality, and dignity. The negative impact can be financial, such as when your bank account information, credit card number, or offering envelope is mishandled by a church worker, allowing criminals the opportunity to steal your personal financial information, defraud you of your life's savings, or ruin your credit. This is why privacy laws and regulations are stringent.

8. How can I get good at protecting privacy so I don't hurt those I care about?

The only way to get really good at privacy is to learn more about it and practice. What do I mean by learning? You're reading Chapter 1 right now, and you have other very interesting chapters ahead. Friend, you're going to learn so much. Practice means you're being more sensitive to people's concerns and proactive about applying what you've learned, not only when someone complains or because your boss or ministry leader is watching you but because you genuinely care. And you're doing this for the benefit of others and the good of your church community. Understanding privacy and taking the initiative to protect others is a blessing, and it is one of the most wonderful, spiritually sustaining things you can do in church.

9. How can I learn about privacy so I can be a good steward of personal information?

How can you know about God unless someone teaches you (Romans 10:14)? Remember that Scripture? The same applies here. How can you know if I don't teach you? This book is a good place to start improving your stewardship. The resources and tools I provide will help you and your church address specific issues you're dealing with. The role of a good privacy steward is to lead their church to the privacy resources and tools available. At www.LearnChurchPrivacy.com, you can add the name of your church and email to request a free privacy Q&A session and secure training to learn about best privacy practices and the privacy laws in your state.

## A Church Lady Gets Sued Over Privacy

10. Why do we need privacy laws at all?

It's against the law to not pay taxes. You didn't always know that. Someone had to tell you. Right? That's a good lesson you learned. You may not remember who told you, but you're grateful that the IRS has no reason to look for you. If you're like me, you still fuss about taxes from time to time. It seems unfair that so much is taken from your paycheck, regardless of whether you're a large or average earner. But Jesus paid taxes (Matthew 17:24–27), right? And he never complained. That's what he taught you and me (his church) about complying with laws and obeying earthly authority. Privacy laws protect you and your loved ones from a long list of problems, which you'll learn about in the upcoming chapters. After reading each chapter, you'll be thankful that there are privacy laws and regulations. Think of privacy laws as insurance. You don't think much about it or even think it's important until you need it. Read on.

11. Is privacy really a church problem?

That's exactly what I'm saying. Privacy is a church problem. Some people prefer I not say anything about church privacy or the lack thereof. "It's for businesses and major corporations," they argue. Not true. Any problem that happens to a church member, visitor, employee, or volunteer is a church problem—an issue the church should look into and address in a timely manner. For example, the fact that a church has a program that offers rehabilitation to drug abusers or alcoholics doesn't mean the entire church abuses substances. It just shows that the church has identified specific needs that folks have and is meeting them. Same with privacy. We all have this need in church. And it affects every member Monday through Sunday 24/7. The church needs a privacy program. Preserving privacy has to start in churches.

## Privacy Principles

Privacy regulators have principles they expect individuals and organizations to follow. If you're wondering how you're supposed to handle other people's personal information, handle it with these privacy principles in mind:

- **Lawfulness:** Is the activity you're doing with someone's personal information legal?

- **Fairness:** Is it fair to the person? Did you give the person false hope that you'd adequately protect their personal information?

- **Transparency:** Do they know what you're doing with their personal information? Were you open and honest with them about it?

- **Purpose limitation:** For what purpose did you inform them you needed the information? If they agreed with the purpose, are you limiting your use of the information to that purpose?

- **Data minimization:** Did you collect personal information that's specific to the purpose, or did you collect and use more than you needed?

- **Accuracy:** Is the information correct? Could this inaccurate information negatively impact the person? Did you check and confirm with them?

- **Storage limitation:** Are you keeping or storing personal information you no longer need?

- **Integrity and confidentiality (security):** Are you keeping personal information safe?

A Church Lady Gets Sued Over Privacy

- **Accountability:** How are you holding yourself and others accountable to ensure you're addressing all these principles consistently and effectively? Who is in charge of privacy?

> *Let every person be subject to the governing authorities.*
> *For there is no authority except from God, and*
> *those that exist have been instituted by God.*
> (Romans 13:1 ESV)

## Privacy Is Essential and Lawful

The church does a lot of good. It saves lives. But does the church lock its office doors on Sundays? Yes. Is the preacher's office left unattended and unsecured because it's located inside a church? No. Are the cars in the parking lot locked when their owners are inside the church worshiping, serving, and praying? Yes. Are the car windows rolled down because the owners have "nothing to hide"? No. They need privacy.

Do church folks use technology to tithe and give offerings? Yes. Can a website like eGiving.com and similar apps be broken into on a Sunday and credit card numbers and other personal financial information be stolen? Yes. But upon finding out about it, should the church wait until Monday to respond? No. The church will need to alert members, call in experts, notify the authorities, and prevent further damage so the thieves won't bleed congregants' bank accounts dry and cause them distress. In this situation, will your church know how to respond or what the first step is to comply with privacy laws? Is privacy a church problem? Yes.

Not every privacy violator and invader is a thief. Not all privacy offenders are online. Privacy protects you in different ways. It protects you emotionally, mentally, and spiritually. It keeps you from negative distractions—if your need for privacy is to focus and reflect. It keeps you from losing your peace. Privacy gives you the focus you need to handle your priorities. It helps you feel safe and allows you time and space to heal. Your body, mind, spirit, and soul all need the security and confidence that privacy offers. And your wallet needs it too. Without privacy protection, your identity and your financial information are up for grabs.

Keep in mind that everyone's privacy temperature is different depending on the situation. One day, a friend who was about to go through premarital counseling texted me. We chatted about the counseling formats—group or one-on-one. She's a people person, and I wasn't surprised when she said, "I love group discussions on marriage, but . . ."

"But what?" I asked.

"I'd prefer not to discuss topics I consider private in front of a group. Those discussions should only be held privately with a marriage counselor," she replied. What she felt was right. A one-on-one format would give her the peace of mind and focus she needed to work on her premarital relationship. She learned that her fiancé wouldn't have minded a group discussion. But we all have different privacy preferences. In relationships, unless you tell someone what your privacy preferences are, they may never know or respect them. Isn't it great that the church gave them options? Privacy is about choices and having control over your information.

Let's consider the role of the church as a good steward of our spiritual health. It is, after all, a place of faith, healing, and hope—the headquarters of people's needs. The responsibility to care for and protect each other spiritually and lawfully falls on me, you, and all members of the church community. What affects one person in your church affects everyone in your church. Remember, we're one body.

## A Church Lady Gets Sued Over Privacy

Violating someone's privacy is one lesson where experience is not the best teacher. Robert Orben once said, "If you think education is expensive, try ignorance."[11] Agreed. I believe it's cheaper to obey the law. It's cheaper to learn more about privacy. It's cheaper to do the right thing, no matter what your state's privacy law requires. It's more expensive to plead ignorance of the law in court. It's more expensive to leave the courtroom with a Hefty trash bag of fines and penalties, a damaged reputation, a perpetual existence in court records, prison time, or worse.

Has Sister Bodil's case changed her church?

Yes, quite a lot has changed, as would be expected. One thing is for sure: they don't make excuses about privacy. They know better than that. They now value privacy education. They now understand that having a privacy officer is as essential as having doors, windows, locks, sermons, and fellowship.

*Many are the afflictions of the righteous,*
*but the Lord delivers him out of them all.*
(Psalm 34:19 ESV)

# 2

# What Is Privacy?

*All Scripture is God-breathed and is useful for teaching, rebuking, correcting and training in righteousness, so that the servant of God may be thoroughly equipped for every good work.*

(2 Timothy 3:16–17)

## The Unknown Need

Privacy is not for the self-centered, selfish, and immature. Privacy is about many natural needs. But it is first and foremost about people and the personal matters people naturally need healthy control over. It protects your general sense of well-being. Also, privacy is about sensitive personal information and issues that, if exposed, misused, or stolen, will embarrass, cause distress, or harm you—like information about you or your family's health, opinions, beliefs, bodies, or identities. Privacy means protecting yourself from those who may misjudge you based on their conclusions about you without having full knowledge of the facts and context of your situation.

Privacy is also physical—such as closing the door when you're about to undress or shower. It's using your body to block other people's view when entering your bank card PIN at the ATM. Privacy is putting the Do Not Disturb sign on your door handle in the hotel. It's all of these. But there's so

## What Is Privacy?

much more to privacy than the physical need; it's also a spiritual, mental, and emotional need. You don't call it *privacy*, even though you deal with many different types of privacy issues throughout your day. You may not consider them privacy issues, but you know when privacy is given to you because you feel free, respected, peaceful, in control, and valued. And it's not surprising that when it's not given, you feel like your needs are squashed—you're violated, invalidated, shamed, invaded, disrespected, or demeaned.

### *Privacy has many definitions and uses.*

When you want space to decompress, pray, meditate, reflect, or just unwind, that's privacy. When you crave quiet or solitude or want to get away from prying eyes, that's privacy. When you need to talk to God candidly and you go into a room alone and shut the door, that's privacy. When you sit in your car and let your brain process your moment or day, that's privacy. When you check the caller ID and ignore a call, that's privacy. When you want to relax alone and binge-watch movies, that's privacy. When you don't want to be accessible to others, when you want to be left alone, when you don't want to talk, be heard, be observed, or be touched—these are all privacy needs. You also need a level of privacy to share your opinion, express your misgivings, or vent without fearing consequences.[1] These are privacy needs, but we don't call them that.

According to one of America's modern-day scholars and privacy pioneers, Alan F. Westin, you need privacy to manage your bodily functions, your sexual functions, and certain displays of affection. Privacy is also when you're being still, resting your mind, spirit, or body, reflecting, taking personal *inventory*, and planning your next moves to make a comeback. Privacy can help you release pressure. He calls that "emotional release." Westin said, "Privacy also allows individuals to deviate temporarily from social etiquette when alone or among intimates, as by putting feet on desks . . . letting one's face go slack or scratching wherever one itches."[2] Being selective also applies when you only allow certain people to see you cry, grieve, and go through a traumatic experience. When you're mad or irritated and need a harmless outburst, privacy is often what you need for that.

Privacy is being respectful of other people's boundaries, space, needs, and what they do or do not want to share with you. Privacy means protecting what someone shared with you in private.

### *Is there another word for privacy?*

Andrea, a client, asked me if I could tell her another word that describes privacy—what it *really* is. That is, a word a layperson can relate to that covers *everything*. I'd never been asked that before, and I've been researching privacy for a long time. It was a great question. After giving it some serious thought, I came to the conclusion that we are all laypeople when it comes to privacy. We deal with privacy issues several times a day, in all the ways I mentioned above, but we don't use its real name. Besides, the word is quite broad. We need several names, not just one, to describe each privacy need or issue.

An alternate phrase we often use comes from the Bible. Scripture describes privacy as "your own business" (1 Thessalonians 4:11). At first, I typed the Scripture reference as *Thessalonions* in error, and then I stared at the last six letters of the misspelled word—*onions*. It was the confirmation of a revelation for me because in Chapter 4 and later chapters, I describe the concept of privacy onions, which is a model with which to create your inner privacy circles. These onions allow you to add people to the different rings of each onion so you'll never be confused about who to share your business with.

# What Is Privacy?

## *Does the Bible have another word for privacy?*

Even the Bible is short of one catchall word or phrase for privacy. But a few words you'll find are very specific or have more than one meaning of privacy: *nakedness, tattling, gossip,* and *your business*. The Bible talks about nakedness, which covers bodily privacy, vulnerability, and emotional, mental, and spiritual privacy. Scripture says to mind "your own business." Minding your personal business here pretty much covers *communication* and *information privacy*—including breaching confidence, backbiting, gossiping, eavesdropping, and slander. And it also talks about physical boundaries, for example, when it instructs us to go into our room or house and close the door to pray (Matthew 6:6). Nehemiah rebuilt the walls of Jerusalem for many reasons, including territorial privacy—for maintaining control, security, and peace and for denying access to attackers and bad influencers. He said the builders were doing this for their children, wives, and homes (Nehemiah 4:14). Technically, they were protecting their private lives and securing their territory from observing adversaries.

> *Enter your rooms*
> *and shut the doors behind you;*
>
> *hide yourselves for a little while*
> *until his wrath has passed by.*
> (Isaiah 26:20)

## *Does the meaning of privacy depend on who you ask?*

Yes, it does. But it all comes back to being about fundamental human needs. Your constitution (national or state) details your privacy in the civil rights or fundamental rights you've been given. What privacy means to the authorities is further defined in laws and regulations to protect you from intrusion. I defined fundamental human needs in the previous chapter in the Privacy Q&A and Principles section.

Merriam-Webster defines privacy as follows:

> a: the quality or state of being apart from company or observation: SECLUSION
>
> b: freedom from unauthorized intrusion // one's right to privacy.[3]

When we look at these definitions, we can conclude that privacy is the freedom from invasion of our mind, soul, spirit, body, personal information, communication, and space. And privacy allows us control over who has access to us and our personal information.

Privacy fulfills and satisfies many nameless needs you may not even realize you have. It is truly an unknown need. Sadly, it's highly underrated, misunderstood, and misconstrued—all because you've never been taught at home, school, or church what privacy is and why it's important. You don't call your many life's issues and the problems that arise from them *privacy* issues. They're everything but privacy issues.

## Reflect

- Have you ever ignored calls, even if you were at home doing absolutely nothing?

- Have you ever prayed for forgiveness because you didn't pick up a clergyperson's call? I have.

- Have you ever regretted giving a relative a good friend's phone number?

- Have you ever given your friend a relative's number—and peace has evaded you since?

## The Point

There's no denying that God is right. Westin and the Constitution are right. We need to be let alone sometimes, in different ways. Privacy is a natural need. We need to protect it. Even public figures and celebrities have this need.

> *You don't know when you're being watched.*
> *That's one of the weird things about celebrity.*
> (Denzel Washington)

**There is a private cost to being a public figure.**

When celebrities, public figures, or people in the public eye walk down the street or enter a room, they know they may be recognized and watched. When someone says to me, "You look familiar," I assume they took one of my courses or heard me speak at an event or at their company. You might be a celebrity, public figure, or renowned clergyperson. You might be a celebrity to your Sunday school students, or as a leader in your church or your family, or anywhere else you're admired and celebrated. But there comes a time when you want to go unnoticed, unrecognized, and unobserved and feel completely at ease. You need privacy.

**There's no privacy in the public eye.**

When you're finished playing the roles that life requires you to play, do you appreciate retreating to your home to recharge, meditate, listen to music, and maybe sing along at the top of your voice or dance around to blow off steam?

# Church Privacy 101

Whenever I teach a sixteen-hour course in two days back-to-back, I become mute on the third day. I try my hardest not to talk to anyone. This is my way of recalibrating and decompressing. Other times, you might need to shut out noise, people, and things—so you can recharge, reflect, rejuvenate, relax, refocus, or dream—to see your vision more clearly.

Privacy for you might look like a change of location or locale. Just because you lead a church doesn't mean you don't crave escape to a church in the middle of nowhere just to listen to another leader minister the truth to you. This temporary change of venue can open you up to a new church community and fellowship from a congregation that will wholeheartedly welcome you, even if they don't know you or your ministry accomplishments (and you don't care). That's privacy.

I once heard a preacher lament over Acts 2:17, saying, "Our sons and daughters can't prophesy. Our sons can't see visions and our old men can't dream dreams because they have so much noise and demands going on—on their smart phones, on social media, and on YouTube."

He had a point. It's hard to renew when our power button is always on. Have you noticed your computer works better when you restart it or power it down for a bit? It's the same for us. We have to shut down to recharge. How does that translate to privacy? That can mean recharging from social engagements, work commitments, relationships, or even just being in public. You might need to go home, kick off your shoes, and binge-read or watch your favorite content. Or take a deep breath, exhale, and slouch in your car for a few minutes to gather yourself before you start the engine. You might need to power down your hectic day to connect with God. Maybe you're feeling rundown and need a spa day to refresh yourself physically, or you need a mental recharge to focus on that book you're writing. If we're constantly on, we're courting a breakdown. If we're constantly powered up, we will become overloaded, stressed, and empty. If we are empty, we can't pour out love, support, gratitude, information, or advice into the lives of our friends, loved ones, or family. We need privacy to be able to function fully to help others and to serve God and our church community.

## *There is sanctity in solitude.*

Although your life may be in the public eye, that doesn't mean you want strangers going through your garbage bins, accessing your medical records, misusing your credit card information, or taking and sharing photos of you without your consent. If you're a celebrity or public figure, it's difficult to maintain privacy when your fans want to know all about you. For some celebrities, that could mean no privacy for you in public, unless you're in disguise. In some cases, you have no privacy, even when you're at your home. You may think you're alone or lounging by your pool, but meanwhile, there's a photographer with a high-scope lens shooting photos of you that they'll later sell to a tabloid or post online.

We not only crave solitude; we *need* it. Because it renews and refreshes us. It gives us an emotional release. When you're stalked by an ex or when you're in church just trying to get your worship on but you keep getting interrupted, these are privacy issues. Since privacy is an emotional need, when it's denied to us, it's abusive and harmful. The absence of privacy affects our well-being and how we relate to the world around us. For instance, a narcissistic parent, sibling, friend, or spouse can deny you privacy when they disclose, misuse, or compromise your personal information. Also, a colleague, employer, neighbor, or church member can do the same. As a result, you don't feel safe or at peace because you're no longer in control of your personal space or private information. These are all privacy concerns, but we don't call them that. When these needs aren't met, they create problems in our lives, but we don't even realize they're related to privacy.

According to Daniel Solove, professor of law at the George Washington University Law School, "People don't acknowledge certain problems, because those problems don't fit into a particular one-size-fits-all conception of privacy. Regardless of whether we call something a 'privacy' problem, it still remains a problem, and problems shouldn't be ignored."[4]

### *There is relief in emotional release.*

Solitude, or alone time, allows us emotional release. We all practice some form of emotional release. For instance, solitude engages you with yourself or with God and allows you to focus, reflect, and meditate on or ponder decisions and ideas. In the workplace, you probably have personal and mental health days known as work retreats where you leave the workplace environment. Churches do likewise. Church leaders don't invite congregants to every meeting—especially church leadership meetings—because *a lot* of emotional release goes on there. You're not privy to elders or leaders presenting and negotiating ideas or making decisions. You don't hear their heated arguments. You don't know which clergyperson steps out to let off steam before she goes back inside to agree on a decision and later adjourns the meeting with a warm prayer. Everyone needs an emotional release in a safe and private place. It's all done behind closed doors for a reason. At the right time, depending on what is discussed, that final decision is then shared with the congregation. But the leaders decide and control how much information to disclose, when to disclose it, and which medium to use. This is also a privacy need. They are calibrating their privacy thermostat when they do this.

*And to aspire to live quietly, and to mind your own affairs.*
(1 Thessalonians 4:11 ESV)

# What Is Privacy?

*Privacy is good medicine.*

Because of its many health benefits, privacy is like good medicine. But it's not only for when you're sick or have a particular health issue. It's like medicine you take for general well-being. Any deep human need, when met sufficiently and in a timely manner, is like a tonic—it's restorative and energizing. It takes care of any present ailment and prevents others from sprouting up. That's privacy—preventative and corrective.

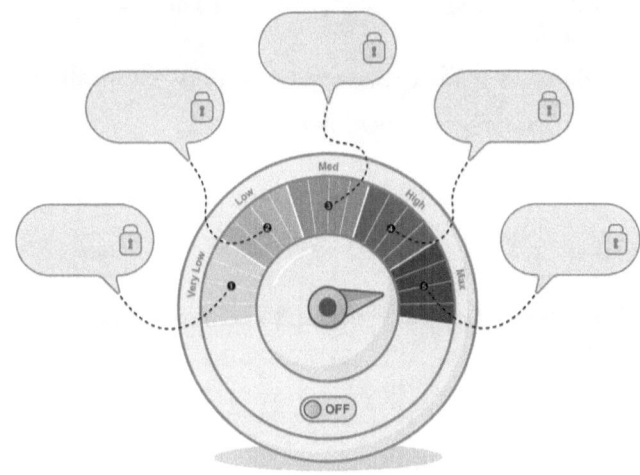

*Figure 1. Be aware of your privacy thermostat.*

In addition to being good medicine, privacy is also like a personal thermostat. What do you do when someone walks up to you while you're having a private conversation with another individual? Even though you may not realize it, you adjust your privacy thermostat (PT for short). Take a look at the illustration. That thermostat is in your head right now. You control your PT. You can turn it down or keep it on low if you're with friends, family, loved ones, or a trusted confidant. And you can turn up your privacy to the max if you're in public with people you don't know. That means you turn privacy up or down depending on many factors, including the following:

- what's going on—your present circumstances and your personal choices

- the day or the time

- who is around

- where you are

- the question somebody is asking, and who is asking it

- how much information is enough, and what's at stake

- which emotions or feelings you need to express physically or outwardly (sadness, embarrassment, shock, anger)

- if the value or benefit of disclosure or transparency outweighs your need for privacy

- how you feel at the moment—not up to being seen, heard, watched, and identified

***Privacy is about having choices.***

Privacy gives us choices. Having control over our privacy affords us good judgment and discretion. It allows us to manage our expectations and those of others. As seen by the privacy thermostat illustration, we can turn it up or down. We can control privacy by choosing what we share and who we share it with. If we're asked questions, we can decide if we are going to answer them or not—or give the most diluted version possible. Privacy is the option to choose who is allowed access to our home or our personal life. Also, it's what we can comfortably share once we've considered that the value of disclosing an aspect of our personal life or situation is greater than withholding the information. Privacy is the understanding that on a particular day we may feel one way about these choices—around a certain person or place—and another day we may feel another way. Sometimes we choose to interact with others anonymously, like when we use alternate identities or anonymous user accounts in online forums. Also, church donors sometimes give anonymous gifts—small or large amounts. Anonymity is not only a need the wealthy or celebrities have. At some point or another, we all crave anonymity. It's all privacy. Whether you're the one needing or giving privacy, intentional choices should be made, discretion should be used, and responsibilities should be fulfilled.

## *The drama of life is at play.*

Privacy is role-based. You can adjust your privacy thermostat many times in the day and from moment to moment. The roles you play change several times a day, and so do the people you're dealing with. This makes life in general a bit of a drama.

William Shakespeare famously wrote, "All the world's a stage."[5] What Bill meant was that every day has a multitude of mini-dramas, and we wear different hats or faces to fill roles and play different characters. We put on different personas to satisfy those roles. Life hands us multiple roles and scripts daily. Properly playing them takes mental, emotional, spiritual, and physical effort. For instance, on any given day, one person can play all or many of these roles:

- church leader
- congregant
- ministry volunteer
- usher

- youth leader
- teacher/professor
- spouse
- parent
- sibling
- daughter-in-law or son-in-law
- grandchild
- guardian or mentor
- employer or employee
- manager/supervisor/director
- freelancer or consultant
- driver or passenger
- neighbor

I know someone like this—me, with the exception of four of these roles. Which roles do you play on a given day? Whether you realize it or not, for each role, you adjust your privacy thermostat accordingly. It is natural and intentional, even if you're not aware of it. With your thermostat, you're adjusting privacy limits. In each role, you control how close or distant you'll be, how much access you'll allow, or how much or little you'll share or confide in others. Automatically, you create the right privacy temperature. Doing so means you're controlling your physical, mental, emotional, and spiritual comfort for a given role throughout your day.

## What Is Privacy?

Control is at the heart of privacy. It's a healthy control. We all exercise control subconsciously. Even the most transparent people have control.

## Reflect

- How do you control your privacy?

- Who do you invite into your home? Do you invite coworkers into your home on a regular basis? Why or why not?

- Who stays in your house until late at night? Do your coworkers or neighbors stay at your house until late? Why or why not?

- Who can sleep on your sofa because it's too late to go home? Do you allow your coworkers, neighbors, or love interest to crash on the sofa, or do you even invite them at all? Why or why not?

- Would you respond to a Facebook friend request from the pharmacist at your neighborhood pharmacy who just filled your prescription a couple of days earlier and was super friendly? Why or why not? (This actually happened to someone in my Twitter feed.)

## The Point

Each scenario in the reflection section shows how you might turn your privacy thermostat up or down. Have you ever heard that familiarity breeds contempt? This comes from Proverbs 25:17. It says, "Seldom set foot in your neighbor's house—too much of you, and they will hate you." When you separate certain relationships and conversations from your personal space and life—for the sake of your peace, freedom, and self-respect—that's privacy, and you're using your naturally built-in privacy thermostat.

*Familiarity breeds contempt.*

Jesus didn't perform as many miracles in his hometown as he did in other towns. Folks back home weren't as excited about him as strangers were. Instead, they wanted to ruin him because of what they knew about his humble beginnings. They weren't just going to ruin him or chase him to the bus stop so he could catch the next ride out of town. They were going to toss him "off the cliff" (Luke 4:29).

Even with the miracles they heard he performed, some still remembered him as the controversial baby born to an unwed teenage Mary (before Joseph, her fiancé, married her). I believe those hometown people probably thought, *He hasn't found out yet who his real daddy is, and he's starting another controversy—who does he think he is?*

I can imagine the looks he got when he healed a few people there and how his town's folks felt they'd had enough of him when he declared he was a prophet. Some questioned, "Where did the man get all these ideas?" "How can he perform these kinds of miracles?" "Isn't this the carpenter's son, the son of Mary?" (Mark 6:2–4, author's paraphrase). That was their way of saying, "This boy grew up around here, went to the same daycare as our kids, got sent home from school because teachers thought he was a bit of a smart aleck, drank pomegranate juice like the other children, and loved fig pizza. Just like any other kid—there's nothing special about him." Do you know people like that? People who consult your past to determine your present or future because they don't understand or believe in you—that you can become anything great?

Too much familiarity breeds contempt and ruins privacy.

# What Is Privacy?

*Privacy affects our close and intimate relationships.*

We all need space from time to time. Even from our loved ones. Spouses included. You may be married to the best spouse in the world and have the greatest kids, but you still need physical, mental, and emotional space. Let's say you're a boss. Without having control over what your subordinates know about you, you risk becoming too familiar with them and losing their respect. For instance, if they all have unrestricted access to you or your home to snoop in your medicine cabinet, look around your bedroom, and be privy to your intimate conversations or personal business, they'd see you less as a boss and more as an equal or lower. You need a certain level of privacy to help you succeed in certain roles and meet your personal needs.

In a different way, we need privacy from our family, children, spouse, partner, or significant other. Love them, but find space and time to retreat and recharge. For a marriage to be healthy, it needs limits and space to create a sense of privacy for growth. But this needs to be mutual and sustaining, not a way to get away from your spouse to spite them. It's not a license to keep secrets or live a double life. Privacy is a way to connect with yourself—to unsaddle some emotional, mental, physical, and spiritual loads—so you can be your best self to those you love. As a result, you can impact their lives in a loving and nurturing way. Marriages thrive on privacy.

So I get this question a lot: "Grace, why can't I have privacy from my spouse?"

Nine out of ten times, when the person elaborates some more, the word *phone* comes up. Even if they don't say the word, I ask, "Is this about you locking your spouse out of your phone with some top secret password? Do you have a phone-hiding routine before you step into the shower or before going to sleep?"

If that's the case, I say, "Don't claim privacy. You don't need privacy. What you have is a *secret* you're keeping. Call it a secret. Don't give privacy a bad name."

Here's the thing. Watching sports and gaming in a man-cave is privacy—from the wife and kids. A spa day with the girls, curling up alone with a cup of tea and a good book, or a retreat out of town is privacy—from the husband and kids. That's healthy. But *secret* phone calls, texting, virtual coffees, dinners, or contact with others are not. God champions privacy in marriage. More on that in Chapters 11 and 12.

So how does anyone choose what to be private about? Here's my answer: "Whatever is true, whatever is noble, whatever is right, whatever is pure, whatever is lovely, whatever is admirable—if anything is excellent or praiseworthy—think about such things" (Philippians 4:8). It's simple. If your secret isn't about any of these things, let go of your secret. You don't need privacy for that. Every spouse or couple who approaches me with phone privacy issues goes through my Philippians 4:8 test. If what you don't want the other person to see on your phone fails the Philippians 4:8 test, you have a different issue, not privacy. Remember, God sees, hears, and knows everything.

> *Therefore a man shall leave his father and his mother and hold fast to his wife, and they shall become one flesh.*
> (Genesis 2:24 ESV)

In Psalm 139:7–12, King David realized that there was no privacy with God. So, in this spiritual poetic tribute, he asked God to disclose even one place he could possibly hide from God.

# What Is Privacy?

> *Where can I go from your Spirit?*
> *Where can I flee from your presence?*
>
> *If I go up to the heavens, you are there;*
> *if I make my bed in the depths, you are there.*
>
> *If I rise on the wings of the dawn,*
> *if I settle on the far side of the sea,*
>
> *even there your hand will guide me,*
> *your right hand will hold me fast.*
>
> *If I say, "Surely the darkness will hide me,*
> *and the light become night around me,"*
>
> *even the darkness will not be dark to you;*
> *the night will shine like the day,*
> *for darkness is as light to you.*

David answered his own questions in Psalm 139:16. He said, "Your eyes saw my unformed body; all the days ordained for me were written in your book before one of them came to be." God knows everything—your password included. There's no privacy or secret with God. He knows what you're doing inside your locked phone.

### *Enjoy a day of rest.*

Privacy not only allows us to rest safe in the knowledge that we can be ourselves and that we aren't being observed, but privacy *is* the rest we don't always need a bed for. It can be your rest from not playing roles, not doing

# Church Privacy 101

things, not being accessed or watched. Privacy is life's weekend—that happens any day and any time it is needed. Put in biblical terms, it's your mental, emotional, physical, and spiritual Sabbath. It's the kind of rest God is talking about in Psalm 46:10: "Be still, and know that I am God." This is another way of saying, "Chill and sit down. You're safe and protected." Leviticus 23:3 also reminds us that the Sabbath is a day of rest: "There are six days when you may work, but the seventh day is a day of sabbath rest, a day of sacred assembly. You are not to do any work; wherever you live, it is a sabbath to the Lord."

### *Privacy provides focus.*

Rest allows you to be alert and carefully set out for the week, months, or year ahead. Privacy allows you to rest, reflect on your needs, and take stock of where you are in life. These are times when you're honest with yourself about your values and flaws, when you consider what strengthens you emotionally and spiritually. Alone time allows you to ask yourself the following questions:

- What do I *want* when I don't *need* anything?
- What drives my peace? Is it being alone for blocks of time during my day, or do I enjoy calling a friend to catch up?
- Do I sometimes need to share concerns with a confidant?
- What are my deep fears about what people know about me?
- What personal information do I want others to have about me, or not have?
- How much knowledge of my life am I comfortable sharing?

- Do I categorize people in my life according to what I'm comfortable sharing?

Categorize people? I'm glad you asked. You should categorize people. It's a helpful privacy habit. I call it putting people on the rings of your onion. I go into detail and show you how to do this in Chapter 4. If losing control of what people know about you can rob you of your peace, it stands to reason that you can rob someone of their peace if you're careless with their personal information. Privacy is a give-and-take.

## Reflect

- Do you ever take time to pause so you can recharge?
- Do you make time to reflect on how you're doing spiritually, mentally, emotionally, and physically in the course of a day?
- Have you ever called in sick to work when you weren't really physically sick but because you needed a mental health day?
- Have you ever used an excuse to gain privacy?

## The Point

Mindful and intentional solitude allows you the privacy to be replenished, refreshed, and energized to take stock of what's going on in that moment of your life. That way, you change what needs to change and realign priorities. It not only benefits you, but it also allows you to better take care of your loved ones and serve your church community. Remember, you can't pour from an empty cup. Some employers are now open to letting you use your sick leave hours for mental health breaks. When it comes to your friends, let them know you need a break. You don't need to give a lot of details or excuses.

### *Is sharing or disclosing personal stuff healthy?*

Of course, sharing is healthy. There's a lot of that in church. While privacy is an essential need, disclosing personal business is also necessary. Think of privacy as a coin. One side of the coin preserves and protects your personal business. The other side is called *transparency,* or *openness*. Both sides give you control and are good. Except that too much of a good thing is bad. Let me explain. One hundred percent openness is bad for you, and one hundred percent privacy is also bad for you. You should always be mindful of what you share, how you share it, when you share it, and with whom you share it. That's why it's helpful to have trusted friends or confidants with whom you can safely share your thoughts, discuss important decisions, and seek advice. Someone you trust will hold you accountable. I talk about this more in Chapter 5: Finding Confidants in Church. If you're going to be transparent with someone or with a group, first consider what you need your openness to accomplish. For instance, will it encourage, alert, motivate, or help you and others in any way? How much detail do you need to provide to accomplish this? Being intentional about sharing gives you control, and helps others. You can then share what you need to share without regret.

Do you have a confidant? Or two? I do. The fact that we need a confidant at times shows how important privacy is. It might seem strange to think of *sharing* as privacy. But sharing is one healthy way we can maintain our private lives. If we didn't have a sounding board or someone to open up to, we'd be fraught with the burden of having to make difficult decisions all on our own. Our confidants can give us their perspective, gleaned from experiences we

## What Is Privacy?

might not have. They might have specialties we don't have—their knowledge is invaluable. They are also not as emotionally attached to our personal issues. And that distance allows them to have a more objective and analytical view of things. Confiding and confessing also allow us to vent our frustrations and unload what might be an emotional or spiritual burden. If we don't have a friend, loved one, or confidant as an emotional outlet, we are weighed down with life's burdens. But these burdens—physical, emotional, or spiritual—are lighter when we have someone to help us carry them. Nobody can help us if we aren't open.

Jesus had twelve disciples he could reveal things to that others didn't know about him and his father (God). The beauty of privacy is that when you share, where you share, what you share, and how much privacy you need are different from person to person, situation to situation, day to day, and hour to hour.

## Reflect

- Have you ever felt conflicted about confiding, confessing, or sharing because you were still waiting on God's directed timing?

- Have you ever needed to seek solace after hearing bad news or because you needed a break from playing all the roles you play every day?

- Have you ever sought counsel because you were burdened by an issue or needed advice?

## The Point

Folks in biblical times dealt with privacy concerns and needs. More specifically, Jesus did. So privacy is not a new idea. It's about setting limits around your life, your space, your home, your friends, and your*self*—or at work or on the subway, bus, or airplane. It's about making sure your sensitive thoughts, experiences, and information are under control.

But consider all the privacy needs you've read about so far. How many of them have anything to do with your private information being in the hands of the government or tech firms?

My focus is you. I want you to own your privacy. Own your needs. Privacy is about your well-being, discretion, decisions, choices, transparency, and protection, which apply in your physical, virtual, and digital life in and out of church.

Whenever I mention the government or privacy authorities in this book, I want you to know that they make laws to protect you, and it's helpful that you know what your privacy rights are. Besides, the government holds organizations, including churches, accountable for their privacy practices. When I bring up tech firms and businesses that collect your personal information, I do so to help you become aware of why you should maintain control of your privacy as a consumer.

At the end of the day, privacy is about you and your decisions and how some of your decisions impact others, and vice versa.

### *Dealing with organizations regarding your privacy is important.*

Earlier in the chapter, I gave you several scenarios to help you understand privacy in your personal life and intimate relationships. But what about when you're dealing with organizations? Below are a few scenarios:

## What Is Privacy?

Let's say a company encouraged you to use their services to chat with friends and share photos. They promised that if you deleted your private chat, it would be gone forever. You deleted your private chat. Later, you found out it wasn't gone forever. The company unlawfully accessed the information and used it. Such a deceptive practice is a privacy violation. They lied.

You thought your personal information was safe on social media, conferencing platforms, shopping, and credit monitoring sites. But your identity was stolen, and charges were racked up on your credit card. You now have to spend time and to reclaim your name and good credit. If you research the Federal Trade Commission's list of regulatory compliance cases, it's easy to spot reputable companies that cut corners instead of properly securing your personal information. Privacy regulators call the practice of not applying appropriate safeguards to protect privacy "unfair" practices. Rightfully, because it's unfair to you. Treating you unfairly is a privacy violation.

A business has been compiling information about you and monitoring you. They've been observing your credit card usage and your location via your phone—all without your knowledge or consent. They then shared this information with their third-party affiliates, including your spending and decision-making patterns, your locations, your contacts, your health data, and your preferences—all without your knowledge or consent. Another problem with that is that even if they don't share this information, if they don't store it securely, it can be stolen or leaked into the wrong hands. Unlawful collection and processing of your personal information without your consent is a privacy violation.

Your child was a prodigy who might graduate college before the age of fifteen. You kept it hush within the family and his school. One day, someone told the press, and reporters gathered outside his school to interview him and take photos of him. You saw photos of him in the media, indicating that he'd been followed and that these photos had been taken without his knowledge or consent. People who barely knew him were giving details about his life in interviews. You noticed his personality change almost overnight. He was depressed, and he no longer wanted to leave the house. His once-promising future was now in question, and his life was put on hold due to the constant unwelcome attention. Ambushing him in his school (where he would expect privacy), taking his photos without consent, and publishing them is a privacy issue.

Your ex had intimate photos of you or sensitive information you didn't want him to share with anyone. He wanted you back in his life and was threatening to post the photos or embarrassing information about you online if you didn't cooperate. Threatening to publish or expose sensitive information is a privacy issue. It's also blackmail.

A credit reporting agency's affiliate gathered your private information for Equifax, Experian, TransUnion, and other credit reporting agencies. The information they compiled and reported was incorrect. As a result, you got turned down for a mortgage because neither the affiliate nor the agency addressed the obvious inaccuracies. As a result, you now have inaccurate information on your credit report—with errors on your report including a duplicated debt you don't owe, the misspelling of your name, and an incorrect birth date. It's illegal for a credit reporting agency or affiliate to knowingly report inaccurate credit information. This is also a privacy issue.

The government created a profile of you based on information they gathered from digital surveillance of your searches on Google and your payment history. Because of the type of books you bought online and your interest in spy thrillers and military covert operations, they suspected you were involved in intelligence activities for a foreign power. One day, while you were at the airport trying to get to your son's graduation, you were told you'd been put on a no-fly list. You'd lost your right to fly. You ordered an Uber to return home, but your card was declined. You called your bank, and customer ser-

## What Is Privacy?

vice told you your accounts had been frozen. All because of a computer or machine-based decision, not human knowledge of the truth or your actual situation. It took months to undo the damage that had been done. Plus, you missed your son's graduation. Profiling is a privacy issue.

Let's say you were in a witness protection program. You were given a new identity. Your very life depended on privacy. You prayed daily that hackers wouldn't access any witness protection computer systems and leak your real identity. If your personal information got out, it would put you and your loved ones in mortal danger. Hacking is a privacy issue.

What if you're just plain scared of speaking your mind or sharing your political opinion about how and why the government is a pain—or that you love the current regime? You're scared to go to a political rally. You won't participate in a demonstration, even if you really want to. You're scared to be affiliated with political organizations. You don't go to church or synagogue because you fear the consequences for you or your family. You've basically given up your civil liberties and right to free speech. To make matters worse, your church is divided on political views. This, too, is a privacy issue.

I extracted these examples from real stories. They happen more often than you can imagine.

## Protect Your Privacy

Identity thieves can use your personal information to create a profile of you, impersonate you, or even clean out the funds in your bank accounts. Keep your precious documents out of your car and out of sight at home. This information can potentially harm you if you're careless about it. If I asked you to empty out your bag, wallet, or pocket, after ruling out things like sanitizer, gum, and mints, you'd be left with items that have your personal information, and that's what you should protect. That would include your cell phone with texts, call logs, voice mails, emails, and videos; your contact list; your Internet search history; your receipts—especially those from oil changes and your car dealership; and your bank cards, ID cards, and anything else that has the following information:

- full name

- gender, race, ethnicity

- home and work addresses

- email address and/or home phone number

- driver's license

- mobile phone number

- family photos

Now let's look at your home. You also have important documents you don't usually take with you when you're out and about. They shouldn't be left unattended. They should be put away, if not under lock and key, at least not made easily accessible, especially if you routinely have visitors and guests to your home and if you live in an apartment. Your apartment manager might stop by with the plumber, electrician, or potential new tenants if you're moving. Make sure you don't keep these important documents out in the open:

- anything with your birth date (month, day, and year)

- passport

- wallet or credit and/or debit cards

## What Is Privacy?

- insurance beneficiary information
- employment files
- passwords (social media, work, and personal devices)
- information about your political affiliation
- credit reports
- personal documents
- fingerprints
- background check information
- computer, laptop, or iPad without password protection
- Social Security number (SSN)
- health and medical records and prescriptions (past, present, and future)
- bank or retirement account numbers or personal checks, which include your routing information

Don't assume that someone won't try to stuff one of those into their pocket or bag when you're not looking. But why stuff their pockets when they can take a photo of it? Thanks to cell phones, someone can quickly snap a photo of your documents without you even knowing. In April 2019, a visitor to a celebrity's home discreetly snapped a photo of a private portrait of her children and posted it online. This privacy issue is not limited to celebrities. I've helped apartment dwellers who were victims of passport, photo, designer shoes, and Social Security card theft. I always wonder what else the culprits might have taken a photo of that the apartment dweller didn't even realize.

Have you ever wondered why someone would steal your personal information? For the same reasons a thief would steal your TV, camera, laptop, or phone. But your personal information is worth considerably more. Marijuana is not the only product sold or distributed on the dark web, the Internet's black market. Your personal information is in demand, like weed. Below is a range of prices your personal information could sell for. These prices may have increased due to inflation.

- diplomas $100–$400

- driver's license $20

- US passports $1,000–$2,000

- medical records can go for up to $1,000

- online payment information $20–$200 (including Stripe, PayPal, Square, Cash App, Zelle, and others)[6]

Just as it is common for legitimate services and products to offer deals, there are also "combos" or "bundles" in the black market or dark web. If the thief has your full name combined with "SSN, birth date, account numbers and other data that make them desirable,"[7] this gives the buyer more information to access your finances and clean out your bank account. A bundle has equity. The buyer can use the information to create credit card accounts in your name. A bundle can sell for as little as thirty dollars. The far-reaching negative effects of this identity theft on your financial and personal life, however, will cost you a lot more than thirty dollars.

This is a major privacy issue.

Be ready to hold any person, business, or organization you've given personal information to accountable, because that's what the law does. Since it's your information, your participation is vital. The more you know about pri-

## What Is Privacy?

vacy, the better. You'll think twice before you fill out forms online or offline. You won't be fooled by a so-called bargain like 40 percent off in exchange for you completing a survey or form with your full name, mailing address, email, phone number—you name it. And instead of focusing on fluffing pillows and washing dishes when someone is coming over, you will first put away your personal information.

### *What types of personal information should your church protect?*

Another important privacy concern is managing and controlling the personal information you give your church when you establish membership, during your membership, and after you leave. Your privacy is protected by laws and regulations, and your church must comply. What type of personal information is involved depends on the information processing activities of your church, not just the size of the church. Let me elaborate. Some churches collect and store more personal information than other churches. The scale of the activities matters. Some churches do more with personal information than other churches—they analyze, profile, monitor, transfer across international borders, share with their branches and partners, and sell personal information—meaning they may have a higher risk of violating people's privacy. All these activities are called *processing activities*. The risks these activities present matter to regulators and can increase the legal and regulatory obligations of your church. Typically, most churches create, collect, maintain, and store some of the personal information below. And your church should know that the law requires them to protect it. Check out the companion book, *Church Privacy Team*, for an extensive list.

- a directory (with email, home address, phone number, and current photo)
- birth and death records

- church leadership voting forms
- conference registrations
- counseling records
- donor financial information
- education/course records
- health records—church clinic visits
- leadership position forms
- marriage records
- membership and ministry forms
- mental health records
- published prayer requests in church bulletins
- senior and youth contact information or profiles
- tithing or offering envelopes (with credit card details, full name, and membership number)
- volunteer sign-up forms

These should be lawfully secured, with the church members', visitors', and donors' privacy guarded.

### *Privacy doesn't mean only one thing.*

Sometimes it's hard to imagine a business being interested in your personal information or misusing it. Why would someone need your identifying

## What Is Privacy?

information? If you don't know why businesses work so hard to get it, it's because you don't understand its value. They do. Their business success depends on how much they know about people or consumers. That goes for organizations that are constantly pressuring you for more of your personal information.

On the Internet, in the hands of a church or a business, our personal information is like a hot, out-of-the-oven dessert left unattended. It's too risky to be left out in the open—someone it wasn't meant for will devour it. Remember, privacy is about a living, breathing person. It's about you. Not being aware of your privacy needs and concerns can be costly. Knowing what privacy is allows you and your family a level of control and protection you can cherish.

I mentioned earlier that the word *privacy* is a bit of a catchall and has many meanings and categories: information, communication, physical, psychological, spiritual, and digital, among others. Privacy is broad. Now you have a better understanding of the different aspects and types of privacy and why they are important. You can use the tools and resources in the upcoming chapters to address your own privacy issues and protect the privacy of your loved ones, your church family, your colleagues, and your employees. Understanding what privacy is and does and how it functions across many different mediums and contexts can help address many of your earthly and spiritual needs. Shall we?

> *Be alert and of sober mind. Your enemy the devil prowls around like a roaring lion looking for someone to devour.*
> (1 Peter 5:8)

# 3

# Five Things the Bible Says to Hush About

*Set a guard over my mouth, Lord;*
*keep watch over the door of my lips.*

(Psalm 141:3)

## Does the Bible Value Privacy?

You bet. How does God demonstrate that in our lives?

Well, he says he hides certain things from us (Matthew 11:25–27). We have to go through Jesus and the Holy Spirit to access what he hides. That means that having knowledge of Jesus and God is important here. God chooses to be obscure at times to carry out certain missions or commissions (1 Corinthians 2:9), possibly to keep us from messing up his plan. He doesn't reveal everything at once, and definitely not to everyone. There's a time for revealing everything that's private (1 John 3:2). He chooses to show his attributes in both seen and unseen things (Romans 1:19). And he reveals them through his Spirit, who researches and vets the hearts of those who receive the revelations (1 Corinthians 2:10–11). Also, God wants us to know and understand that he has freely given us information about himself (1 Corinthians 2:12). To sum these up, God values privacy. He reveals

## Five Things the Bible Says to Hush About

certain things to some people and not to others. He is particular about the timing, where he reveals information, and how much information he reveals about himself.

Many in the Bible protected their privacy from invaders and violators. Who is a privacy violator or invader? This can be a person who talks too much or someone who enjoys listening to a person who talks too much. I don't mean *too much* in terms of the number of words but about issues that are none of their business. It's also someone who violates other people's personal space or snoops through their things—including their information. Other than invading other folks' privacy, the Bible says you should hush about a number of things.

Let's focus on five of them. Below are five things you should keep private. The first are your prayers, which are your conversations with God. The second is your fasting. The third is your offering and charity. The fourth is your body, and the fifth is the sexual functions of your body and sexual intimacy.

## Your Prayers

Have you ever prayed about issues you couldn't talk to anyone about? Prayers are your personal conversations with God. Prayers are private, intimate thoughts you tell God or questions you ask him. They are personal, private, and confidential. Prayers are about your needs and requests. They might be your confessions, sort of like you turning yourself in, and you might get deep into the details because you know God saw what you did or thought. You beg for mercy. And whatever it is you're talking about, you know God won't judge you. But people will. For that reason, you keep your prayers and confessions private.

# Church Privacy 101

I appreciate prayer privacy. You know, sometimes I'm mad at God because things don't go my way. Guess what? Not many people admit that they sometimes feel that way toward him. There's nothing wrong with arguing with God or having a disagreement. It shows God you're paying attention and that you're aware that he's in control, not you. You're like that kid a teacher appreciates because you ask questions and challenge her, while other kids are passing around notes, giggling, and not paying attention.

One of my favorite gospel artists is Aaron Shust. His songs "Give Me Words to Speak" and "My Hope Is in You" are both very deep prayers. In a radio interview, Shust gave listeners words of encouragement when he said, "It's okay to fight with God. . . . Be real with him. God wants your real."[1] He believes God honors arguments and a little bit of wrestling. It's one of the ways we show him that we believe he is real. You can do all that with God. Yes, you can argue and question, just as many biblical heroes of faith did, in a safe and private place. And God won't be angry, and he won't tell anyone. Whatever happens in prayer stays in prayer. Guaranteed.

> *When you pray, go into your room, close the door and pray to your Father, who is unseen. Then your Father, who sees what is done in secret, will reward you.*
> (Matthew 6:6)

Seclude yourself, even if there's no door to be closed. That doesn't mean you'll never again hold other people's hands and pray aloud in a group. There's time for that too. You have public prayers—in a church, temple, synagogue, chapel, or sanctuary—and you have private prayers—in your room or car, at your desk, or kneeling over your flower bed. But prayer shouldn't be a show. A prayer is not a performance. Your real audience is God. He knows your heart.

## Five Things the Bible Says to Hush About

*When you pray, don't be like the hypocrites who love to pray publicly on street corners and in the synagogues where everyone can see them. I tell you the truth, that is all the reward they will ever get.*
(Matthew 6:5 NLT)

He already knows what you need before you speak, so word choices, adjectives, synonyms, clichés, and digging deep into supporting details don't really matter. He wants you to surrender your control. An example of that is when Jesus parabolically hacked the prayers of two men at the temple to demonstrate to his disciples that prayer reveals us to ourselves (Luke 18:10–14). Years ago, I started analyzing my prayers to see if they were mostly about me or if they also added value to others' lives. That observation changed and redirected me. Prayer is a gesture of surrender, showing that you trust God and believe he hears you and has all the answers.

## Reflect

- Have you ever prayed in public or in a group like you were auditioning for a part in a movie as a prayer leader?

- Have you ever chosen words and phrases that would yield the most "Amens"?

- Have you ever prayed to demonstrate your knowledge of the Word of God?

## The Point

Not every issue you take to God and the experience God wants to have with you is made for public prayer. And if you aim to impress people with your transparency, you'll likely violate your privacy and not experience being real and intimate with God—you may not have clear, revolutionary takeaways from your prayers.

> *I will answer them before they even call to me.*
> *While they are still talking about their needs,*
> *I will go ahead and answer their prayers!*
> (Isaiah 65:24 NLT)

## Your Fasts

Have you ever been on a fast that was torturous to your tummy and mood? When I first started fasting, it was rough. Every time someone said, "Are you okay?" I resisted telling them I was fasting. That question was my cue. I knew it was time to fix my face, not look so hungry, and be strong during my fast. The second thing the Bible says to keep hush is when you fast. Don't use it as a conversation starter. Act normal. Be yourself. The only thing that's changed is that you're a little hungrier. You're turning down your plate so you can focus spiritually. "And when you fast, don't make it obvious, as the hypocrites do, for they try to look miserable and disheveled so people will admire them for their fasting. I tell you the truth, that is the only reward they will ever get" (Matthew 6:16 NLT).

Of course, you're supposed to have a headache and feel a little tired. But haven't you felt worse when you don't fast? What's the problem? God says, "Don't make a federal case out of it." If you can't handle a dry fast with no food or water, try other fasts. Read Daniel 1:12–16 and try the Daniel Fast. Skip meat, drink only water, and eat only veggies.

Your fasting is a personal decision. It's still private even if it's a group fast.

When I was writing this chapter, I wondered how to define fasting with one word, without preaching. I opened my copy of *The 40-Day Surrender Fast* by Dr. Celeste Owens, and the word *surrender* jumped out at me. *Surrender* is the perfect word. You're surrendering to God. It's a decision you make at a set time. Because it's your choice to eat mainly spiritual food, you should hush feeling sorry for yourself. In case you didn't know, in your physical weakness when you fast, God's strength is what supports you.

> *And when He had come into the house, His disciples asked Him privately, "Why could we not cast it out?"*
>
> *So He said to them, "This kind can come out by nothing but prayer and fasting."*
> (Mark 9:28–29 NKJV)

It sounds to me like if you fast, pray, and hush, you can make particular miracles happen.

## Your Offering

Ever notice how discreet you were when you used to give little, and that didn't change even when you started giving a lot more to your church? You're not wrong. The Bible says to be discreet about your giving. This means tithes, offerings, donations, and gifts. Even charity outside the church and giving of your time are included. Keep these hush, whether you give them as cash or through Cash App, Zelle, PayPal, or Stripe.

# Church Privacy 101

> *When you give to someone in need, don't let your left hand know what your right hand is doing. Give your gifts in private, and your Father, who sees everything, will reward you.*
> (Matthew 6:3–4 NLT)

Don't announce how much you give. Practicing privacy equals all kinds of rewards from God. The Bible says that God will supply all of your needs—your need for a stronger relationship with him and your need for wisdom, salvation, faith, health, strength, life, justice, peace, contentment, growth, and other rewards and provisions.

What should you do if a church leader or preacher asks members to give $100 toward renovating the church nursery? This is not a donation you can keep quiet about—everyone who has chosen to participate is giving $100. But that's okay. There's a particular goal and a specific expectation. It's a special request. You may also choose to give $200, but you can keep that extra $100 between you and God. However, in the unlikely event that a church leader asks how much you gave and the amount you gave was less than $100, don't lie. Remember the couple who dropped dead in church when they lied about (Acts 5:1–10)? They said one thing but did another. Also, don't lie if you gave $200. You didn't advertise it; they asked. Tell them.

What about parts of the world where people tithe with items and not with cash or credit cards? During a business trip in 2015, I worshipped at a church about twenty miles from Nairobi, Kenya. When it was offering time, people headed for the altar with roosters, fresh eggs, and some of the freshest fruits and vegetables I'd ever seen. They gave their most valuable things. These were also items they knew the church and the congregation could use. It humbled me. I could tell they were giving their best—they were joyful. God says we should all give cheerfully. It's not a competition. This brought back memories of my parents being posted as missionaries in different places. The congregation did the same thing there—my mom would tell me. Members of fishing communities brought their best catch. Farmers brought their harvests, and craftsmen brought furniture—chairs, tables, and benches. It's a beautiful expression, but not everyone is a fisherman, farmer, or craftsperson.

Ultimately, it's not so much what is being offered. It's about the heart of the giver and the spirit in which the gift is given. It's the attitude toward God. For instance, are you giving cheerfully or out of compulsion? Are you giving for others to see? God judges the heart, not the gift. He says it's best to keep it quiet.

*Each one must give as he has decided in his heart, not reluctantly or under compulsion, for God loves a cheerful giver.*
(2 Corinthians 9:7 ESV)

## Your Body

The fourth thing to hush about is your body, which should be kept covered and private. The Internet may seem private, but it's not. Even when spouses send intimate photos to each other, their bodies may be private, but the electronic transmission is not. The book of Leviticus hashes out *nakedness* and its consequences more than any other book in the Bible. It says that when our nakedness is seen by others (meaning someone we're not married to), it brings shame. What I think this means is that giving publicity to one's nakedness is shaming and shameful.

Of course, nakedness is not limited to your physical body. It includes the bareness of your decisions, your behavior, your choices, and your thoughts that you don't wish to expose to others or allow them to observe. When

# Church Privacy 101

Adam and Eve fell out of their good standing with God, they hid behind bushes. Their excuse? They were ashamed and scared. Their private spiritual closeness with God had been invaded and violated by Satan, the serpent in the garden. Adam and Eve had traded their privacy and intimacy with God for new ideas and knowledge. It turns out it was a fraud. They got evicted from the Garden of Eden. The culprit shamed them and ruined their future. What a snake!

***Even when you're not strutting your stuff, you may be watched.***

Bathsheba took off her clothes to bathe. Who doesn't? But that's not why her bath was recorded in the Bible. She was bathing in her courtyard, where, as was customary, she would normally have an expectation of privacy, with no one observing her. However, an idle spectator saw her. It was as if she'd posted revealing photos online in the public domain. She had no immoral intentions, but King David, a person very devoted to God, was strolling on the roof of his high-rise palace, people-watching. "One evening David got up from his bed and walked around on the roof of the palace. From the roof he saw a woman bathing. The woman was very beautiful, and David sent someone to find out about her" (2 Samuel 11:2–3). It sounds like he looked up her profile. "The man said, 'She is Bathsheba, the daughter of Eliam and the wife of Uriah the Hittite'" (2 Samuel 11:3).

David was interested, but she was married. Her husband was off fighting a war. But David thought, *What has that got to do with me?* That was selfishness kicking in. As military commander, he was supposed to be on the battlefield, defending his territories. Instead, he let his soldiers handle the war. He totally forgot his values and his standing with God. It was all about his evil desires. He contacted Bathsheba, and she responded. "Then David sent messengers to get her. She came to him" (2 Samuel 11:4).

## Five Things the Bible Says to Hush About

I'm not faulting Bathsheba, but your nakedness can arouse others—even if you don't intend it to. When you display yourself, especially your naked body, you attract attention, good or bad. Strutting your stuff may mean different things to different people. In the Bible, it's not a compliment. "The LORD says, 'The women of Zion are haughty, walking along with outstretched necks, flirting with their eyes, strutting along with swaying hips, with ornaments jingling on their ankles'" (Isaiah 3:16).

Bathsheba was definitely naked, but in her own private courtyard or bathroom. When David saw her, he could have looked away and gone about his business. Instead, he sent for her, knowing what would happen when she got to the palace. Maybe she'd bathed alfresco several times before and had never been seen by anyone. But when the king commands an audience, you dare not say no. When the king's men arrived to pick her up, she went along out of respect and duty. It could have been for any reason that David sent for her—such as news from the warfront where her husband was fighting. He was her husband's boss after all. Unfortunately, it turned out this invitation wasn't about national security at all.

How does this translate to privacy in our day and time? It's the same as taking photos of your nakedness for your personal use. If another person knows the photos exist, they may view them without your knowledge or permission and exploit them for their own desires and uses, even if you don't intend for other people to see them. Now you're facing the consequences of their actions, and everyone judges you. You wish you'd never taken those photos. This takes me to my next point.

*Marriage should be honored by all, and the marriage bed kept pure,*
*for God will judge the adulterer and all the sexually immoral.*
(Hebrews 13:4)

## Sexual Intimacy

The fifth thing you should keep private is sexual intimacy. In the Bible, God prescribed that two people have sex as husband and wife behind closed doors. What happens and what is seen (by them) in the bedroom stays in the bedroom. No third parties are allowed. There are limits that everyone is expected to respect, no matter who they are in a person's life. If your title is not "spouse," it's not your business.

If what happens in your marriage bed is posted online, you're inviting an audience—a third person. A third person contaminates. That's what *defilement* means. Some people, "adulterers and sexually immoral," are serial contaminators—emotionally, visually, and physically. God hates privacy violations of the marriage bed because the third person involved ends up drawing the husband and wife apart, and the bed loses its integrity. Privacy is about respect and honor. It's better to keep that aspect of your life out of reach and away from prying eyes.

> *But I say, anyone who even looks at a woman with lust has already committed adultery with her in his heart.*
> (Matthew 5:28 NLT)

## Situational Privacy

Now that you know the five things God says to hush about, let's discuss the different situations surrounding them. Now, what if privacy is not about honor but about timing or a particular situation? It's still privacy and a valid need. I sometimes call this "situational hushness." In the Bible, Jesus healed two sufferers: the blind and the lame. He then asked them to refrain from telling anyone that he had healed them. But they told *everyone* they met. Can

## Five Things the Bible Says to Hush About

you blame them? They were so overjoyed that they wanted to shout it from the rooftops. And what about those who knew people who were healed? Imagine if you saw someone who was crippled a few hours before, and now they're miraculously healed and walking. Wouldn't you be curious?

But there was a reason Jesus asked certain people who were healed to keep it quiet for a while. He was always very intentional about privacy. One reason was that he knew it might draw negative attention too soon, especially from critics who were always arguing against his theology. But he was so compassionate that he couldn't turn away the sick because people would use it as ammunition against him for breaking certain religious laws. So he healed them, and it drew attention, both good and bad. This type of privacy was about timing and situations. Jesus had a goal for his ministry. Between sermons, prayers, and healings, his schedule was tight. Distractions were not an option. He had better things to do with his time, including helping more people rather than answering religious critics. Privacy helped cut down on distractions and bought him time.

*And they have defeated him by the blood of the Lamb*
*and by their testimony.*
(Revelation 12:11 NLT)

A testimony is not a bad thing. The devil is defeated when we testify about what Jesus has done for us. However, every detail is not important in a testimony. Plan what you want to say and share information that will not compromise your safety or privacy or someone else's. "So faith comes from hearing, that is, hearing the Good News about Christ" (Romans 10:17 NLT). Sharing the problem you had and how God intervened increases your faith and the faith of the hearer. Otherwise, "how can they believe in the one of whom they have not heard?" (Romans 10:14)

What about privacy for the individual? Remember the story of a father asking Jesus if there was anything Jesus could do for his epileptic son? He started his request by saying to Jesus that others had tried but couldn't help him. Basically, he was saying he'd been to others, but they just couldn't get the demons out.

People who went to Jesus were desperate to be healed, but not because they wanted the whole world to know they were sick. They were seeking healing, and privacy ceased to matter to them in that moment when they saw the possibility of getting healing from Jesus. Coming to Jesus publicly was mortifying. But people didn't want to lose their lives or a loved one's to disease. That included the father of the twelve-year-old girl, the centurion whose servant was sick, the woman with the bleeding issue, the demon-possessed man, and the father of the epileptic boy.

They had exhausted the resources they had at the time—herbalists, healers, priests—and nothing had worked. So they went to a public place to try their chances with Jesus—the healer and deliverer everyone was talking about. They were healed publicly but still maintained their private lives. Public healing didn't mean they perpetually gave up their privacy. They spread their own story of healing, even when Jesus asked them to hush (Matthew 8:3–4). In other situations, he allowed people he healed to spread the word about their healing right away (Mark 5:18–19).

Remember the faith of the centurion, or army commander? His sick servant never met Jesus but got healed *remotely*. The idea of receiving healing from a distance, or remotely, is the same today (Luke 7:1–9). In our day, people post photos of afflicted body parts online, and others stream healing services to get healing or testify that they received healing—but they're not forfeiting the privacy of all aspects of their lives. I believe something unexplainable happens between the desperation to get healing and getting the healing. One of the most popular healing places in modern times is the

## Five Things the Bible Says to Hush About

Synagogue, Church of All Nations. By 4:30 in the morning, thousands of people have already lined up. Some sleep nearby for a chance to get in line. This is what blind Bartimaeus had to deal with: an overwhelming crowd (Mark 10:45–52).

Some of these folks who gathered, waiting for healing, had gone through several surgeries and were dying. Those whom medical doctors had given up on came to receive healing, even if it was in public. Once they got healed, they announced to the world how Jesus had healed the disease or sickness they had hidden from people for years or had been ashamed of. Would you hush if you couldn't walk for years and now you could?

It's hard to remain silent when a blessing or miracle is so profound that it knocks all thoughts of privacy out of your head. You can't really put a lid on God. With God, privacy is not absolute. Just as with the few he asked to keep hush about the miracles he performed for them, he may ask you to keep hush for a time, but it won't be forever. That is situational privacy.

Situational privacy is about you discerning what God leads you to share and what he expects you to keep to yourself for a time.

## Reflect

- Do you always feel the need to disclose your conversations with God to others?

- Do you share to encourage others spiritually? Why do you share?

- Are you often very outspoken about how much you give to churches or charities?

- In what ways have you not been private about certain aspects of your physical body? Are you seeking attention for a reason?

- What habits do you have right now that expose or give public attention to your marriage bed and its activities? Have you invited a third party into your marriage bed? What is one big step you can take today to stop it?

## The Point

From the Scriptures in this section, it seems clear that God wants you to use discretion about your praying, fasting, giving, body, and sexual intimacy. When you give, God wants that to be just between you and him. You can, however, encourage others to follow your example and give by faith. When I didn't fully understand giving in church, Sister Marlene explained her own giving habits to me, but she shrewdly left the amount she gave the church out of our conversation. I still got the value of her tutelage without knowing the exact amount she gave. Others have taught me about praying and fasting in the same way—without divulging everything.

Concerning your body and sexual intimacy, always think about the impact your decisions about your body have on you and others. The story of David and Bathsheba didn't end after her privacy was violated or after spending the day together. It also involved adultery, an unexpected pregnancy, public shaming, a ruined marriage, several deaths, rapes, and a lot of lies to cover up the scandal.

> *In the shelter of your presence you hide them*
> *from all human intrigues;*
> *you keep them safe in your dwelling*
> *from accusing tongues.*
>
> (Psalm 31:20)

*Five Things the Bible Says to Hush About*

# Church Privacy Myths

God expects us to hush about certain things. But what does that mean in the church? Let's debunk a few church privacy myths. You'll find this helpful when you're unsure about asking for privacy from church folks.

### *Myth #1*
Wanting privacy is a waste of time because nothing is hidden. "There is nothing concealed that will not be disclosed, or hidden that will not be made known" (Matthew 10:26).

### *Truth*
Scripture is true. But does it say that privacy is a waste of time? No. I believe Matthew 10:26 is talking about God's knowledge. It doesn't suggest that your life should be an open book. God is ever-present, omniscient, and all-seeing. This is a blessing because God is not the reason we need privacy; other people are. God will not use what he knows to harm us. People will.

### *Myth #2*
Privacy is influenced by a self-centered or individualistic culture. It is for those with selfish and immoral desires searching for any way to hide their sins. Privacy is born out of a legal rather than a spiritual need. It doesn't belong in the church.

### *Truth*
Privacy is a physical, emotional, mental, and spiritual need. Jesus needed it, and so do we. That need doesn't change in relation to the church, which is, at times, our second family. It's hard to be a part of our church family or community without trust. It's hard to share openly or give to the church without

# Church Privacy 101

trust. Privacy is one way to ensure trust. And it is one of many humanitarian needs churches have the opportunity to meet. The duty to meet privacy needs is not driven primarily by law. The law has its place and its expectations. Privacy is also spiritual care. When we're discussing privacy within communion and fellowship, it is wholly personal—physically, emotionally, mentally, and spiritually.

### *Myth #3*

Privacy rights are not biblical. There's no such thing. Worldly people made this up.

### *Truth*

It depends on which Bible passages you're reading. Some people don't like using the terms *right* or *privacy right*. To them, this word and phrase sound like notions unbelievers or the government invented. Even if that were the case, what's wrong with a *right* anyway? As long as it doesn't lead you to justifying or covering wrongdoing, it's okay.

For instance, when you drive, aren't you glad you have a rule called *right of way*? It saves you from drivers who don't have the right of way crashing into you. It stops them from cutting you off and causing injuries or even death. Privacy establishes limits. A person's violation of your privacy limits could also cause injuries. Although blood or broken bones are absent in many cases, you still have emotional, mental, and spiritual wounds to deal with. For instance, Esther Salas, the New Jersey federal judge, was targeted by an armed attorney who posed as a delivery guy. He shot her son to death and left her husband in critical condition. She was left with a lifetime of emotional injuries. Someone who didn't agree with her court decision obtained her home address and other personal information and then attacked her and

## Five Things the Bible Says to Hush About

her family. The person violated privacy limits. Should you have *privacy rights* to protect you and your family?

The Bible talks about the *right* of the firstborn. God made sure Abraham gave Ishmael his due inheritance, even though he was born out of wedlock—that wasn't Ishmael's fault. Jesus said it's a form of wickedness when a husband wants to get rid of his wife because of his own selfishness. Jesus mentioned that Moses was fed up with such men, so he required that they at least make it official. That is, show respect and honor the wife's *right* to a certificate of divorce, possibly so the woman would be free from societal condemnation—shaming, rejection, discrimination, assault, and other related consequences. God himself invented and granted fundamental *rights*.

Let's say you move into the beautiful home of your dreams. It is over your budget, but you believe it will be worth it in the long run. But as soon as you hang the first blind in your window, your homeowner association orders you to take it down because this is a zero-blind neighborhood. Would you hop on your laptop and search for the *rights* you have? Would you claim your privacy rights in this situation?

If a neighbor near your church plants spinach on the land where the church intends to build a parking lot in three weeks, how will your church react? Will they wait for the spinach to mature and be harvested? Will they say *rights* are unbiblical, forget the parking lot, and let the neighbor grow spinach? I don't think so. Your church will claim its *right* to the land. The church will point out the land's boundaries or limits to prove that the land belongs to the church. Because the land belongs to the church, the church gets to decide how it should be used, who they will share it with, and how much of the land is shared. And what if the neighbor refuses to uproot their spinach? They'll hear from the government. That's how the state will respond if the church is found by the authorities to have breached its privacy duties to the public or violated a church member's privacy by neglecting to apply privacy principles and requirements to protect personal information. Regulators won't say the church shouldn't be held accountable because privacy is unbiblical. They will uphold the *rights* of the individual.

## Myth #4
If you want or need privacy, you've got secrets.

## Truth
It depends. Not telling everyone in your church community what's going on in your life doesn't mean you're keeping secrets or hiding something. Neither are you a fellowship wrecker, pushing people away from getting close to you or stopping them from expressing their genuine love for you. Wherever privacy is misunderstood, people will think this way. This is also a way to guilt you into oversharing or even pushing your boundaries. Privacy is about choice. You control how much or how little you feel comfortable sharing, with whom, and at which time.

## Myth #5
It is wrong to commit to helping someone who asks you to keep what they share with you private. It shows they don't trust you. Otherwise, they wouldn't give you such instructions. They must be hiding something, and you shouldn't get involved in secrecy or help them.

## Truth
*Privacy* and *secrecy* have different meanings. Some people use one when they mean the other. They're similar because, in both, personal affairs or knowledge are undisclosed. For example, you may just want to take it easy and not go to a birthday party. You're not mad at anyone. You just don't feel like

## Five Things the Bible Says to Hush About

mingling or being social on that particular evening, but you don't tell anyone why you aren't attending. Privacy is about self-care. On the other hand, secrecy is not a natural seclusion of oneself from others for a mental break. A secret is created—by act or invention. I'll explain. You, another person, a situation, or an organization can create secrets—intentionally and unintentionally. A secret is information, an object, a person, or an event you're hiding. It could be the surprise party you're planning for a member of your ministry, your spouse, your fiancé, or your boss. You warned everyone to keep it a secret. Businesses have secrets. They're called trade secrets—strategies, recipes, methods, formulas, codes, and ingredients—which keep businesses competitive. For instance, KFC's fried chicken recipe is a trade secret. The government also has secrets and secret agents for national security purposes.

There are good secrets, and there are bad ones. We often say someone is keeping a secret when we think they're hiding something negative. For example, someone may be hiding an immoral or illegal activity and attempting to keep it hidden forever to evade justice or consequences. Other examples include extramarital affairs or unhealthy relationships, destructive habits or behaviors, theft, murder, drug trafficking, and other crimes. David's secrets were his adultery with Bathsheba, her pregnancy, and his order for Uriah's death.

If you're on social media enough, you've seen tweets or posts every day saying, "My relationship is private, but my lover is not a secret." This is a declaration that the person's need for privacy doesn't mean they're doing anything questionable—or hiding who they're courting or married to. They just want people to stay out of the details of their personal lives.

There's nothing wrong when someone says, "Don't tell anyone," before sharing their confidence. They're just reminding you about limits. Because sometimes we do forget limits. If you're going to be a good confidant, work on your memory. Don't be forgetful. It's hurtful when you betray confidence. Don't let a reminder offend you.

## Reflect

- Have you ever disclosed private information and then immediately regretted it?

- Have you ever betrayed a trust? Did you apologize for it or make an excuse? Maybe it sounded like "Sorry, I told him. I didn't know you didn't want him to know. I thought you guys were close."

- Have you ever forgotten that the information you had about someone was private and you spilled it? You could have really used a reminder.

- Have you ever thought a friend in church was secretive, self-centered, and spiritually immature all because she asked for privacy?

## The Point

Understand why someone asks for privacy. They may need space or time. Privacy means peace—the absence of distraction that comes with many people knowing what the person isn't ready to share. Isn't it your hope that God will use you to identify other people's needs and meet them? Well, here you go. Privacy is a need. It's also a fundamental right. There's nothing wrong with a promise of confidence to someone. One day, you might need it. Everyone needs it. In some cases, that promise is either spoken or written. In others, it's implied but expected. The law recognizes that not every promise of privacy is written, spoken, and/or on a signed contract. But the fact that

## Five Things the Bible Says to Hush About

it was implied or expected due to the type of relationship or situation gives it weight.

More on that in Chapters 4, 5, and 14 when I go deeper into privacy in our relationships.

I've made a living reminding employees of corporations that they signed and promised to keep their employer's confidential business affairs hush during and after employment. No guesswork there. I've never seen an employee complain or quit their job because they felt my being invited to talk about privacy meant their employer didn't trust them. Everyone needs to be reminded every now and then about their promise to hush—even in church.

### *Be intentional and discreet.*

Expressing your need for privacy shows you're aware of your needs and value your private life. You're your own personal information factory. You want that factory to be well-managed—classified and categorized. That means certain privileges are reserved for a few close people, for example, your *real* friends and confidants. You use wisdom and discretion. When information leaves the factory, it is what you allow, including the quantity and the timing you're comfortable with. It doesn't mean your life is on absolute privacy lockdown, that you don't enjoy your other friends who are not as close, or that you'll never share anything with anyone other than the select few. It means you're intentional and discreet. These two Bible passages approve rather than criticize discretion and wisdom:

> *When words are many, transgression is not lacking,*
> *but whoever restrains his lips is prudent.*
> (Proverbs 10:19 ESV)

*Know this, my beloved brothers: let every person be quick to hear, slow to speak, slow to anger.*
(James 1:19 ESV)

# 4

# Managing Your Circle

*Whoever can be trusted with very little can also be trusted with much, and whoever is dishonest with very little will also be dishonest with much.*

(Luke 16:10)

## Making Onion Rings

Let's talk about onions. Not the kind you tuck into a burger, toss in a garden salad, or caramelize and fold into your mac and cheese. I mean the kind we use to manage our privacy. Privacy onions and their rings are a privacy model I created to manage privacy. I use them to help me decide who is in my privacy circle. I add people to different rings in different onions to manage my discretion, or who I tell what and when. It makes sense to me. A good way to remember this model is to remember that people in your life are like onions—they can be sweet and season your life, but even the ones who don't mean to hurt you can make you cry. It's a fairly simple system. Each ring represents the level of private information you divulge to the people in that onion. You'll give deeper personal information to people on some rings and not-so-personal information to those on other rings.

One onion won't work in every situation. Your life is divided into a thousand compartments and choices. Each compartment requires a different decision. You have people in your inner circle you seek guidance and counsel from, share with, and confide in. No one person has all the answers, especially if it's not a situation they can relate to or have any experience with. This is why you have more than one confidant. This is also why your health information, career decisions, and relationship decisions should each have their onion. Sometimes you need different people for different private concerns in your life. The colleague you excitedly tell about your interviews with two major firms might not be the friend you confide in when you're not sure you can date someone or accept a marriage proposal. The people in your onions will change. They can be suitable in one season or situation and not in another. This is normal. Most onion rings are situational and seasonal. But each person on your ring needs to earn their spot. Where they land depends on whether they are high risk, medium risk, or low risk. Why should you worry about risks? All relationships that are not merely surface relationships come with some risk. Let's unravel how you should manage onions, people, your privacy, and risks.

*Preparation is key.*

If you have a well-thought-out onion, you won't need to guess who you should add and why you should add them. Draw an onion on a piece of paper with different rings spiraling out from the center. It should look like the illustration I'll share shortly. The center, or core, is where you put God because you confide all things in him—besides, he already knows. On the next ring right after that center ring is the person you trust with the most private information that this particular onion represents. For instance, if this onion represents the next house you're considering purchasing, the people on that ring could be a friend who's a real estate investor, your realtor, a financial/tax advisor, and other related experts. These are people you tell how much

## Managing Your Circle

is in your account, how much you can afford, how much debt you have, and the real personal or financial benefits you want from your future home. On the next ring are the people who are always excited for you and cheer you on when you're taking a big step or making a hard decision. You share some details of the neighborhood you have your eyes on. They know the type of house, garage, flooring, and garden you'd like. You share how much you'll save on gas commuting to work and church. But you never get into your personal financial decisions or the asking price of the house.

In general, each ring in your onion signifies a group or a person and can be general: siblings, parents, close friends, church leaders, and small group members. Or you can get specific: the name of your mom, your bestie, your neighbor, or a trusted colleague. Please never tell someone in the course of an argument, "That's why you're on the thirty-seventh ring of my onion." Your onion rings should be private to you. Don't use this to insult others.

The locks indicate that your confidants' lips are sealed—they're protecting your private matters from leaking off of the individual rings or out of the whole onion.

Don't despair about filling up all the rings in your onion with people you're close to.

No—that's not the point.

Some situations in your life may require you to use only three rings. For example, let's say another onion is about your future trip to Israel and then Dubai. You already know who you don't want in your business. But who will you tell that you're out of town and that you'll be traveling for a while? Because I travel a lot for work, I use three rings for travel: first, God; second, the person I've hired to drive me to the airport; and third, the friend who has keys to my place. No, I don't always tell my mom—it depends on why I'm traveling. See? You don't have to use many rings either. But for births, deaths, weddings, retirements, graduations, surprises, and other private occasions, definitely draw more rings for each of these onions.

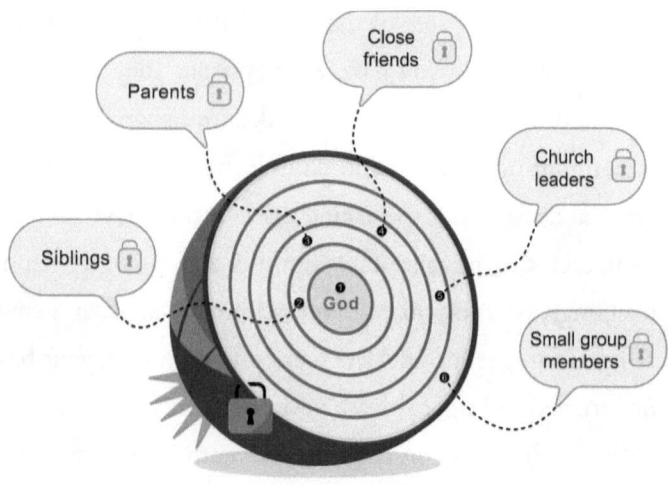

*Figure 2. Onion rings with trust assigned according to individual groups*

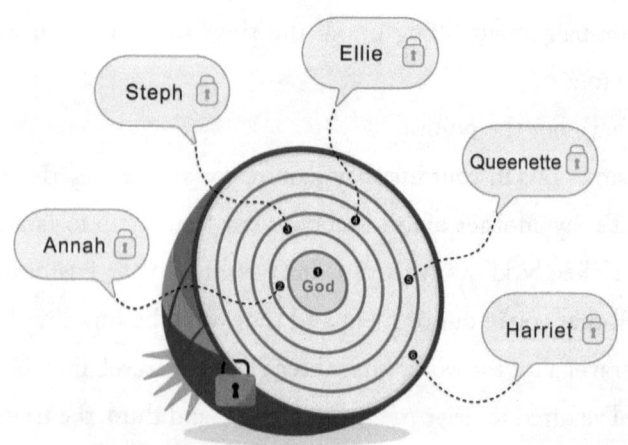

*Figure 3. Onion rings with trust assigned according to individuals*

## Reflect

As you plan your rings, ask yourself the following questions:

1. What is this ring for (surprise party, pregnancy announcement, engagement announcement, or "I messed up and need accountability")?

2. Why have I put someone on a particular ring?

3. Is there anyone I trust or who is in my circle but isn't included in this onion?

4. Did I remove someone from my onion? Why?

5. Did I move someone up or down a ring or two? Why?

6. Did I bring someone back into this onion or to a specific ring? Why?

## The Point

Don't make rash or emotional decisions about adding or removing people from your onion. That includes not making those decisions under the influence of

- anger
- guilt
- romantic feelings
- happiness or excitement
- confusion

## Plan for Change

Expect changes in people and situations. Sometimes people in your life change for the better and you confide in them more. Other times they remain the same. Some become untrustworthy. Forgive, but confide in them less or not at all. Planning who you confide in will keep you grounded and intentional about what you share and who you share it with so you can protect your privacy. The rings of your onion will change, sometimes for the better and sometimes for the worse. Some people you're friends with may not make it into your onion at all. That's not because of your lack of trust in them but because of who they associate with—people you don't find trustworthy. This means you need to reevaluate your onions and each ring now and then.

### *What happens next?*

Don't brag about who made it into your onion. Don't tell people where they fall in your onion—don't even use it as a compliment. They shouldn't even know you use onions. If certain people start asking why you don't tell them what's going on with you anymore, you can tell them your privacy policy has changed. Jokes aside, it's true. A good response is "There's nothing to share," completing the sentence in your head, "with you."

I have many onion success stories I could share. But let's look at how folks in the Bible handled discretion and privacy. Friend, you're going to be excited about what you learn.

### *The wise men understood that a privacy breach could get a baby killed.*

Three wise men were searching for where baby Jesus had been born. Their unpredictable navigation system (a peculiar star) took them straight into King Herod's palace. Wrong turn! They were lost in their search of the new

## Managing Your Circle

king, "the King of the Jews." The news of a new king didn't sit well with Herod, but the shrewd king decided to play along. He hosted the wise men and secretly gleaned more info so he could have the baby killed. Herod requested the wise men report back to him about the location of the baby so he could pay homage. When the wise men stepped outside and mounted their camels, they probably discerned that Herod could not be trusted. I don't know. But if they did, they were right. After all, I'm sure Herod asked prying questions. They'd made a huge mistake. They had trusted the wrong person and had given him an important piece of personal information.

The wise men were directed to Bethlehem. They found Jesus there, worshipped him, dropped off some gifts, and said farewell. They started their return journey. But God showed up in a dream and warned them about Herod (Matthew 2:1–12). They booted Herod off their onion ring and took a different route home. The rest is history.

Privacy protects you against someone maliciously using personal information you entrusted to them—including your location data—to hurt you or a loved one. God was intentional, and the wise men were intentional about preserving Jesus' privacy. Imagine if they'd been so excited to have found baby Jesus that they posted a few selfies, which Herod found? The story would have a different ending. Thankfully, they used discretion, wisdom, and good privacy judgment.

> *To the pure you show yourself pure,*
> *but to the crooked you show yourself shrewd.*
> (2 Samuel 22:27 NLT)

### Queen Esther's privacy prevented discrimination and distraction.

The word *secret* has gotten a bad rap. Sometimes when people want to deny your need for privacy, they may accuse you of keeping secrets. The bad kind—

the ones that hide immoral, criminal, and unethical behavior. Wanting privacy is not the same as keeping a secret about anything bad. Your desire to be alone or to keep your needs, thoughts, and personal information to yourself is a human need and a personal right.

What was Esther's secret? While in King Xerxes' harem, she hid her faith. How? Her name was changed from Hadassah to Esther—a Babylonian name—before she got there. Her name would have associated her with her ethnicity and religion, and she didn't disclose to anyone she was a Jew. Why? She feared discrimination and persecution. In Babylon, the Jews were a marginalized group. Esther was an orphan. Her cousin Mordecai, a man of discretion and wisdom, saw the dangers ahead of Esther, and he changed her name. His decision gave her the protection and peace that allowed her to thrive and adjust to the strictly Persian environment she was forced into. For twelve months, Esther was with hundreds of women in Xerxes' harem, all of whom were auditioning to be his new wife. Esther didn't ask to be there—neither was she there to compete. She protected herself by keeping a low profile. What happened next was the really surprising part of this story.

She was the only one who got a callback after her one night with the king.

At the right time, as queen, Esther was bold and transparent. She made known her faith. She was intentional with her transparency. With it, she petitioned the king to save her life and that of her people from mass killing—the annihilation scheduled to be carried out in every province where one of the king's wicked officials had posted an edict to kill all Jews. Esther's cousin Mordecai, by hiding her identity, proved that privacy is a lifesaver.

Even today, privacy laws and public policies are in place to help protect people against discrimination based on race, religion, socioeconomic status, political party, or other affiliation. Adolf Hitler's misuse of personal information is a modern example. His violation of privacy was the catalyst for the terrible event that was the Holocaust. His acts of discrimination, abuse, and killing—a human rights violation of more than six million people—spurred the many human rights and privacy laws we have today.

## Reflect

- Like the wise men, have you ever sought help from someone who later used personal information you shared in a malicious way to hurt you or another person?

- In Esther's story, do you see timing as a factor, that privacy is not just about what you share but how much is shared and also when you choose to share it?

- If you're a parent, do you talk to your children about protecting their privacy?

- As an uncle or aunt, do you talk to your nephews and nieces about privacy?

- As a member of the clergy, do you talk about discrimination and why it was important for Esther to hide her faith for a time?

***Check your heart before you share people's private business.***

Some churchgoers dress up their ill intentions with the right actions. For instance, they'll use prayer. They'll request prayer to learn more about a fellow churchgoer's personal matters.

"I'd like to ask you all to pray for Angie, her job, kids, and—has anyone else heard from her lately? Just wondering . . ."

Unfortunately in some fellowships, someone will volunteer details about the last conversation they had with Angie—what her personal issues are. At that point, twelve or more people are privy to Angie's private information, which she would not have shared.

Other times, a churchgoer will do what I call "gossip-prayer." That's when you ask for prayer for someone else just to draw attention to that person's private issue and include details that are not even relevant to the prayer request. It's a self-serving act—with the intention of either showing how much you know the person or to shame them. You may sound caring and spiritual when you share that information with others, but check your heart for the real motive or intention. How will you know you have the traits of a gossiper, a backstabber, or worse? It takes two to do this, a speaker and a listener. No worries, I've got a solution for both. Continue reading.

## The Gossip Detection Test

The speaker: before you speak, ask yourself the following questions:

1. Will God be happy with me sharing private information I know about this person?

2. Did the person specifically say he needs my help sharing it?

3. Will anything catastrophic happen if I don't share it?

4. Is there an emergency that requires me to share?

If you answer "no" to any of these, there's a problem. You may have just diagnosed yourself. If you have bouts twice a year, yours might be a mild case. But it still needs to be addressed. When you're on one of Angie's onion rings, under no circumstances do you have the right to open the onion or onion ring for others (at a prayer meeting or anywhere else) to come in. You have

## Managing Your Circle

no right to reassign people's privileges in that onion. Gossip-prayer does exactly that and is damaging. It destroys trust.

The listener: before asking follow-up questions, ask yourself these questions:

1. Will God be pleased with me asking follow-up questions about someone's private life?

2. Will anything go wrong if I don't know the details I'm asking for?

3. Is there an emergency that requires me to know?

4. Am I willing to tell the speaker, "I think that's private to him. I can't justify discussing this"?

If you answer "no" to any of these, there's a problem. You and the person speaking have the same privacy invasion issue.

What if you're not the one oversharing, but you're more like a gossip enabler? Once you hear about the privacy violation, you ask questions you shouldn't—questions that excavate more dirt on the subject. A gossiper needs a listener to enable them. Otherwise, they can't be effective.

Do you know people who ask probing questions? Some pretend they are asking innocent questions. They are invasive and disrespectful in a tactical way.

You might be tempted to think that if you're not the one doing the talking, you're not a gossiper. But the Bible begs to differ: "So pay attention to how you hear" (Luke 8:18 NLT), which means the gossiper and her listener are in the same boat. They share the responsibility to stop.

We've all done it at some point in different ways, right? Thanks be to God, we're reformed. You're not like that anymore. That's why you respect other people's onion rings.

> *What you do with other people's trust determines what you get.*
> (Luke 16:12, author's paraphrase)

## Privacy and Betrayal

In the Bible, people betrayed each other's confidence. Relationships can be complicated. Ahithophel, King David's chief advisor—who was in David's onion on the ring right after God's—ditched the king to back the king's contender on a campaign trail (2 Samuel 15:12; Psalm 41:9; 55:12–14). It worked.

Absalom, King David's son and contender for the throne, revolted and conspired to dethrone his dad (2 Samuel 13–19). He must have heard through the grapevine that the prophetic succession plan to the throne wasn't in his favor. Absalom had already burned the bridge in his relationship with his father when he killed his oldest brother. Desperate, Absalom wanted to take the throne by force. Spears and arrows weren't enough to do the job. He wanted the king's personal information. He wanted it from an insider. So he made his dad feel the pain of betrayal by stripping him of his chief advisor, Ahithophel. Without throwing any blows or punches, Absalom gained control. After many years of serving King David, Ahithophel had personal information and knowledge of the king's war strategy, behavior, strengths, and weaknesses. And he spilled them to Absalom.

A few more double agents in the Bible include Judah and his brothers, Joseph's siblings who colluded and sold him to human traffickers so Joseph wouldn't fulfill the dream he told his brothers about (Genesis 37). It worked because they had very private and very valuable personal information about Joseph's dream—enough to make them jealous and bitter.

# Managing Your Circle

If King David, Jesus, and Joseph were giving a TED Talk, I think they'd all quote Matthew 10:36, "A person's enemies will be those of his own household" (ESV), and Psalm 41:9, "Even my close friend in whom I trusted, who ate my bread, has lifted his heel against me" (ESV).

I wish these two passages were not true. Sadly, they are.

To make sure that it wouldn't happen to Solomon, the heir of his kingship, King David warned him. He even went as far as dropping a few names—Solomon's brother Adonijah, Joab (former commander of David's armies), and Abiathar, the royal high priest wannabe. David warned Solomon that they were not to be trusted with personal business or his life. David had been burned many times by such people—those who claimed to fear God. He learned his lessons on privacy, discretion, and wisdom. He had a lot to share with Solomon.

He probably said, "Privacy is power. What people don't know, they can't ruin." He may have quoted the tweet from the Idil Ahmend of his time and said, "Just because you don't share it on social media doesn't mean you're not up to big things. Live it and stay low-key. Privacy is everything."[1]

David lamented about his privacy in a way that resonates with most people. Imagine eavesdropping on David's self-talk:

*It is not an enemy who taunts me—*
*I could bear that.*

*It is not my foes who so arrogantly insult me—*
*I could have **hidden from them**.*

*Instead, it is you—**my equal**,*
***my companion and close friend**.*

> *What **good fellowship** we once enjoyed*
> *as **we walked together** to the **house of God**.*
> (Psalm 55:12–14 NLT, emphasis added)

Poor David—this brother was hurting badly. Enemies and haters get all the flak—all the time. But quite often, it is those closest to us who betray us or violate our privacy. *In the house of God.* David needed onion rings. In his lamentation, David cried out, "I could have hidden from them" (Psalm 55:12). He meant he didn't see it coming; nothing prepared him for it. King David was a warrior from childhood, fighting and conquering enemies. When it came to war, nobody knew strategy like King David. He built an impressive résumé of war victories. He never lost one. For each war, he was intentional and had a plan. Sadly, this mighty warrior won many battles against his enemies but suffered privacy violations. He was a victim of relationship drama—betrayals by friends, family, confidants, bosses, and spiritual acquaintances.

This is why it's wise to be intentional about your privacy.

**Privacy invasions and betrayals occur in your church.**

In case you don't know, church folks are not all godly. The devil goes to church too. In a sheep vest. I'm talking about church attendees who are as gentle as sheep and well-intentioned on the outside but "ravenous wolves" on the inside (Matthew 7:15 ESV). For them, it's not about people's personal needs. Or God's purpose. They're not members of the church on the inside, meaning they are not walking in obedience, fostering healthy fellowship and relationships, or working in cooperation with the mission of the church body or community. They definitely test positive on the Gossip Detection Test.

Managing Your Circle

# Reflect

- Do you know that familiar people in your life can try to stop you from fulfilling your God-given purpose, destiny, or calling? How do you protect yourself?

- What do you think they could use against you? Could it be personal information they know about you?

- How might they ruin you? Is it with a personal experience you shared with them?

**When admiration turns to envy, privacy is at stake.**

David's life was a classic office drama. When Saul hired David to lead the army of Israel, it was on merit. Although very young, as a military freshman, David defeated more gigantic war opponents than Saul did in his entire military career. Saul applauded David, but he became insecure instead of seeing the victory as a team accomplishment. He believed David wanted his position, his throne. To kill David, Saul planned to marry his daughter off to David to spy on him, having his servants speak kindly about Saul so David would trust these servants and marry his daughter. Wasn't that a violation of privacy? Yes. This was gross disrespect and an invasion of David's privacy. But Saul didn't care. He was monitoring David's every move.

David was in a bind with such a paranoid boss. But he had information that saved his life. David and his family kept hush about an important piece of personal information. As a boy, David was privately anointed by Samuel, God's prophet, to succeed Saul (1 Samuel 16:1–13). That was before he and Saul worked in the same office. David didn't want to be the boss. But God wanted it. David eventually fulfilled his destiny. Kudos to his confidants—his father, his brothers, his wife Michal, his brother-in-law Jonathan, and his spiritual advisors and prophets, Samuel and Gad. Let me ask you, "Who are the people in your onions?"

## Reflect

- Does David's story sound familiar? Have you ever worked for a boss or supervisor who celebrated your accomplishments at first but then felt threatened?

- Have you ever been hated and suspected of wanting a position or role you didn't want?

## The Point

Let me ask you this again: who do you have in the onions of your life—colleagues, church members, siblings, parents, friends, in-laws, neighbors, members of the clergy? Make sure you've carefully selected people who can pull their weight in controlling what they share with others about you when push comes to shove. You need people who will protect your peace.

*The trials of Joash were originally privacy battles.*

When Joash lost his dad, King Ahaziah of Judah, he was only a baby. His wicked grandmother, Athaliah, went on a rampage. She killed all her son's potential royal heirs so she could seize the throne. While this was going down at the palace, Joash was still at daycare. The sitter heard the ruckus. She grabbed Joash and bolted to the temple. There, the priest protected them for

## Managing Your Circle

six years. The temple personnel kept it hush all those years. That's the beauty of the church community and privacy. Not a word was said about him. Only the clergy knew. Church members and worshippers had no clue. Here's the best part.

Joash turned seven, and the church decided it was time for the big reveal. The church planned his inauguration and the surprise party that followed all in private. Not one drop of information was leaked. When the public announcement was made and Joash was crowned for all to see, his wicked grandmother finally heard. She wasn't having it. But it was too late. Joash was already sworn in, and he kept his position for forty years and fulfilled his destiny, all because church folks kept hush. Privacy is about timing and choices. It saves lives. With godly wisdom, discretion, good planning, and strategy, anything is possible.

### *Moses escaped death.*

Moses was hidden in a basket. His mother, Jochebed, put him there. It was a life-or-death situation. She chose life for baby Moses. She got a papyrus basket and coated it with tar so it would float. She then secured baby Moses inside and dropped the basket in the Nile. With the massacre of baby boys, the mourning, the commotion in her neighborhood, and the chaos of people running from soldiers, Jochebed didn't risk letting friends in on her plan. It would have leaked. And the entire family would have been killed. Even little Miriam, Moses' sister, knew the basket idea was to be kept private. The stakes were that high.

Not only did Jochebed keep it from the church community, but she fooled the enemy, the destructive pharaoh of Egypt. Privacy helped Moses grow up peacefully and be protected as a prince in the enemy's own territory—the pharaoh's palace. It gave Jochebed access to royal resources to care

# Church Privacy 101

for her son (Exodus 2:1–10). God had plans for Moses. But he still needed to be protected and covered by someone. He needed privacy protection. And his family made it happen.

## *Personal information is in the hands of malicious former friends.*

You can understand baby Moses in a basket. But what's Paul, a grown man, doing in a basket? Same thing. Life-or-death situation. He needed privacy protection. Paul was hiding from people who were friends turned frenemies. He was a wanted man. Every inn, goat market, threshing floor, and manger probably had Paul's wanted poster on the wall. He was wanted dead or alive. Preferably dead. Converting to Christianity was his crime, according to his former friends—his colleagues and the high priest, whose mission Paul didn't carry out.

One minute they were part of the same team persecuting Christians, and the next minute Paul had left that life. To them, he was a traitor. In those days, becoming a Christian was not a bed of roses; it often meant running from persecutors. He stayed low-key and private for a while. That wasn't enough. To stay alive and fulfill his calling, Paul needed good confidants—people who could hush and help support his need for privacy. Here he was, new to church, looking for people to trust with his privacy—his life. But this same community couldn't trust him with theirs, given what they knew about his past. Paul needed privacy to survive the murderous intentions of his old friends. People in the church community needed privacy to survive persecution—some weren't sure if Paul was honest with his conversion or if he was a double agent. In his case, privacy cut both ways. The giver and the keeper of information need to trust each other.

## Managing Your Circle

### *Samson shared his password.*

You can't have a catnap when it comes to your privacy. You snooze, you lose. Your peace and life depend on it. No one knew this better than Samson. He's a great example of someone who fell from grace because he neglected his privacy. Samson, one of Israel's judges, met Delilah while out of town, and he fell in love.

It turned out that Samson trusted the wrong person. He let his guard down. Delilah probably seemed like a nice person. But a person being nice isn't always a guarantee that they have your best interests at heart. Unbeknownst to Samson, Delilah was conspiring against him. It wasn't originally her idea, but some Philistine governors (Samson's enemies) approached and lured her to bait Samson. They knew he trusted her and that she was the weakest link in his life, so to speak. Let me ask you this: "Who is the Delilah or pretender in your circle?" All it took to get Delilah to betray Samson was cash. But how did she succeed in hacking the secret to Samson's strength? She pouted, nagged, and fussed at Samson when he wouldn't reveal that aspect of his personal life, until he finally gave in and divulged everything. As soon as Samson got tired one day—and needed a peaceful lap nap—Delilah took advantage of him (Judges 16:19).

It's a red flag when someone nags you to get on your onion ring. The only people in Samson's hair onion were his parents. He was fine until he added Delilah.

> *After putting him to sleep on her lap, she called for someone to shave off the seven braids of his hair, and so began to subdue him. And his strength left him.*
>
> (Judges 16:19)

Samson was tired in the wrong place, at the wrong time, with the wrong person, and said too much. He was sick of evading Delilah's constant hounding about the source of his strength. It was like divulging the password to the source of his strength. His gorgeous braids were God-ordained. As he slept on her lap, I imagine Delilah messaged a man (possibly at the neighborhood barbershop). The barber showed up and went to work, shearing Samson's seven locks. What a major privacy violation! How would you feel if a trusted friend did that to you? There's something about his deep sleep that doesn't sit well with me. Scripture says she lulled him to sleep. Scripture doesn't say this, but I suspect she laced Samson's drink.

She then handed him to the Philistine authorities and collected her .

This was the end of Samson's twenty-year career as a judge. His eyes were gouged out, and more punishment awaited him at the prison's grain mill in Gaza (Judges 16:21). Philistine law enforcement finally got their man, and he was going to pay.

## Reflect

- Whose lap have you been having a nap on—without even taking a peek at your onion rings?

- Do you easily choose convenience over protecting your God-given privacy?

- Is downloading a bunch of unnecessary apps your way of taking a lap nap—because it's convenient? You have apps you never use. Like Samson, you're giving tech companies a way to shear off every strand of your power and privacy rights. You're powerless because you checked the "accept all" box when you signed up. You slept.

- What private information are you feeling lazy about protecting? Or neglecting it because it isn't convenient?

- Is an enemy close to someone you consider a friend who gives them access to you?

## The Point

Realize that seemingly good people will befriend you, but they can easily betray your confidence for their own interests. Some people will allow others access to the same personal information you've entrusted to them. It may be unintentional or calculated. And it can happen while they're still close to you or after they've departed from your life.

**Does God have privacy? Does he protect it?**

Yes. "God is mysterious" is not a cliché. It's truth. The Bible uses the word *mystery* a lot to describe God's love, knowledge, salvation, the conversion he offers us, his relationship with us, and more. A few of those Scriptures are

> *The mystery of Christ.*
> (Colossians 4:3)

> *The mystery from which true godliness springs is great.*
> (1 Timothy 3:16)

> *This is a profound mystery—but I am talking about Christ and the church.*
> (Ephesians 5:32)

> *The mystery that has been kept hidden for ages and generations, but is now disclosed to the Lord's people.*
> (Colossians 1:26)

*I will fearlessly make known the mystery of the gospel.*
(Ephesians 6:19)

What has God shown us about privacy in his own nature? He is intentional. He doesn't do anything without his onion rings. He keeps a lot of things to himself. He's selective when he reveals mysteries—only to those he calls his people. "To them God has chosen to make known among the Gentiles the glorious riches of this mystery, which is Christ in you, the hope of glory" (Colossians 1:27).

When Jesus was asked when the world would end, or when he would return, he answered, "But about that day or hour no one knows, not even the angels in heaven, nor the Son, but only the Father" (Mark 13:32).

Yes, God cares about timing too. And as I'm sure you've learned by now, privacy is about timing.

### *Does God violate privacy?*

He doesn't violate privacy. He just knows things—he can't help it. "For there is nothing hidden that will not be disclosed, and nothing concealed that will not be known or brought out into the open" (Luke 8:17). When God wants to save someone from destruction or danger ahead, he can leak information through a dream to the person. He warned Joseph and the wise men in their sleep when Herod was going nuts, wanting to kill baby Jesus. God leaked his motive.

For folks who challenged God's sovereignty, God leaked their dreams as a reminder that God is boss. He would humble them by leaking the dream or its interpretation to his prophet or someone with whom God had a very close relationship—for example, Daniel, Joseph, and the prophet Elisha.

## Managing Your Circle

**Daniel** narrated King Nebuchadnezzar's troubling dream exactly as the king had dreamt it. He then told the king what God wanted him to do to save his life and his Babylonian throne.

**Joseph** interpreted Pharaoh's dream about an impending seven-year famine. Egypt was spared a serious economic disaster. Joseph also interpreted the dreams of his prison cellmates.

**The prophet Elisha** revealed to Israel's military the top secret battle plan of their opponent, King Ben-Hadad, the king of Aram. Like the proverbial cat, the enemy's game plan and murderous attack strategy were out of the bag, word for word. Fired up, King Ben-Hadad figured that the person with access to his private information was more dangerous than the entire army of Israel. So he abandoned his attack on Israel and went after Elisha. He sent his whole army to capture him. But that didn't go very well—not the way he'd hoped (2 Kings 6:8–23). Again, God knows everything. Even things we think nobody knows.

*The king said to Daniel, "Surely your God is the God of gods and the Lord of kings and a revealer of mysteries, for you were able to reveal this mystery.*
(Daniel 2:47)

# 5

# Finding Confidants in Church

*A man who has friends must himself be friendly,*
*But there is a friend who sticks closer than a brother.*

(Proverbs 18:24 NKJV)

## Partners in Privacy

If genuine friends and confidants were a product you could buy in the store, would you buy just one? A dozen? I'd buy a whole box, then sign up for the subscription. Everyone wants someone they can trust. At times, we need a second opinion to help us make a better decision or someone to help put our views in perspective. Of course, some are friends, and others are confidants. At a certain point, some friends graduate to confidants. Others don't. Some confidants are deemed so by their role as clergy. I believe some friendships as well as confidant relationships develop fairly quickly in the church community compared to other environments. Shared values and beliefs have a way of speeding up the connection and bonding. It must be that pure and unique love that folks shower on each other in the church community.

Although we crave and need them, genuine relationships are increasingly difficult to develop these days. It doesn't seem to matter which church you attend. And with privacy needs, how do you trust people beyond a superficial level—how do you make friends in church?

Even with all that authenticity, remember, churchgoers are people. They're holy, not always holier than you. They're human just like you and have the same needs you do, such as a need for trust and a sense of community. You go to church because you expect they'll be different. And they are—but God is still working on them, just as he is working on you. What sets them apart is their humble confidence in God's will and their inner hope and joy—that's not a façade.

> *This is the confidence we have in approaching God:*
> *that if we ask anything according to his will, he hears us.*
> (1 John 5:14)

Even when churchgoers face challenges, they have faith—the confidence that God is aware of whatever their problem is and that he can fix it. Of course, people make mistakes—some more than others—as they grow spiritually. Unless they're taught, corrected, or helped, they can repeat those mistakes. You have to be intentional about making every friendship what you expect it to be, for you and for the other person. It's easy to think of trust as one-sided, but trust takes two. Other folks in church want to make friends with you and be able to trust you too. Assuming you're seeking God first in church, that's easier.

How do you make genuine friends and confidants in church? Let's start with your attitude. How you show up in life determines the types of people around you and the relationships you create and sustain. Your attitude can either help you make good friends or cause you to lose potential lasting friendships. It all comes down to you. Making friends will be difficult in the following circumstances:

- You arrive at church, and you're suspicious of everyone.

- You arrive expecting to be judged by other people, or you feel judged.

- You isolate yourself, sit far away from people, or are standoffish.

- Your mind is on what you personally want out of this particular church. You don't plan to contribute your time, talents, or resources so everyone in the community benefits. You feel the church owes you.

> *The best way to find out if you can trust somebody is to trust them.*
> (Ernest Hemmingway)

## Be the Friend You Want to Have

Without trust, genuine friendships will evade you. It's hard to build a close relationship without trust. Even if a particular faith or church community is not what you want, you never know when God might have that diamond-in-the-rough friend for you. You have to be open to making friends. But that doesn't mean you share all your intimate details with them—be observant. Be intentional about what you share with someone you don't know very well. As the friendship grows, make your privacy expectations known so you'll be comfortable opening up to them.

Not all my close friends are in my church. They're from the 101 churches, chapels, and synagogues I've visited both in my travels and at home. Some are people I've observed doing very selfless acts for others in their communities. Their acts of faith challenge and inspire me to mature in my faith. They've earned my trust in church and outside. Many of them are in my various onions. I can go to them for sage advice and counsel. They've overcome many of the difficulties I'm still struggling with. But I didn't meet them by not being friendly or by not trusting them with my friendship. The opening Scripture of this chapter says it all: "A man who has friends must himself

## Finding Confidant in Church

be friendly, But there is a friend who sticks closer than a brother" (Proverbs 18:24 NKJV).

If you want to cultivate a genuine friendship, you must be a genuine friend. To receive friendship and fellowship, you must first give them. You'll be amazed at the strong bond you can create when you make yourself the friend you desire in others. You don't wait for friendship to happen. You create situations where you can show genuine friendship to others.

The Holy Spirit doesn't run a friendship drive in church parking lots. You need to hustle a little. Bring value to the table. Be genuine, trustworthy, helpful, and nurturing. Never leave others the way you found them.

> *God is spirit, and his worshipers must*
> *worship in the Spirit and in truth.*
> (John 4:24)

Since church is one of God's houses, my spirit gets excited when I'm there. I bring church to church. I don't leave the same way I arrived. It doesn't mean my life's journey is a bed of roses or that I have it all under control. But I intentionally bring value and purpose to church that change my experience and the experience of those around me. I expect that something magnificent will happen because I'm there. What I bring is intangible. It can be felt in the spirit. It's that joyful anticipation of the miracle of fellowship, and it shows and positively impacts those around me. This is how you should enter into a friendship. That incredible alignment and connection can and will happen—because you're purposefully there and you're being yourself. Radiate your joy and friendliness. Give freely of your warmth and joy without expectations. Be the friend you want to have, and you'll be surprised at how often your actions are reciprocated and what strong bonds you'll create with others.

## Reflect

- What can you do to make yourself more approachable to people who want to make friends with you?

- Is it your expectation to spot a great friend and confidant in seconds?

- Besides the friend and confidant part, are you looking for growth and accountability?

## The Point

Whether you're new to church or you've always been in church, the formula is the same. Get involved in church ministries, activities, and services. Get to know people at different levels and in different situations—in jeans and T-shirts versus suits. Know them in fold-up chairs versus pews. Sitting side by side on Sunday morning does not give you the same knowledge about someone as volunteering together to help the church make 400 sandwiches on a Saturday. That bond deepens even further when you journey out together onto troubled streets to feed people who don't know where their next meal is coming from. And you pray together for others.

***People add value.***

People can add value to your life, whether they're close confidants, friends, or fellow volunteers. The key is to make a distinction based on shared values. You can discover whether someone is committed to growing spiritually and if they will hold you accountable. Pay attention to how a potential friend or confidant acts and note their outlook on life. When they speak, read between the lines. Are they positive and upbeat, or dour and negative? Do they show up fully in life or do the bare minimum? How do they speak of others? Are they judgmental and critical, or are they affirming and speaking well of others? How much do they share? Are they discreet, or do they overshare? Do you think they'd expect the same from you?

Keep in mind that if someone is overly transparent about their lives and it embarrasses you or makes you uncomfortable, it doesn't mean they're not worthy of being your friend or that they won't add value to your life. But be aware, and consider that it might be harder for them to keep what you tell them private—so practice discretion with them. You can't change them. Everyone has a weakness; some people are privacy-deficient.

It's wise to have a good mix of church friends with different personalities and interests, as well as friends outside of church. Keep this in mind: a friend is not an instant confidant. There's a difference. Most times, you befriend great people based on their interests or life experiences. Sometimes it's simply because the person is fun to be around. If there's trust and growth in the friendship, a friend can eventually become a confidant.

On the flip side, a confidant doesn't need to be a friend. And your relationship doesn't always start because you share the same interests—hobbies, beliefs, or careers. My dentist and I get excited whenever we discover a new thirty-minute dinner recipe, and we share tips. But that's not why I became her patient. Some people are confidants because they have expertise you don't have but need, meaning what connects you with them is that they provide you with care and value your privacy. For example, therapists, doctors, financial planners, tax preparers, or counselors are your confidants because of their expertise—without having to befriend you first or know you for a long time. Other people are your confidants because they're older, wiser, and more discreet. Others are confidants because of life experiences or their track record of handling private information well.

# Church Privacy 101

## *What are the benefits of a church support network?*

Church people are great cooks! The meals and fellowship they share are always delicious and unforgettable—Scripture prescribes participation. Of course, the church has many other benefits. After a long, hectic week, your church family gives you something to look forward to. Release. The church is a shelter, and a place of comfort and celebration. People are usually happy to see you. It's the hub for hugs, fist bumps, and praise. Having a church community reminds you that you're not alone—you're family.

Your church family supports you in prayer for your career, school, parenting, marriage, and anything else. The church and its members have a wealth of expertise and resources. For instance, members share ideas about health, exercise, and careers, and they offer advice to new parents or newlyweds and counseling to couples. In a church family, you find doctors, nurses, lawyers, pilots, chefs, construction workers, mechanics, and other experts. They inspire, guide, and support you. I especially appreciate taking courses at church. Classes foster spiritual growth and also support members with different needs. Those opportunities are transformational. They are a network of love, ideas, wisdom, and hope. A great sermon anywhere can lift you up for a few hours. But a great church family keeps you lifted all the time. They envelop and comfort you when you're sick, lost, or alone. It's called a church family for a reason. When you're there, you're family.

## *Is everyone in church trustworthy?*

Of course not. But there are more people you can trust than those you can't. Also, it depends on what you're trusting them with. Church communities are unwavering in meeting great spiritual and humanitarian needs around the globe—with excellence. Still, certain needs are not met well in most churches. They don't intend to harm anyone. It's mostly because they've misunderstood and ignored certain essential human needs and could use some awareness and education. Privacy is one of those misunderstood needs. Some churches are learning about privacy, while others haven't started yet. Regarding privacy, churchgoers and church workers are just like anyone else. We can be the most wonderful, caring, and supportive people, but we make mistakes when we don't know better. We're all on this journey to be better, but we haven't arrived yet. What should you do? You need to manage your own privacy expectations. I strongly believe everyone wants to be trusted. They want to give and receive trust. But not everyone is able to do a good job of keeping what you've told them in confidence.

What does that mean for you? Take control and make your privacy a priority. You can avoid their indiscretions when you're intentional about managing your privacy. You can do this either by not disclosing private information to certain people or by telling them what you expect privacy-wise. Being honest about your privacy needs creates a positive space and provides transparency for good relationships to thrive.

If you've never been intentional about your privacy, don't worry, there's hope. I explained how to create a privacy model in Chapter 4. It's called The Onion Model. If you skipped that chapter or need a refresher, check it out. You'll find an illustration of an onion and its different privacy rings. Before you face a situation where you need to control your private information, use your onion. Assign people to the rings, which symbolize your varying privacy circles. These details create peace for you and others because you're not pushing your privacy needs on someone who's unable or unwilling to fulfill them.

This practice creates harmony in your private life because you're clear about your privacy needs and expectations, and you know who you can trust with them. The goal is to cultivate healthy, trusting, and lasting relationships.

Be direct. You can tell a friend she's the only person you've confided in about a particular concern—if that's the case—so she knows to keep it hush. A great confidant will not be offended by occasional privacy reminders. Equally important, you can tell her she's the first person you've told and that you'll share it with others later. Follow up and update her when you're beginning to disclose the information to others—you may or may not say to whom. It all depends on your relationship and the situation.

> *Discretion will protect you,*
> *and understanding will guard you.*
> (Proverbs 2:11)

## *Can you have a trusted confidant without a close relationship?*

You can't really know God beyond a superficial level if you don't spend time with him. It's the same with people you want to be close friends with. That said, a confidant can also be a clergyperson. For instance, in certain denominations, that could be a priest in a confession booth. You could visit a confessional in Paris, Chicago, Las Vegas, Detroit, or any place in the world. You don't need a close relationship to do that—that's the person's expertise and duty. You're there to unburden yourself. The priest doesn't need to be your close buddy. For other confidants, you need connection and fellowship.

God is omniscient and all-knowing, but we're not. The only way we can truly get to know a person—who they really are and what's in their heart—is by spending time with them, listening to them, and observing them in different situations and with different people. "A good person produces good things from the treasury of a good heart, and an evil person produces evil things from the treasury of an evil heart. What you say flows from what is in your heart" (Luke 6:45 NLT).

## Finding Confidant in Church

*Read between the lines to uncover their trustworthiness.*

You know not to badmouth your former employer in a job interview. Even if you aren't openly critical in your answers to interview questions, your prospective employer will still scope out your attitude, temperament, and what they're getting into if they hire you. They'll know if you're bitter about getting laid off or about not having the opportunity to grow in your previous position. They will read between the lines of your responses. That's Luke 6:45 in practice.

They do this because they don't know you. You appear trustworthy—because you look the part, you use the right industry lingo, and your résumé shines. The only way they can get to know you in the short amount of time they have is to get you talking and engage with you. Then they can use that information to make a decision about whether to trust you or not. If Luke 6:45 helps corporations find people they can trust to work for them and help manage their businesses, why can't you use it to manage your private life?

*How does God make friends?*

Think about Psalm 91. I've recited that psalm every morning for years. Every time I do, certain words stick out to me. They're in bold below.

> *He that dwelleth in the **secret place** of the most High shall abide **under the shadow** of the Almighty.*
>
> *I will say of the LORD, He is my **refuge and my fortress**: my God; in Him will **I trust**.*
>
> *Surely he shall **deliver thee from the snare** of the fowler, and from the noisome pestilence.*

# Church Privacy 101

*He shall **cover** thee with His feathers, and **under his wings** shalt thou **trust**: his truth [**faithfulness**] shall be thy **shield and buckler**.*
(Psalm 91:1–4 KJV)

Many of the words in bold mean shelter, hiding, safety, covering, protection, reliability, and an experience between God and a person that's unobserved by others. They all produce trust. All these happen because time is spent together. This is how God makes friends. My close relationship with God would be nonexistent if there were no secrets (private experiences with him), trust (surrendering to him and being present in the moment when I'm with him), covering (of the many naked truths about me), faithfulness (his reliability and commitment to not bolt on me), truth (his communication with me through his Word, the Bible), shield and buckler (protective covering against my enemies), and his promised peace. How does this translate into friendship and privacy? To help build my church family, I'm extending the same value that God gives me to others in many ways, including preserving their confidence and privacy. I can be faithful, reliable, and trusted. And I can be a shelter and covering where someone can hide emotionally, mentally, and spiritually so they're not exposed—the same thing God does for all of us.

### *Should you trust all good friends and confidants equally?*

No. Get to know people first. Love people, but don't rush trust. One confidant will not be the headquarters for all your private life's issues. It could be one or two concerns set aside for a particular confidant or confidants. If you don't tell all your confidants the same things, that's perfectly normal. Some have unique experiences that prove helpful in different areas of your life. Same with friends. That's why you use The Onion Model.

## Finding Confidant in Church

People in church are generally very loving. So cherish every unique relationship. You never can predict how or when God will bring valuable people your way when you're in need. So be open and lead with love, but be discerning. That's how trust works. It's either given or it's earned.

## Reflect

- Let's say your employer was featured by *Fortune* magazine as "The Best Place to Work." Does that mean every employee there will be kind and treat you with respect?

- Will you go to work and share the laundry of your life just because it's the best place to work? No, you won't. You'll use wisdom and discretion. Right?

- Has anyone ever stated their expectations before confiding in you? That's totally fine.

- Has anyone ever prefaced what they're about to share with "I don't remember if I told you this already," "Maybe it wasn't you I told," or "I don't know if you've heard . . ."? Or are you that person? If so, have you considered how telling that is about your carelessness regarding privacy?

If you're the person who can't remember who you confided in last, it's evidence of acute onion ring deficiency. You're unintentional about privacy. And disorganized. Privacy is not a math problem you can solve in your head. Start on paper with your onion rings until you commit who you shared with to memory. When you're disorganized about privacy, you make others nervous. Here's how. First, others may suspect you've betrayed their confidences too, since you don't track who you talk to. Second, suppose your personal business gets leaked, and you're not sure who might have been indiscreet. You'll suspect or blame innocent people in your circle and put your long-standing relationships or friendships at risk.

Then you'll end up crying to God, "Where were you, Lord, when this happened?" His reply might be, "Where was your onion?" or "Again and again I sent all my servants the prophets to you" (Jeremiah 35:15). True, he sent you this book.

## The Point

You're not indiscreet in your office. You don't discuss your personal business at the coffee station with people you don't know. If you are not careless in those places, why do it in church? Where is your discretion in church? Don't use trust to curry favor. Don't share your personal business hoping to gain trust. Don't use trust as a lazy currency to gain approval. Don't pay for friendships with your privacy. There're no refunds. Not everyone can handle your transparency. This doesn't mean you can't be a very friendly person. But when it comes to trust and privacy, they're not bargaining chips.

People should only have the personal information you allow them to have. Granted, those outside the church will not get the level of trust you give people you know in church. But even your church family has to earn your trust. And if you happen to hear a sermon that says, "Trust everybody equally," I'm sure they meant to *love* everyone. Don't let that guilt-trip you. Don't trust blindly.

### *Can privacy needs stop you from enjoying fellowship in church?*

No. You can fellowship with anyone without worrying as long as you've established your trust and privacy onions, set limits, and have good boundaries

## Finding Confidant in Church

with your church family. It works the same way in church as it does anywhere else: at work, in your marriage, and with your friends in your social circle. For instance, does protecting your privacy stop you from going to work or socializing with your friends? In church, it doesn't stop fellowship. Consider the following:

- Having privacy or healthy personal boundaries doesn't stop you from fulfilling your purpose in the church and enjoying fellowship with others.

- Having your privacy protected by your employer doesn't mean you can't be the best employee, manager, supervisor, director, VP, or team leader.

- A good corporate privacy policy at your job doesn't weaken the spirit of teamwork; likewise, privacy will not erode fellowship in church but can enhance it.

- Being married and maintaining privacy and healthy boundaries doesn't prevent you from having a full life of fellowship in church. It also doesn't keep you from enjoying great friendships outside the church or your marriage.

- Maintaining privacy as a member of the clergy doesn't mean your life's calling, assignment, or role will suffer. Or that you can't have fellowship.

### *There's a privacy rock star in you.*

I know of many rock stars. They may not grace the cover of *Rolling Stone*, but they do a fine job gracing the pages of the Bible. Daniel is one example. When King Nebuchadnezzar conquered Jerusalem, he captured Daniel and his three friends, Shadrach, Meshach, and Abednego. Since they were bright, well-read, and preppy, the king's chief court official slated them to work as full-time civil servants. When they arrived in Babylon and it was time for

Daniel and all the captives to have their first dinner buffet, Daniel said no. He wasn't eating the Babylonian cuisine, especially the meat, not because it was too spicy but because it was food sacrificed to idols.

He wanted a different kind of food. He could've been killed for that! He was supposed to eat what the king set before him because captives have no choice or say.

Not Daniel. He respectfully insisted that he and his friends exercise boundaries, not only about diet but also in honoring the living God. Long story short, the chef had to clock in again and whip up some vegetarian recipes. Under the circumstances, eating vegetables was more spiritually peaceful for Daniel and his friends. So they spoke up and detailed why it was important.

Daniel didn't stop there. While other civil servants took breaks, Daniel took prayer breaks. He got into his apartment and prayed privately by his window. He was an awesome guy among other believers.

The book of Daniel highlights his achievements as a person who loved God. It also highlights the fact that God was very excited about Daniel's commitment to his faith in God.

> *Then this Daniel became distinguished above all the other high officials and satraps, because an excellent spirit was in him. And the king planned to set him over the whole kingdom.*
> (Daniel 6:3 ESV)

Many of Daniel's challenges in Babylon came from his competitors, people who didn't have boundaries themselves and despised his private life. They couldn't figure him out, so they opted to destroy him. Isn't that how people who value their private lives inside and outside of church are being snubbed today? Preserving your privacy is a healthy boundary. Others may not like it, but it is healthy.

## Finding Confidant in Church

*Even if that person wrongs you seven times a day and each time turns again and asks forgiveness, you must forgive.*
(Luke 17:4 NLT)

### *Should you forgive someone who has violated your privacy?*

Of course, you should forgive. Several childish years ago, I would have said no. But I know better. I've grown spiritually. You should forgive. Don't hold grudges. But upgrade your onion rings, especially if that was someone you had assigned to a ring and they bombed. Remember, people should earn their place on the ring and in the onion. Love and forgiveness have nothing to do with it. Your onion is for your protection. So with love, boot them out of your onion if they prove to be a liability.

But keep in mind that if their violation is a misdemeanor, felonious, or a criminal privacy violation, the government may not forgive them—even once.

### *How do you create fellowship?*

You can't live a joyous, fruitful life alone. My church emphasizes fellowship. We have a zero-tolerance policy for just showing up to worship, hearing a sermon, and then vanishing without a trace until 9 a.m. the next Sunday morning. You should contribute, at the very least, your time, joyful energy, good cheer, faith, and goodwill for the benefit of others. And if you make slamming sweet potato pie or the crispiest fried chicken, contribute that too. If you can work the grill better than Steven Raichlen, create fellowship out of that—to entertain and educate others, feed a homeless family, or host members of your home Bible study group. Eating, feeding, serving, learning, playing, and uplifting others are all part of fellowship. You have many more ways to create fellowship and friendships.

# Church Privacy 101

Give a family a ride home from church, but don't ask them invasive questions just because they're riding in your car. Host a game night at your place or virtually. Attend a singles or couples ministry event. Share a testimony or story about your life to encourage someone. Fellowship is asking for prayer for a family member or for you to get a raise at work. Fellowship is asking your group to pray that God blesses you with coworkers who actually show up at work to work—so you don't have to pull their weight, work late, miss fellowship, or feel bitter. Fellowship is asking if anyone knows a good plumber. You're still that person who needs and values privacy, and that person who can tell everyone you were able to replace your car and that you're glad you found a great car dealership and a helpful salesperson. You don't share that you spent $1,000 more than your budget, but people can still relate to your joy without you oversharing. That's fellowship.

### *Should I share when I fellowship?*

Yes. But are you comfortable? Or are you being transparent because it's the culture of that particular church? Why are you sharing—is it to give someone hope, or are you sharing out of guilt? What are you sharing? Have you thought about it and organized your thoughts, or are you just excited about that moment? Is it something light or serious? Are there other people in your story you should not mention by name? Who is there listening? Is a camera rolling—and is that okay with you? How are you sharing—virtually? Notice that these questions are not discouraging transparency. I'm just getting you ready so you're more intentional, comfortable, and organized before you say a word.

I have fun with fellowship. However, not every fellowship environment is the same. Some are smaller and more intimate than others. Some are public, while others only include certain groups within the church. If you want to

## Finding Confidant in Church

limit your transparency to a particular group, do so. Share your expectations and your *need* for privacy with that group. Of course, don't say, "Privacy is my right." Yes, it is, but explain what it means to you. They'll get it when you share why it's important to you and how it will affect you negatively if people spread what you share.

In my years of wrangling privacy concerns, I can say with confidence that people and organizations that identify with your privacy needs protect you with more compassion than those who identify only with the fact that you have a *right* to privacy—and their concern is not about protecting you; rather, it's about avoiding penalties. That means those who understand the why behind your need are more committed to protecting you. So manage your privacy through good communication with friends, confidants, and those in your fellowship. You'll have more peace and freedom when you do.

*Let us not neglect our meeting together,*
*as some people do, but encourage one another.*
(Hebrews 10:25 NLT)

# Confession Privacy Sacred Confidence

*Therefore confess your sins to each other and pray for each other so that you may be healed. The prayer of a righteous person is powerful and effective.*

(James 5:16)

## Between You and God Alone

I'm not sure about you, but I'm still wired to think about the Catholic Church first when I hear the word *confession*. Growing up Protestant, I wondered why Catholics committed so many sins. I was young and didn't understand until I desired to be closer to God. I studied the Bible more and grew in my understanding and meditation of Scripture. I discovered that Catholics don't necessarily sin more often. They just have a more managed James 5:16 process. They handle confession with a formal procedure, similar to Lutherans, Anglicans, Orthodox, Methodists, Latter-Day Saints, Presbyterians, and Jews.

God specifies righteous standards and principles we should live by. Sin is when you don't comply with God's expectations or directives for your life. That means you served your own desires and did the opposite of what God

## Confession Privacy Sacred Confidence

instructed. It's when you're being disobedient and fall short of God's standard. Yet when you miss the mark, it's not the end of you. God requires you to address it. How? Confess.

Confessing and receiving forgiveness are standard practices (Matthew 6:9–13). Confessions of sin should be part of your prayers. You can confess anytime. Even if your church or synagogue has no special time slots for confession, the fact remains. We all sin daily. I do. You do too.

> *If we say we have no sin, we deceive ourselves,*
> *and the truth is not in us.*
> (1 John 1:8 ESV)

That said, confession is not just you confessing to another person—whether they're your confidant, friend, clergyperson, or the person you sinned against. In most cases, it means you receive forgiveness, prayer, restoration, and accountability. Confession also helps you grow spiritually above those particular temptations or sins. As you grow closer to God, temptation may increase against your conscious effort to live a holy life. Your sensitivity and resistance to temptation and sin may also grow. You need people you can trust to hold you accountable. But who do you open up to?

> *I have hidden your word in my heart,*
> *that I might not sin against you.*
> (Psalm 119:11)

Do you attend Bible studies? Do you worship on Sundays with the church? Do you attend prayer meetings or events? Do you make an effort to meet people and make friends who will someday hold you accountable? That doesn't just happen automatically. Accountability happens through relationships with others. "You're called to be relational," Minister Eugene Howie, a passionate Sunday school teacher and author of *The Awakening*, stressed in his class. "What are your plans for other people in your future?" Trust, accountability, and peace are on my list.

You can trust God. Praying and confessing are simply talking to God. You can speak your mind or talk for the sake of talking. Ask for forgiveness, and "with confidence draw near to the throne of grace, that we may receive mercy and find grace to help in time of need" (Hebrews 4:16 ESV). You'll not be sin-free because you confess, are forgiven, or spend time with God. However, you'll get to know him better and build better resistance to sin. And the beauty of this is privacy.

> *After he had dismissed the crowds, he went up on the mountain by himself to pray. When evening came, he was there alone.*
> (Matthew 14:23 ESV)

Everyone commits sin in some way. "For all have sinned and fall short of the glory of God" (Romans 3:23), and "Indeed, there is no one on earth who is righteous, no one who does what is right and never sins" (Ecclesiastes 7:20). Sin is our nature—and our greatest challenge. But the game changer is confession (or acknowledgement that we sinned), genuine remorse, and a willingness to change (James 4:6). God is not interested in us wasting away physically and spiritually because of the guilt and consequences of sin. Bottling them up or trying to hide them does just that. Confession is important, and privacy gives us the confidence to confess.

> *Let the wicked forsake his way,*
> *and the unrighteous man his thoughts;*
> *let him return to the* L*ord, that he may have compassion on him,*
> *and to our God, for he will abundantly pardon.*
> (Isaiah 55:7 ESV)

# Confession Privacy Sacred Confidence

*Whoever conceals his transgressions will not prosper,*
*but he who confess and forsakes them will obtain mercy.*
(Proverbs 28:13 ESV)

Do I confess my sins? Of course, to God all the time, and sometimes to others. But not to everyone. Confession isn't necessarily an enumeration of all your sins. It can be kept general when you convey it. For example, 100 individual sins could be narrowed down to one particular issue or type of sin as the root cause. Pride. Envy. Greed. Lust. Anger. Gluttony. Sloth. So confess to God and get set free, no matter how many of them you've committed. Math is unnecessary. There is no need to get into the gory details when confessing. Preserve privacy.

Not long ago, I called a friend—not for legal advice, even though he's a lawyer, or for clergy advice, even though he's an ordained clergyperson. He's a friend. And I needed accountability. When we spoke, I laid it out. I told him I was struggling with a decision and my motive. I wanted to ensure that my heart and attitude were in the right place and that I was sensitive to any negative impact my decision might have on others. I didn't want to do things my way and later invite God to participate. If there was even an ounce of self-centeredness in the decision I was contemplating, I trusted that my friend would squash it. We mulled it over. Then we prayed. He enlightened me with Scriptures and words of wisdom. At the end of the call, I was secure in the choice I would make. That's how I personally approach confessing to others. It's not complicated.

Confession keeps you in check, but you still need trust and privacy to confidently practice openness. Confess to someone who will do one, some, or all of the following:

- listen with understanding

- give you godly wisdom on what you can do differently, or help direct your view if it's wrong

- share lessons from their own experience

- remind you that God's love for you lasts longer than his anger about anything you've done or will do—"For his anger lasts only a moment, but his favor lasts a lifetime," (Psalm 30:5)—and that he always makes an allowance for you to receive his forgiveness

- hold you accountable

- protect your confidence or privacy by not discussing your confession with others or rubbing it in your face later when they're angry with you

- pray for you—asking God to forgive and purify you and that you forgive yourself too

You don't need to keep a sin log. Confessions happen in many ways. In some church environments, I've heard people confess sins during Bible studies and then request prayer. I've observed people who responded to an altar call—after a teaching or sermon was delivered, they confessed their sins and asked for prayer. There's no one way to go about it. There's no right or wrong way. Some confess openly; others do so privately. Everyone is different. God hears them all.

## *The Race of Your Life*

Guilt and shame can weigh you down while you're running the race of life. Acknowledging your sin to God cleanses you, replenishes your spiritual strength, and refreshes you to keep running. However, saying all your sins are between you and God doesn't quite work. It means you're practicing absolute

## Confession Privacy Sacred Confidence

privacy, which is quite unhealthy. I empathize with people whose privacy has been violated before. They tend to remain closed after a series of privacy violations. But there has to be another human you can trust and discuss some things with to help lighten your load. Also, regarding sin, if you feel you've wronged or sinned against someone, you should apologize—that's openness. Some sins afford us more opportunities to hide than others. If your sin is a crime—a privacy violation, murder, sexual offense, arson, computer crime, or illicit drug use, for example—you've pretty much sold your privacy to your state and have made a public record for yourself.

Whether it's a physical or spiritual crime, it doesn't matter to God. Once he forgives your sins, he deletes and forgets them (Acts 3:19 and Hebrews 8:12).

*I will remember their sins and their lawless deeds no more.*
(Hebrews 10:17 ESV)

While God promises he'll remove your sins "as far as the east is from the west" (Psalm 103:12), not so the state. Despite your confession to God, law enforcement will chase you from the east to the west to make sure justice is served. Expect legal consequences for sins that break the law, such as privacy violations. The state has a duty to protect people from you or deter others like you, depending on your crime. People whose sins are not considered crimes are not better people. They're still violators. We all need confession.

Protect your privacy during confession. You need it. Confession doesn't mean you have to publish your sins or speak transparently with the wrong person just for the sake of confession.

I recently read Ellen Boegel's legal article "The Seal of Confession and Mandatory Reporting: A Survey of State Laws." It was an enlightening read. In it, she writes that St. John Nepomucene Catholic Church in

New York City was named for the fourteenth-century Bohemian saint John Nepomucene. He was considered the first martyr of the seal of confession.[1] Spiritually, his lips were sealed with crazy glue. Nepomucene wouldn't betray anyone's confidence, even on the threat of death.

That's truly a gift. Those who bear others' burdens are also exercising their obedience to God's standards and principles, not just the state's.

*Bear one another's burdens, and so fulfill the law of Christ.*
(Galatians 6:2 ESV)

## Reflect

- Do you confess your sins to God?

- Is being genuinely held accountable and growing spiritually important to you? Do you actively seek these traits from friends and confidants? Who is your "one another" (mentioned in James 5:16) whom you can talk to candidly?

- Have you ever regretted confessing your sins to another person? Are you worried a clergyperson or church member may betray your confidence?

- Have you ever repeated a sin or found it easier to repeat sins you covered up because you had not been open to someone about it, confessed it, or addressed it?

- Do you wish you knew a Saint Nepomucene in your church? Or at the church you used to go to? And do you wish you had a few close Christian friends who were like Saint Nepomucene?

## The Point

I've never gone to a formal confession—in a booth. If your church does formal confessions, fine. If not, I know it can be tough. I struggled with James 5:16 for a long time. I wondered if it meant confessing to any random person. But here's what I discovered: confessions are trust-based. If there's someone trustworthy you can confess to, fine—not every single sin, though. But know the person well. Trust, but verify that the friend, confidant, or clergyperson has what it takes to be helpful. Read and reread the seven qualities I recommended you look for in people you confess to. But first things first, confess your sins to God. If you're still justifying to God why you did this or that, that means you haven't learned anything. I'm talking about candid surrender. Approach God with genuine repentance. Fess up. Know what you're conceding. Say you're sorry. Don't justify anything. He knows the situation. He was there.

*Do your homework.*

If you've been let down in the past by someone you confessed to, I'm sorry. That hurts. Be even more intentional about your privacy. Observe and note the person you open up to. Is she humble? How does he handle other people's information—based on what you've heard him say? Is he judgmental and talkative?

You already know you'll sin one way or another. Get organized about it. Line up your confidants. Be an organized sinner and get expedited grace. Select the person ahead of time if your church or synagogue doesn't have formal or scheduled confession sessions or counselors. Even if it does, this is a personal decision you need to make. Suppose we were hit with another pandemic and churches suspended confessions. What would happen to your

# Church Privacy 101

sins? I remember when I read that New York churches shut down confession booths—unless the confessor was dying. Of course, you shouldn't lie about dying—that's another sin entirely. Los Angeles shut down the Blessed Sacrament, including confessions, with the exception of doing last rites. Correct, unless you were dying. Miami and San Francisco parishes held theirs by appointment only. Miami "benched all priests over 65 or with a compromised immune system."[2] New Orleans churches coordinated confessional drive-throughs. That's out of your control; that's why I'm preparing you. No matter what goes down in church, turn to God, and check your confession onion rings.

### *DIY confession is flexible and gives you privacy control.*

When I realize I've sinned, I pray right there and then. I apologize to God ASAP.

Confession isn't rigid. Learn what works best for you. Once in a while, I talk to different people about different faults or sins because I value objective insights. How do you start? What do you say?

For me, more often than not, it just comes up during a good conversation, and I take the opportunity. Other times, I've texted friends to say, "I need to confess something. Pray ahead for wisdom!" The first part is my prompt that this be kept private. The second part is a prompt to say I expect them to bring godly wisdom, not their own, and to be objective.

My close friends are curious beings in a good way. I'll get anything from "Give me thirty minutes" to "Sure, let's do this! When?" to "Mmm . . . where are you—can you talk now?"

When we connect, I typically start the conversation with "I need to confess." I cut to the chase. "Hey, I need you to hold me accountable. . . . Here's what happened. . . . After that, I did ABC. . . . Maybe I should

## Confession Privacy Sacred Confidence

have done DEFG, but part of me really wanted HIJ. . . . I'm convicted by my understanding of Scriptures XYZ that I wasn't wrong for doing ABC; maybe I was wrong for doing ABC first. Plus, my motive was wrong-ish. I've prayed about it. But I still feel a need to chat with someone." Then I shut up and leave the person to analyze or respectfully probe deeper. I never choose a person because they will tell me just what I want to hear—that's not accountability. If that were the case, I would confess to a salesperson at a car dealership. Their advice would simply be, "You're due for a new car!" That's not accountability. When I'm playing the role of listening to another person confess, I'm careful to listen without judgment, and I always keep their confessions private. Trust, protection, dignity, openness, truth, and freedom from misjudgment are all part of privacy.

> *Love one another with brotherly affection. Outdo one another*
> *in showing honor. Do not be slothful in zeal,*
> *be fervent in spirit, serve the Lord.*
> (Romans 12:10–11 ESV)

The conversation that I just outlined is what I call do-it-yourself confession. It means planning and organizing your confession for best results—even if you prefer going to the booth or church for formal confessions. Overall, you're planning your privacy. Know and keep confidants around like extra batteries: people who will build you up when you miss or suspect you've missed the mark on God's principles for your life.

> *As iron sharpens iron,*
> *so one person sharpens another.*
> (Proverbs 27:17)

In the absence of a priest, pastor, minister, counselor, reverend, or rabbi, turn to your "iron" person. Pencil the people you choose into your privacy plan so that when you no longer have confessionals, prayer meetings, small groups, or however you usually confess or seek accountability, you're covered. If you travel as often as I do, these formal confession occasions are not always convenient to turn to anyway. That's when I turn to my onion rings.

If you've already been in the habit of assigning friends and family to different privacy levels—who you tell what and when—you're already ahead of the game, whether your church is open or closed.

## Can Your Private Confessions in Church Go Public?

Yes, they can. But under different circumstances. Let's look at three scenarios. First, this can happen if you're transparent with the wrong person or clergyperson—especially one who likes to air grievances or anything sensational. A wrong person is someone who airs out your confession when you're no longer on good terms. That's why I stress planning privacy or onions ahead of time. Second, this can happen if the law in your state has specific disclosure requirements that your church must comply with. There are some sins or acts that are criminal (even if you don't think so), and states deem them reportable. Remember, it's the state's duty to protect the public. Third, carelessness with information management at your church and the lack of privacy policies and processes can lead to a breach of your confession or personal information.

Over the years, there have been a few clashes between churches and states. For instance, the Catholic Church and the state of California were at odds about confessions. The Catholic Church has always followed the state's requirements for reporting child sexual abuse and neglect. Actually, the church supported strengthening those requirements, and it even helped draft parts of the amendment to make the reporting requirements stronger.

The problem started when the state wanted extra access to confessions. It wanted access to all confessions, regardless of what the confessions were about (in addition to confessions of child sexual abuse and neglect). That's where the church disagreed with the state.

The church was concerned that some added language in the amendment would potentially compel clergy and church workers to disclose other sins shared during confessions. Allowing the state to have unlimited access would violate privacy. It would break the ancient *seal of the confessional*. In other words, it would deny Catholics their religious freedom. The church fought back. California pulled the bill, mostly due to public opposition. More than 100,000 Catholics spoke up in favor of confession privacy and put their signatures on letters opposing SB 360.

For the church, it was a major win for religious freedom. It makes sense since some churches require confession (James 5:16) just as they do Communion (Luke 22:7–20). They didn't want their members to abandon confession for fear of the state's privacy invasion or losing their religious rights. You have rights regarding confession. Know what they are in your state.

The state of New Hampshire is strict on this issue. No matter which denomination or nondenominational congregation you belong to, New Hampshire's law requires any clergyperson in a church or synagogue to report suspected child abuse and neglect to the state's Department of Health and Human Services. Again, requirements vary by state.

Although churches support the requirements of their states and do report confessions of child sexual abuse and neglect, in some churches, clergypersons or church workers can be fired or excommunicated for disclosing certain private information about confessors.

## Reflect

- Would you report child abuse that someone confessed to the church? Does your church have an internal process for handling such cases so children and other abuse victims can be protected?

- Not all places of worship have formal or structured confessions. Does your church have a structured confession process? Are there any privacy guidelines? Are they being followed?

- People confess sins and ask for prayers in the sanctuary, in small groups, or during Bible studies within the church. Are there church privacy guidelines set up that you know of?

- If you're the person confessing, would you like others to follow the privacy guidelines?

- Are you scared of confessing? Why? What's your alternative for accountability?

## The Point

Know the people you decide to trust. Be aware of what's going on in your state. If you don't like it and want to rely on confessing to individuals, remember to plan. What's not a good alternative is taking your confession to TikTok, Facebook, Twitter, Instagram, WhatsApp, LinkedIn, or your free (unencrypted) email provider. These are public domains and are subject to police surveillance and the court of public opinion. Even if your church leader requires you to go on a social media platform with your confession, speak up about how you feel about your privacy concerns. You're a member of the church for such a time as this. Raise privacy awareness in your church.

## *Prophesied confessions are public but have a benefit.*

I was streaming a church service when the minister prophesied, "Someone in our midst needs to confess to killing a friend." By the way, a prophecy is spiritual advice or a warning. An intense hush fell over the congregation. You could hear a pin drop.

The minister continued, "You're feeling tormented by your act. You can't sleep, and you're scared. You might end up killing yourself if you don't come out now."

The five-thousand-plus-member church remained mute.

"Please come out for a prayer of forgiveness and deliverance. Don't take your life. God loves you!"

Perplexed, I thought, *Would someone really step out?*

You won't believe this. I kid you not, someone came forward and confirmed the prophecy to be true. He confessed that he had killed a friend. He had felt tormented since the act and was contemplating suicide. All this played out with the church camera rolling, YouTube streaming, and congregants watching in disbelief. Only the Holy Spirit can make someone do this. The prophecy was "for the salvation of his soul," as the preacher put it, and for him to take responsibility for his crime.

What the church does when this happens is counsel the confessor and get them on track, not just spiritually. Depending on the severity of a confessor's case, church leadership will encourage him to turn himself in to the authorities. In some cases, they'll accompany the person to the police station after meeting with lawyers. This leader saved a man from committing suicide, helped him confess, addressed his spiritual needs, and encouraged him to face the consequences.

> *Let each of you look not only to his own interests,*
> *but also to the interests of others.*
> (Philippians 2:4 ESV)

You may be thinking, *But what about privacy? Did it have to be so public? Doesn't God's forgiveness and grace know how to hush?*

When God wants to heal and deliver a soul, he doesn't look at privacy in the same way that we do. He is not exposing the person but rather the evil spirits behind their sinful behavior. For example, Jesus called out a rich tax collector, Zacchaeus (Luke 19:1–10). To the Roman government, Zacchaeus held a role similar to that of the chief of the Internal Revenue Service. But in his community, he was an infamous sinner for being a tax collector, or tax fraudster, amassing wealth at the expense of innocent taxpayers and the poor. Zacchaeus confessed and repented of his sins. Publicly, he stopped his sinful acts and paid back all the people he had defrauded. Not in a thousand years did anyone think they'd see Zacchaeus as a changed man or that they'd be reunited with their cash. It was a miracle, not only for Zacchaeus but for everyone who witnessed it.

## Reflect

- Have you ever witnessed a Zacchaeus situation? Has preserving your privacy ever been unsuccessful, but you were blessed because of the exposure?

- We're called to be witnesses of the miraculous works of God. Has somebody else's miracle (that you would have kept private if it were you) been helpful to you and increased your faith in God's power?

## The Point

Sins have consequences. So does carelessness with your confessions. God is a spiritual being who sometimes makes exceptions and prompts public confessions to prove a point. Zacchaeus is a great example of that. But he wasn't forced. The Spirit of God tugged at his heart to surrender.

> *Therefore, if anyone is in Christ, he is a new creation.*
> *The old has passed away; behold, the new has come.*
> (2 Corinthians 5:17 ESV)

***There are risks to keeping secrets in church.***

The church is not where sinners and criminals hide or are encouraged to dodge the authorities and consequences. It's where people can seek God and are loved despite their errors. If someone is a danger to others and the church is aware, it has a duty to warn and save others from that danger. Privacy is not about criminal, unethical, or immoral secrets. Knowing about certain risks to people and not properly responding to reduce the impact of those risks is a liability to the church. Keep in mind that some of your privacy rights are not absolute. For example, when it involves the state's interests—crime, safety, public health, or a life-or-death situation—the church may not have the control to protect all your privacy rights. It is critical that church policies address these issues.

The idea behind confession is for sins to be exposed and forgiven (James 5:16). Basically, you're offloading a burden. The clergy's job is to reconcile people to God. This helps turn a new leaf in people's lives emotionally, spiritually, and mentally so they can get back into a good relationship with God—even behind bars. "The priest who hears the confession is merely Christ's instrument of forgiveness."[3]

# Church Privacy 101

*Watch out for the confession culture.*

In some churches, a fellow church member or friend can tell on you if you confide in them about your sins. In this culture, snitching is a virtue, and members have an obligation to report sins to church leadership. Plus, they have your best interests at heart. It's a holy snitch so that the church is aware and turns to church doctrine and principles to help counsel you, the sinner, and deal with your sins accordingly. In this environment, you know to expect this style of accountability. If this culture doesn't work for you, then confess to friends who attend other churches. You can still have accountability.

This brings back memories of my church when I was a kid. A serious sin would be addressed from the pulpit, usually after someone was reported to leadership. The clergy tried to help the person privately, but to no avail. Short of options, the leadership would address the church, with the person standing the entire time. If this was a repeat offender, he didn't sit with the general congregation. He was benched in the back of the sanctuary, where nobody would sit near him. I don't recall how long he was supposed to be there, but I believe it was until he showed genuine repentance and confessed to the entire church. He didn't need any introductions to church guests. Anyone who walked into church on a given Sunday and saw him sitting there knew he was under church arrest until he was fully reformed.

Whatever form confession takes in your church, with people you know or with total strangers, the goal is to address the confessor's sins, not to expose or shame the confessor's private life. Reconcile the person to God while protecting the person's confidence, even as you hold them accountable. This protects their spouse's and their children's privacy—and that of other people, when names are not discussed.

Don't feel you can bring up discussions about church confession privacy practices in your church? Share this chapter with your church. You'd be amazed by how people feel about privacy. You can't change any church issue if you're in denial about it. Privacy is one of them.

> *Where the Spirit of the Lord is, there is liberty.*
> (2 Corinthians 3:17 NKJV)

*Even on Sundays, confessors need privacy protection no matter when, where, and with whom they confess.*

Some churches have a staff person who counsels confessors or talks to people seeking support. The person may advise confessors on their relationship with God. Confession takes two steps: acknowledgement of sins and repentance. For new believers, confession includes acknowledgment of Jesus as Lord and Savior. Both steps happen during worship services, in Bible studies, during Sunday school, and at any church event or fellowship when an invitation is extended to the attendees. Sometimes I am that person who helps inform and guide the confessor to understand what Scripture says about where they are spiritually—after I've heard everything they have to say. Sometimes there's also someone in the church who is a licensed counselor. The church will call on that individual to intervene when a member is going through emotional or mental health issues or crises—whether it's sporadic, short-term, or long-term.

For instance, perhaps someone responds to the sermon and needs to confess their sins and receive prayer about specific needs. The member confesses to abusing substances or being afraid they may hurt themselves or others. In my church, I'm trained to invite a licensed counselor to take over the discussion at that point. Regardless of the counselor's rank and stature, respecting privacy is paramount when handling confessions of any kind.

## Reflect

- Does your church have a licensed counselor who handles issues that may require more specialized support?

- As a church volunteer, do you assume you know how to handle these types of scenarios and all the privacy concerns that come with them? Why?

- Would you share a confessor's personal information with others who know the person—because in your church there are no rules about sharing? An example would be asking folks at a prayer meeting to pray for John not to hurt Sandra, as he mentioned in counseling.

- Have you ever approached the leadership for help with how to handle a church member who was living a destructive life contrary to God's standards? Did you handle it with careful consideration of the person's privacy?

- Would you give personal information and notes to the police or respond to a court order about someone you've counseled in church? Does your church follow a privacy standard for reporting?

## The Point

When the church puts the word *counseling* in your title or role, ask the church for training. You may feel justified jumping into the role of counseling people because you're gifted at encouraging others. That's not enough. The role comes with unique responsibilities and obligations that have legal consequences. It's the same when members of the clergy take up a counseling role by virtue of their leadership role, but they have no expertise in counseling or related privacy training. Don't do it.

## Helping to Heal

You're vulnerable to making damaging disclosures about others if counseling is not your expertise. You don't do counseling every day, you don't have an advanced degree in it, or you're not paid to do it. Even if you're called to counsel in church, education and best privacy practices matter. If you're called to counseling, be equipped to do this with excellence and without harm to others. Pay attention to policies and what the law requires.

No matter our education or lack of counseling training, in church we get to hear some of the same personal details that licensed professionals listen to and handle all day. The danger in church is that we can handle it the wrong way.

Licensed professionals know how to handle personal information. Church members who are not trained or licensed but are in counseling roles are often lax—to them, it's just church. They have no stake in the matter. They're not paid by the church or its members for their counseling services and are not held accountable by industry codes and standards. You should take your counseling responsibility in church seriously. If you worked at a hospital, would you be indiscreet about your patients' personal health information? Of course not. You'd be worried about privacy laws and about losing your job. The same applies when you're counseling people in church—the church is a hospital (Luke 5:31).

One thing I learned from one of my professional codes of conduct is to never take on a job you're not competent or qualified to do. Simply put, competence means "know how." How are you going to *know* if you haven't effectively studied how to carry out your role with excellence? Consider this book as your first resource. Respect people's dignity by protecting their privacy, even if the church doesn't acknowledge or reward you for doing it. To be an effective counselor, you need specialized training, supervision, and ongoing professional development. Being a member of the church for thirty years doesn't qualify you as a counselor. Being a member of the clergy is not a qualification to serve as a professional counselor.

If the church doesn't have policies and training regarding counseling, help make that happen. Suggest them to the church. Be willing to see it through. If you're in church leadership, don't let the lack of resources cause you to give counseling roles to members without first equipping them. This can create situations that attract liability, negligence, and malpractice. Plus, it is unfair to those seeking help from the church. Lawfully speaking, the church demonstrates diligence in protecting people when it puts policies and procedures in place and adequately trains its counselors.

***A court order can require an investigation and the release of church records.***

What if you get a court order to provide information about a church member you've been counseling because the court believes it will be helpful in supporting a case? What should you do? Well, first, read the order. Understand what's being asked. Don't rush it. Just because it came from the court doesn't mean you should respond immediately or divulge private information without a second opinion. Talk to your supervisor, church leadership, and/or the church attorney first. Your church should retain an attorney before it needs one. The client or church member you counsel could sign a release to disclose information or decline (an attorney will best handle this process). Refer to the companion course for more guidelines on handling church business processes.

> *Let us then with confidence draw near to the throne of grace, that we may receive mercy and find grace to help in time of need.*
> (Hebrews 4:16 ESV)

# 7

# Financial Privacy
# Money Matters

*Whoever can be trusted with very little can also be trusted with much,*
*and whoever is dishonest with very little*
*will also be dishonest with much.*

(Luke 16:10)

## Lack of Discernment Will Cost You

When it comes to personal finance and financial privacy, God cares. But there are certain things he expects you to handle with godly intuition, wisdom, and discernment (1 Thessalonians 5:21–22). We're supposed to use those skills to examine things, decisions, and people, but sometimes we don't. You know how you pick up an apple in the grocery store and appraise it to find the slightest bruise or dent? "I had a feeling something wasn't quite right with those apples," you say, putting down the apple and buying an avocado instead—that's you doing your diligence with your observation and intuition. Other times, you need just a little more awareness and knowledge, so you make bigger financial decisions with the help of an objective confidant or expert. Smart! The same idea applies, but spiritually. This may seem elementary and common sense, but in the heat of the moment or under

## Financial Privacy: Money Matters

pressure, we all make errors in judgment. Some of the stories in this chapter illustrate how a lack of discernment, not trusting that inner voice, neglecting your observation, or neglecting due diligence can exact a hefty cost. If an opportunity seems too good to be true, it probably isn't true (Matthew 4:1–11). If you're confused about an opportunity, pray about it and do your research. Ask someone in your financial onion for their opinion. Do this before you make any rash financial decisions. Read on to understand how good people make really bad financial mistakes and violate other people's financial privacy. Unfortunately, when this happens, they're too embarrassed to talk about it. This leads others to make the same mistakes. When we don't share lessons from our experiences, both the good and the bad, we don't help others learn from them.

### *Harold's story*

Harold was a hard worker—kindhearted, great sense of humor, good work ethic—and he treated his coworkers as friends and family. Harold and his friend Sandra co-owned a small business that brought in passive income. Both of their names were on the business account. One day, James, Harold's coworker who was in the process of starting his own business, asked Harold if he could have his client deposit a large sum into Harold's business account. It was urgent. He had the capital but had not yet opened his own business account. The deposit had to be done with a business account. James promised a percentage as a gratuity for the favor. Harold trusted James. He'd known and worked with him for over a year and wanted to help. Besides, Harold could also use the he would make from the gratuity to help lift their business off the ground. How could that lead to anything bad? He discussed the idea with Sandra, and she agreed. It seemed like a safe bet because the would be withdrawn from the account once it cleared. They decided to help James.

# Church Privacy 101

James deposited the check into Harold's account. Two days later, the funds were available. Harold excitedly texted the good news to his colleague. James said he needed $10,000 of the to buy supplies for his business. Harold gave James the —after all, it was just a fraction of the total amount he deposited. That same day, Harold wrote checks to cover expenses related to his own business.

The following week, the bank called Harold. It was urgent. The bank was suspicious of Harold and Sandra. The check James deposited had not cleared—it had bounced. All of Harold's bank accounts were frozen, as were Sandra's personal accounts at the same bank. The last thing Sandra needed was zero access to . She was eight months pregnant. She and Harold were under investigation. The bank demanded $10,000, which neither Harold nor Sandra could produce. They were both implicated. And for some reason, James was unreachable. He wasn't picking up Harold's calls and didn't show up to work. It was a mess. Harold was left frantically trying to raise the —from his fellow church members—so the bank would unfreeze Sandra's personal accounts.

## *Etta's story*

Etta was pressured by a family member to change her substandard lifestyle. Her cousin insisted she deserved better. Months later, the cousin approached Etta with news that a close friend's relative had died and left the friend an estate in another country. His friend was working on selling the property and having the wired to an account in the US. He asked Etta if his friend could temporarily use Etta's account as a surrogate for the transfer. He promised Etta would get a six-figure reward. But that wasn't all. Before he could divulge more details, he asked Etta to sign a nondisclosure agreement. What for? His friend needed privacy.

## Financial Privacy: Money Matters

That would dramatically change Etta's life. She could even buy a bigger house in an affluent neighborhood. Tempted but not convinced, Etta called close church friends and confidants and got their thoughts on the situation. Most of them told her it sounded fishy. Etta decided not to go through with it. As it turned out, she got an amazing, high-paying job a month later that positioned her to do better financially. Are you seeing this? If she had succumbed to temptation, accepted her relative's offer, and been caught in the middle of a scam, she would have had a negative financial background check as a result of a possible frozen account and unpaid bills, which would have jeopardized her credit report and the possibility of getting a new job or buying a future home.

### *Keep your financial business quiet.*

Harold's and Etta's stories illustrate how people close to you can target and exploit your generosity and good heart with bad opportunities. In the end, you have more to lose than they do. Like Harold, the idea may come in the form of helping someone, but the risk is on you. Most of the time, they entice you by manipulating your need for and then lead you to make a bad decision, one that jeopardizes your finances and your privacy. This type of decision is made for folks in your onion—they should help you make decisions. Etta consulted her onion. Make an onion for your finances if you haven't already. Your financial life is personal.

Not everyone needs to know you're trying to get a business off the ground. I'm not blaming Harold for attracting a scammer; we're all targets and are all vulnerable. But if we practice discretion, it's less likely we'll be exploited. Your bank account is personal, plain and simple. Like your password, you shouldn't share your bank account with anyone. That's why financial banking laws exist—to protect your . Too bad banks can't protect you from your own mistakes. If you're a parent, not even your kids should have access to your financial accounts. If you're single, nobody should have access. Your bank account is not a public storage center. Anyone who needs to deposit should get their own account. Etta was blessed to have used discernment and her onion—with me as a member—before making a potentially devastating financial decision. Harold wasn't so fortunate.

### *Don't give with expectations.*

Privacy and can be tricky at times. Some people actually don't mind being recognized for being the biggest giver in church. Honestly, if you're like me, you may not really want to know who that person is. You might be tempted to treat them with deference or partiality. You'll find one of these stories in Chapter 18: People Who Leave the Church.

In a church in New York, there was a millionaire who was a big giver, and church leadership wouldn't do anything until he blessed their decision. He could do no wrong by them. Everyone else seemed insignificant, and he went along with it. In another church, no one knew who the biggest giver was because he was such a low-key and humble guy. They found out about his giving only after he left the church to pursue another ministry calling. He was missed mostly for how he treated people and the time he poured into many ministries and activities of the church. Members didn't know he was also a very generous giver financially. They only knew he was a greater tither of his time, energy, and presence.

In a different church, the biggest giver used to threaten to leave when he didn't agree with a particular stance or decision of the church. The church had lost members and was struggling financially. He'd mention his monetary contributions when pushing his ideas. The leaders were at his mercy. They gave in time after time to please him in order to get the church bills paid.

## Financial Privacy: Money Matters

He stressed out the leadership, who were constantly walking on eggshells around him. One day, they took a stand, and he left. The church struggled financially for a couple of years. Then the clergy pulled themselves up by their bootstraps and changed a few approaches to their community outreach. More people came out to the church and joined. The church grew organically and thrived. As a result, the church leadership was less stressed.

This reminds me of what I once heard a preacher at a megachurch say about big givers. He used to announce the names of donors and partners for the church's special projects. He'd also announce the amounts they gave. After many years, he felt in his spirit that he should stop. The year after he stopped announcing the biggest givers, the donations dwindled. Some donors vanished. What does that say about the reason behind their giving? Some people appreciate privacy when it comes to their giving. Others, not so much. It appears they want the praise and attention in exchange—their giving is more transactional. I don't know how it feels to be that person, but I'll tell you more about that in a moment.

### *Privacy is peace.*

Privacy is a *choice*. Sometimes, if an organization or church is the big giver, they appreciate the recognition because it shows they're working in partnership with other churches, projects, or organizations for a greater good. In that context, *transactional* is not as bad as it may sound. Individual giving is a different story altogether. Big givers, if known, sometimes have a tough time in church relationally, even those who want to remain anonymous. As a privacy expert, I appreciate knowing when someone gives significantly, but I prefer to have no clue who that person is. I don't need to know. I appreciate that their giving encourages me to step up and entrust to God more of the financial resources he's given me. Their anonymous donations show that they're not interested in praise or acknowledgment but only in obedience—as I should be, whether I can only give $1 or $10,000. I always say privacy is peaceful. The peace that privacy offers you means not being singled out or treated more favorably than others who don't give as much as you do. It also means not having church members swamp you for loans or bailouts because of your *known* giving to your church and charities. There's more. Peace means people aren't pressuring you with ideas about organizations or causes that need your . Peace means not being discriminated against when you're in a bad financial situation and can only give a little.

Whether you give openly, privately, or anonymously, your church leadership should respect your privacy, but you need to expressly request it.

### *Helen's story*

Helen knew how to coordinate her outfits and always looked put together; not to mention, her hair was a statement of its own. She was used to being doused with loads of compliments after church services. One particular Sunday, as a small group of women gathered in the foyer to chat, once again, Helen's outfit and hair garnered a lot of praise. Sandra, one of the women, scoffed, "That's because she doesn't have children! She can spend her on clothes and hair. I have kids to get ready on Sunday mornings, and she has lots of time to make herself look good." If you didn't know what was going on with Helen privately, that may have sounded like a harmless comment. But Helen had struggled unsuccessfully for years to have children. Sandra had unwittingly disclosed something not only personal but painful for Helen. What could have been a special moment of bonding turned into a reminder of what Helen desperately wanted but didn't have. Helen was torn between letting those who were present know she had been struggling

## Financial Privacy: Money Matters

to have children or keeping this personal information to herself—letting the hurtful comment go. She swallowed her pain and said nothing. Sadly, people often think they've figured out why other people spend their the way they do. They're openly speculating, misjudging, and comparing themselves to that individual—this violates privacy.

### *Kelly's story*

Kelly's friend April was in a financial bind and needed a loan. Unfortunately, it was bad timing because Kelly was in the market to buy a home, and every penny she'd saved for the purchase was going toward the required down payment. Although she'd loaned April in the past, she couldn't lend her at this critical time—interest rates were rapidly dropping and the housing market was favorable to buyers, except down payments had skyrocketed. She told April about the house she was about to purchase and even apologized. To her surprise, April became upset and retorted, "You don't have kids like I do. Definitely no school fees to worry about. You don't have a mortgage yet. With your salary, what do you spend your on?" Kelly had a perfectly legitimate reason for why she couldn't give April a loan, and she didn't think she needed to explain her private spending decisions or give additional excuses. April distanced herself from Kelly in church and limited her responses to Kelly's calls. Kelly bought the house. Other friends showed up to celebrate and pray over the house. April was a no-show and didn't even acknowledge Kelly's invitation. It's too bad her friend used what she knew about Kelly's salary—her private business—to manipulate her and violate her privacy.

### *Allison's story*

Allison wanted to support Layla, an entrepreneur in church. She didn't know her personally but preferred to support businesses within the church community. She contacted Layla to discuss her services and prices, but mostly to explain what she needed and discuss options. But Layla was more focused on how much Allison's budget was. When Allison disclosed her budget, Layla's next comment surprised her. "That's not very much. You're not married. You don't have kids. You should have a higher budget." Allison ended the conversation. Although Allison's budget was low and Layla's fee was high, that was beside the point. A budget is a budget and is set for a reason. Even if you choose to negotiate to find a middle ground, not having kids or being single shouldn't be a part of a sales discussion or negotiation, especially when a client or customer is trying to support your business. Layla could've shown more privacy grace.

*Avoid judgment without knowledge.*

Jesus said no to giving preferential treatment because someone looks put together (James 2:3). I interpret that to also mean don't judge or invade someone's privacy because they look like they have more or time than you do. That's what happened to Helen, Kelly, and Allison. They were not spending their the way others wanted them to. That angered some people.

The critics in the stories had *information* but not *knowledge*. They lacked knowledge about what these ladies were going through privately or what went on behind the scenes. They judged based on their outward appearance and their perception. James 2:3 goes both ways.

Can you relate to Helen's, Kelly's, and Allison's stories? Can you relate to people making judgments about you based on what they see, not what they know? I can. When I finished my undergraduate studies, moved off campus, and started working, I kept my living situation private from many people. They knew I was gainfully employed and traveling the world, but they had no knowledge that I was living in my former professor's garage that he'd turned

## Financial Privacy: Money Matters

into an affordable studio. I wanted a home. I was saving to buy a house—not just buy, but invest. I was content with my Mini Cooper rideshare on weekends and with hopping on and off trains, planes, and buses during the week to achieve my goal. If I had shared my vision with too many people, some would have discouraged me and told me I deserved a large, fancy apartment, a big car, and more. People had certain financial expectations of me, but I didn't meet those expectations. They had information about me but not knowledge. Most times, that's how we view others. We look at the exterior without knowing a person's struggles, hopes, and dreams.

### *These Houston, Texas, church stories are about privacy, not just cash.*

Has your preacher ever called a guest to the altar and introduced or endorsed them to the congregation? And they were a financial advisor, businessman, investor, or social capitalist? They professed to be a believer and talked passionately about their beliefs, your Christian financial heritage, and how they're in the business of making your investments exponentially profitable to you, your church, and your community. Or was that person the featured expert at your church's financial empowerment seminar? Either way, what they didn't say was that they misled your clergy—and now you. Because when your church leaders endorse anything, you're all in. No argument there. No questions asked.

At a church in Houston, Texas, a member of the clergy persuaded its members to invest in historic Chinese bonds. Following leadership advice and the endorsement of an investor, the members invested nearly $3.5 million in the bonds, but the investment wasn't legit. The bonds had no value.[1] The congregants lost their investments. Lawsuits followed. And the acting attorney general determined that the clergyperson had abused the trust of the church members. As a result, the clergy member who misled the congregants paid $2 million in restitution to the members and was sentenced to six years in federal prison.[2] This particular Houston, Texas, congregation was the hardest hit. In Atlanta, ten members sued New Birth Missionary Baptist Church regarding a fraudulent investment. Some churches were targets, notably the fastest-growing megachurch in the US, Lakewood Church, and some members were exploited.

What a truly tragic tale. The church did nothing out of the ordinary. I've visited at least two churches where the church communities were collaborating on investments, including bonds. People trust church leadership with these decisions. Sure, they probably prayed corporately about this. But buying bonds is also a private decision. First, you do your research, and then, if it still doesn't sit well in your spirit, pass on the opportunity. It's not disobedient to the leadership. A mistake made as a group is still a mistake. If it's fraudulent, you all pay the price—both clergy and members. And the criminals who mislead the clergy typically disappear with the funds.

## Reflect

- Like Harold, has someone ever come to you with a desperate plea for help or a proposal that sounded so profitable you forgot to consider the implications on your personal life?

- Like Etta, have you ever been faced with an idea from a close family member who made you lucrative promises that required you to allow them access to your bank account?

- Like the church members in Texas, have you or anyone you know ever been a member of a congregation where the clergy encouraged specific investments?

## Financial Privacy: Money Matters

- Are you sensitive to Helen's needs and the comments that might invade her privacy?

- Like Allison, do you feel church folks misjudge you because you're single, young, or financially secure? If you were Layla, would you have negotiated professionally with Allison to help her see the value of your services and the available options she should consider?

- Like Kelly, has anyone ever put you in a position where you had to explain how you spend your ?

- Have you ever known folks who were big givers in church? How did you know? Were you supposed to know? Or did someone violate that person's privacy? Was it a church member or clergy? Or did the leadership always praise the big giver openly? Have you ever targeted a big giver when you had personal financial issues? If you're a big giver, has a clergy member ever sent people to you for help when they had personal financial difficulties? How did that make you feel?

## The Point

Helen was already suffering trying to have a child. Sandra's careless words added insult to injury. Even if you don't think a compliment is deserved, it's best to let the compliment be given and allow that person to enjoy it. Regardless of the context of your remarks, be careful when reminding people who have fertility issues that they don't have children. That's a personal, private, and sensitive issue. Besides, not all truths need to be told to a person in front of others.

A single, married, childless, or divorced person shouldn't have to explain to a married person, a parent, or anyone how they spend . You never know.

# Church Privacy 101

She could be feeding more mouths around the world than the number of children in your household. She may be funding the education of multiple kids and communities or building schools in distant countries. Comparing yourself to another person in this situation is really saying you don't think they deserve the life they have. Personal financial information isn't in the public domain; people have the right to live without judgment or criticism. We can never know enough about someone else's financial situation to judge them, even if we have information. Scripture says don't judge.

Church folks can be a trusting lot. All it takes is undiscerning and misled clergy who compel members to make bogus investments. Trust your leaders, but verify their choices. Do your research and ask questions. And always do your research before encouraging members to participate with their and personal information—not limited to bank information, addresses, phone numbers, and email addresses.

Come to think of it, losing cash is one thing. Are you going to get all that personal information about you back? No. Where does it end up? As a privacy expert, that concerns me even more than the cash you'll lose. Another fraudster could be waiting for the right time to capitalize on that. I hope these stories inform and educate you. I'll leave you with this: "A smart person learns from their mistakes. A wise person learns from the mistakes of others."[3]

*We must help the weak, remembering the words the Lord Jesus himself said: "It is more blessed to give than to receive."*

(Acts 20:35)

### *Lending to friends comes with its own privacy complexities.*

Lending to friends is a risky business because we often get burned.

## Financial Privacy: Money Matters

We say we're lending, but then it gets awkward. We don't want to bug our friend about the loan when it's not repaid on time. We may even avoid spending time with them. We also don't seek advice from anyone before we lend—to preserve their privacy and our decision to lend the . But resentment builds. We feel like we're gossiping if we talk about it. That's understandable. It's private. But the problem is not in talking about it. The issue is that we're talking about it with the wrong person. We must be sure the person we choose as a confidant is someone who doesn't know our friend and is shrewd with . The right person is objective, discreet, and will give sound advice without sabotaging our relationship with our friend. An interesting concern when considering lending is whether we should lend or refuse to lend. In lending we may lose friends, and in refusing we may lose friends.

It's a blessing to give to others. And we shouldn't always wait until we're asked. Actually, it's more of a blessing to give than to lend—if we can afford it.

### *Don't let your giving turn into an enabling gesture.*

Iris was a good friend who was in a tricky spot. She'd been lending to her friend Deborah ever since Deborah's husband, David, was laid off. That was four years ago, and David had long since lost his motivation to find another job. They had two kids, and  was tight on only one income. Whenever they needed groceries, childcare, mortgage , or gas, Deborah borrowed  from Iris. Deborah and Iris also kept these loans a secret from David. Iris wanted to tell Deborah that she couldn't keep lending her , but she was afraid it would ruin their friendship.

For years, Iris indirectly enabled David not to be a provider in his house. She also enabled Deborah to keep it a secret. Iris thought she was respecting their privacy. But she was enabling the issues in Deborah's marriage. Deborah didn't want to confront the issue and get help. Maybe she didn't want to cause tension. Avoiding the issue wasn't helping anything, and she was not only enabling David's behavior, but she was also transferring the risk to Iris, who had become almost her insurance policy whenever Deborah and David found themselves in financial emergencies. I get it. Iris wanted to help her friend. But true friends don't put you in that type of situation.

Are you enabling a friend or a loved one by always lending them or bailing them out of endless financial situations? If they need it, you give it, even if they rarely pay you back or take steps to change their situation. But what if anything bad happens to you and you find yourself in a financial fix? You'll have to borrow from someone. Right? Do you realize how much pressure you put on a friend when you ask for a loan? If you're the person constantly lending to a friend, be honest with the person and let them know you don't want them to go through feeling pressured to pay you back all the they've already borrowed; therefore, you are going to stop lending. It's not only about the ; it's also about preserving your relationship with a friend or relative, whatever your unique case may be.

When you give, you're giving up time, , and energy you could spend to help someone else. It's a blessing to give, but it can quickly turn into enablement, which is not surprising considering the many downsides to lending: guilt, shame, indebtedness, and resentment from either the lender or the borrower. Whenever possible, it's better to give than to lend . And whether you give or lend, always preserve the privacy of the borrower. Keep in mind that when you give or lend, it doesn't have to be the requested amount. For example, you could offer $100 as a gift instead of the larger amount they are requesting as a loan.

If you can't afford to lend any , you can say you don't have a budget for loans. Your has a purpose—and you didn't set aside to loan, but you have to give. You need to handle it carefully. You don't have to go into detail about

Financial Privacy: Money Matters

why you can't. They may not understand, or they may not want to. That's not your concern. But this also gives you insight into their character.

*Lending and borrowing require trust.*

Privacy and transparency go together. The lender doesn't need to explain why she doesn't have the $1,700 to lend. The borrower doesn't need to divulge everything they'll use the for, but they should be transparent depending on the amount they need—unless both individuals are very close or the reason is obvious. The lender needs a reason to lend, which encourages the person to make a sacrifice for the borrower.

If you say, "I'm in trouble," that may not be enough for some people to help you with a large sum. Try telling that to your bank. You won't get a penny if you put that reason on your loan application. Is it for your house, medical bills, or your child's tuition? Did you get laid off? Say so. As a borrower, this person is likely in your onion or about to be. Be transparent.

# Reflect

- Have you ever loaned to someone to the point that they depended on you all the time? Did it matter to you what they used the for? Did you feel you had a need to know?

- Did you stop lending or continue to enable them out of guilt? Did you get professional or objective advice, or did you vow absolute privacy with the borrower?

- What did you do to help them break out of this cycle? Or did you do nothing?

- What do you typically tell people you don't want to lend or give to?

## The Point

If you think the borrower has a problem and you're still lending, you also have a problem by not breaking the secrecy cycle. Privacy is not secrecy. They may have told you that you're the only one they trust to borrow from. That might be true. But don't try to live up to their praise (or flattery) by not confronting them about their financial life. "Hey, you said you trusted me, right? Great! Then trust me when I say you need a long-term financial solution to this situation you're in. I have some suggestions. Let's talk about it." This goes beyond preserving their privacy. Their privacy isn't the problem. The problem is that keeping their secret is bleeding your wallet dry and making them dependent on you. Either way, it's unhealthy—it takes away your peace and theirs. I'm not saying you should tell everyone about it. Who do you trust? Get help for yourself so you can better help the person. Seeking advice or help doesn't have to mean a privacy violation. Look within your onion and get advice. You don't have to disclose the name of the person you're helping to an advisor. Refer the borrower to resources about management. If they are not employed, volunteer to review their résumé or be a job reference. Otherwise, you are enabling the spirit that's afflicting them.

*Save your friendship.*

Don't let the guilt and shame of not being able to pay back a loan cause you to lose a good friend. Don't claim privacy. Answer your phone when they call, text them back, and reply to their email. If someone was kind enough to lend you, you should do your best to pay it back. And if you can't do it right away, tell them. Forget your pride. Let the lender know you're struggling to

Financial Privacy: Money Matters

pay the loan back and why—they'll understand. When you start avoiding and ignoring them, that's unfair and irresponsible. Your friendship is worth more than the sum of you borrowed. A good friend is priceless. is not the most valuable thing a person can give you. But a friend who selflessly lends you is a good friend. A keeper. They're probably already on your onion ring, or should be.

## Reflect

- Have you borrowed and not repaid because you found a way to justify not paying, or have you just felt ashamed because you were unable to pay?

- Do you lend to your friends' spouses? What risks could that present to your relationship and theirs?

- Do you spend based on what you feel you deserve, want, or need? Could comparing yourself with others and spending to keep up rob you of your peace and freedom?

## The Point

If lending to someone's spouse requires secrecy, don't do it. That's not privacy. But don't shame them—just let them know your stance. However, if you notice abuse in their marriage and the abuser has control of the , that's different. You can give the victim . Giving is always the best option if you can afford to give. To be on the safe side, don't give to the opposite sex. You're better off giving or lending anonymously. Try not to keep secrets with someone else's husband, wife, fiancé, girlfriend, or boyfriend. Why? Once you get involved, they'll automatically make you a member of their relationship onion when

# Church Privacy 101

you have no business being on it. And you'll be told about private matters you don't even know how to handle. Plus, you could be blamed for causing their relationship issues.

*You shall not charge interest on loans to your brother, interest on , interest on food, interest on anything that is lent for interest.*
*(Deuteronomy 23:19 ESV)*

# 8

# Personal Privacy Emotional and Physical Well-Being

*Beloved, I pray that all may go well with you and that you may be in good health, as it goes well with your soul.*

(3 John 1:2 ESV)

## Health Privacy

Imagine a doctor giving an examination without actually looking at the patient. The doctor would have to base his exam on touch and imagination. I know this has never happened to you. If it did, your physician would be in jail. But that's how health privacy rolled in the 1800s—a gynecologist could not conduct a vaginal exam. A woman would stand facing her doctor while the doctor knelt in front of her and felt his way up her long, flowing skirt to find and examine her reproductive organ. In those days, there were strict privacy boundaries. A physician could not lay his eyes on a patient's organ or reproductive system, especially not a female's. In general, the body was carefully guarded, and so were doctors' notes and reports about women's bodies.

Fast-forward to 2017. Diane is in her gynecologist's office, sitting on the examination table. Dr. Powers hasn't seen her since the previous year, and she's here today for her annual checkup. He makes some small talk before asking several medical questions. After that, she expects him to leave the room and give her time to change into an examination gown, but what he says next surprises her.

"It sounds like you're doing great. You don't seem to have any issues. There's nothing to worry about. I'll examine you next time."

Diane is confused. She is there for her annual checkup, and he's assuming everything is fine based on her answers and expects her to wait another year.

"Dr. Powers, will my insurance pay you for this visit?" she asks.

"Of course."

"Then you should do the job you're paid by my insurance to do. I didn't wait a whole year to make sure I'm healthy just to have you put me off for another year. Anything can happen in a year. I'd rather be safe than sorry." She picks up the gown.

"You didn't even give me a breast examine today. But you know I've had issues in the past."

Dr. Powers stands up and walks to the door. "Of course, Diane. My apologies. Please take your time and undress. I'll be back in a few minutes."

Diane is the patient we all need to be at every doctor's appointment. In the past, I've been shy about asking doctors to give me the full examination I'd gone in for. Have you done the same? I'll never do that again. Back in the 1800s, patients and physicians were very concerned about privacy. That's valid even today. It was tough for doctors to conduct "compromised" examinations, as they were called then. But it turned out to be detrimental to women's health. It also hampered gynecology research because of the limited access to women's private parts. The need for health privacy still exists today, but things have changed for the better since the 1800s.

## Personal Privacy: Emotional and Physical Well-Being

While health privacy is good for personal and religious reasons, you must give full disclosure to be examined. That's what you're doing when you fill out the health screening paperwork. You're giving consent. And you're not being disobedient or unruly by insisting on knowing what's going on in your body. It doesn't mean you're of little faith. On the contrary, if you're not transparent about your body or health, that's when there's a problem. Your physician should be a VIP member of your health onion.

In the same way, your lawyer should be a VIP or priority member in some of your other onions. Like doctors, they're trained to be discreet. They're a safe sounding board and can help calm your fears and give you direction on critical decisions. Say, for instance, you're afraid of being sued for violating someone's privacy, you're in the process of being sued, or someone violates your privacy, and it results in reputational damage, emotional distress, loss of a job, being stalked, or being defrauded, among other harms. Your lawyer not only provides a safe place to talk about what doesn't feel safe for you to disclose to others, but they also listen with understanding and have more objective and informed answers that address your concerns. They have your best interests at heart—same as your doctor or therapist. Another VIP is your accountant or tax person—who is also trained to protect your privacy. Transparency with experts leads to good and reliable privacy. You're not without anyone in the world.

*For no one ever hated his own flesh, but nourishes and cherishes it, just as Christ does the church.*
(Ephesians 5:29 ESV)

God expects you to love, nourish, cherish, and maintain your body the same way Christ loves, nourishes, cherishes, and maintains you—the church. If you don't care, something is wrong in the sense that you don't know who and whose you are or the purpose of your physical and spiritual body.

# Church Privacy 101

> *Do you not know that you are God's temple*
> *and that God's Spirit dwells in you?*
> (1 Corinthians 3:16 ESV)

Let your privacy be invaded for *temple* maintenance purposes. Don't miss doctors' appointments. This applies to guys too. Use your health insurance. That's what it's there for. Have you ever heard about someone suffering from a health issue for years that, had it been caught sooner, would have been easily resolved? At my church, Sister Shana's daughter, a mother of a few young kids, was in a major car accident. In the process of being treated for her injuries, the hospital found a tumor the size of an orange in her head. She didn't have much time to decide, if she wanted to live. The church was on its knees, praying while she was on the operating table. She admitted always focusing on everybody else's health but hers. That's the point. Sometimes people don't get the care or checkups they need early, and things get out of hand.

What does that teach you? Transparency is not your enemy. Being forthright is a good thing. Preserving privacy isn't the absence of transparency. But it's all in the timing and sharing with the right person—especially your healthcare provider. Transparency in the nick of time can save your life, reduce distress, and prevent death. It can open up opportunities for others to offer you support if you're dealing with alcohol and substance abuse, a mental health crisis, or depression. Also, transparency can help you feel less overwhelmed by the loss of a loved one, your marriage, your job, and countless other losses. Transparency can help save you from yourself—more on that in the next chapter, where I talk about illusions of perfection. But you should also have limits on transparency and openness. Here's why. Being transparent and open with your doctor or a helpful confidant is different from sharing with everyone else. Put a limit on it. For instance, consider the way you overshare your health information, including on social media, or your DNA

## Personal Privacy: Emotional and Physical Well-Being

information and other related health information on genealogy sites. Let's dig deeper into DNA in Chapter 10: Medical Privacy.

Our modern life has both helped and complicated things. It appears your privacy needs don't really exist. But they do. More than ever. Today, during a visit to the doctor's office, you undress from the waist down or waist up. Other times, everything has to come off, and you have to wear those awful gowns with your butt barely covered in the back.

These days, you take printouts of your records and a summary of your visit home with X-ray or ultrasound results, prescriptions, referrals, reports, you name it. Then you leave those papers or items lying carelessly in the car or on your dining table, or you toss them in your recycling bin.

That's not all.

Health insurance companies do their share. To cover your payment for a doctor's visit, they need information from your doctor. Physicians don't talk to them directly; they get information through your physician's billing partner. Insurance companies then generate their own information and share that with their business partners. Also, you share certain health information with your employer to justify sick leave or a doctor's appointment. On and on. This sharing is legit. It gets you the service you paid for. And it helps keep you employed.

You store all kinds of health information online via your devices, further chipping away at your health privacy. Healthcare institutions and providers now store information on portals, making for one-stop shopping for you and criminals alike. But sometimes the problem with privacy isn't only about the excess of health information. Quite the contrary. The problem can also be that you aren't transparent enough, and your physician doesn't have all the information he needs to treat you or direct you to other specialists. It's a fine line.

## Emotional Health and Wellness

Listening is not only important in the doctor's office. It is vital to listen closely to others for what is unsaid to help discern any wellness issues in them. This happened to me when Debra, a hardworking and accomplished acquaintance of mine, called me after we hadn't spoken in a while. She has this big sister personality—very protective of me and sweet. We had our usual talk about how many miles of cycling she did that day and the refreshing citrus, arugula, walnut, and cranberry salad she made after. I noticed she was a little down. I heard frustration in her voice, and she wasn't trying to cover it up. I asked her how she was *really* doing. The long pause that followed confirmed she was about to divulge a very difficult and private matter. A moment later, she mustered the courage and spoke. "Last night I started drinking again."

*Again?* I didn't know she drank alcohol at all, much less had a problem with it. But, of course, I didn't express my thoughts. Instead, I listened as she vented her inner struggles with alcohol. I'd never had this kind of transparent conversation before with anyone. I didn't know what to say. I could only imagine how difficult it was for her to share this. When she finished, I told her I was proud of her. She seemed almost surprised. Then she broke down and sobbed.

"Do you realize how hard it is to do what you just did? I am proud of you for sharing this with me," I reassured Debra. "I don't have answers, but we can sort this out. I'll hold you accountable. If you have other bottles left in the house, dump them out now." She agreed.

That was a year ago. She hasn't had a drink since and is in a program that's helping. I don't think I was the only one she reached out to for help. But she had to take the first step and be open, or transparent, with one person first. This is hard, especially when you live alone and nobody notices what you're doing. I was honored that she entrusted me with her concerns.

## Personal Privacy: Emotional and Physical Well-Being

Helping her helped me to be more informed and sensitive about alcohol and substance abuse and addictive behavior—should another person in my circle have the same concern. Plus, I got a promotion in Debra's onion. It's something she said—something to do with how she felt that day talking to me. She felt she could be more transparent with me and trust me. I can't articulate it here, but it feels good knowing someone can trust you in their critical private moments.

While privacy is important, in some situations, you might be tempted to use it as a cover-up or excuse. You shouldn't. You'll hurt yourself without realizing how badly. Don't destroy yourself in silence for the sake of privacy if you need help in any way. If you don't have someone you trust, call a helpline. Get a professional to help you if you don't want anyone you know involved initially. Professional help is not as bad as we make it sound. In our society today, when we say someone needs professional help, we sometimes mean that as an insult. No wonder people who need help reject support. A professional—counselor, therapist, helpline worker, or psychotherapist—is a specialist. They also tend to be objective, discreet, empathetic, reassuring, nonjudgmental, and informed. They can help you get back on your feet and become the person that God designed you to be. Preserving your privacy is a huge part of their job. They should be in your health onion.

## Reflect

- Have you ever had an addiction or an addictive behavior? For instance, under stress, you chose a self-destructive habit, and now you feel stuck? Do you think it might get out of hand and impact those you love?

- What's that habit for you? We think of addictive behaviors as being only about substances like drugs or alcohol. But they can also be food addictions, bingeing or purging, overspending, or destructive behaviors like enabling people who abuse you emotionally or physically.

- Do you feel that these struggles are your private business?

- Do you believe you can help yourself without anyone else being involved?

## The Point

No Scripture supports keeping a drinking problem private. Yes, you have the right to drink. The Bible shows that it is a personal decision but also talks about the consequences of addiction. When you're addicted to anything, you should seek help. Don't let an addiction compromise your dignity, spiritual life, or growth. Remember, privacy is about personal choices and decisions, but it is also about dignity and respect. If you're overconsuming alcohol, you may find yourself behaving in any of the following ways:

- making bad choices or decisions (Proverbs 20:21; Ephesians 5:18)

- acting out of character and making a fool of yourself; self-shaming (Genesis 9:21)

- becoming disorderly, including doing disgusting things like vomiting in public or getting into fights (Isaiah 28:7–8)

- aggravating work and health issues as well as doing illegal things like driving under the influence (1 John 3:4)

- stealing, lying, sleeping in the wrong bed with the wrong person, or hurting others, including raping and murdering (Romans 13:13)

## Personal Privacy: Emotional and Physical Well-Being

- hurting people or saying things you will regret after you're sober (Matthew 24:49)

- setting yourself up to be victimized, especially these days when onlookers will snap photos or upload videos on social media (Proverbs 23:35)

In the Bible, abuse of alcohol and drunkenness are often linked with immorality, sexual misconduct, foolishness, reckless indiscretion, and negative behavior (Ephesians 5:18). In these digital days, all of those can be posted online and mercilessly violate your privacy.

As the saying goes, "You can do bad all by yourself." I know people can do everything on the list without being drunk. But booze can be a bad influence if you let it. And it adds fuel to the fire.

> *I have told you these things, so that in me you may have peace.*
> *In this world you will have trouble. But take heart!*
> *I have overcome the world.*
> (John 16:33)

### *Don't let domestic violence and abuse become your secret.*

Demanding privacy is just a cover-up when you aren't open about a domestic violence situation that you're in. Stop endangering yourself and hurting others—especially if your children are in that situation. Domestic violence, whether caused by alcohol abuse or not, isn't a situation in which you should practice absolute privacy. Sure, we live in a world where some people can't keep things to themselves, but it's important to be transparent with the people who can help you. Professionals are the best. You don't need to worry about others knowing until you're ready to share. But professionals need to know. Don't keep secrets. Don't wait.

# Church Privacy 101

In the US, the nationwide help number for domestic violence is 1-800-799-SAFE (7233), TTY 1-800-787-3224, or (206) 518-9361 (video phone only for deaf callers). They'll connect you to agencies in your home state. It won't cost you a thing. And your privacy stays intact. These are not the only hotlines. If you're on the other side of the Atlantic, browse https://ec.europa.eu/justice/saynostopvaw/helpline.html for a directory designed for European countries. You'll find phone numbers and more. If your life or someone else's is in danger, there's no privacy about that. Get help first. And fast.

### *Identify dangerous people and situations.*

Abuse comes in many forms, including mental, emotional, and physical. Learn to recognize when you're in a dangerous situation or with a dangerous person who may be abusing you one way or another. For instance, you're in danger when you're pushed, shoved, punched, choked, or slapped, or when someone has a dangerous or sharp object pointed at you. You or a loved one is in danger when the person you're with gets angry and punches the wall, kicks in the door, curses or yells at you, or makes you feel unsafe or afraid. You're in danger if someone constantly insults you, shames you, or threatens to break up with you if you don't do what they want. You're in danger when you can't sleep because of these disturbances to your peace or when your kids are punished unnecessarily, yelled at, beaten, threatened, or injured. You're in danger if your belongings are destroyed or trashed. That's also abuse.

It doesn't matter if the abuse is caused by alcohol, ginger ale, anger, depression, Netflix, or sugar—call the cops. You might be criticized by friends or others, but it's not their life in danger; it's yours. Call the cops and call a good, trusted friend too—you need their support. You may be worried about calling the cops or getting the authorities involved, but don't play with your life. This has nothing to do with forgiveness. Forgive the person, but

## Personal Privacy: Emotional and Physical Well-Being

protect yourself and your children (if there are any involved). Take threats seriously. Many people are harmed by spouses, romantic partners, and loved ones. If you feel unsafe, get away and stay with a friend or family member. It's wise to spot danger ahead and protect yourself (Proverbs 22:3). As a zealous Sunday school leader, Oláolu, puts it, "Getting away is not enough. Get law enforcement involved to ensure the person doesn't do this again. Calling the cops means protecting other people you may not even know. This is not only about you. Stop thinking your problems are only about you." Having once been in a church where a minister, an abusive husband, eventually killed his wife, Brother Olá says this from a place of empathy, experience, and wisdom whenever the topic of domestic abuse and forgiveness crops up in Sunday school. Dangerous people and situations are not only about you or your private life. They're a public concern, and the authorities should know—they're counting on you to notify them.

## Reflect

- Are you ashamed of what someone else is doing to you? Are you embarrassed for them?

- Do you find that you don't want anyone you know to know about it? Understood. But did you know you have options? Did you know you can call someone who won't judge you—someone trained to handle this sort of issue? They'll listen. Let them guide you on the next steps.

- Are you worried about what your neighbors will think if they see cops at your house? Why?

## The Point

Get help. Don't let your challenges or problems embarrass you. Don't blame yourself—you don't deserve abuse of any kind. Call a helpline. Call the cops. If it happened to your neighbor, she'd do the same thing. Don't worry about her judging you or what she'll say. Why should you be ashamed of somebody else's dysfunction? If you're in this situation and keep quiet, this is not privacy; instead, you're keeping a destructive secret and enabling abuse. Privacy is supposed to protect you—that is, if you're applying privacy the right way. It should allow you to be in control of information or a situation. That means not everyone should know your business. But at the same time, control means not keeping information to yourself indefinitely. Control means making choices about who, when, and where to disclose that information for your own benefit. That includes getting help to ensure the peace, safety, health, and well-being of you and your children. Here's what keeping this a secret does: it protects the abuser's harmful behavior and the toxic environment they've created. A secret hides your hurt and feeds your fears. It takes away your control and eats away at your peace, safety, and health. You're not the first Christian or believer this has happened to, nor will you be the last. Don't cover up abuse. That's not privacy.

> *The godly may trip seven times, but they will get up again.*
> *But one disaster is enough to overthrow the wicked.*
> (Proverbs 24:16 NLT)

**Impotence is private, but healing begins when you talk—to the right person.**

There's no absolute privacy about this. You don't want to tell anyone your business or your man's business? Agreed. Not every friend will care enough

## Personal Privacy: Emotional and Physical Well-Being

to keep it hush. Some will be bewildered, and others won't know to advise you to seek help. But you have options. Whether you're a man or a woman, you have options. Start by making a doctor's appointment—you can trust a doctor to protect your privacy. Your church family? Not so much, unless you have a licensed counselor in your church. Even so, it's best to consider counselors outside the church. This is a top-tier personal issue.

So how does impotence translate to church privacy? I've seen these types of issues turn into domestic violence and spousal abuse, with the churches involved making excuses, mishandling the information, oversharing, gaslighting one spouse openly, and, in the end, splitting marriages.

Talk to a specialist who can actually help without spreading the news. Privacy is peace. In this type of situation, peace is critical for healing. Mental serenity—not people's random, unsolicited, and unfounded opinions—will allow you to focus and solve this problem. Miracles do happen. Impotence doesn't solve itself. Pray about it, and in the meantime, avoid bootleg Viagra or Cialis. If medication is necessary, get it from your board-certified, not Internet-certified, doctor. They have to be prescribed by a legitimate source.

Impotence is destructive on many levels. It hurts the person afflicted, and it can damage all his relationships—work, marriage, church, and beyond. It's also not an easy topic to discuss. Let's say a husband is impotent. He might pull away, even though he doesn't mean to be rude. Impotence, or erectile dysfunction, can lead to anxiety, depression, and even isolation. Whatever you do, don't tell him to "man up!" He's sensitive to every word spoken, no matter what you mean, and every word or behavior from others, even if it's not intended to insult, can be perceived as such, making him feel more insecure. Both men and women feel anxious and uncertain when this problem exists. They may also feel disappointed, frustrated, or inadequate. It's worse for the man. This is very personal.

You can be the most supportive spouse and still be treated harshly by your husband, who's struggling with impotence. You can't fill that void in his self-worth. More often than not, you might even be accused of having an affair or cheating, even when your spouse is the one distancing himself. Deep private issues abound. But try to get help for you and your spouse. There's counseling for couples and for individuals. Don't use privacy as an excuse for not getting help. Proper privacy and transparency speed up healing.

## Reflect

- Men: are you avoiding going to bed because you're scared she may have a need that you can't meet?

- Men: do you watch TV longer and spend the night in the living room, trying to avoid being put in a situation where you can't perform?

- Women: does your spouse obsessively worry about you going out and who you speak to or meet up with socially?

- Women: is your spouse isolating himself and you by turning down invitations to spend time with other couples?

- Men and women: Is your spouse angry, moody, combative, argumentative, or feeling worthless? Could this have anything to do with impotence?

## The Point

The person suffering from impotence feels insecure and even ashamed. You, their spouse, walk on eggshells. He may withdraw from your normal social activities and friends. He may suffer mood swings, depression, and anxiety.

## Personal Privacy: Emotional and Physical Well-Being

One or both of you may feel angry, despondent, or critical. Get help. Don't let this quietly ruin your relationship. Impotence is nobody's business but your spouse's and your doctor's. And how else do I propose you solve this problem? Get knowledge and make an onion.

> *Getting wisdom is the wisest thing you can do!*
> *And whatever else you do, develop good judgment.*
> (Proverbs 4:7 NLT)

### *Knowledge is power.*

Knowledge and wisdom won't fall from the sky. You need to do your research. That reminds me to ask: which search engine do you use? I use DuckDuckGo .com, as do most privacy enthusiasts. That way, you're not tracked according to DuckDuckGo's claims. When I searched the terms *erectile dysfunction* and *impotence* with other search engines, can you imagine how many weeks Cialis ads popped up on my computer screen? Also, don't use your work computer for personal searches. Try DuckDuckGo instead—no endorsement intended.

As you do your research, you will be surprised at how many people have the same issue. It's more common than you think and is a serious health issue. Don't self-diagnose and call it a day. Preserve your privacy, but make an appointment with your doctor. Doctors will point you to the right specialists who can help and won't judge. The Mayo Clinic website states that one of the first steps a doctor might take is screening for depression and a number of possible psychological causes of erectile dysfunction.[1] Depression can be a cause. But impotence can also *lead* to depression and stress. Erectile dysfunction can be brought on by both physical and psychological issues. This is serious stuff. If this is you, I know it's embarrassing, but put your faith to work on this. Get help. Of course, your privacy should be intact as well. Your relatives don't need to know about this.

Not every church has programs to educate you and give you the help you need on this particular issue. Rightfully, you don't want people talking about your business in church. That's why you should consider websites and hotlines you can get information from. Learn how to handle this issue the right way. Privacy is about choices. You're not stuck. Choose carefully whom you tell and where you get help. This is private health information. Let only professionals handle it. Pray to find the best specialist and therapist to help you and your spouse get through this. When you're helping a spouse with this complex issue, you also need to get professional help yourself—separately.

### *Keep your onion small.*

Use a small onion and manage your privacy wisely. If your privacy is not giving you freedom and peace, chances are it's not really privacy to begin with—you're keeping secrets. Everyone is going to face privacy risks and private battles in different aspects of their lives. Manage these risks by identifying who you're going to tell and when. I mentioned you need a small onion for this. It could be just three people. That's what onion rings are for—they make you think this through. If you're feeling embarrassed and don't feel you can talk to anyone close to you, fine. It's okay to use only two rings from your onion—add God plus a couple of professionals. You don't need a crowd. Onion rings are not just for friends. They're for the right people you need at a specific time—those who can give you the support and guidance you need to overcome a difficult situation. Here's what you'll get with professionals: an objective, empathetic, and trained listener who will give you their full attention during your appointment. A professional won't judge you based on what they know about you the way a friend might be tempted to form an opinion about you. An expert won't carelessly cast their personal opinions on

Personal Privacy: Emotional and Physical Well-Being

your issues. But they will use expert knowledge and wisdom to help you take the next steps forward.

> *Whoever walks with the wise becomes wise,*
> *but the companion of fools will suffer harm.*
> (Proverbs 13:20 ESV)

## Dangerous Decisions

One of the first legal analyses and memos I penned in school was when I was the pretend prosecutor on a court case about a man named Mr. Davenport, a businessman who texted himself to death. How? As I mentioned earlier, sometimes something you misuse in private becomes dangerous. Jamie Davenport, of Knoxville, Tennessee, was driving on Route 1 in Princeton, New Jersey. He was speeding at seventy-five mph—twenty above the posted speed limit of fifty-five mph—texting, and not wearing a seat belt. Real-life story. Shortly after, Mr. Davenport died in a car accident, leaving the woman in the car in front of him with dozens of life-altering injuries. When text records were disclosed during the investigation, it turned out Mr. Davenport was texting his lawyer back and forth about a new business deal. She knew he was driving and speeding. Long story short, neither of them acted responsibly.

Texting while driving is your personal business; at least that's what people believe. So they're scared to warn you because they fear you might bite off their head. But when you text and drive, not only are you endangering yourself, you're also risking other people's lives. Nobody corrects you. This is an example of how respecting someone's privacy is applied incorrectly.

A woman had a meeting with me. Afterward, I walked her back to her car, only to find the front of the car was almost gone. Totaled. I stared at the car, perplexed, knowing she was seven months pregnant.

"Someone hit your car? Were you in the car when this happened? Are you okay?"

She laughed. Confused, I repeated my questions.

"No, I went off the road and hit the ramp. No biggie; I was texting. I text all the time."

Are you serious? No biggie? All the time? Do I really need to tell a grown woman not to text while driving because it will endanger her baby, other drivers, pedestrians, and herself? Apparently so! This seems like common sense, but it clearly isn't. I gave her my candid disapproval and held her accountable—with love, of course—and hoped for her baby's sake she listened.

*An open rebuke*
*is better than hidden love!*
(Proverbs 27:5 NLT)

## Reflect

- Do you obey some laws more than others, even though you know your choices endanger lives and can change the course of your life and health?

- Do you keep quiet even when you see people in your circle or church make dangerous decisions?

## The Point

We all indirectly contribute to the dangers surrounding others' lives and health. Maybe you drive recklessly, or you don't speak up when someone else is because you're preserving your good rapport with that person. You don't

## Personal Privacy: Emotional and Physical Well-Being

want them to see you as someone who meddles in their personal business. Remember this: it's never helpful to honor privacy when it's harmful to you or others. My friend Steph in the UK tells her students that if they make her aware of any situation that poses a danger to them, by law, she can't guarantee privacy. For Steph, it is crucial to report abuse or a harmful behavior to the authorities, meaning she's committed to being involved in getting her students help quickly from the right sources. You may not be a teacher, but this should apply to your personal circle. Helping doesn't mean putting the person's privacy on blast. Preserve privacy, but honor safety and well-being. Honor the law in the process, where applicable. That's what privacy is about.

*Live as people who are free, not using your freedom as a cover-up for evil, but living as servants of God.*
(1 Peter 2:16 ESV)

# 9

# Mental Health Privacy
# The Illusion of Perfection

*Love your neighbor as yourself.*

(Matthew 22:39)

## Don't Judge a Book by Its Cover

Ever wonder why, when you enter the church sanctuary, members always seem so perfect? Or at least they look perfectly fine? They're laughing, hugging each other, and filled with gratitude. Some never seem to struggle with complex life issues like the ones you're carrying. When you say, "Good morning, how've you been?" the response will most likely be "God is good" or "I'm trusting Him" or "I'm blessed." Rarely do people say, "I'm sick.... It's not a good morning" or "I'm depressed" or "I'm still really traumatized by what happened to me this week." I've certainly never heard anyone say, "I'm confused and suicidal" or "I plan to end my life as soon as I get home." They say they're fine. But they're not.

Here's the truth. People's lives are not as perfect as they seem. But don't expect that kind of candidness. They might be more open if they weren't so afraid that their personal business would get leaked. Sadly, some think everyone in church is supposed to feel and look like everything is going

## Mental Health Privacy: The Illusion of Perfection

great—as proof that they're righteous. So they pretend all's well. And their pretense is a defense mechanism that protects their feelings from being hurt by someone who may react negatively to their personal issues.

For most people in the church, interaction with others only happens in the sanctuary, in Sunday school, and during midweek church gatherings, and they may not feel as connected or close enough to people to share. The Bible says we should not neglect fellowship. Churches meet a lot. We've got the meeting part down. But true fellowship happens when we engage others and build trust through deeper conversations. What about observing a member, pinpointing that there's a problem, and gently intervening with encouragement? If you sense an issue brewing in another person, you should reach out and offer support, guidance, and, if they're willing to share, nonjudgmental encouragement. This opens doors to building friendships, creating deeper connections, and supporting each other.

Society has this stigma around mental health. There is a misunderstanding of what it is. The truth is, the many things that contribute to how you feel, relate to others, or think affect your choices and decision-making processes, as well as how you handle stressful situations. These all relate to your mental well-being. If you don't fully understand what impacts your mental health, you won't be able to help yourself or others.

Mental health concerns are common and varied. The shocking part of the problem, according to Mental Health First Aid USA, is that mental health struggles or disorders are more common than heart disease, lung cancer, and other types of cancer combined.[1] It can happen at any time to anyone from any walk of life. It doesn't depend on how good a person's life looks on the outside. It doesn't consider your social or economic status, your age, or your race and ethnicity. That's why a perfect-looking, rational, broke, financially secure, Christian, Jew, unbeliever, man, child, or woman could be struggling. It can come in the form of anxiety, trauma, depression, and/or distress. It could lead to suicide, or the afflicted person could hurt others. Some people get depressed and become withdrawn and unproductive. Others can be depressed but high-functioning and achieve their goals. Anthony Bourdain, Robin Williams, and Abraham Lincoln are good examples. They were high-functioning and likable individuals, just like many biblical examples, including Jacob, Job, King Saul, and King David.

> *Not giving up meeting together, as some are in the habit of doing, but encouraging one another—and all the more as you see the Day approaching.*
> (Hebrews 10:25)

### How depression creeps in is unreckonable.

Depression can be caused by many factors. Loss of a job, divorce, loss of a loved one, sexual assault, rape, prolonged illness, loss of mobility, loss of a business, loss of opportunities, loss of possessions or property, or even a major life change can trigger mental health issues or make them worse. Some are genetically triggered, meaning it is a prevalent health issue in the person's family.

Speaking of family, Absalom was a rebellious pain in the neck. He drove his dad, King David, into distress and depression. Absalom wasn't discreet about David's private life. Instead, he shouted it from the rooftop to shame his father (2 Samuel 16:22). And it went viral. His misbehavior was definitely a violation of both David's privacy and the honor clause of the law (Deuteronomy 5:16). David's top confidant sided with Absalom. The loss of a confidant, the subsequent betrayal, and the violation of privacy drove David deeper into anxiety and depression. It reminds me of how Jezebel stressed out the prophet Elijah so badly that the prophet fell into despair and depression. This led Elijah to make a shocking proposal to God (1 Kings 19:1–14).

## Mental Health Privacy: The Illusion of Perfection

He prayed the first-ever suicide prayer in the Bible. Elijah was so afraid of Jezebel's threats to cut off his head that he begged God to take him out. He was on high alert. He felt unsafe.

A prolonged illness and chronic pain were unbearable for Job and his wife. It appeared as though Job and his wife were both depressed. They were emotionally and mentally weak but spiritually strong. Job had little dignity left. Who has dignity when their life is out of their control, they smell terrible, they look hideous, they are covered with boils, and dogs are licking their sores? His wife suggested he was better off dead—to preserve the little dignity he had left—and gave him an idea on how he should end his life: "Curse God and die!" (Job 2:9). But Job chewed her out.

What do these folks have in common? They were loved by God, but they all had mental and emotional health struggles. We're all vulnerable. There's no shame in this struggle. We should recognize the signs, give help to others, and seek help for ourselves when needed.

### *Offer support and guidance to someone who needs it.*

Years ago, I signed up for mental health training. I thought it could help me better help others during my ministry activities, lectures, talks, and consultations. A lot of that training came back to me as I recently completed my certification as a mental health first aid responder. These skills can quite literally save lives. With them, I can help someone facing a mental health crisis. People don't always come out and talk about what they're going through. Most of the time, it is for privacy reasons—they're afraid of judgment, and they feel ashamed about their struggle.

The COVID-19 pandemic left people worldwide struggling with anxiety and depression from the loss of jobs, businesses, and family members and the inability to move around freely or travel to be with family. Globally, we're probably all still suffering from the trauma of COVID-19 in the form of post-traumatic stress disorder (PTSD) and the uncertainty of the future. So don't ignore the critical signs of depression in people around you. And it goes both ways. If you have mental health needs, be open to getting help. You need to have the willingness to share, but at the right time, with the right person, and in the right place.

That's not all. There's much more to mental health than depression. There are many different types of disorders we often don't even think about, such as obsessive-compulsive disorder (OCD), eating disorders, bipolar disorder, and schizophrenia, among many others. Take five minutes to look up one of these and get to know the common symptoms and behaviors. Knowing the signs will help you become intentional about helping preserve a friend's, loved one's, or church member's privacy and dignity. The church should be a place where people are treated with understanding. But too often, it isn't. Instead, people get judged for not being well. We need the church to be a place of understanding, guidance, and support—a place where privacy is respected and transparency is embraced.

## Reflect

- Can you identify with Job's frustration and feelings of hopelessness?

- Is someone around you dealing with a prolonged or recurring illness? Since you know that prolonged illness can trigger depression, how might you help them?

- Is anyone going through a life-changing situation or crisis? Have you noticed?

## The Point

Always preserve mental health privacy. Never blurt out to someone that they have mental health problems—even if they're difficult to deal with at the time. That would be ignorant and rude. Instead, based on the circumstances, ask caring questions such as the following:

- Ask how work, school, or business is going.

- Depending on their response, if you sense a specific issue, ask if there's anything they would like to talk about.

- Ask if you can talk about the pressure or stress they've expressed or that they are feeling.

- Gently mention any changes you've observed in them, and let them know you're concerned.

- Encourage them to see a physician with whom they'll feel more comfortable opening up about the issue. Part of caring is relinquishing control to better help the person. Offer to go with them.

- Ask how they are feeling (listen closely if they mention depression or other conditions).

- Depending on the response, if you've proven yourself trustworthy, you may have an opportunity to ask if they've had suicidal thoughts or ideas.

- Take mental health first aid training so you can learn more.

# Church Privacy 101

*Doing God's work also means accepting responsibility for preserving privacy.*

People in crisis need you to respect their health privacy, even if they don't say so—their hearts are looking for someone to trust. So treat their mention of thoughts of suicide as a life-or-death situation. If you end up on someone's onion ring, be ready to make tough choices for their benefit. One of those choices is speaking up at the right time. Being a member of an onion ring is more than keeping things hush. No. In a privacy context, it can mean speaking up and taking action to preserve an individual's destiny and build up their life—openness is the other side of privacy. If someone ever calls you to say she wants to kill herself, treat it like an emergency because it is. Don't brush it off. Think fast, and put your faith into action. You can't help save her soul if she's no longer alive, can you?

To prepare yourself for situations like these, you could take mental health first aid training, like I did. Ask your church to sponsor you, then share your experience with other members. Until then, I'm sharing what I learned with you.

Thankfully, not every mental health crisis or issue requires suicide prevention. But it doesn't hurt to have a few hotline numbers at hand:

- National Suicide Prevention Lifeline: 1-800-273-8255 or 1-800-784-2433

- Boys Town National Hotline: 1-800-448-3000

In Europe, the International Association of Suicide Prevention (iasp.info) has all European countries and their hotlines. And their individual online live-chat pages are available.

Don't you just hate it when someone reveals something private about you and says, "Sorry, I didn't know you didn't want anyone else to know"?

## Mental Health Privacy: The Illusion of Perfection

No matter the issue, you should always be discreet and protect the privacy of the person you're helping. This doesn't mean you won't get them professional help. It means you will protect what they've shared with you. Don't share it with others. You may not have a privacy title in church, but God expects love, integrity, and respect for others from you. Protecting privacy shows you genuinely care by preserving the dignity of someone who is in the middle of a difficult time in their life. In some situations, you might need to contact the church for resources. Perhaps a member of your church has education and experience in this area and is better equipped to handle it. Other than that, don't discuss their details, lest they be misjudged, isolated, and discriminated against. How would you like to be treated when you're in a crisis? Having mental health issues doesn't define us—but a premature exposure of the fact can be damaging. If you break someone's trust, you may close the door to them opening up again and getting help. When you have any title in church, that's God plugging you into his divine onion ring. Do your duty with due diligence. Protect all those who have been assigned to you. When you care for people, you're doing this as a duty to God. You're doing God's work by preserving privacy.

*Love must be sincere.*
(Romans 12:9)

*Honor privacy choices even when private information about a person is known.*

Let's say all is well now. The person you helped has chosen to testify in church. If she calls you out from the pews and says you were very instrumental in her journey to getting better, what should you do?

Smile, nod, and stay quiet.

What if she insists you say a word or two? Piggyback on what she said, but don't add a bunch of new details. Don't hog the mic. Be brief. For example, you shouldn't start with "There were some details left out of the testimony. The part where . . ."

It's hard to believe, but if she wanted to share that part, she would have. Honor her story, no matter how it's told or what's left out. Privacy is about what you share, with whom, the level of detail you're comfortable sharing, and the timing. And giving them that "right time" control is one of the best gifts you can give someone when they need privacy. Hand over the story and the control to the owner, even if you played a part in it. It's theirs to reveal to the world—their issues or victories. After all, it took them a while to get to the point of sharing with others. Sharing means it's the right time. Revealing the information means she feels at peace sharing it with others outside her onion.

Let's use you as an example. Some people in your onion may know you were so broke at one point in your life that you were discreetly helping yourself to food from the church pantry. Others in your onion ring may have only known you weren't doing well financially.

Then time passed, and you were back on your feet financially. Ten years later, you wrote a memoir, and in the book you stated, "I wasn't only broke, but it was a desperate situation, and only the people who were close to me knew the extent of my desperation." Then someone in your onion began to tell others who weren't even close to you, "Yes, she's right about that. All the food she ate for ten months was taken from the church pantry—it's amazing how she did it without anyone noticing. I'm happy for her that she has a job now." This would be a violation of your privacy and of the onion ring you added this person to as a member. Honoring privacy means sharing a lot less than you know about someone.

## Mental Health Privacy: The Illusion of Perfection

*By wisdom a house is built,*
*and through understanding it is established.*
(Proverbs 24:3)

# Dealing with Loss

Strangely enough, when it comes to grief and grieving, even though we've gone through it ourselves, we can be a bit judgmental at times—and it makes us terrible comforters. Like Job's three friends. We're the Eliphaz, Bildad, and Zophar who don't offer real comfort in our friend's crisis (Job 42:7–8). We have logic, opinions, and Scriptures brewing up before we really listen effectively with our ears and hearts. Did you know you could use Scriptures at the wrong time, with the wrong motive, and in the wrong situation? I learned that from Job's friends. Usually, instead of helping the situation, the grieving person sinks deeper into the hole of depression, anger, or despair.

It's hard to see that if you're overly focused on cause and effect—talking about or justifying why the situation happened. Here's how God answered such a person: "I am angry with you [Eliphaz] and your two friends, because you have not spoken the truth about me" (Job 42:7).

To their credit, Job's friends did some things right. First, they showed up when they heard he was sick (Job 2:11). Second, they felt his pain: "they began to weep aloud, and they tore their robes and sprinkled dust on their heads" (Job 2:12). Third, they spent time with him. They spent seven days sitting on the ground with him in silence before they offered their advice (Job 2:13).

Later, after they gave him many insensitive speeches, Job prayed for forgiveness for his friends. He didn't unfriend them, despite how they'd treated him. I suspect he may have shuffled them around his onion rings a few times during their brawl. Job was hurt. You would be too. But he prayed for them and forgave them. God must have spoken to his heart to keep these friends.

If someone loses a loved one, you can focus on helping them lighten the burden, not on eliciting information. Ask, "How are you today?" not "How did it happen?"

I didn't used to mention grief at all. *It might trigger sadness*, I thought. Even though I've had mental health first aid training where I was taught to mention the deceased person's name to their grieving loved one during a conversation and ask them about their grieving, to me it still felt triggering. Recently, that changed for me. Cara, a colleague of mine, and I were talking. She mentioned she'd lost her son Justin a few years before we'd met. This broke my heart. To protect her from the pain she'd already lived and relived, I withheld asking questions. One day, I came clean about my hesitation. I explained to Cara that I wanted to know more about Justin but didn't want to cause her any more pain.

"No, talking about my son isn't painful," Cara said.

"So it would be okay for me to say Justin's name and for us to talk about him?"

"I love talking about my son!" Cara said. "It reminds me of him and how much I love him. People think it will make me sad if they ask me about my grieving or mention his name. But it's exactly the opposite."

Cara told me that after Justin's death, nobody talked to her about him or mentioned his name. Feeling isolated and lonely in her grief, she took to social media. There, people were posting their memories of Justin and wanting to talk about him. Members of his sports team raved about him there. Teachers and classmates posted messages about missing him. They uploaded their favorite photos and videos. Cara found relief there. She couldn't see or read enough about Justin. Social media became her support system. People

## Mental Health Privacy: The Illusion of Perfection

posted and messaged her about Justin, and Cara responded. She looked forward to these daily exchanges.

Meanwhile, like me, the people closest to her were too cautious to mention Justin's name or dig more into how Cara was coping with her grief, afraid to upset her. They assumed they were giving her privacy or space. When they noticed her activities on social media, they were puzzled. They asked why she was putting her business out there with total strangers. They meant well, but they failed to ask Cara if she needed the type of privacy where she didn't talk about Justin or if she needed a different type of support—and what that support would look like. You shouldn't confuse privacy with inactivity or silence. Privacy is not the absence of activity or engagement. It helps to ask the other person what they need. If I'd never asked Cara, I'd still be avoiding mentioning Justin's name around her. Now I know what she needs most. So even on Justin's birthday, I respected privacy on Cara's terms. I remembered what Cara needed most. I texted her a birthday card in celebration of Justin's life. She called. We talked about him for almost an hour, laughing out loud.

*The loss of a loved one can lead to decisions one shouldn't have to explain.*

When my friend Carlese lost her child, she was broken. I should say devastated. Shortly after, she put her house up for sale, and her husband transferred his job to another state. When she told me she was moving, I responded with a big smile. "Wow! That's so exciting. A change might be good for you." I never asked her why. Even though my heart was already feeling the void of them leaving, this wasn't about me. Months later, she told me what my response had meant to her. It was one of the best things she heard during that period of grieving and moving. She felt my sincere support, and it strengthened her. Most people she told bombarded her with questions she couldn't answer. And they then expressed their disappointment. They meant well. They cared. But that made her feel bad about her decision to move. Collecting information or putting someone in a position to always explain their choices is an invasion of their privacy, especially during a time of loss or grief.

## *Till death do us part?*

If a friend, neighbor, or colleague is grieving the loss of their marriage or going through a divorce, be supportive. Don't pry. Intrusive questions are a no-no. Don't ask, "So what's the house worth now?" "Have you thought about selling or investing?" "After you sell, what are you going to do with all that ?" "Can I take it off your hands?" "Did she leave any debt?" "I hope you're not planning to move out of the area."

When people are grieving because of a divorce or a breakup, they need privacy and healing. And how we approach and respect their privacy can make all the difference. If a friend needs privacy, don't respond by not reaching out to them at all. That would be retaliation. They might just need some mental space to process the situation, but they don't want to lose your friendship or support. Feeling sad, grieving, or experiencing depression or a mental health crisis doesn't mean they're not the person they were before. They're going through different phases of something incomprehensible and complex. You can help with their recovery. Jesus' mission included caring for the brokenhearted (Isaiah 61:1).

You can show genuine concern without being invasive. Ask what they want to talk about. Create a trusted environment for them to open up and share when they're ready. If you don't know what to say, listen without speaking. Your silence is powerful. Silence is not the absence of words. Your presence, availability, and approachability speak volumes. Silence means sup-

## Mental Health Privacy: The Illusion of Perfection

port. It means you're listening. And when you do speak, try to avoid these privacy-invading questions:

- "Are you going to remarry?"
- "How long did you two know each other or date before you married?"
- "You didn't know her long enough, did you?"
- "You didn't see any sign that she was selfish, a gold digger, or hot tempered?"
- "How long was he a Christian? Was he baptized in our church or some other church?"
- "Did your families get along? Did your parents approve of the marriage?"
- "How much did you spend on that wedding?"
- "Aren't you glad you two never had kids?"
- "You're still young. What are you doing grieving? Why don't you find someone else?"
- "You're grieving her; how do you know she's not out there already with somebody else?"
- "He's moved on, and you're still mourning and feeling sorry for yourself?"

These questions are invasive, thoughtless, and hurtful. If any of the people on your onion rings ask these types of questions, ask them to read Job 2:13 aloud to you. Be easy on them and learn from their mistakes. Squeezing information out of a grieving person way too soon does not aid the person's emotional healing or preserve privacy. If this happens to you, reconsider and re-evaluate your choice of onion members. Better yet, create an onion for grief support. It should include only people who can genuinely help you heal with their words and actions.

Children go through similar issues with privacy invasion during a divorce. Realize that children of divorced parents, whether old or young, go through stages of grief as well.

*Cosmopolitan* magazine ran an article titled "18 Things You Should Never Say to Someone with Divorced Parents," which included the following invasive questions:

- "Which parent did you side with?"

- "Do you think they'll ever get back together?"

- "So you probably have pretty bad trust issues, huh?"

- "Who's going to walk you down the aisle at your wedding?"

- "At least they're both still alive, right?"[2]

**The loss of a job is a delicate matter and seldom makes sense.**

When someone loses a job, be cautious with insensitive and privacy-invading questions. You mean well, but consider how your questions might be received—especially when the timing, situation, or location is wrong. *HuffPost* put out an article titled "20 Things You Should Never Say to Someone Who's Just Lost Their Job," and it included the following examples:

- "Not a great time to be looking for a new job."

- "It could always be worse."

- "Have you been applying for jobs?"

- "As one door closes, another opens."

## Mental Health Privacy: The Illusion of Perfection

- "It was a terrible job anyway."

- "You just need to stay positive."³

Hurtful. From a privacy perspective, I'd add these to the list of things not to say:

- "Exactly how much were you making there, anyway?"

- "With that salary, you must have put a lot aside—no less than fifty percent in your savings."

- "How are you paying your bills?

- "Did you get into a brawl with your boss? Are you going to sue?"

Just because they've lost their job doesn't mean their privacy is up for grabs. Privacy is about control. Let them have control over processing their losses. Having a conversation with them should make them feel better, not worse. So allow them to control what and how much they want to share, where they want to share it, and with whom they want to share it. How? You could do that by offering to take them out to dinner or lunch. If they choose to share, just listen. If they don't, let them know you're there if they need to chat. When they share with others, still keep what you're told private. Ask if you can request prayer in church on their behalf or if they want to request the prayers themselves in order to control the amount of detail that is shared. Next time, you can piggyback on their request and ask everyone to continue to pray for them. Don't add details to their prayer request.

*My dear brothers and sisters, take note of this: Everyone should be quick to listen, slow to speak and slow to become angry.*

(James 1:19)

# Church Privacy 101

***Listen intently to others.***

Not long ago, during a phone conversation with an acquaintance whom I'll call Ann, unrelated to our conversation, Ann told me that she hadn't showered all week because she was depressed and lethargic. It wasn't lost on me how much courage it took for her to share this. Her voice shook with emotion. I felt her lips quivering and tears rushing out of her control, blocking the words from her lips. She seemed to be laughing and crying at the same time, apologizing for being "lazy." If I hadn't pinned back my ears to listen intently to her words, I would have missed the pain in her voice. It was clear that she didn't want to see another twilight still not showered or still feeling this miserable.

"Hey, I'd rather you tell me stuff like this than not," I said to ease her embarrassment. But I also wanted to help more. I figured that if she had people readily available in her onion rings, she wouldn't be telling me this.

"Sounds like we've got a lot to catch up on," I added. "How about we both go and take a quick shower and call each other back in forty-five minutes?"

"Sure! That'll be great! Let's do this!" Ann said, with a smile in her voice.

And we showered. Then we returned to chatting as planned. I found out she was carrying a lot on her shoulders—a traumatic month without a job, anger and depression setting in, parenting, and financial responsibilities getting the best of her. It was heavy stuff, but I could feel her energy was different and lighter. We prayed and promised each other we would take virtual showers on difficult days. I could tell that she felt better. I thought about this call later when God brought me Sam, a very kind psychologist on my project team. What follows are some of her tips for managing depression: "If you can manage, brush your teeth and change your clothes. When you have those *off days*, remembering hygiene is important. If you can find the energy to get out of bed, make sure you change your clothes and brush your teeth.

## Mental Health Privacy: The Illusion of Perfection

I promise, you'll feel a thousand times better if you do. If these tasks seem too much, find what you can do and do it. Can you only bring yourself to change your shirt? Your underwear? That's perfectly fine. You'll still feel better than if you hadn't done anything at all. Plus, sometimes, simply starting a task is the hardest part. Maybe you're dreading brushing your teeth, so you opt to just floss instead. You may then encourage yourself to go ahead and brush your teeth since you're already in the bathroom. Today is all about survival."

I could see why God placed me in Ann's path the day we talked. By *off days*, Sam was referring to those days when you wake up and don't feel right, don't think right, or aren't capable of carrying out your normal daily activities. There are days when you feel overwhelmed, disconnected, hopeless, worthless, and unmotivated. You don't want to look at yourself in the mirror. You don't like that person who looks back at you in the mirror. You're fearful, sad, irritable, tripping, and moody, and sometimes your motion or movement is slow—you're dragging. You feel as though everyone's life is great except yours. During those days, you lose interest in people or activities you normally enjoy. And you don't know why or how to get out of that numbing feeling.

Depression comes in many forms. What Ann was experiencing wasn't laziness (as she referred to it), but a real health issue. You could be the one who needed to hear these tips when you woke up this morning. It happens to all of us in different ways, but we dismiss it as feeling lazy. Because we dismiss this in ourselves, we don't notice these signs in others. And because we don't notice when it's happening to other people, we neglect their needs and neglect to respect their privacy. I can't imagine the courage it took for Ann to get out of bed that day, pick up the phone, and call me. She was desperate to confide in someone and to garner enough encouragement to shower, brush her teeth, or change her clothes. These may not seem like much on days you're feeling normal, but when you're in a crisis, these small achievements will enable you to keep surviving and thriving—whether you're grieving a job loss, divorce, financial instability, or the loss of a loved one.

Don't distance yourself from a good friend because they're being distant. First, think about their circumstances. Their need for space is not always a sign that something is wrong with you. Tell them you're concerned about them and ask if everything is okay, but don't hide behind just sending them text messages. Let them know you care about them. Be available and intentional about showing up fully in their life while respecting their privacy. What will it take? Anything. That includes taking an extra shower that you didn't need to take, but you took it to encourage another person to come out of a depressed state. Recognize when someone in need extends an invitation to you to be on their onion rings to save them in a particular moment. Pray for them, and God will give you discernment and all the right words to speak.

# 10

# Medical Privacy
# Your Body Is the Temple

*Your body is the temple of the Holy Spirit.*

(1 Corinthians 6:19 NLT)

## Family and Heritage

I've been curious about my genealogy for a long time. I still am. After all, I watch PBS. My love for their theater, music, fine art, and history is uncompromising, and there's no cure. But let's face it, their genealogy musings are world-class edutainment.

Have you ever watched the *Finding Your Roots* series? Check out the guests—Tamera Mowry-Housley, Viola Davis, Carol Burnett, Cyndi Lauper, Niecy Nash, Julia Roberts, John Legend, Martha Stewart, Stephen King, and many others. PBS is sincere in saying that the host, renowned scholar and professor Dr. Henry Louis Gates Jr., "guides influential guests into their roots, uncovering deep secrets, hidden identities and lost ancestors." You'll notice it is all done with consent, respect, and "humor, wisdom, and compassion."[1]

Are you an enthusiast of ancestry or genealogy tracking services? I understand the appeal, but be careful about exposing what your relatives would prefer to keep private. It doesn't hurt to discuss it with them or explain what you want to accomplish by discovering your ancestry before you go searching for your roots. Get consent. Use wisdom and compassion. Always do what promotes peace. Don't do anything that comes between you and your loved ones just because you're excited to share DNA information with a genealogy company or the public on social media.

In 2018, *Fast Company* reported that the Federal Trade Commission was investigating DNA companies over privacy.[2] A year and a half later, the *New York Times* ran a story on the Pentagon's warning to military personnel about the privacy risks of home DNA tests from firms such as 23andMe, Ancestry.com, and others.[3] As you consider finding your roots, consider the risks.

If you are your family's self-designated historian, remember that sometimes too much truth is not good for everyone. Just because it's the truth doesn't mean everyone appreciates it being shared. That's privacy—don't make assumptions about others. Not everyone is equally excited about disclosing personal information, even members of the same family. It's okay to want to find unknown kin; just make sure you don't lose the known kin in the process.

## Reflect

- Did you read the terms and conditions of the genealogy tracking company?

- What promises have they made to you about securing your data?

- What are your rights, waivers, and more as you dig into your roots?

## Medical Privacy: Your Body Is the Temple

- Do you understand everything you've signed away? Are you also allowing these companies to sell or share your genealogy and DNA information? You should consider if and how they're monetizing the data. Who do they disclose your information to?

## The Point

Did you know that law enforcement accesses Ancestry.com, MyHeritage, and other genealogy databases? Is that fine with you? I'm not saying not to use them if you choose to. But at least now you know. You may not have had any brushes with the law or have anything to hide (as most people would claim), but law enforcement can wrongfully link you and your relatives to crimes. They can plug DNA into genealogy websites to crack cases, like the murder of Janet Hylton. Ricky Davis, who was wrongfully arrested, charged, and convicted of her murder, was exonerated after fifteen years behind bars.

*Be careful with your DNA.*

A DNA search using genealogy databases also led to the arrest of murder and rape suspect Joseph James DeAngelo, also known as the Golden State Killer. This was a huge win for investigators. However, it could turn out to be a nightmare for you if you're innocent but implicated in such probes, especially if you're linked to someone who committed a crime. Or worse, you're wrongfully suspected.

In my Twitter archives, I found @HeatherEHeying, a revolutionary biologist who tweeted on November 9, 2019, that a judge approved law enforcement access to search DNA on genealogy sites unbeknownst to the owners of the DNA. Heying was referring to Joycelyn Kaiser's article "A Judge Said

Police Can Search the DNA of 1 Million Americans without Their Consent. What's next?"[4] The truth is, even if you don't agree to police searches when you sign up on these sites, you can still get searched by law enforcement. I believe what's next is for you to rethink your privacy. Can you live with that level of privacy invasion?

If you ask Peter Aldhous of *BuzzFeed News*, he'd probably say, "Forget the police for now. Worry about hackers." On July 22, 2020, Aldhous penned an article alerting readers that the same genealogy database, GEDmatch, that led to DeAngelo's arrest was hacked. Profiles of more than a million users, including the ones who had privacy settings to hide their records from police, were visible to all users.[5] Two days later, MyHeritage was hit.

In January of 2020, before these incidents, DNA services such as 23andMe laid off workers. The company said that consumer DNA tests were waning. One of the major reasons was privacy concerns. This means people want to know their family tree, but not at the expense of their privacy. Folks are wising up and erring on the side of caution. Was it because, in December 2019, the *New York Times* reported the Pentagon's warning that military personnel guard against home DNA tests? That news, of course, was trailed by major news shows, including a recent report by *60 Minutes*: "How China Is Racing to Collect Americans' DNA." These might have deterred home DNA test enthusiasts, resulting in more people paying closer attention to their privacy needs. Are you?

> *Buy the truth and do not sell it—*
> *wisdom, instruction and insight as well.*
> (Proverbs 23:23)

Medical Privacy: Your Body Is the Temple

## Privacy and Hospitalization

At some point, any of us may have a health crisis and may need to have surgery or an extended stay in the hospital. And church members and friends are super caring. As the patient, you don't want to appear ungrateful, but you don't want everyone showing up in your hospital room after Sunday morning worship service. What are your choices? What are your privacy options?

It's totally okay to inform the clergy and ministry facilitators that you don't want church members visiting you in the hospital right away, or maybe at all. God is not going to withhold your healing if you decline visits. The smart thing to do is to be specific about what you want to happen. Be intentional about privacy. For example, if you want just clergy to visit but not members, say so. If you don't want anyone there, you can indicate where they can send cards or who to call on your behalf to get updates. Simply put, you need privacy and peace while you're healing. You're human.

Use the word *privacy* a little more often. The church leader may not understand privacy or think it's a natural need. Don't fret. Don't try to school them. Let them know you're just not ready yet for visitors. When you get well, you can explain privacy to them if they inquire. Many of us struggle with honoring our own needs. And it's even harder to say no to our church family because they're brimming with love, warmth, and irresistible saintly expressions. Some of us avoid the two-letter word to the extent that we would rather say, "I'll pray about it" than "That's kind. But I really need privacy and prayers" (PAP for short). You could also say, "That's really thoughtful, but I'm not ready for that yet."

When you're in the hospital, you don't always have the luxury of praying about that decision. Make the decision right away. When you drag your feet, you put yourself and everyone else in an awkward situation. The earlier you let people know your preferences, the better. They can adjust to and respect your needs. That means you get your much-needed peace early in the process so that you won't feel guilty when someone has already driven to the hospital and finds out the hard way that you don't want them there.

## Reflect

- Do you feel like God will punish you for not saying yes to all good gestures?

- Have you ever been in a hospital and someone informed you that so and so was downstairs and asking to come see you?

- Have you ever been that sister or brother who didn't ask before driving ten miles to the hospital with forty dollars' worth of yellow daisies and get-well balloons only to get upset because you were not allowed visitation?

## The Point

Knowing how God works is important. He knows when you're sick and when you don't feel like being seen by anyone other than your doctor and nurses. God makes allowances for privacy. But you have to let friends, family, and your church family know what you need. They'll understand, or maybe they won't. It's okay. After all, you're the one who needs healing. You shouldn't have to worry about how they feel. They should be concerned about how you feel and give you a chance to heal.

## Medical Privacy: Your Body Is the Temple

*Be a good hospital patient.*

You'll feel less guilty about saying no if you have a plan in place. What can you do to manage the expectations of potential visitors? You can think of it as managed love. You're managing the love people want to heap on you while also allowing for your privacy at a time when you need it. What else do I suggest you do?

- As soon as you can, ask your nurse to inform the visitors' desk that you do not want visitors. Ask that only specific individuals visit or engage with you. Give her a list of names. Let those individuals know so they don't bring others.

- The nurse will relay your choices to potential visitors and those who call about you. This saves you the hassle, awkwardness, and guilt of telling them yourself.

- Don't think since Sister Ellie let everyone from church, including you, visit her in the hospital a few months earlier that you should return the favor. Privacy is not a favor. That was her *choice*, and she was comfortable with it. If you're not comfortable, don't do it.

Assuming you're conscious and aware of your surroundings, text the one person you want to discuss and coordinate updates with. This person should update everyone else in your family on your behalf. Usually, that's also the person you want to visit you. This way, you don't need to respond to every text that comes from well-wishers. You don't need to answer every inquiry, no matter how thoughtful. Such activities take time and effort away from recovering and focusing on your treatment. You're in the hospital to get well, not to keep people happy. That's your priority.

# Church Privacy 101

## *Be a good hospital visitor.*

If you're planning to visit a hospitalized member of your church or a friend, be sure to ask first. Some well-meaning folks believe that if you want to help someone, you shouldn't have to ask for permission. I understand the rationale, but it depends on the relationship. I don't have to ask my mom if I should order her flowers for Mother's Day—because I'm not violating her privacy. If she requests that I don't send them without first asking her, I'll respect her wishes. I won't show up at her doorstep without letting her know, unless she's ill or I'm planning a surprise.

Don't think only about what *you* want to do. Also think about the needs of the person you want to visit. Showing up unannounced in a church member's hospital room when she's in a hospital gown could be embarrassing for both of you. Asking for permission is better than having to offer an apology. Asking first will make a hospital visit more meaningful. The person you're visiting will expect you and prepare for your visit. This will make for a more enjoyable time together.

How do you ask?

Don't say, "Wouldn't you like for me to come visit you?" Don't put words in her mouth. Instead, make it easy for her to say no—if that's her true answer. When you phrase your request that way, she's put on the spot to accept it. Many people don't like to say no to kind gestures such as visits. So you're actually doing a good deed by saying, "I'd love to come see you. Let me know when you feel up to a visit." Don't act as if you're waiting for an answer right then and there.

Until they're ready for visitors, leave a get-well balloon, card, flowers, their favorite snacks, or a stuffed animal at the desk for them. This will show you're thinking about them without pressuring them.

## Medical Privacy: Your Body Is the Temple

Even if his answer is not what you expect, don't complain about Brother Ralph's decision when another person asks if you visited him. You could say you spoke to him, and he sounded better than he did a few days ago. Then encourage the person to keep praying for him.

On the flip side, don't assume the patient wants privacy. No, I'm not contradicting myself. You might *not* visit Brother Ralph because you assume he doesn't want visitors. You could be wrong. The point is, it really doesn't hurt to ask.

I made this assumption about a lovely older lady who wasn't a member of our church but was a devout volunteer for our neighborhood outreach services. Let's call her Joy. When I found out that Joy was in the hospital, I drove over and dropped off balloons, flowers, and a card. Surprisingly, I was driving away when Joy called to thank me and ask that I visit with her. Well, I hadn't bothered to call from the nurse's desk because I didn't want to disturb her. She was undergoing chemotherapy, and I thought she'd be resting. I also knew her to be a very private person. But it turned out she needed company at that moment. When I walked into her room, her face lit up with a smile. We chatted, did crossword puzzles together, and laughed out loud. After her discharge from the hospital, she honored my request to visit her at her home. On a windy autumn afternoon, we chased leaves together with rakes in her front yard, and I met her lovely family. I had wonderful visits with Joy, until months later, when she transitioned to heaven. Her passing was very difficult, but I was blessed to have spent many memorable moments with her.

Later on, it occurred to me that there were many people she'd known much longer who didn't enjoy these final months as intimately as I did. They assumed that because she was a very private person, she didn't want to see anyone during what was such a difficult time in her life. I'm glad I was available to her when she needed *company*, not *privacy*. I've heard many stories of church members who wanted to have visitors while they were in the hospital or at home, but no one came to see them. Nobody asked; they assumed. At first, I did the same.

### *Bring good cheer and laughter.*

Let's say you didn't assume; you asked, and now you're visiting with Brother Ralph. What do you say, especially if he's feeling extra terrible on the day you're visiting and isn't saying much? Even better. That's why you're there. Drive the conversation. That's your role. And you probably know two kinds of drivers in life: responsible and reckless. You're the responsible driver. For privacy's sake, don't discuss his condition in a way that elicits private information you don't need to know. That would be reckless. If pain is all he's talking about, that's where you park. Stay on that point with him and show empathy, even if you've never experienced what he's going through. Keep away from prying questions. Don't stare at him as if he's dying, even if the doctors say he is. If he's not in pain but is a little down, bring him some joy and laughter. After all, he's in the hospital. Keep the conversation upbeat. Be cheerful. Use humor. Maybe stock up on some silly jokes beforehand—preferably related to his hobbies (camping, fishing, or grilling). Get him smiling and laughing. If you're allowed to bring him some outside food that aligns with his diet, find out what he likes and bring it. It might be the best meal he's had that day. (I have nothing against hospital chefs. They are essential, but I've never heard patients compliment their cooking.) You can bring his favorite snack, as long as it doesn't compromise his treatment or diet. Unless you're asked to stay longer, keep your visit short. Your aim is to leave him in a better disposition than when you arrived.

# Medical Privacy: Your Body Is the Temple

*Whoever keeps his mouth and his tongue
keeps himself out of trouble.*
(Proverbs 21:23 ESV)

## *Be sure to protect personal health information.*

During your visit with a patient, be sure to excuse yourself when a doctor, nurse, or other medical professional comes into the room. Give them privacy. Typically, I also let the caregiver know that I'm not a relative so that personal health information isn't accidentally shared with me. Roam around in the hallway far enough away to not hear their conversation. Wait until the care provider leaves the room. Then ask the patient (before you re-enter the room) if they're ready for you to come back in. Usually, the provider will tell you when you can go back in the room. Still ask the patient. When caregivers come into the room, don't ask the patient if they want you to leave the room. Don't put them in that position. You can tell them you'll be in the hallway or that you're going by the restroom. You could also ask if they'd like you to get them an item from the gift shop. Even if they motion for you to stay, leave anyway.

Patients' diagnoses and treatments—past, present, and future—are deemed *protected health information*. If you're not family, you shouldn't be privy to that sensitive information or be in the room when the doctor or nurse examines the patient. Unless the patient willfully shares this information during your visit, don't ask about health information, medications, or treatments. Forget the law for a minute. If the patient doesn't voluntarily share this with you, this information is private. Don't ask about prescriptions, medications administered in the hospital, medical conversations with caregivers, medical records, or diagnoses—they are personal health information. When you're in a hospital room, don't read the personal information on the

# Church Privacy 101

patient's medical wristband or chart or any other personal information on their IV bag. Focus on the patient.

### *Out of the mouths of babes privacy can be violated.*

Don't take children to the hospital. They are curious little beings. My sister "Cupcake" has one of those curious ones—and another one on the way. My very bright and outspoken niece is unfiltered. She speaks her mind gloriously. It's great if you're taking her to shop for real estate. In a heartbeat, she'll candidly tell you everything that's wrong with your house choices—like she did at five years old when we all went house-hunting with my sister "Luvie." At a particular open house, she shook the realtor's hand, introduced herself, and let everyone know the place stunk. It happened so fast. It got out before we could cover her mouth. She was right, though. The place reeked. She didn't expect her auntie "Luvie" to buy a stinky house. So we left.

Sigh.

That won't work well in a hospital room. Children tend to speak their minds and ask very invasive questions. They are attentive, investigative, and innocent in their actions. Unfortunately, they are also oblivious to how it will make the patient feel. They want to touch everything and may ask difficult questions about what they see and smell. However, in my experience, some adults are far worse in that regard than children. Do you know an adult who's as inquisitive as a child? Don't take them with you on a hospital visit, either.

Hospitals are also places with strict rules. Children are full of energy and get bored easily. They want to run around, they don't have volume control, and they want to explore *everything*. They may also wander off to peek into other rooms. Monitoring them will make it difficult for you to have a peaceful and focused visit. Of course, if it's a child in the patient's family

## Medical Privacy: Your Body Is the Temple

or the patient has a great relationship with the child, a short visit will bring both of them joy.

> *Out of the mouth of babies and infants,*
> *you have established strength.*
> (Psalm 8:2 ESV)

### *Selfies and photos are private even if patients say yes to taking them.*

Selfies are invasive in hospital rooms. Unless the patient asks, don't take them. Don't take photos and share them with other people in church, and definitely don't post them on social media. The patient may say yes, trying to be polite. But they may not mean it. Again, take photos only if the patient specifically asks you to take them. I once visited a member of the clergy in the hospital. He'd had an emergency surgery due to the location of a tumor close to his brain. The incision started on the back of his neck and extended up to his skull, where he wasn't able to see it. He'd been in the hospital bed for days and had no idea what the incision looked like or if it was healing well. He was curious. The best way to help him was to take a photo. He asked me, and I took a photo to show him. I could feel the relief that washed over him. He didn't have to keep imagining what it looked like. He saw the stitches and how far the incision extended. Every time I went to see him, I took a photo so he could see the progress of his healing. It helped him feel better, and I believe it helped him get better faster. Our photo sessions were very meaningful to him—and private for a time. When he was healed and back on clergy duty, he shared those photos with the church and his family as a testimony of how God intervened so the tumor didn't cause damage to his brain. Wow. Being transparent was his choice. He shared when he was comfortable doing so and with the people he chose.

## Reflect

- Can you relate to any of the patients I've discussed? In what ways have visitors invaded your privacy in the hospital?

- Have you ever made a hospital visitation mistake that left a patient feeling violated and discouraged?

- How did you apply what you learned from your mistake the next time you visited someone?

## The Point

Be intentional. Plan how your visit can be uplifting to a patient. Consider what they would like and need. Determine to make them feel better when you're there, even if they are in pain when you visit. It's unkind to leave a sick person angry or disappointed when you could have just stayed home.

> *Let each of you look not only to his own interests,*
> *but also to the interests of others.*
> (Philippians 2:4 ESV)

**Praying is almost always appreciated, but sharing without consent is a different matter.**

If the patient shares with you their diagnosis and treatment, refrain from calling everyone to share it. If asked, say she's making progress or that her progress is slow. But keep things general unless you've been given permission to share details. Even when asking others to pray for her, be discreet.

Much of this depends on the patient. It's a matter of *choice*. Some people are very open about sharing their health situation; others aren't. It also

## Medical Privacy: Your Body Is the Temple

depends on their condition. Are they aware of what's happening to them or that they're in the hospital? Are they conscious? Their family can control visitation on their behalf, but be respectful of what you see and hear during your visit.

### *Is there conflict or tension?*

Say, for instance, that you had a conflict or tension with someone who's been admitted to the hospital. What do you do? Hopefully, you weren't the cause of their hospitalization. Regardless, you should expect that, in most cases, they won't want to see you. That might be hard to hear, but this person is the one in the hospital going through a tough time. Be patient and understanding.

If you had a disagreement of some sort before or during the hospitalization, or just don't see eye to eye on something, don't just show up. Regardless of your warm intentions, wait. You may be ready to make amends, but this is not about you and your needs. Give them privacy to heal. It's not the time to make them feel like you're the better or bigger person. Allow them to be comfortable in that difficult, private space. It helps their recovery. Send a card or an apology (if one is due) through another person. Drop off a gift at the front desk or text your well wishes. Let them know you're thinking about them. It might prompt them to ask that you stop by to visit, but don't have that expectation. If they don't respond, that's okay. Don't tell others how the person responded or give the impression that you're a better and more reconciliatory person. You'll just be showing them the terrible condition of your heart (Matthew 15:18).

If you're genuine about making amends or reconciling, you'll wait. You'll be understanding. God worked on me regarding this recently. It was tough to not visit a friend who no longer felt friendly toward me. I knew her condition was bad and she needed support. But she wasn't ready to see me, so I waited out of respect for her privacy. Instead of visiting, I prayed for her healing and prayed to not make it about me. I tried not to overdo it, but I sent my sentiments and waited. In the meantime, I asked other friends to join me in praying. In the end, she called and told me that she knew how much I genuinely cared about her. She thanked me for respecting her privacy and for not giving up on our friendship. Think about the other person's needs the next time you feel like pushing your good deed or visit on them. If you love them, you'll wait until they're ready.

## Health Tests and Privacy

You may not know who Henrietta Lacks is, but she changed the course of medical history, and she never knew it. On January 29, 1951, the thirty-one-year-old Lacks complained of a "knot" she felt in her womb. She visited Johns Hopkins, went to the hospital's unit that served Black patients, and had samples taken. Mrs. Lacks had cervical cancer but was misdiagnosed. She didn't get the treatment she urgently needed. Meanwhile, unbeknownst to her and her family, the doctor harvested her cancer cells for his personal research without her consent. Mrs. Lacks' story was featured on the *Oprah Winfrey Show*, and HBO made it into a movie. If you've read *The Immortal Life of Henrietta Lacks* by Rebecca Skloot, you're familiar with her story. If you haven't, I'll give you a little sliver of what happened next.

*Mrs. Lacks was a modern miracle who changed history.*

Henrietta Lacks' cells lived on after they were harvested from her body. No human cell had ever done this. They wouldn't stop growing and reproducing. The lab couldn't keep up with her cells. Before then, medical science had exhausted its efforts trying to find such a remarkable human cell. As you

## Medical Privacy: Your Body Is the Temple

might imagine, when this happened, it was news worldwide. Her doctor was being interviewed by media outlets. Her cells gained international notoriety and made billions of dollars in the years that followed, while Mrs. Lacks, a mother of five children, was dirt poor. She was a former tobacco farmer with no job, she was discriminated against, and she couldn't afford treatments for her cervical cancer. Meanwhile, her cells helped to create the polio vaccine.

*Time* magazine compared the similarities of the polio epidemic and the COVID-19 pandemic—104 years apart. Cities and facilities were shut down, and people were quarantined. Imagine living through the polio epidemic and being quarantined in the summer when most homes had no air conditioning. You couldn't work remotely. There were no cell phones—definitely no Netflix, Amazon, Twitter, Facebook, Instagram, or YouTube to keep you distracted.

Imagine your body producing the first-ever human cell that was capable of helping develop a vaccine for polio. But it was harvested without your consent. It saved countless lives, but you weren't informed—the name of the cell was altered so nobody would know the cell came from you. Billions of dollars, pounds, and yen were made from the creation of the vaccine and the subsequent medical breakthroughs that came from your cells. Meanwhile, you're penniless and dying of cancer. This is what happened to Mrs. Lacks.

***Genetic information abuse is a critical privacy concern.***

Henrietta Lacks' "HeLa cell" is the oldest and most commonly used cell in medical studies. Many scientific landmarks and accomplishments were made possible using her cells, including cloning, gene mapping, and in vitro fertilization. These breakthroughs were immensely profitable for physicians, scientists, and medical institutions. But Henrietta was bedridden and too sick to work. She certainly couldn't care for herself or her five children. When she finally received treatment for her cervical cancer, it was too late. The disease had spread too far throughout her body. She died in agony months later. All the while, she was a human guinea pig for her doctor, who was taking cells and samples from her body for his own research and sharing his breakthroughs with the world. As if that wasn't enough, the doctor asked Henrietta's husband for her body parts. Not knowing they'd already procured samples from his wife's body—without consent—when she was still alive, he agreed. He didn't realize what he was doing. Think about it. If you struggle to understand medical privacy consent forms today, imagine how much harder it was for a tobacco farmer and steel worker to comprehend in the 1950s. They did not understand what they were agreeing to or signing away.

The hospital then started paying visits to the family under the guise of cancer prevention screening. They took blood and other samples from Henrietta's children and from other relatives. Unaware of the deception, the family cooperated. Every opportunistic researcher and cell smuggler was flying from different parts of the world into Baltimore. The amazing Henrietta Lacks put Baltimore on the map. Her family was stalked for her miraculous DNA. The cell-growing business was booming worldwide because of Henrietta's cell. Some researchers and scientists lied to steal more of her immortal cells to boost their cell farms. Food, health care, health insurance, education, and the welfare of Mrs. Lacks' children and family weren't a concern to those who took advantage of her peculiar cell. Her relatives found out about her stolen cells twenty years later—from the media, not the hospital.

Theirs is a long and heartbreaking story of genetic information abuse. Although European countries are often seen as leaders in preserving privacy and human rights, European scientists published Mrs. Lacks' genome, or DNA sequence, online in 2013, which further violated her family's privacy. This could have caused problems for her successors—health insurance denials, employment discrimination, you name it. Did you know that your

## Medical Privacy: Your Body Is the Temple

DNA sequences and genetic information that are in the hands of health insurance companies means you might be denied coverage for pre-existing conditions? This could happen if they deem you high-risk for cancer, which is what Mrs. Lacks died of. In response to her family's protest, the National Institute of Health ordered the European researchers to take down the DNA information out of respect for the family's privacy. That year, the family was finally granted private rights in medical research.

The Lacks family eventually sued Johns Hopkins Hospital for invasion of privacy. Hopefully, after their decades-long ordeal with medical and health privacy invasions, they will find peace, justice, restitution, and much needed privacy.

A few years ago, at the Global Privacy Summit, Rebecca Skloot, author of *The Immortal Life of Henrietta Lacks*, was a keynote speaker. When she discussed the horrific privacy violations Mrs. Lacks and her family experienced, the audience gasped. We were shocked by the rampant, unchecked, and callous disregard for Mrs. Lacks and her family's privacy. And keep in mind that it happened less than sixty-five years ago. It's still happening today. I hope it's not happening to you.

### *Are you signing your privacy away?*

In church, we're taught not to meddle in medical matters. We let the doctors handle them. Besides, you believe that doctors, hospitals, and staff members always have integrity. But when a loved one dies, you wonder if the hospital did what was best for your loved one or if there were privacy violations. Were physicians transparent about all their activities, and did they respect your loved one's privacy needs and rights?

When you go to see a doctor or when you're hospitalized, it's not just about you getting treatment. Someone can take your bodily fluids or tissue and uncover patterns regarding what your body has or has inherited—disease-wise. Tests and scans can show the risks of particular disorders, sicknesses, and diseases, as well as how your body functions. While you're praying that the treatments work, your provider has unrestricted access to your private health records and DNA, and you have no idea how they are being used or if they are being shared.

## Reflect

- Do you know if a sample taken from your body was taken for other purposes than to treat your condition without your knowledge or consent? Maybe you were given a paper to sign concerning privacy. Did you read it all before signing?

- Do you know the privacy laws that protect your genetic information? Have you read them?

- Have you ever sensed something didn't seem right about someone's hospitalization or treatment, but you dismissed it? You think the hospital is the safest place and has patients' best interests at heart. Right?

- When someone has passed away, have you wondered whether the hospital's treatment was fair and if all treatment options were considered?

- Who has your DNA in their files or records? What are the terms and conditions? And is it traded or shared?

- Do you read treatment agreements closely to make sure you're okay with them? Do you ensure you're in control of your protected health information?

## The Point

In life, nobody will steal anything from you that isn't worth something, even if for only a minute, and even if you won't miss it. Samples taken from your body contain personal and highly private medical information, such as your present health conditions or potential diseases. The privacy risk is this: using this information, employers or health insurance companies might discriminate against you. That's why genetic information is private and protected by law. Physicians and medical institutions can monetize it and profit from it. That's why you should be careful with your genetic information and make sure it is never used without your consent.

Be more cautious of what hospitals are doing with your bodily fluids and samples. Read the fine print before you sign the consent forms. Find out who has your DNA on record and what they're doing with it. Maybe this doesn't seem important now. It will after you find out what happened to John Moore.

## *John Moore's story*

In 1976, John Moore was diagnosed with leukemia at a cancer center in Los Angeles. His doctor told him that it was necessary to start treatments quickly because his spleen was swelling to the point of endangering his life. John agreed and signed the necessary papers and consent forms. He made a choice. He wanted his spleen removed and cremated. Several times a week, he followed up at the health facility for treatments. On one of those visits, the doctor took out his spleen—it was damaged. He also took samples of blood, urine, sperm, and other bodily fluids.

Later on, John decided to move to Seattle, Washington, approximately 1,200 miles away from Los Angeles, California. What about his treatments? He did what you and I would do. He found another health-care center.

Then the unexpected happened. John's doctor in Los Angeles offered to pay for John's airfare so he could commute to appointments in LA. How considerate! That's probably what John thought, so he took his doctor up on his offer. However, it wasn't out of the doctor's concern for John. To the doctor, John was a lab rat. By moving to Seattle, John had unintentionally cut off his physician's access. His DNA, fluids, and other samples were a treasure trove for the doctor, who was secretly harvesting samples for his own personal research. He then created products based on the research findings and monetized John's DNA.

When John discovered this privacy invasion, he sought legal relief—he sued, claiming *conversion*. Let me explain. In his lawsuit, John wanted his share of the the doctor had made from John's property—his body. John's civil suit was what's called a *conversion tort*. In this context, this means claiming a "proprietary interest" in the products that were created as a result of the physician's use of John's fluids—and whatever else the doctor took that belonged to John. It's basically profit sharing. To some degree, we may all be Mr. or Ms. Moore and not even be aware of it. It's not a bad idea to follow the , which is what John Moore did. Unfortunately, Henrietta Lacks didn't get to sue or follow the made at her expense. She didn't even know what was happening behind the scenes. Neither did her family—until about twenty years after her death. Stories like John's and Henrietta's make you skeptical about hospitals, doctors, and care providers. I respect caregivers who honor privacy. It's the few bad apples that spoil the reputation of the many good ones.

But you've got to ask questions. Some health privacy laws require that people be told about the uses of their bodily fluids, health information, and more. Of course, that means that, as early as possible, health-care providers should let patients make choices they're comfortable with. Privacy means deciding on and exercising your choices. You get to freely choose what you

## Medical Privacy: Your Body Is the Temple

want to happen to you or your body during treatments. You should be in control of your protected health information.

Can someone force you to donate your organs while you're still alive? No. That's the point. Make sure your relatives read medical releases and agreements before signing. Even if you're dead, it's still your decision or your family's decision. For example, if someone removes your eyes after you die, that's not a donation. That's theft. A friend of an amazing friend sued and won when, at her brother's final viewing, she discovered his eyeballs had been tampered with. His irises had been removed without his family's consent.

Medical facilities shouldn't allow physicians' research when it involves anything taken from your body without your understanding and express consent. You should be informed about physicians' personal research interests. Some facilities have third-party services that go over the health-care facility's research practices with patients so patients won't feel pressured. I suggest you speak up and ask what they'll do with the samples once they've been tested. Don't be bashful. Ask questions about health information privacy. Know your choices and options. You have more power over your privacy than you think. Exercise it. Start by asking questions. Share what you learn along the way with your fellow church members. If you're a medical doctor, this might be a great opportunity to educate your church members about health privacy. Share resources. This is your contribution to building a more informed, aware, and healthy church community.

*My people are destroyed for lack of knowledge.*
(Hosea 4:6 ESV)

Body parts or body components are a hot commodity, which is why they're often stolen. If they weren't, there wouldn't be a black market for bodies, bones, tissues, organs, skin, body parts, and fluids. It's called the *Red Market*. I'm spooked! Journalist Scott Carney wrote the book *The Red Market* about this and more. Records show that in a span of nineteen years (from

# Church Privacy 101

1987 to 2006), more than 16,800 families took legal action against the illegal sale of their loved ones' body parts, which was "estimated at $6 million."[6]

Other than doctors doing their share of stealing, body part brokers and funeral homes unlawfully exchange body parts for cash. It is not surprising that cremation doesn't always yield the ashes of a loved one. How much is the human body worth? Some sources say you can't measure its value. Others estimate $25 million or $45 million based on selling the parts. I wonder what the value of Henrietta's cells would be for all the medical and scientific breakthroughs they garnered and all the lives they saved.

There was a time when it was common practice for "for-profit blood-collection centers [to be] located in almost every poor neighborhood, somewhat like payday loan centers are today."[7] Talk about an invasion of privacy! People have been exploited because they lack privacy awareness and education, and things haven't changed much.

You're part of the church. Think of yourself as an organ or tissue that makes the church body function as it should. You should help the church address the needs of its community. One thing the community needs is protection from exploitation in exchange for putting food on the table. That's where the church, you, can be the voice of privacy awareness—getting the word out so others can learn and do better. Can you help your church do that?

You can't put a dollar amount on the body, also known as the temple where God's Holy Spirit dwells (1 Corinthians 3:16–17). How much value God places on a person's body is clearly explained in many Scriptures.

*So God created mankind in his own image,*
*in the image of God he created them.*
(Genesis 1:27)

## Medical Privacy: Your Body Is the Temple

You have supernatural DNA. You're a walking powerhouse of miracles waiting to happen. Your body is that *temple*, and not only spiritually. Pay attention to your bodily privacy. Know your rights and the rights of your loved ones. Don't assume healthcare organizations and care providers always make ethical choices or respect individuals' privacy.

About Jesus' missing body in the tomb, Mary said, "Sir, if you have carried him away, tell me where you have put him, and I will get him" (John 20:15). She was pretty much saying, "I need answers, Mr. Gardener. Where's the body?" That's how outspoken, strict, aware, and engaged you should be about what's being done to your body and your loved ones' body parts, fluids, organs, and cells. Ask care providers what they've done with them. Don't sign anything and everything put in front of you. Don't waive your privacy rights, whether it's for you, your family, or a church member. Read it first. If you don't fully understand it or feel right about it, ask questions.

*Do you not know that your bodies are temples of the Holy Spirit, who is in you,*
*whom you have received from God?*
*You are not your own; you were bought at a price.*
*Therefore honor God with your bodies.*
(1 Corinthians 6:19–20)

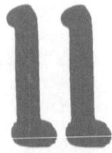

# Privacy in Marriage and Courtship

*My command is this: Love each other as I have loved you.*

(John 15:12)

## A More Perfect Union

Romantic relationships can sometimes be as difficult to navigate as a minefield. My friend Donna cuts to the chase with her potential suitors by asking two questions: "Do you have a job?" and "How's your relationship with God?"

Blunt? Yes. Effective? Certainly.

Getting to know a potential partner takes patience and work. It helps to have solid information before moving out of the dating stage and on to courting. For a serious relationship such as marriage, it helps to know who your potential spouse *really* is. What are their hopes and dreams? How will you know if you're a good match emotionally, spiritually, and mentally? Do you share the same outlook on life and plans for the future? This information is personal, and these questions should be asked when someone expresses romantic interest. Unfortunately for many of us, we start asking questions after they pop the question or have said yes to the question—too late. Why should

## Privacy in Marriage and Courtship

you start early? You don't just want answers; you need time to prove the answers. You need enough time to observe that their answers and reality align.

### *When should you start asking questions, and what should you ask?*

First, let them know why you want to know more about them so they can expect it and understand your purpose. You both need an understanding and an agreement. It is fair to let them know how you will use their personal information. It's like giving a privacy notice before you collect information, and it goes for both parties. Some make this a condition for moving forward with courtship. That way, you don't even get to pop a question or answer a proposal without first knowing that the other person is really who they claim to be.

Are you uncomfortable when it comes to asking personal questions? It feels awkward, but if you aren't open with each other from the start, it will only become more difficult later on.

### *Make smart moves.*

As a former landlady, I've used TransUnion's SmartMove app to vet rental applications. I could check potential tenants' backgrounds in a matter of minutes. All they had to do was accept my invitation and consent to the credit check online. SmartMove checks credit reports, criminal records, evictions, and financials. I wish it were that easy to do a background check on the finances, credit, and criminal history of a prospective spouse. Even if you've done that, you have to do the next best thing and ask questions. Keep in mind that you can't always trust the data you pull on a person from other sources to be 100 percent accurate. You need to find things out on your own and align them with what's out there. Like I've said before, information you have about a person doesn't necessarily equal knowledge of that person.

Ask questions. Observe them and let them show you who they are. Do your due diligence and gather information. It's one thing to know; it's another to decide based on what you find out. A risk is a risk is a risk. Maya Angelo said, "When someone shows you who they are, believe them the first time."[1] The problem with our human emotions is that we see danger—in credit reports and a background check of a potential spouse—but we still hope we can change them. The most difficult tenants I had were the ones whose credit reports had red flags, but I decided to believe their sob stories instead.

If he is dancing around questions or if she hesitates to give you information, that may be a red flag only if you have both expressed your intention to marry. And if you don't have an interest in marrying someone, don't ask for personal information. If you're interested and they don't respond, take a hint—they're not ready or as serious as you are. Transparency is going to be needed for your relationship to grow and to build trust. In every stage of the relationship, decide what types of information to share and why. Don't think, *What if the whole purpose of my life is to help this person straighten up or reach their potential?* Your life's purpose is not to fix the person you want to marry. Maybe they will change, but that's not a risk you should be willing to take.

If the person you're dating is seeking a marriage relationship, you need to know certain things about them. You've got to see through the haze of *feelings* and ask tough *questions*. Keep in mind that after you exchange personal information, you'll need to respect their privacy, even if you decide to walk away. Even if they're on the credit bureau's most-wanted list, that's their private information. You're not a better person by telling everyone their business. Keep their personal information hush. I'm not saying you'll never tell your best friend about your decision not to pursue a relationship with this person. Your closest confidant may want to know what happened. Open

## Privacy in Marriage and Courtship

up as you're comfortable. Your family might pressure you to discuss it, but you don't need to. You can just say, "I changed my mind," just like you say at IKEA when you return an item.

Okay, let's say the credit check and criminal check both look good. Now you know about the places they've lived and accounts they've had, including debt and credit cards, and especially if they're still legally married elsewhere but separated. How long has it been since they separated from their previous love interest or former spouse? This is very important information. Know if they have children and if they're taking that responsibility seriously.

Next, get tested together for sexually transmitted diseases. Yes, this is very private, but some STDs could kill you or make you miserable for a lifetime. States used to require blood tests before issuing marriage licenses. These days, you have to manage your own risks. Labcorp will provide a report for whatever you specify and report back to you. Each person opens it in the presence of the other and destroys it after you've discussed it. (I'm not saying good people don't have diseases—usually from someone they once trusted.) You can now both make an informed decision about your potential future together. Knowing them better won't stop here. It's a process that requires more sharing of personal information.

What if your prospective spouse doesn't want to go through this discovery process or thinks you're paranoid? That's fine, because you're not trying to impress them. If they're pestering you to engage in kissing, sex, or any type of touching, say it's not happening. Run like Joseph.

The decision is yours. You can decide if they should be in your life or not. If you decide to do an independent background check on them, don't rush to Spokeo. Spokeo is a search engine just like Google, but for searching people. For a minimal fee, Spokeo will divulge someone's *public* records. Spokeo specializes in gathering and organizing public data and linking it to people.

Their sources include social media, deeds, court records, and personal contact information. They match records to people and people to records all day. But there's always plenty of room for error.

For example, in 2010, Thomas Robins sued Spokeo for posting incorrect personal information about him. Spokeo showed that Robins worked where he didn't work, had a career he didn't have, had wealth he didn't have, held an advanced degree he hadn't earned, and was married with kids. In reality, he was a single man with no kids and was unemployed. Spokeo had the wrong age and even the wrong profile picture.[2] If a prospective spouse was searching Robins' information on Spokeo, it would have been a disaster. Be careful about the information you find, and prove every report.

For the health and well-being of your relationship, it is vital to know your potential partner's temperament, character, integrity, spiritual maturity, selflessness, and sexual purity. These are huge potential blind spots. Decide whether or not you can live with what you find out. Observe it and note how it makes you feel.

### *Premarital counseling rarely goes in depth on critical privacy matters.*

I went to a premarital counseling service near me and asked what the counselor discussed with couples. She delightedly gave me the rundown of everything she covers, but privacy was not on the list. I then considered how I could create a formula for new couples looking for advice on handling their private lives that I could then expand to privacy plans for managing relatives, marriage, children, the workplace, and friends. I've visited many counseling programs, but I always leave wanting more. These programs rarely ever take privacy into account in these areas of life. But I observed that privacy is at the heart of many family and relationship issues and feuds. A disagreement often starts because someone's privacy is violated. Communication and

## Privacy in Marriage and Courtship

conflict resolution are common discussion items on almost every premarital and marital counseling agenda. I asked if, during counseling, counselors discuss privacy with regard to how the couple communicates marital business with their relatives, friends, and coworkers and how that can impact conflict resolution in their relationship. The response I got was, "No, not really in that sense."

Premarital counselors cover many helpful topics. When discussing family planning, they ask couples to consider whether the children will go through certain ceremonies, such as baptism, christening, first Communion, confirmation, or bar or bat mitzvah. However, one item about discussing problems in the relationship stood out to me as a direct privacy concern. Counselors talk about keeping both the bride's and groom's parents out of a couple's relationship matters, but they rarely address privacy in other relationships a couple may have—siblings and other relatives, coworkers, best friends, church friends, and the like. Certain issues in your relationship are private, and if you share them with others, that might not sit well with your spouse. I believe the focus on keeping parents out of your marital relationship might have to do with Genesis 2:24: "That is why a man leaves his father and mother and is united to his wife, and they become one flesh." But you also need to keep out others.

Our parents may treat privacy according to the beliefs they were taught when they were growing up. Those beliefs shaped them, and they also shape us. I have seen people who have unspoken loyalty to their parents divulge personal details about their marriage that their spouse might have wanted kept private. Some parents and relatives expect your loyalty to them because they gave their loyalty to their parents—they expect you to tell them your marital business. You don't owe them.

***Know who you're marrying.***

Before marriage, you should know how private or transparent your potential spouse is regarding privacy and sharing personal information with others. This also includes how they share your personal information and private life with others. Factor that in. Observe. Are they of the school of thought that they've got nothing to hide? Will they tell anyone who is willing to listen to everything about them and about you?

## Reflect

- If you're courting, how many privacy disagreements have you had because one of you doesn't want to share personal information?

- If you're married, have you ever said, "You didn't need to tell your mother that," or "I can't believe you told your sister that"?

- Privacy issues shake up marriages in many ways. Have you refused to call it out as the underlying issue in most of your conflicts?

- Were you raised to be ashamed to speak up when your privacy is violated? Are you embarrassed to tell your spouse that you're uncomfortable with certain things they share with others?

## The Point

Managing privacy in a relationship is healthy. Ignoring it isn't. Privacy issues are as common as fights over the temperature in a couple's bedroom. A little understanding and accommodation will resolve the issue. With privacy, all it takes is a little transparency. It's best to discuss privacy early in your relationship. It helps you get used to talking about it and respecting the other person's needs. Better yet, I created this helpful list of discussion points you can use if you don't know how to start. Shall we begin?

## Discussion Points

You've learned how important it is to handle private information *before* you tie the knot. But what should you discuss? Consider the examples below:

- How will you handle each other's personal information (past, present, and future)?

- *Personal* could have a different meaning for both of you. Get an understanding.

- When you have a misunderstanding or conflict, who can you vent to? Privacy is about choice and preferences. It is better to communicate your preferences *before* your other half violates them. Your prospective spouse may not mean to violate your privacy, but it still hurts, and the damage is done. How will they know how to prevent it if you don't share with them which privacy violations will be most damaging to you?

- Discuss what personal information should be entrusted to close relatives and friends *before* you marry. Maybe you agree not to keep secrets from certain family members or close friends who will help you navigate your decision to marry. Define what personal information could be too personal or damaging to share with the people who really care about you.

- What personal information should be entrusted to relatives and very close friends *after* you're married?

- How much of your personal financial information should be shared with your best friends or relatives?

- Know what not to share with your coworkers. People tell coworkers about fights with their spouses. They walk into the office and wait for someone to ask them what's wrong so they can vent. Some will tell everyone who's willing to listen. I remember a colleague who did that. Soon, everyone started voicing their opinions. Even colleagues who were single added their two cents. A coworker labeled the colleague's wife a gold digger and advised him on how to run his relationship. He loved his wife with all his heart, but when he let everyone into his personal business, it left him confused. Some of his coworkers even called him a pushover or soft and started treating him with disrespect. Their insults weighed on him and influenced how he viewed himself, his wife, and his marriage. Please don't be that person.

- Decide who you'll call for advice. Is there a spiritual counselor in your church who would be neutral toward both of you? You should both know about this person and decide if you're comfortable talking with them. If you don't have a counselor in your church, designate a professional who understands your spiritual values. That way, your conflicts stay protected and outside your church community. I can't emphasize this enough: a preacher or clergy member is not your counselor if that's not their specialization. Have a professional marriage counselor handy. Agree on one or two counselors ahead of time, before you have a conflict.

- Will you visit your doctor alone or together? Eliminate any surprises. Say how you feel about it early—no matter how silly you might think it sounds. If it's important to you, it's not silly to make it known. Anticipate your privacy needs ahead.

## Privacy in Marriage and Courtship

- Are you okay with having friends, church members, and relatives drop in on short notice? Some cultures and families are perfectly fine with no notice or short notice. My parents were missionaries. Our house was an open door to relatives and strangers. It may have just been the nature of the work. However, your spouse may not be okay with it. Every couple and family needs privacy. If your spouse is like me, they need prior notice and details: time, day, length of stay, and dietary requirements. Finding this out early is good for my privacy.

- Are certain parts of the house closed to friends and relatives? Maybe it's your bedroom, bathroom, or home office? When I was growing up, my parents' bedroom was a sacred place. You could visit us for months and never step foot in that room. Do you both have that understanding? Or is it assumed? Do either of you have a relative who will go through all your papers in your home office and bedroom if you leave them alone and say they were helping you organize? What are your plans for that relative? Be proactive; don't wait for a privacy crisis to happen that could negatively impact your marital relationship. You know your relatives better than anyone else. Plan for that.

- Financial secrecy or privacy doesn't work well in marriage. Anything you both share requires transparency—house, , car, investments, phone, you name it. Decide what level of detail you'll share with other people, including church members, friends, and relatives. If you know that the church treasurer, an award-winning CPA, shares people's personal financial information around the church and is helping your prospective spouse with their taxes, this is an opportunity to say that when you're married, you won't be comfortable with that individual doing both of your taxes due to privacy concerns.

- When you need solitude or *me time*—to reflect, pray, retreat, or hang out with close friends or siblings—be clear about where you are going and who you'll be with, even if your phone is on silent. Some couples take me time only when there's a conflict, which seems more like a time-out. You should still tell your spouse where time-out is taking you. If you take more alone time or privacy time when you need to, you might eliminate many of those marital conflicts and the need for a time-out.

- Has someone shown up to a cookout that you didn't expect? Did it lead you to ask, "Honey, who invited him?" Or did either of you say, "Babe, I wanted this to be just us"? These situations can lead to hurt feelings and conflict. Reduce these types of invasive surprises. Set your privacy needs early.

- When might it be necessary to step away from your spouse's presence to take a call? This could happen when someone of the same sex calls who you and your spouse both understand needs your counseling, especially if you are a professional or church counselor. Or it could be someone in trouble who might require the assurance of confidentiality. Maybe your relative needs to speak to you one-on-one about their personal situation. Maybe it's a work call with privileged or proprietary information. All are acceptable situations where stepping away for privacy may be necessary. The point is, do you have an understanding ahead of time?

- Avoid going into another room for privacy's sake if a person of the opposite sex calls just to socialize—even if they're your work colleague or fellow volunteer in a ministry. The caller should know you're married and should not expect privacy for that call. Talk openly (in the presence of your spouse) unless the conversation would be an interruption to your spouse's activities, in which case you should keep it short.

## Privacy in Marriage and Courtship

- If the person on the phone wouldn't share the conversation with or around your spouse, you shouldn't share that individual's personal details with your spouse. In general, let your spouse know that this person needs your support, advice, or whatever they may need, and why. Details are not necessary except in special and limited circumstances. And remember to ask your spouse to keep it hush.

- A breach of confidence can be damaging. Being married doesn't mean that friends, church members, or family cannot confide in you as they once did. And don't share other people's personal information to prove how much you trust your spouse. If your spouse makes you feel guilty because you don't share every private detail about someone, help them understand that you're simply about respecting their privacy.

- You might be the hope that someone needs in order to handle a difficult situation. First Corinthians 6:19–20 says you don't exist to please yourself. Basically, your time and ears belong to God, not you. So be of service to God by being a confidant of someone who needs your help.

- If you don't desire to have the family's opinion in your marital and financial decisions, what rules have you come up with to keep you both on the same page? Realize that certain private issues can't be taken back once you let family in. Don't let your family decide what you do with your investments, especially during marriage.

- Don't hide assets or put your relatives' names on your accounts to protect your wealth. Your family loves you. But if you're about to marry the right person—post-screening—why let your family plant doubt? How would you feel if the person did the same to you? If they are high-risk (considering their credit, criminal, eviction, driving, or other records), that's different. Then, either reconsider the marriage or accept the risks.

## Church Privacy 101

If you decide you're not willing to accept the risks, walk away. Pastor John K. Jenkins, senior pastor of First Baptist Church of Glenarden, is blunt about couples who don't share their or assets in a marriage because they think it's their , their house, or their account: "You don't mind exchanging bodily fluids, but you won't share your ? It doesn't make sense!" Agreed. Why go into a marriage union if you don't trust your potential spouse? Marriage is a *trust* relationship. When marriage trust is selective, conflict is sure.

- Background checks are necessary to clear any worries you have that your prospect might take advantage of you financially. Decide to go over credit checks together annually to keep each other accountable and transparent.

- There's no bank account privacy when you marry. It doesn't mean you have to show receipts for every taco or Sprite you buy. You should both decide that you need your own spending allowances or budget. Your accounts are shared accounts, no matter whose name is on them. Of course, if a credit report shows that your spouse is abusing family funds, then it might be necessary to restrict access or secure the monies in that account for the benefit of the relationship (and children). Seek the help of a professional to help you handle this. Sort it out so that your spouse gets help and accountability. Again, it's wise to plan ahead.

- Should you tell family members about financial abuse in your marriage? It depends. Will they be helpful? They may forgive your spouse, but they won't forget long after the issue has been resolved. Both of you should decide ahead. Options should include talking to a professional or a specific confidant who will give you actionable advice without judging either of you. Go with a professional when you can.

## Privacy in Marriage and Courtship

- We evolve in relationships for the good or for the bad. You'll have bumpy seasons and conflicts. Plan how you'll respond so you don't vent all your personal business to the wrong people. If you need to vent, make sure it is to the right people. This is a perfect time to choose onion ring members you can both agree to before you need to vent.

### *To each his own?*

Should you hold on to your passwords until you've tied the knot? Yes. Then you can share them after you've discussed how to protect them and have both agreed. If, after marriage, you can't take a nap on the patio while your phone is in the kitchen unattended, ask yourself why you're so protective of your phone. What are you afraid of? Sit down and take inventory. Why are you sweating over your spouse touching your phone? Cell phone privacy remains one of the most prevalent issues among couples I've talked with.

### *Dealing with trust issues can be tricky.*

Here's a case in point. Jeffrey was having some serious conflicts with his wife, Jean, mostly because he didn't think he could trust her. He was so concerned that he refused to tell her the address of his new job or the name of his employer because she would at times fly into a rage and threaten to show up at his job, cause a scene, and get him fired. When the couple received counseling at their church and Jean got anger management counseling, they were reconciled. After that, Jeffrey was transparent and shared everything with her, which was how he'd wanted their marriage to be. Jeffrey's trust issue was justified—for a time.

On the other hand, David almost peed his pants when his wife asked him for his password. She was updating all the computers in the house with the latest antivirus software. He had done everything he could to keep his wife away from the laptop that he brought into the marriage (which was now *theirs*, not *his*). She had never read anything into it. On this occasion, he awkwardly told her no and tried to make an excuse. It turned out he was hiding a pornography addiction that he had also brought into the marriage. He'd stay up all night pretending to study the Bible while secretly visiting porn sites. His wife gave him all the privacy he needed, not wanting to interfere with his personal Bible studies—thinking she had married a man who was constantly in the Word. She didn't understand why he was so protective of that particular computer and the password for it.

There was a pattern here. She paid $200 to Geek Squad to restore one of the laptops he had, unbeknownst to her, killed with his perverse surfing. When she showed up with her husband at the repair center to pick up the computer, the technician was too scared to tell her the reason why all the laptops in her household were infected with malware—from all the images her husband had downloaded and sites he'd visited.

Your personal computers and phone passwords should be off-limits to your relatives and kids, but not to your spouse. If your spouse is unreasonably protective of their password, phone, or computer, something is amiss.

## Reflect

- Other than because it's a work computer or phone, what's your real reason for restricting access to your device—especially from your spouse?

- Is your quest for privacy just a cover for immorality?

- What don't you trust about your spouse? How do they feel when you don't want them near your computer or phone?

## The Point

I've heard many sermons that ended with "If you won't share your or wealth with the person you'll marry, don't marry them." Apply that same principle to spousal privacy. If you would be uncomfortable sharing your passwords with them, don't marry them. Why be nervous for the rest of your union? Why do you need that kind of privacy from your spouse? If, in the dead of winter, you have to take a call outside from a friend of the opposite sex, there's a problem. It's unfair and immature to ask your spouse to accommodate this behavior. You're keeping *secrets*. That's not privacy.

It's the same with social media. For example, having a Facebook or other social media account that your spouse doesn't know about or having one that is not in your real name is a red flag. If you're married and you're only friending single people who wear skimpy outfits, exactly what privacy are you protecting there? Be honest with yourself. It's a secret, and you're open to flirting and perhaps more. Also, regarding social media, there's the danger that these new "friends" aren't who they appear to be. They may not even be people, but bots programmed by hackers to lead you on and get your personal information after you accept their friend request.

Again, the only acceptable reason to keep your spouse from using your computer or phone is if it's company-owned equipment. Those come with acceptable use, confidentiality, and privacy stipulations. Your employer is also likely to be lawfully monitoring your use of company equipment. They can fire you for too much non-work-related activity, including shopping and visiting porn sites—even if you visit them with your spouse.

### *Is social media driving up divorce rates?*

Facebook and other social media usage is cropping up more than ever in relationship counseling. A recent study published in *Cyberpsychology, Behavior, and Social Networking* was the first to look at actual break-up rates. The study "found a correlation between relationship health and Facebook use that may cause more people to want to switch off the computer and smartphone in favor of spending more time paying attention to their spouses."[3] A law firm in Houston, Texas, used this study in its article "Facebook Has Become a Leading Cause in Divorce Cases." The study also "found that people who use Facebook more than once an hour are more likely to 'experience Facebook-related conflict with their romantic partners'. That conflict could then lead to a breakup or divorce."[4] Social media usage is even more problematic for the partner who is *not* using social media. Why? There is "a strong correlation between Facebook use and relationship stability. . . . The correlation probably stems from jealousy and arguments about past partners related to social media snooping."[5] They're looking for indiscretions, such as who they friend and interact with and what they "like" or "love" on people's posts. This surveillance often turns into misunderstandings that lead to irrational feelings of jealousy, anger, and eventually arguments, especially about past partners they may be connected to on Facebook. Facebook or social media "makes it possible for users to reconnect with others, including past lovers, which could lead to emotional and physical cheating."[6] Even if you're only looking, lusting, or thinking about what would have been, that is adulterous (Matthew 5:28).

## *The devil is in the details.*

I was privileged to hear Nona, a preacher and author, speak at a women's conference about her beautiful marriage as well as her temptations. She'd been traveling extensively to speak around the country and was physically and mentally exhausted. When she flew home, she asked her husband to let her go away on a retreat to decompress her brain a little. Her birthday

## Privacy in Marriage and Courtship

was that week, and he didn't want her going away so they could celebrate together. She insisted, and he reluctantly agreed. She went to her favorite beach retreat to reconnect with God. Not getting phone calls was totally fine. Her family knew how much she needed the tranquility. That was the point of the trip after all—to retreat. Then her birthday arrived. When her husband didn't call that morning, she thought he'd call later. He didn't. Nona assumed he would at least acknowledge her birthday, whether she was on a retreat or not. Or did he forget? How could he forget? She had cut off all social media use while retreating. But in that moment of vulnerability, she logged in. She received many birthday wishes from people on social media, including a guy she used to date. He sent a thoughtful birthday wish and wrote that he was just checking up on her. How devilish and timely was that! Judging from his location, he happened to be just a couple of miles from her beach resort. Her thoughts went wild: the man she had dumped remembered her birthday, but the man to whom she had given her best years and children did not. Hmm.

Nonetheless, she waited. Still no call from hubby. The more disappointed and impatient she grew, the more she kept reading the other man's Facebook post. As the day dragged on, she forgot the purpose of her trip. She watched her phone. Nothing. Tired of going back and forth to read the same message her ex-lover had sent on Facebook, she called her husband. Her call went to voicemail. Really? She called again. He replied with a text that he'd call her later. That was just adding fuel to the fire. Furious, she called and left a voicemail telling him to call her ASAP. When she didn't hear from him, she called again. He answered and whispered that he was in church at a men's fellowship meeting. Not satisfied with his answer, she asked him to step outside. At the end of their exchange, he admitted that he'd forgotten her birthday. It happens to all of us sometimes. Maybe that was his coping mechanism because she went away the week of her birthday. I don't know. But let this be a lesson for men. Don't forget.

The point Nona was making was that during a moment of vulnerability, the devil will use a past love interest to make you feel special, admired, and loved—especially on social media—while making the person who is in your life look like a failure. During that moment of her disappointment and anger toward her husband, she subconsciously compared the two men. She thought along the lines of, *I let him go, and he remembered me. But the man I gave my heart to forgot me.* And how did it come to be that her ex (her temptation) happened to be so conveniently close by? As some would say, "That's nothing but the devil."

**Don't succumb to temptation.**

That's how it starts. Small. Then it builds until it's blown completely out of proportion. And a good and strong person becomes vulnerable and succumbs to temptation, only to regret it later. It can happen to anyone.

According to the American Academy of Matrimonial Lawyers, "four out of five lawyers used evidence derived from social networking sites in divorce cases, with Facebook leading the pack."[7] They suggest, as I did earlier, discussing the risks of social media before you tie the knot. Discuss your choices and set boundaries for the different aspects of your marriage and your private life. What I've observed is that some people want their spouse to identify them as their spouse in their social media profiles. That could be accomplished by a photo together or occasional posts with the spouse and kids. Others work out different arrangements. Half a plan is better than none.

Some of the most frequently used pieces of evidence by family law attorneys include content from Facebook, Twitter, Instagram, and social media sites. The judge will come to a verdict according to what they see. How will this affect the spouse caught behaving irresponsibly? It will affect their negotiations for alimony, child custody, and the division of assets. You don't want

## Privacy in Marriage and Courtship

a judge to see your social media posts and draw the conclusion that you're irresponsible.

You'll find these articles in the Additional Resources section. Read them with your significant other or prospective partner:

- Focus on the Family, "Social Media: Signs of Negative Impact on Marriage"

- Family Life, "4 Ways to Avoid Being a Social Media Marriage Casualty"

- Perspectives of Troy, "Is Social Media Ruining Your Marriage? (Signs to Watch Out For)"

- McKinley Irvin, "Effects of Social Media Use (and Misuse) on Marriages & Relationships"

- Only You Forever, "Social Media Is Destroying Your Marriage"

***Revenge porn is not always about payback.***

After seven years of living together, Bethany Austin and Matthew Rychlik were engaged to be married. They seemed to be looking forward to their wedding. Then things took a dramatic turn. Bethany found out that Matthew was cheating. He was exchanging salacious text messages with a neighbor. Matthew's texts with the neighbor—let's call her Jezebel—showed up on Bethany's linked iPad. What do I mean by "linked"? As a couple, Bethany and Matthew shared an iCloud account. Texts and pictures sent to or from Matthew's iPhone showed up in their shared iCloud, to which Bethany's iPad was connected. Matthew and Jezebel knew this would happen. Weird, right? Especially since some messages were not words. They were beyond words. They were photos of Jezebel's private parts. These exchanges went back and forth.[8]

Bethany saw everything. Feeling betrayed, she pulled out of the wedding.

Matthew, knowing he'd been exposed and fearing the public perception of Bethany's decision, told everyone they both knew that he dumped Bethany—before she could give her account of what happened. He said that her cooking didn't measure up and that she wasn't marriage material. Hurt not only by Matthew's affair but also by his lies about why they were no longer getting married, Bethany reacted. She sent the nude photos to family members to prove why she'd called off the engagement. It was proof positive, but it didn't end there.

Because Bethany texted the photos to family (or others) without her consent, Jezebel reported Bethany to the state of Illinois for violating her privacy. She indicated she was a victim of "revenge porn" because she would otherwise not have shown her nudity to anyone other than Matthew or the person the photos were intended for. The state agreed. There was a victim in this love triangle, and that victim wasn't Bethany. It was the court that decided who the victim was—Jezebel.

## Reflect

- Armed with those photos, what would you have done if you were Bethany?

- Would you have deleted them and handled the situation differently with your family? Would you have shown them the photos to explain what really happened?

## Privacy in Marriage and Courtship

- Are you a Matthew? What have you gained and learned from victimizing Bethany?

- Are you Jezebel, a fiancé-swiping neighbor? Do you think a man who does this with you while under the same roof as his fiancée respects you? And is he worth being entangled with?

- If you were Matthew's parents or relatives, would you support Matthew's behavior to prevent shame on your family, or would you rebuke him? This was probably not his first time, nor will it be his last.

## The Point

The state of Illinois sued Bethany. At the time of this writing, about forty-five states have similar laws to those in Illinois.[9] Bethany's case dragged on for a few years and even made its way to the Illinois Supreme Court as of 2019. Bethany said the photos were made available on her own device—on her shared iCloud with Matthew—and that's where Jezebel sent them. Plus, she wasn't trying to hurt anybody—she just wanted to tell the truth and clear her name. I totally get that. But the judge said it didn't matter what Bethany was trying to do or her motive. Distributing nude photos for any reason without the consent of the person depicted in the photo is a crime. Depending on the particular circumstance, you're talking felony or misdemeanor.[10] Bethany was charged with a felony and also fined. Of course, Bethany argued she was just exercising her First Amendment constitutional right to free speech. The court bought it. But when the state appealed, Bethany's argument didn't work. She was back to square one.

It can happen to anyone. When someone has betrayed your trust and lied about you, yet you have this really nice piece of evidence that can clear your name, it's tempting to do what Bethany did. Even if you're strong in your relationship with God, betrayal-related emotions are strong and painful. What you do with emotions matters.

You'll find out quickly that attempting to clear your name can easily turn into a fight with your state. Why? Trying to tell the truth with nude photos as evidence—without the other person's consent—is a crime. It's called *unconsented pornography* or *revenge porn* regardless of your reason, even if *revenge* never crosses your mind. Not getting the consent of the person in the photos before distribution is deemed a violation of privacy.

What this means is that you're the one spending the and time to fight the state, even up to the highest court. The person who wronged you doesn't have to spend a dime. You can't move on and enjoy a better relationship (with someone who will appreciate you) because you're still fighting the state.

If you're Matthew, you need serious deliverance from yourself. If you're Bethany, Matthew isn't worth your life being dragged through national news. If you're a friend of Bethany, give informed advice—calm her emotions down and consider the legal consequences of reacting rashly. It's not by accident that you're reading this story. If you know a Jezebel, warn her against having an affair with an engaged man and sharing nude photos via text (or sexting). She can't take back those photos.

If you're a parent, youth pastor, or youth minister, teach boys and girls to refrain from taking nude photos. Even if it's not sent to anyone, it becomes public as soon as you take it. iCloud and other cloud storage services are owned by companies, and you've probably given them your consent and the right to your images. Also, having a nude photo of someone on your phone or in your possession doesn't mean you can share or forward it, which could easily get you into legal battles.

A crime of passion? That doesn't work when it comes to anything connected to the Internet, including your phone. Self-defense doesn't work

## Privacy in Marriage and Courtship

when it violates somebody else's privacy in this way. The courts have no sympathy. The law is the law, and two wrongs do not make a right. Even though Bethany was unfairly treated and Matthew lied about why their relationship ended, which cast Bethany in an unflattering light, it didn't matter in the eyes of the law.

Being cheated on or being unfairly treated hurts. That's undeniable, but think before you react emotionally. Thoughtless or vengeful sharing of photos, messages, and information on cell phones, social media, and online communication in general has caused numerous insecurities, destroyed relationships, and gotten perpetrators fined or sent to prison.

It's much better to walk away than to correct every lie told about you. It's better to be jilted than spend your savings, life, and time in court. Time will tell. God sees, hears, and knows your misery and the truth (Hebrews 4:13). You need to start praying, "Vindicate me, my God, and plead my cause" (Psalm 43:1), before you do anything foolish.

You may think the law was unfair to Bethany. I also believe she didn't knowingly break the law. The irony is that research on revenge porn, or nonconsensual pornography, "shows that 3 in 4 victims are female, and 9 out of 10 female victims suffer intimate image abuse.... Male victims of sextortion [using sexual content to financially blackmail the victim—usually by hackers or criminal gangs] reported feeling little shame and self-blame and were able to move on quickly from their experiences. Female victims of intimate image abuse [when an ex-partner uses a photo to control or exact punishment on the victim], on the other hand, reported much longer-lasting social and emotional impacts, describing their experiences as sexually violating."[11] The irony is that revenge porn, or nonconsensual pornography, laws were put in place to protect women from men. While victims of revenge porn vary, men are the ones who share the most nude photos of women without the women's consent. In most cases, people (mainly men) use nude photos as psychological blackmail to keep their partner or ex-partner from breaking up with them, from pursuing full custody of their children, or as a threat to stop them from going to the authorities to report rape, involvement in the sex trade, or physical abuse. The law was meant to stop the humiliation and psychological injuries that victims suffer—and punish the offender.[12] In this unique case, a woman, Bethany, was the one defending her actions against criminal charges. Even though her situation was not the typical revenge porn case, the law still applied.

If it can happen in Illinois, it can happen anywhere. If it can happen to Bethany, it can happen to any woman or man, even in the church community. It can happen to you. The law allows you to freely take a photo of your buttocks. That's not illegal. It is freedom of expression. However, just because you share it with another person doesn't mean you want to have it shared with anyone else without your consent.

But before you snap that photo, think about who may see it—not only who it's sent to but also whatever medium or service (Apple, Android, Verizon, AT&T, T-Mobile, Sprint) has access to the information. Don't forget that their suppliers also get an eyeful as well as text message app providers, iCloud providers, and whoever else works on these services. At the end of the day, they all have access to the data you generate.

According to the law, you're free to snap photos of your private parts. After all, you're grown. But keep in mind that the Lord says, "All things are lawful for me, but not all things are helpful; all things are lawful for me, but not all things edify. Let no one seek his own, but each one the other's well-being" (1 Corinthians 10:23–24 NKJV).

***Just because you can doesn't mean you should.***

## Privacy in Marriage and Courtship

The first revenge porn case to reach a jury verdict in the state of North Carolina was Elizabeth Ann Clark's. She was awarded $3.2 million in a revenge porn lawsuit. It was a long legal journey, and I'm sure if you asked her, regardless of the settlement, it's one she would not wish on anyone. You can fight it, like Elizabeth did, if someone distributes your nude photos without your consent. But prevention is even better. Elizabeth sued her ex-husband, US Army Major Adam Clark, and his new girlfriend, Lieutenant Colonel Kimberly Rae Barrett. Elizabeth said that her ex posted revealing photos online, spread lies about her, and stalked her. Elizabeth's lawyer mentioned that Kimberly was "under military investigation for adultery" and other allegations, including "accessing the medical records of Elizabeth Clark and her children."[13]

Are you thinking what I'm thinking? 1 Corinthians 10:23–24. *Just because you can doesn't mean you should.* Most people who share nude photos of others claim they have First Amendment rights or *free speech*. The reason that argument doesn't carry weight is because the person in the photo didn't agree to the sharing. That's how the law sees it.

Well, don't you have freedom of speech over information you lawfully possess? Only if you're spreading information that could benefit the public. Nude photos don't. When everything was going well between you two, you understood that the nude photos you'd taken were private. Now that the relationship has soured, you've forgotten that quickly. As attorney Paul Larkin puts it, "Intimate photographs are shared under circumstances giving rise to an implied agreement of confidentiality between the parties."[14] Let me say that differently. Your emotion and the devil got the best of you. You betrayed the other person's trust. The law will hold you accountable for that type of betrayal. It may not bother you, but the judge, the jury, and Jesus will hold you accountable regardless of what the other person did. In the words of Daniel Solove, professor of law at George Washington University, "The permanence of information on the Internet carries a past insult or injury forward, potentially forever, making an original sin into an eternal one."[15]

Romantic relationships aren't easy. If we want to succeed at them, we must be willing to put in the groundwork. Don't allow Cupid to cloud your vision and make you skip your due diligence. Remember to always do a thorough background check and treat your disagreements with the reverence they deserve. Don't act out of pettiness, spite, anger, or even revenge. Take privacy in your marriage and courtship seriously. Failure to do so can lead to consequences that will haunt you forever.

*Marriage should be honored by all, and the marriage bed kept pure, for God will judge the adulterer and all the sexually immoral.*
(Hebrews 13:4)

# 12

# Parenting and Privacy at Home

*For those God foreknew He also predestined to be conformed to the image of his Son, that he might be the firstborn among many brothers and sisters.*

(Romans 8:29)

## Protecting Your Children and Their Privacy

Every family has privacy violators and offenders. Those are the people who promise privacy but then betray your confidence under the guise of it being for your own good. Maybe you have a family member who informs everyone of personal details that you'd rather not disclose. It's not always about private information being repeated. It's also about how you're treated by your family members after the disclosure. Judgmental reactions are worse in dysfunctional families, but every family has trust and privacy issues. No one is exempt. Don't think that it's only affecting you—it hurts every person being violated, whether a child, teen, or adult. If God promised to move you to a new family, which family would you select? Even your favorite TV and YouTube families have privacy issues.

Anyone in a family can cause privacy issues, and anyone in the family can suffer the impact. Let's focus on the immediate family (parents, children, teens, young adults, and adult children) as well as relatives and extended family (aunts, uncles, grandparents, and other relatives).

**Children, teens, and young adults are often denied privacy.**

If you're a young person in the family, almost all the adults are privacy offenders. Do you agree? There're two sides to this. First, it is part of growing up—that is, if you're committed to growing up around people, especially since the human population is made up of people. Second, it is sometimes done to save you from your naiveté and to help you avoid life's hard lessons until you're an adult. Now that we're grown-ups, many of us adults are grateful that we didn't get everything we wanted when we were teenagers, including 100 percent privacy. If you're a teen or preteen, the seeming invasion of privacy may feel unfair, but all hope is not lost. You'll thank the adults in your life later.

In some families, adults say privacy shouldn't exist. They don't see the negative impact that ignoring privacy needs has on trust, esteem, and confidence in younger family members or fellow adults. They discount any privacy complaints from anyone even a year younger than them. When you become an adult, it's easier to forget how much privacy invasions hurt you. How does a young person view privacy, or the lack thereof, in their family or home? Here are a few chief complaints I got from social media.

- "My mother will be on some 'can I come in?' while walking in."
  - @Lerumo (female)

- "Mom even kept some linens and table cloths in my wardrobe (closet) just to make sure she has access to my room." - @Korops (male)

## Parenting and Privacy at Home

- "This is so true :) I caught my mom reading my sister's diary and she didn't even feel guilty." - @Amahle (female)

- "My mom used to read my diaries too . . . really annoying"
  - @Nolu (female)

- "My mom used to barge in the room, decide that the wardrobe (closet) was untidy, and haul everything down. My dad, on the other hand, has been a knocker and respectful of private space." - @Dube (female)

- "That's every dad, mom are the ones who respect no privacy."
  - @Kairi (male)

- "Dads aren't invasive cos they're absent" - @Wendy (female)

- "Sure, Dad's invading privacy is not going to be a huge problem as 40% of households are headed by women. Men can't invade privacy if they are not there in the first place." - @Njabulo (male)

- "Not excusing it, but in many households moms are the only ones doing any parenting at all—they're parenting their offspring as well as their husband/partner. So yeah, dads really do get to be the 'cool parent' cause they're carrying out the BARE minimum of the parental toiling."
  - @Wande (female)

Agreed. These are definitely parental invasions. But sometimes kids are actually up to no good. I slept over at a friend's house when we were teens. She wanted to sneak and make a phone call, although it was after lights out. She went into the kitchen, pretending to get us some water, and then snuck the cordless phone from the kitchen wall into her pants. She tried to keep a straight face while heading for the stairs on the opposite side of the living room where her parents were watching the news. She was halfway across the living room, when the phone rang. Her parents looked up to see that it was her pants ringing, with the phone numbers all lit up. She ended up being the real evening news that night, and I was an eyewitness to that segment. I would have executed that plan differently. Sometimes kids invite privacy invasions and then blame their parents for being nosy.

I was guilty of a privacy invasion with my ten-year-old nephew. "Hey, you wore this suit to church this morning. Why is it on the floor?" I asked, looking through his closet. What I really wanted was for him to stop playing video games and clean his room. I wasn't thinking about privacy. I want him to be a tidy person when he grows up, and I'm willing to commit a few privacy invasions to get him to be that person. He might have been annoyed, but my gut feeling tells me he'll love me rather than see me as an offender. I know this because, shortly after he put down the video game, he asked me a question.

"Did I tell you I told my entire class about my summer vacation?"

"Oh, what exactly did you tell them?"

"About Canadian privacy."

"*Really?*"

"Yes, Auntie. Remember when me and grandma visited you last summer and you talked to me about privacy?"

"Of course I do," I answered.

"You gave me that book to read. And all that stuff you told me?"

"And you did a mini-talk in your class about it? That's super!" I gave him a hug. "I'm so proud of you."

He is learning fast from what I tell him about privacy. But not all our privacy lessons are good ones. One day, his father chewed him out about something he did. I jumped in and agreed, using an example of a behavior I'd already warned my nephew about. Later on, when it was just us in the

## Parenting and Privacy at Home

kitchen, I asked him how he felt about what his dad said. His answer surprised me. He said, "Auntie, if I answer you, you'll just tell Dad. He's your big brother—you'll tell him!"

I was stunned. I felt like I'd failed him. I didn't argue or defend myself. I love my nephew, and it was clear that I'd hurt him. Siding with his dad and mentioning a conversation that we'd had in private was what had upset him. It wasn't the way a privacy-preaching aunt should act, I admit. But I wasn't going to force trust. I decided to leave it alone. If I was to have his trust, I wanted to earn it. He had the right to choose whom and when to trust. Thirty minutes later, he came back and confided in me as if nothing had happened. Well, that was settled pretty fast.

My nephew reminds me of myself as a kid. With privacy invasions, I was more forgiving of aunts and grandmas than of my parents. Those relatives' long absences cured all the wrongs. I want to say it's just the way family is. People who are closer and whom you see often hurt you more deeply. No wonder parents are accused of more privacy violations than other relatives. And moms more than dads. Maybe it's just the relationship we sometimes have with our parents.

### *When parental intrusion is important.*

I had my own room after I turned fifteen. Before that, I shared a room with my sisters. For some reason, I thought I had absolute privacy because I had a key to my room. I was wrong. One day, I walked in, and there was my mom lying on my bed. She was waiting for me like a cop. Like in the movies, I said, "How did you get in here? How long have you been here?" I got that look, as though she was saying, "Last time I checked, my sweat and blood built this house. Plus, you don't pay rent." So I said, "Welcome to your house, Mom. What's up?"

"What are you doing with pot in my house? Are you using or selling?"

I chuckled.

"What pot? You mean the stuff that guy downtown got in trouble for growing?"

She snatched a clear glass bottle off my dresser and said, "This!"

It was a bottle of dried leaves that I had brought back from boarding school about a month prior. "I heard it strengthens and grows hair. I bought it off campus," I said. "One of my classmates took me there. The guy selling it was rolling them up in paper. I thought it was a waste of time. So I just asked him to sell it to me in bulk. I didn't want mine rolled. I saved some . I was going to make my own hair product with it. It's called Indian hemp."

My mom wasn't born yesterday, and her sense of smell had never failed her. She believed my naiveté but wasn't taking any chances. She was right—it was weed.

"Okay, get rid of it before you start smoking it. Now!" She handed it to me.

She probably went through my stuff after finding the dope. You know, like the cops do. I'd given her a *probable cause*. Her priority was my well-being. She wasn't willing to compromise on that. She didn't want me to abuse substances. I got it. We sat on my bed in silence for a minute and then laughed at how I stockpiled her old perfume bottles on my decorated dresser to give the impression I had an array of perfumes—they were all empty. We chuckled about how I was faking glam. That was the last I heard of my near-weed use—it stayed just between me and my mom. When that dialogue was over, she changed the subject and told me why she was in my room. She just wanted an escape to reflect and didn't want to be where anyone might look for her—she needed privacy. I believed her.

## Parenting and Privacy at Home

If my mom had ignored my dope, that would have possibly given another person a chance to convince me to smoke it. Since I didn't know what it was, maybe I would have tried it out of curiosity. As a teenager, you're prone to experimenting with what your peers say works or is trending. At fifteen, looks and self-image were my priorities. I was seeking exponential hair growth beyond what God had already given me. Those dried leaves were the answer. I didn't know I had contraband in my possession that could hurt me if I misused it or get me in trouble with the law. I never heard about drugs or drug use on the news. I wasn't watching the news. I never saw people smoking anything beyond Marlboros and Newports. I didn't know more than three smokers in my entire life. I was in boarding school, hundreds of miles away from home. I know she was praying her heart out for me.

Other privacy issues involving kids include not only schools unlawfully collecting information on students and their parents but also when a parent feels a child is old enough to receive their own report card without a parent needing to sign it. When my parents didn't ask for my report card, I skipped classes I hated. I was praying that my freedom would last forever. But now I'm glad that the unintended privacy my parents afforded me for a semester was short-lived. I was outgoing but focused. However, having that much control without accountability was eventually going to negatively impact me, even though I was a good kid.

A parent shared with me that his son was booted from the track team for not showing up. His son didn't tell him, so he didn't know what had happened until he volunteered at a track meet. That might be fine with one parent and not another. The concern for a parent would be that if he wasn't at track all those times, where was he? Not every kid is the same, but all kids are vulnerable to danger because of information they're not sharing with adults. Parental privacy intrusion is not all bad.

## Reflect

- What was privacy like when you were growing up? How was privacy in your immediate family?

- What is privacy like in your family or home now?

- Do you find yourself repeating privacy violations with your own kids that your parents did when you were younger?

- Has your child, teenager, or young adult complained about privacy, and how did you respond? What did you say to help them understand why you were invading?

- Have you used an argument more nuanced than

    - I brought you into this world,

    - I carried you for nine months,

    - Move out if you want privacy, or

    - I pay the bills in this house?

## The Point

It's tough. Tough love and privacy sometimes wrestle with each other, and tough love usually wins. Tough love can be mutually beneficial. But be gentle. Don't crush their spirits just because you're right. As a parent, it is your duty to make sure your kids turn out well. Then you can exercise your bragging rights—but the success belongs to both of you, and you can celebrate it. Raising another person isn't easy. It's an immeasurable investment that takes sacrifice. Some kids, no matter the resources poured into them to be

## Parenting and Privacy at Home

successful, still go in a different direction. Sometimes it's a direction that turns parents mentally and financially upside down. But still be mindful of their privacy.

### *Balancing privacy and parenting is a must.*

Think about those chief privacy invasion complaints I shared earlier. When good kids distance themselves, sometimes it's because they've lost confidence in adults. In the name of good parenting, the parent may take measures that seem good but lead to a disastrous outcome for the child. To most parents, how the child or young person feels about privacy invasion is important. Those who don't think it's important forget that when a child has low confidence in their parents, it means they'll be seeking trust elsewhere—that's dangerous.

Have you ever heard a child say to a parent, "You invade my privacy all the time, and it's unacceptable"? No.

As a parent, don't wait for them to confront you. They won't (at least not right away). Most likely, they'll internalize it and later take action—just not an action you'd like. Young people act out to get back at their parents. It's a trust thing. Put yourself in their shoes. If your privacy were violated and you had no voice in the matter, you'd be angry. And you'd express your hurt in different ways. As a young person, you would seek people you could trust with your feelings and pain, even if the person you trusted was someone your parents would not approve of—but you valued that trust. If you're a parent, this is not to say that you should be your child's best friend. But they need trust too, just as you do—they need confidence in their relationship with you.

Of course, some kids constantly make decisions that push parents to become full-time privacy invaders, such as hanging with the wrong peers, getting into trouble in school, or carrying questionable items that they don't explain to parents. Out of frustration, parents put these types of kids on surveillance. These parents will talk about their children to aunts, grandparents, and church folks—in front of the children. As a parent, once you do this, going forward, the only trust you'll get is the one you work very hard to earn.

Yes, I understand that children don't make parenting easy. In extreme situations, when children misbehave, sometimes they are inviting the mistrust of their parents. Parents may withhold permissions or privileges, such as using their credit card, owning a cell phone, or attending sleepovers, parties, movies, and dances. Children will think, *My parents treat me like a kid.* But that's usually because they've given their parents a reason to believe they're irresponsible or lack self-control.

However, when this is not the case, parents should be a little more calculated about privacy. What I mean is, you may conduct routine searches and seizures in your kids' rooms, closets, or backpacks, but it doesn't have to be done in an accusatory manner—they're capable of feeling shame and mistrust. Be creative and tactical. You can do a lot of good because you're the first authority in your child's life. But think of the message you're sending. Watch what you say in anger. Think of the risk of your actions. You're risking trust between you and your child—now and when your child becomes an adult.

Have you ever heard someone say to their child, "Well, my parents did the same thing to me, and I turned out okay"? Why repeat ignorance when you have awareness? Okay, by whose standards? It sounds like you expect them to be okay at a later time, when they reach a destination, rather than during the journey of growing up. Don't deal with privacy the way it has always been dealt with in your family. Before you know it, you're just like your parents, and making the mistakes they made. This quote from Stacia Tauscher sums it up: "We worry about what a child will become tomorrow, yet we forget that she is someone today."[1]

## Parenting and Privacy at Home

Their confidence will plummet because of your thoughtless and insensitive reactions. Next time you want to say, "I don't care how you feel; it's my house," think about this: does God care and want you to care?

> *Fathers, do not embitter your children,*
> *or they will become discouraged.*
> (Colossians 3:21)

### Pay it forward.

Being intentional about privacy means thinking ahead. A parent once asked me when she should let her son go into the doctor's office by himself. You may want to be there for your child so they're not taken advantage of. That's smart. You're their protection. You may also feel at ease allowing your child to go alone because you've taught them what to expect. You've given them the confidence to speak up for themselves and tell you if anything seems unusual or uncomfortable. If they go in alone, be sure you're right outside the door in the waiting room. If they're not transparent with you, it may be harder for you to let them go alone. These are hard decisions, and it depends on the child. But trust is not your right as a parent—it must be earned. It doesn't mean you've failed as a parent if they don't trust you with everything. It's not only a trust issue; as a parent, you must understand that your child will have privacy and health needs you're just not designed to provide. And you'll need to let another person or specialist handle those.

Try to let go of control at a certain age and maturity level. Do this incrementally and intentionally. Have a conversation about privacy concerns with your kids, and make them a participant in your privacy concerns or decisions. Be a participant in theirs. Trust is equally a risk for you and for them. Negotiate together in a healthy way so that you don't drive them further away.

# Church Privacy 101

Privacy is about participation and choices—getting your kid involved so they understand why you're concerned is more empowering than you think.

As a parent, you may not know how uncomfortable going to the doctor's office can be for your children, particularly preteens and teens—where their body is examined by someone they don't know. For younger kids, having a parent present is comforting; for teens, it can be mortifying. How do you protect your child while maintaining their privacy? It often depends on what they're going to see the doctor for. Is it specific or general? Or do they have a question they may be embarrassed about? You may not know how they feel about you being in the room unless you ask and give them the option. You can always ensure that a nurse or nurse's aide is present.

At twelve years old, I wasn't convinced that Mom's answers to my questions about general body changes were exactly right. I wanted to know more and talk to someone other than my mom, sister, and aunts. I'd never been alone with our family doctor, so I ruled out that option. When I had questions about my breasts, my mom gave me a training bra instead of talking to me about what was happening. I wore it when I left the house, but when I got to school, I threw it in my locker until it was time to go home. Then I'd put it on. An alternative was to turn to my friends. Yes, there was sex education in school, but that wasn't a subject we came home and talked about to get all my burning questions cleared up. Sex education doesn't mean you understand everything you need to know about sexual health. A teenager doesn't have to be or want to be sexually active to have questions about their bodies or sexual health. My parents didn't discuss this topic at all. They kept two health books on the family bookshelves, and books didn't help. Like many teenagers, I had questions that only a doctor could answer. The problem was that we went to our family doctor as a family (not much one-on-one private conversation happened there). I needed privacy. By the time I turned thirteen, I was finally

*Parenting and Privacy at Home*

able to talk to doctors alone. We'd moved to another part of town, and I was now at boarding school—with a clinic.

Privacy is intentional. Anticipating this for your child is a great move. What do I mean? When you schedule the next doctor's appointment, let your teen know that part of your goal is to give them privacy with the doctor to ask any health questions they want to ask. Help prepare your child to be transparent with a health expert. The privacy and transparency you've gifted them will positively impact how they handle their overall health, even in their adult years.

Another important aspect of health is emotional and mental health. Your child might find peace talking freely to a therapist who is better at asking objective questions about specific issues your child is struggling with than you are. Like adults, some kids need therapy due to illness, self-image, divorced parents, the death of a loved one, child abuse, sexual abuse, substance abuse in the home, bullying at school, and other relational issues. Your child will need to go alone while you wait in another room. Privacy is the independence and peace that'll help speed up their healing and well-being. In practice, you're letting your child create and enjoy their own onion rings and experiences of peace. Help your child trust people who matter.

# Home Privacy

What about when you're an adult dealing with privacy offenders in the family? Okay, so now you're grown. You've left home for another city, state, or zip code. You've been earning your own . You have your own place. There is no need to explain what you choose to splurge on, even if it's a ten-topping pizza. Privacy drama should be behind you, right? Nope. You have different types of privacy issues as an adult. You're now old enough to make your own decisions. You couldn't wait for this when you were a teenager, but as all adults know, adulthood isn't all fun and games. Privacy invasions were just warming up when you were someone's dependent. Now you're old enough to work, pay taxes, and date or court.

What do dating and courtship have to do with privacy? Dating and courting involve two people. If you're one of those two people, you're under the watch of two families, yours and the other person's. Once dating turns into courtship, you'll both get a convoy of unsolicited advice and questions from parents, siblings, and relatives. Don't immediately disregard them or push them away. They love you, and most of the time, they mean well.

Let's say courtship is leading to marriage, and you've taken the steps I shared in Chapter 11. You've proposed or accepted a marriage proposal, and you're looking forward to building a marriage relationship together. You'd better get ready for an onslaught of privacy invasions. Well-meaning relatives will ask questions like, What are your plans for the future? Will you have kids? Where will you live? And let's not get started on the wedding—at least not until Chapter 15. Well-meaning or not, questions like these can test the bonds of love. It's important to know how to protect you and your fiancé's privacy while also not preventing your relatives from protecting your best interests.

***Home sweet home is where privacy lives—until relatives arrive.***

It's not only the newly engaged or newlyweds who are fair game for home privacy invasions. I've been on the receiving end of these loving intrusions many times. A few years ago, I was so excited about owning my own fire-engine red KitchenAid mixer that I immediately came down with a bad case of "baking fever." I wanted to unleash my baking talent, and I took inspiration from the BBC's *The Great British Bake Off*. It became normal to go to church with

## Parenting and Privacy at Home

dessert I'd whipped up early on Sunday morning. I was always guaranteed to go home with an empty pan. After I bought my mixer, I didn't discriminate recipes, even recipes that called for alcohol. I'm not talking about a little innocent white and red wine that you drizzle over a pasta dish. I used Bacardi Silver. I was kicking things up several notches in my alcohol use. Then I got news that my family was coming to visit from out of town.

That week, I ran around the house, cleaning from top to bottom and fluffing pillows. Most importantly, I hid the Bacardi bottle behind my crimson KitchenAid mixer. No one would find it there. I had complied with 1 Corinthians 8:13, or so I had thought.

My family arrived—my mom, my siblings with their kids, and a few relatives. It was a full house. Two days later, I checked on my rum bottle, and it appeared there was slightly less in the bottle than I remembered. The next day, it had clearly gone down by half an inch. Apparently, someone had found my hiding spot! I couldn't complain, confront, or air my grievance for my mom to hear. It was a private matter. My Bacardi was my private decision, even if it was only for baking. But now everyone was a suspect. That's when I saw my little nephew at the doorway, watching my every move. He walked over to me and whispered a useful lead to the suspect. The offender turned out to be a sneaky adult relative. Shame on him for poking around my kitchen.

Let me come clean. Why did I hide the rum? Privacy. I was using Bacardi privately. Of course, I have the right to bake with rum. But also crucial in my decision to hide it was this Scripture: "But take care that this right of yours does not somehow become a stumbling block to the weak" (1 Corinthians 8:9 ESV). I hid it from adult relatives who might have felt uncomfortable about my use, as stated in Romans 14:1. It's best not to become a stumbling block to anyone having a great time at your place. When out of options, always pursue privacy and peace. "Do not cause anyone to stumble, whether

Jews, Greeks or the church of God" (1 Corinthians 10:32). This means that even when you exercise your rights (to use Bacardi, in my case), be considerate of others who may have differing thoughts or beliefs. In short, faith is like a car. Drive it defensively, and be considerate and kind to others on the road. I also hid it from the kids. When children are desperate for juice, they will drink anything.

Should you hide a drinking issue? Absolutely not. If you abuse alcohol or any substance, your motivation for quitting should be for God, your physical and mental health, and the well-being of others you influence. Whether you drink regularly or not, if you find yourself dependent on or abusing alcohol, don't keep it a secret—it'll kill you. Friend, hiding it isn't privacy. Don't try to pretend you're perfect; everyone is struggling with something. You have people or someone who will hold you accountable. Find someone to confide in—a confidant or a counselor. It will still be private if you choose the right person. I wasn't hiding a struggle with Bacardi; I was baking with it.

## Reflect

- Have you ever hidden something when company was on their way?

- Do you hide mail? Documents? What's your Bacardi?

- Did you ever revolt by thinking that hiding something made you feel as if you lacked courage? Did you feel cowardly?

## The Point

Go easy on yourself. It's actually not a bad thing to hide stuff. I once gave a presentation on hiding personal items as a healthy privacy habit when someone is coming over—specifically, how to do it effectively without running out of breath before your guest arrives. It created quite a buzz. The number of early adopters was impressive. So if you ask me, it's quite okay to hide things you don't want to have to explain to relatives, service technicians, or nosy visitors, especially when you know that curious person heading to your place can't resist asking. Save your breath and your time and put them away. The same goes for personal papers and documents. Don't leave private documents or personal information lying around. They can be tempting to corrupt visitors, who could then use them to clean out your bank account or steal your identity. When it comes to privacy, always think ahead.

*All things are lawful for me, but all things are not helpful.*
*All things are lawful for me, but I will not*
*be brought under the power of any.*
(1 Corinthians 6:12 NKJV)

# 13

# Family Privacy and Safety

> *When people ask me silly questions about my private life,*
> *I just say, I don't discuss that.*
>
> (Imogen Cunningham)

## Airing Our Dirty Laundry

How do you manage privacy within your home, and how do you apply those rules and guidelines outside of your home? Merriam-Webster defines *dirty laundry* as "private matters whose public exposure brings distress and embarrassment; called also *dirty linen*."[1] This is what the phrase "airing our dirty laundry" means. Here, *dirty* doesn't necessarily mean lies, deceits, or scandals, but issues, matters, or concerns that should remain private.

Every family as a unit needs protection—that is, protection of private matters. Every family has laundry. Again, not everything that needs to be kept private is necessarily a dirty secret. Just laundry. Not every family who wants to preserve its privacy is motivated by hiding scandals, lies, and despicable behavior. Why, then? Just because information is *true* about a family doesn't mean it must be aired. They want and need the peace that comes with privacy, not having to be misjudged, misunderstood, mistreated, discriminated against, distressed, or embarrassed. Speaking of family and private

## Family Privacy and Safety

affairs, in my experiences with many cultures (although things are always evolving), there was a point in time when these truths were commonplace:

1. Adopted children didn't know they were adopted.

2. Adoptive parents didn't disclose to people in their community that they were raising an adopted child. The reason was to protect the child for similar reasons I just stated—discrimination, misjudgment, mistreatment, confusion, and bullying, among many privacy issues.

3. It was embarrassing to be labeled "barren" or "impotent," whether a man or woman, so adoptive parents kept things hush-hush for their own peace of mind.

4. The birth parent didn't want to be stigmatized for giving up their child for adoption—staying anonymous or unknown prevented embarrassment and devastation.

Their truths were kept with certain trusted people. Here, three kinds of people needed protection—birth parents, children, and adoptive parents. What did they all commonly need? Privacy—peace, freedom, dignity, and protection. They needed to protect their choice to disclose the truth at a later time, when it may have a less negative impact on them and others involved. This was the reason for closed or private adoptions. Society is now more accepting of adoption, adoptive parents, and adopted children, and birth parents are more open.

Although stigmatizing someone for being childless or barren doesn't carry the same shame it once did, I am reminded of Peninnah and Hannah, the polygamous wives of a man named Elkanah in the book of 1 Samuel. Hannah was barren. Peninnah constantly mocked and "provoked her till she wept and would not eat" (1 Samuel 1:7). Others in her community probably looked down on Hannah. But Hannah didn't want to be reminded of this sad truth. This was her laundry.

People suffer from terminal diseases and keep the news within their families. That's part of their laundry. Once upon a time, a person was scared to death about any word getting out to their employer that they were HIV positive or had AIDS, which could result in bearing a stigma worse than death. But even with other less controversial illnesses, a person might not disclose this information in order to be protected against distraction, unwanted attention, misjudgment, discrimination, or stigma. An illness may be factual, but it is laundry, clean or not.

Was it a scandal for President Franklin D. Roosevelt to keep his disability private? He was paralyzed and relied on a wheelchair. He didn't want people to see him in that condition or focus on his health. Why? People are judgmental. Public opinion or perception could have possibly disqualified him from high office. The president requested that journalists take only photos that didn't show his reliance on a wheelchair.[2] His laundry wasn't a scandalous secret. For a time, he needed to conceal his personal struggle from the public—especially from people who could use information about his health to misjudge or criticize him. Family privacy is not always about health issues. Every family has a private struggle they choose to protect.

## Reflect

- Is there anything you think should be kept within your family because it may be damaging, distracting, or worse if shared carelessly outside the family?

Family Privacy and Safety

- What steps do you take to create that understanding so family members don't share that information or so that they discuss it first with those who might be negatively affected if the private information gets out?

- Do you recall anything in your family that you don't have any problem talking to others about but members of your family do?

- Have you, or someone you know, ever mentioned another person's unfortunate beginnings (for example, that they were adopted, abandoned, orphaned, or underprivileged) with the intention of devaluing that person's worth?

## The Point

You may think that protecting family privacy is only for the relatives of the rich and famous. It is not. Every individual has a need for privacy. So does every family. What should be private should be understood and intentionally protected.

***Photos and recordings can help expose and clean up some laundry.***

Taking photos of or video recording a fight, argument, or other sightings with our phones can give us amazing evidence of all sorts of injustices, assaults, abuses, violations, and confrontations. Phone recordings have become commonplace in domestic and global news, from babysitters caught beating, throwing, and kicking infants to caregivers raping their patients to police brutality—such as the video of George Floyd's death in Minnesota and the anti-regime protester's death in Iran. You get in an auto accident, and the first thing you do if you're not badly hurt is get out and take photos. Phone cameras have become a second pair of eyes—an eyewitness. They come in handy in supporting the news media. Regular people take a photo or video and send it to a TV station before the media even gets to the scene. The next thing you know, the footage is used to report the news.

When my neighbor's gutter spout was shooting water toward the side of my house, I was left anticipating the possibility of a flooded basement. Whenever the weatherman reported a rainstorm, I was out there in my raincoat and rain boots up to my knees. I would just rush out and helplessly watch the water gush out onto the side of my house. My kind neighbor is an essential worker. Inviting her to come out and stand outside with me in the muddy puddle to prove this problem existed was not an option. So I recorded the water shooting from her gutter and sent her a video clip worth a thousand words. The problem was fixed within twenty-four hours.

### *Recording conversations is a privacy issue.*

Is it safe to record a phone conversation? Now, that's different. "A minority of states require both parties to consent to the recording of a phone call. If a person tapes in these states without two-party consent, there can be both civil and criminal consequences."[3] Some of these states are California, Connecticut, Delaware, Florida, Massachusetts, Maryland, Michigan, Montana, New Hampshire, Pennsylvania, and Washington.

Federal law allows you to record a phone call with the consent of at least one party if multiple people are on the call. But that doesn't mean that federal law overrides state law in most situations. States have a number of related laws. Besides, the interpretation of the law is different under different circumstances. How consent is requested or how you give the other person notice differs per state, as does how the consent is given. I hope this helps you reconsider any phone conversations you've recorded, shared, and stored—in person or while on the phone with the person—without consent. Research what your state law says.

## Reflect

- Have you ever been so obsessed with securing evidence of what a person said that you secretly recorded a discussion without first letting the participants know?

- Are you or someone in your family in the habit of setting up a phone conversation to catch someone saying things they shouldn't be saying? Have you considered communication privacy laws in your state?

- Are there rules about what kinds of photos not to take, even if you don't share them?

- Do you feel that familiarity with a person or being related to them means automatic approval for recording them, posting the recording on social media, or sharing them with others?

- Have you ever recorded a conversation over the phone but the other person didn't know?

## The Point

Having the ability to record with your phone is great, but make sure you're not recording people unlawfully. Know what's legal in your jurisdiction. Also, make sure you're not recording anything you won't be able to take back once it's distributed.

Thankfully, as I was growing up, I didn't have any way of recording myself or others. When I was eleven years old, I purchased some new underwear while out shopping with a cousin who was visiting from college during her spring break. All the girls loved it. My mom was the least impressed. "The lace defeats the purpose of the panties you bought. You can see right through them. Isn't what I'm seeing through that lace what you're trying to cover up?" She added, "It's so pretty, but it's like you need an audience to admire it."

She was absolutely right. I was looking for an occasion to show off my see-through lace and stone-studded underwear. I'm grateful to Jesus that I didn't have a smartphone then. I would have been tempted. I would have posted or shared a few photos. And those photos would have been misused. Even if I'd deleted them immediately, anyone could have taken a screenshot of them. Then who knows where they might have turned up.

Most teens have a smartphone but don't understand the full extent of the power in their hands. When used irresponsibly, a smartphone can get even an A student in trouble with the law. They'd then have a record before they had a chance to begin their lives. Peer pressure often plays a major role. Ignorance is also a factor. Smart youth and adults make foolish choices all the time. It takes only a moment to make a permanent mistake with a smartphone. Your phone can record anything and everything. What do you think the Bible would say about you and your smartphone? What could you teach yourself and others in your family about what you record inside the family with your phone that could potentially be disastrous? "All things are lawful for me, but not all things are helpful; all things are lawful for me, but not all things edify" (1 Corinthians 10:23 NKJV).

## Family Privacy and Safety

*Blessed is the man*
*who walks not in the counsel of the wicked,*
*nor stands in the way of sinners,*
*nor sits in the seat of scoffers.*
(Psalm 1:1 ESV)

*Suicide is the silent killer.*

What seat are you sitting in daily? What about your kids? Are they violating other people's privacy to fit in or get attention? Shaming, privacy violations, and cyberbullying go hand in hand. Are they knowingly and maliciously sharing private information or photos about a classmate, former friend, or teacher? Are they spreading damaging rumors that will embarrass and cause distress to that person? The teen victim doesn't understand that it's not the end of the world, that she has her whole life ahead of her, or that in a few years none of this may matter. But at that age, high school and middle school feel like her whole world. She withdraws, becomes depressed, and is too embarrassed to talk to her parents, teachers, or the school counselor. She's so distraught that she doesn't want to go on living.

According to the *New York Post*, "An increase in suicide rates among US teens occurred at the same time social media use surged and a new analysis suggests there may be a link."[4] The number of suicides is staggering.

- Suicide is the second leading cause of deaths of young people aged ten to thirty-four.[5]

- In 2021, 48,183 Americans committed suicide.

- Every day, approximately 132 Americans die by suicide.

- Every 10.9 minutes, there is a death by suicide in the United States.

- There is one suicide death for every estimated twenty-five suicide attempts.[6]

More recently, "among teens 15 to 19, the suicide rate was 8 per 100,000 people in 2000 and then increased to 11.8 per 100,000 in 2017. Among young adults 20 to 24, the suicide rate was 12.5 per 100,000 people in 2000 and then rose to 17 per 100,000 in 2017."[7] There is a direct link between "physical, verbal, or online" bullying and the suicide deaths of young people.[8]

Discuss these statistics as a family. Check in daily with your children or young relatives. Ask what's going on in school or with their clique or social group. Sometimes, victims of shaming or bullying don't talk about it. Either they're too embarrassed, or they think talking about being shamed will make it worse. Have you noticed gradual or drastic changes in their attitude or personality? Check for changes in their eating habits and their withdrawal from certain activities. For example, an extrovert may become introverted and avoid social activities they once enjoyed. Maybe they're spending a lot of time in their room and don't want to go out. That's a clear sign they're not okay. Of course, a parent needs to do more than ask what's wrong. You might have to do a little reading between the lines. What you find out might save your son's or daughter's life.

## Reflect

- Is it easy for your family members of all ages to talk about a situation where they are being targeted, bullied, threatened, or shamed online?

- How can you instill in your family members that any kind of shaming of others is inexcusable, hurts others, is against the law, and is disliked by God (Psalm 1:1)?

# The Point

As long as younger family members are in your care, you should make decisions in their best interests. I was on a project with a woman who once shared the signs that she ignored in her young niece just days before her suicide. The niece asked to stay with her. And while she was there, she acted withdrawn, but nobody thought about suicide until it was too late.

*Protecting your children from privacy invasions starts the day they're born.*

Child identity theft is commonplace for parents who are carefree with their children's personal information when they're babies. If crooks get access to your child's Social Security number, they can create a fake identity. That can run up quite a bit of credit using your child's name. How? The perpetrator gives the SSN a new date of birth, one fitting for an adult, and an address other than yours. That's pretty much it.

Children are easy targets for identity theft. Thieves often target children and not adults because a child has clean credit and the criminals might not be detected. Let me explain. Children have no errors on their credit to fix. And babies are too busy eating and sleeping to regularly check their credit report for inaccuracies. Since they don't make any , they have no interest in applying for loans until they are at least eighteen and ready for college. This is perfect for an identity thief because a baby will not find out their identity has been stolen or used until years later. The criminal is buying at least eighteen years before someone sounds the alarm. By then, the damage is done.

Instead of your teen filling out a simple form to apply for credit or a driver's license, you're now spending valuable time and trying to clear their name from thousands of dollars of debt they knew nothing about. And that's no joke. The back and forth from law enforcement to the credit bureau to lawyers can easily clock eighteen months or longer. If you're expecting or already have children, you should read *Child Identity Theft: What Every Parent Needs to Know* written by law enforcement professional Robert P. Chappell Jr.

I advise parents to pull credit reports for their children, no matter how young. As long as they have a Social Security number, do it. You're supposed to get a free credit report annually, right? As you pull yours, pull for the entire household. By law, it's free. You could schedule that as a task to do as part of your family's privacy spring cleaning.

Sister Tricia at my previous church was raising her grandson, Andre. When he turned eighteen, an identity theft issue surfaced. The family knew nothing about this. It was discovered when, out of the blue, Andre got arrested. The police had a laundry list of misdemeanors and felonies associated with him. The church was brought to its knees. We prayed our lungs out. This was a time in Andre's life when he was looking ahead to the next phase of his life—college, internships, and all his aspirations. He was a good kid. But the cops weren't convinced. They thought they had their man, and they treated Andre like a criminal and murderer.

Sister Tricia emptied out her retirement account hiring lawyers to clear his name. This went on for months and months. Soon, two years turned to three. Everything was at a standstill in Andre's life. The church kept fighting the battle on its knees, praying individually and as a corporate body. I wasn't in the privacy industry then. I was a sophomore in college. Watching Sister Tricia and her innocent grandson suffer in this way changed me. I never wanted to see another person endure this again. Having a criminal record threatened everything Andre had set out to do with his life. Although the culprit was eventually caught, it took many years to clear Andre's name, which hindered him from getting ahead. It altered the course of his life and his grandmother's.

### Family Privacy and Safety

*Adults justify the inside job of ruining children's futures.*

Andre's case was not caused by someone he knew or a relative. But what happened to Andre could have easily been caused by someone inside the family's circle, not a faceless, nameless outsider, as was his case. This happens more often than you realize, especially with babies and children. "Nearly 75 percent of identity theft victims know the perpetrators."[9] We often don't see this as a violation of privacy. Well, it is. Be careful who you bring inside your home.

## Reflect

- Have you ever impersonated your child and run up their credit to provide for them?

- What steps can you take to protect your child from being implicated by fraudsters?

- Do you check your children's credit every year?

- Do you realize it might be too late to check your child's credit when they are old enough to apply to colleges, for loans, and for a driver's license?

## The Point

Ana Ramirez was a victim of identity theft. Instead of reporting it to the police, she chose to suffer the consequences of a trashed credit history even as she struggled to raise her own young children. Why? Because the person who stole her identity was her mother. A police report would have meant a better chance of getting her record cleaned. And faster. But no. At twenty-five years old, her dream of buying a house was just that—a dream. She was stuck in a cramped apartment that barely accommodated her family of five. Ana's credit records showed that her credit delinquencies dated back to when she became a homeowner at ten years old. Her mother was responsible for it.[10]

Like with any negative decision you make regarding your children, this one will not only affect the quality of life of your children but also that of your grandchildren. Consider the emotional and psychological anguish of your child keeping your bad decisions and actions secret while watching her children share the consequences of the bad credit you created.

### *Parental wisdom is not old-school.*

These days, kids roam the streets of the Internet without much wisdom or guidance. Their parents wouldn't dare let them carelessly wander around physical streets, yet they have free range on the Internet. They are ordered to go to bed at a certain time. But in their rooms, there's no curfew on the mean streets of the World Wide Web. The Internet never sleeps, and they don't need a driver's license to get there. They give their personal information to anyone who asks online, as long as they get what they want from the exchange. They don't need their parents' or permission.

Where is your child at 1 a.m.? Is he in China visiting a forty-five-year-old woman who wants him to hang out in her bedroom? Is your daughter in Vegas chatting up a grown man until 5 a.m., and is she then too tired to wake up for school? Whose house is she at? Who invited her there?

Imagine if an adult never showed you how to cross the street. Or not to talk to strangers, or not to open the door to people you don't know? How about not answering the phone and not telling the caller you were home alone? What if you didn't tell your parents when someone gave you a gift and didn't get their permission to accept or decline it? Or what if they didn't

## Family Privacy and Safety

teach you that when your friends are making fun of someone, you should remember Psalm 1 and have nothing to do with it? Or that you shouldn't give strangers your home address or your house key? What if they never said you shouldn't bring strangers into your bedroom?

Your kids need and deserve the same guidance to navigate the traitorous online streets.

### *Don't invite strangers into your bedroom.*

Strangers enter your home not only physically but also digitally. Children invite strangers into their homes all the time, even while you're in the house with them. They bring strangers into their rooms when they're online or via chat. Here is a shocking case I recently reviewed of exactly that happening. The events took place in Minnesota in 2014.

The summer that M.J. turned fourteen, she got a job babysitting for a couple whom her parents knew. Not long after that, thirty-four-year-old Daniel Decker moved in with the couple and met M.J. when she babysat for the couple's kids. Decker then became friends with her on Facebook.

One night, while M.J. was in her room, Decker sent her a video via Facebook Messenger at 12:51 a.m. The video showed only Decker's face, and he asked M.J., "[W]hat's up? Shouldn't you be in bed by now?" Decker explained that he was "just kicking it" and "fixing to go to sleep", and winked at the end of the video. Decker and M.J. then exchanged messages for roughly four minutes, until Decker informed her that he was going to finish "what [he] just started before [he] said hey." When M.J. asked what he meant, Decker explained that he was referring to his nightly ritual to de-stress before falling asleep. M.J. . . . asked what his ritual was, and he responded, "[i]t's embarrassing kinda." M.J. did not respond to that message, but one minute later, Decker sent M.J. a picture of his erect penis.[11]

Decker had been masturbating. Fortunately, M.J. had been raised to be aware of inappropriate behavior. She felt violated and told her parents. Decker was charged and convicted of criminal sexual conduct and indecent exposure. Trust me, if it happened in Minnesota, it has happened where you live. It's probably happening right now. The judge said that by engaging with a minor through her phone while she was in her room, it was no different from Decker physically going into her room to drop his pants.

If M.J. were your daughter, niece, or cousin, what would you have done after she brought this to your attention? Would you have dismissed her concern or blamed her? I hope you'd call law enforcement. Who is a potential M.J. in your home or church community who can be struck by an unsuspecting attacker through a smartphone? I'm not only talking about daughters. Sons too. If you stop and think right now, you can imagine at least one potential victim. Worse, some youth do not know when someone has crossed a line. Do you know what your child is condoning and participating in online?

## Reflect

- How would your fourteen-year-old or a teenager in your extended family or church react to this situation?

- Would he or she continue this dialogue with Decker? Would they forward Decker's photo to their friends and find it amusing?

- Would your teen daughter be daring and wild just to prove to Decker that she is a big girl and not afraid of anything?

Speaking of finding nude photos amusing, here's another case that I recently reviewed. Sometimes the habit of recording and sharing can go too far and violate the law. Thirty-year-old Dani Mathers recorded and posted on social media a photo of a naked seventy-year-old woman at the gym while the lady was changing. Mathers did it for laughs with friends, but the judge wasn't laughing. Neither was LA Fitness. The gym revoked Mathers' membership and called her actions "appalling."[12] Mathers was charged with invasion of privacy. Even in a situation that's not at all sexual, it can ruin a life.

## Reflect

- Regardless of your motive, do you ever think something is laughable, but it comes at another person's (privacy) expense and can get you in trouble with the law?

- What do you think might be disrespectful of another person's privacy?

- As a parent, what do you think your kids could mistake as a harmless joke that might get them in legal trouble?

- What can you teach them today about (digital) privacy and respect?

- If you don't have kids, what can you learn from Dani Mathers' behavior, and how can you help those younger than you?

Church Privacy 101

## The Point

These are not the most worrisome privacy violations or cases I've studied. But they can happen to you or someone around you. Adults communicate with your youth on the Internet more than you can imagine. With a snap of the finger, that's who they may turn to, confide in, and allow to influence them. Acceptance is more important to your kids than you think.

*The sins of the fathers hunt the children.*

According to 2 Samuel 13, King David's daughter Tamar was raped by a relative when she was invited to his room and left alone with him—it was a setup. King David was furious, but he did nothing. And because he did nothing, Tamar's brother violently murdered the relative who raped Tamar. The rest of the story is a heaping mess. Who is a potential Tamar in your home or church community? This can happen to both sons and daughters.

## Reflect

- Who is left alone with your daughter or son in their room? Who is entering your child's online room when you're asleep? Are you too tired to keep everyone in the house in order?

- Which Jezebel is planning to friend your son tonight on Facebook, WhatsApp, Instagram, or TikTok and is wooing your son or young nephew with videos and photos?

- While walking back from school, whose room is your niece being invited to enter today on her phone, having been influenced by a friend who says it's cool?

- Do you still believe kids come straight home from school (physically, yes, but virtually, they are in someone else's room or home)?

- Are you only concerned about the bad influences you can physically see and not the virtual ones?

## The Point

If the courts are smart enough to say that what happens on the Internet can ruin our youth, what do you say? Your child should hear from you about the potential dangers of the Internet, their cell phone use, and their online social interactions. The Internet is a new world that didn't exist in our time to the extent it does today. But the rules of a guarded life should also ring true there.

Create the type of awareness that drove fourteen-year-old M.J. to report what happened. An ounce of prevention is worth a pound of cure when it comes to your kids avoiding costly mistakes. And it's not out of your hands to prevent it. It takes only a few seconds to change a child's life forever, for better or worse. "Train up a child in the way he should go; even when he is old he will not depart from it" (Proverbs 22:6 ESV). That training also means the way he or she should behave on the Internet. Even if you don't have a child of your own, you can help other people's children with what you've learned from this chapter.

For kids today, if unchecked, the Web is a veritable playground. They can go almost anywhere with it. They can read about any subject or topic. They're not supposed to go to people's houses they don't know, but online, they can chat with anyone for as long as they'd like. They give their personal details away. They hear self-destructive beliefs and ideologies. They watch videos and buy products that virtual influencers recommend. In today's digital world, kids have no real grasp of privacy or what it means to preserve it.

# Church Privacy 101

In the Bible, the word *nakedness* typically refers to a form of sin—dishonor, perversion, or sexual immorality.[13] It doesn't take much to get naked online or to view a person's nakedness like what Decker did to M.J.

It's a huge mistake to think kids nowadays are smarter. Sure, they're adept at computers and electronics, and they have excessive access to information. But they don't yet have what you have, which is knowledge, wisdom, experience, and a lot more common sense. They need guidance. They need someone like you to remind them that once you take a certain photo, it's permanent, whether you delete it or not. It might be best not to take it.

### *Is there a Decker in your family?*

You may have a "Decker" as a relative, friend, or someone in your church family. I'm not wishing you harm. I'm just saying that most Deckers are family members, friends, associates, or fellow church members. I wish it weren't so.

### *Reforming the likes of Decker in church is a privacy issue.*

Here's something worth mentioning. If your church has a prison ministry or a program that helps reform ex-offenders, such as Decker, you should know about Lester Packingham. Lester was charged with and pleaded guilty to taking advantage of a thirteen-year-old.[14] In North Carolina, having sex or attempting to do so by arousing a minor to satisfy an adult's sexual desire is a criminal offense against that minor.

Lester served his time and was reformed. Wasn't that enough? No.

After a sex offender serves time, he is required to register as a sex offender with the national registry. Some states also have these registries that sex offenders must also register with. Sex offenders don't have much privacy because they're a risk. Registries are public information. You have the

## Family Privacy and Safety

freedom to control your privacy. But a sex offender can only dream of it. They gave theirs up when they committed a sexual offense, and they may not be entitled to privacy rights for thirty years. A state registry is one of the ways the authorities can ensure that minors are protected. They don't want to tempt the offender to commit another crime. This allows daycares, youth camps, kids' Sunday school classes, and others to avoid accidentally hiring an offender. Truth be told, a Lester is closer to you than you think. A Lester is in your ministry—a reformed person in Christ.

What did Lester do wrong after he'd served his time?

Well, in North Carolina, after you serve time as a sex offender, you lose your social media privileges. This means no Facebook, Twitter, or Instagram. In 2008, North Carolina criminalized social media access by sex offenders[15] to keep them from connecting with minors. If you're a registered sex offender, you should not be on any website where minors have accounts or any website minors might be using.

One day, Lester went to court over a traffic ticket, a completely unrelated offense. The ticket was dismissed. Ecstatic, Lester took to Facebook. He posted, "Man God is Good! How about I got so much favor they dismissed the ticket before court even started? No fine, no court cost, no nothing spent . . . Praise be to GOD, WOW! Thanks JESUS!"[16]

It just happened that a policeman was patrolling the sex offender registry for violators. He spotted Lester's testimony. Lester was convicted again—not for contacting a minor but for using social media. Isn't a testimony a good thing? Yes. But he wasn't supposed to use it! See why your church needs privacy awareness?

## Reflect

- Who do you think Lester was addressing on Facebook (possibly his church family)?

- How can you keep the Lester near you out of more trouble with the law while they're getting or seeking reform in your church community? (After all, it's common for offenders to seek reform in church communities.)

- Do you have a fellow church member who is a police officer?

- Can you enlist the police officer in your church to educate the church about social media and related laws for these issues?

## The Point

Did you know the US has 800,000+ registered sex offenders?[17] Some churches have prison ministries. Others do not. Either way, everyone should take advantage of learning. The #MeToo movement has been very vocal about sexual abuse and sex offenders. Our preacher recently dedicated an entire sermon to King David's daughter Tamar's plight (2 Samuel 13) and complimented the bold efforts of the #MeToo movement in our time. Well, the #ChurchToo movement is growing right at the heels of #MeToo. It appears churches are stepping up their sexual abuse and sexual harassment policies and accountability. Privacy is next.

If you're a leader, be sensitive to who in your prison ministry can or cannot legally interact via Facebook and other social media platforms. Lester's uplifting testimony at a Bible study would have been just fine. On Facebook? No. While helping repentant Lesters, please look out for the minors in church communities as well. Children's privacy should be protected online.

## Family Privacy and Safety

Not everyone believes that sex offenders are reformable. But some counselors are committed to working with offenders. According to *Time* magazine, there are roughly "2,350 therapists across the nation who provide court-mandated treatment to sex offenders."[18] Treatments are delivered through state-authorized psychologists or social workers. Prisons offer treatments, but judges can also furnish referrals. Yes, look out for offenders who are reconciled to Christ. Help them break the cycle. But check if your church is authorized to give the appropriate counseling. Don't play with fire. And if the law has taken away their privacy, it's for a good reason. Remind them to comply and to obey authority.

Unfortunately, you can't just look at someone and know their character or what they do in private. Don't make the mistake of thinking a Lester or a Decker is always easy to spot. They come from different ages, ethnicities, socioeconomic statuses, and educational backgrounds. They are public figures. They are in leadership roles. They are on the police force and are members of the clergy. You probably greet or hug one every Sunday, and they're eyeing your little ones. Sometimes these individuals indulge in child pornography until an opportunity presents itself.

Here is a list of offenders by occupation and date arrested or charged for possession of, distribution of, or production of child pornography. It's not only happening in North Carolina and Minnesota, and perpetrators are arrested daily. Pay close attention to their occupations.

- state lawmaker, Pennsylvania, September 2019

- youth pastor, North Carolina, December 2019

- TV weatherman, Ohio, January 2020

- state trooper of the year, Louisiana, February 2020

# Church Privacy 101

- substitute teacher, Minneapolis, May 2021

- priest, Rhode Island, October 2021

- county children's court judge, Wisconsin, December 2021

- former *ABC News* journalist, Virginia, April 2022

- former mayor, Maryland, March 2023

- air force chief master sergeant, Delaware, June 2023

- babysitter, Michigan, June 2023

- school bus driver, Utah, June 2023

- thirteen-year-old boy, New Jersey, June 2023

- high school coach, Ohio, June 2023

- teacher, Texas, July 2023

- capitol police officer, Maryland, July 2023

- seventy-one-year-old man, Pennsylvania, July 2023

- doctor, Massachusetts, July 2023

## Reflect

- Who can you trust these days? Do you trust people mainly by title, age, or occupation?

- Do privacy and dignity make sense to you? Regarding your children's Internet use, is invading children's privacy a minor thing to you?

Family Privacy and Safety

- Do you feel you can't teach the younger generation anything about privacy?

- If you're not willing to teach them, are you willing to bear the risks of careless decisions they make as a result—and what the law could decide about their lives?

- When you give a younger person a smartphone as a gift, do you chat with them about the dangers of using the device?

- Do you feel schools should teach your kids about the perils of technology and privacy?

- What about a situation with a Decker? Are you concerned about the possibility of a Decker showing up at your church event, roaming freely, and interacting with children? What precautions would you take?

## The Point

It happens more often than you think. On January 30, 2020, in Chicago, Illinois, a twenty-year-old man was arrested for sending pornography to a thirteen-year-old girl he had met and exchanged numbers with at a church event in September 2017.[19]

A child can also be arrested or charged for possession of, distribution of, or production of child pornography, even those photos they took of their own bodies or of another child that are exchanged among other kids. They may not think anything of it, but it's against the law.

*Do not conform to the pattern of this world.*
(Romans 12:2)

# Church Privacy 101

*Teach your youth online discretion.*

Don't wait for your church to take the lead. Help the young people in your life be selective and discreet with their social media, online platforms, chats, and apps. Remind them of the values you've worked so hard to drill into them. Your children have many digital privacy decisions to make. These weren't decisions you had to make when you were a child. The next shiny app that comes along doesn't always have their best interests at heart.

Almost everything online is disguised somehow, from people to things. Their value is inflated, and their risks are understated. Just because a product, app, or item offers efficiency and ease of use doesn't mean it's good for you or that it respects your privacy. "All things are lawful for me, but not all things are helpful" (1 Corinthians 10:23 NKJV).

It makes sense not to patronize stores that don't respect you as a customer. You even warn friends and family, yet you conform to unfair and deceptive business practices from app makers. Why not shun them when they don't respect your privacy online or treat you with respect? You're treated unfairly by some tech firms. These tech firms store everything you've typed, shared, talked about, mentioned, searched, opened, downloaded, and read. They sell it to any third party willing to buy private information about you. Even when regulators call them out for it, you're not paying attention. Apps give you terms and conditions, but you don't read the website's privacy notice. *Notice* means you're being notified of how your information is being used and that you might be getting ready to consent to signing away your privacy. They're breaking the law, but you keep allowing these illegal practices. You download the app and give it access. Your children imitate what you do.

*There is nothing free except the grace of God.*
(Charles Portis)

# Family Privacy and Safety

## *There's no such thing as free.*

Don't consume the delicacies of apps and social media platforms and then forget the hazards. Because a platform helps you send personal photos, videos, texts, postcards, announcements, and more doesn't mean you should use it. Especially if you have to give it access to your photo library, text archives, and contact list to do so. I'm not saying to stop using technology completely. That might do more harm than good. But know the risks and try to minimize them. Customize your privacy settings to limit access. If tech firms' unfair practices worry regulators, they should also concern you.

In a lawsuit brought by the state of Arizona against Google for consumer fraud, internal communications revealed that Google's engineers couldn't figure out the company's privacy settings and admitted they were misleading.[20] If their own engineers couldn't figure them out, it means you were not protected the way Google's privacy notice stated. Your location history—meaning your physical location, which can be tracked via a connected device such as a phone, laptop, or wearable technology—was compromised. Sadly, this issue is not limited to Google.

Before you're lured in by the idea of free and start downloading away, ask yourself, "Why is it free? Who is it free for? How is it being paid for, and who is the real recipient of *free*?"

## *There's always a price to pay.*

With respect to the word *free*, there's nothing free in the kingdom of Facebook. While it is the largest social media platform on planet earth, in the words of *HuffPost*, "It isn't a charity."[21]

The social media conglomerate profits from the following:

1. Ads generated based on you using the platform

2. You creating an account that gives them your email address and access to your phone and contacts

3. You not paying attention to the privacy settings of your accounts, meaning you're not customizing your settings so that your personal information remains private

4. You not reading the privacy notice or terms and conditions for anything you might disagree with or question

5. You revealing too much personal information—so it can analyze your behavior, preferences, decisions, beliefs, and affiliations (political, religious, social, and philosophical)—and then selling that to its customers to target you with ads that turn your views, clicks, and likes into revenue

According to *Consumer Reports*, long after you log off a social media platform, they follow you across all your activities on the Internet.[22] Tracking your every move means more revenue for the platform. According to *Forbes*, you have "no truly private profiles on Facebook."[23]

*Forbes* adds, "In some ways, privacy has become impossible on Facebook. . . . The company's ads also claim it's doing altruistic work in bringing communities together, which is, on one level, commendable."[24] Perhaps the social media giant really is bringing church communities together. Also, it's a business and needs to make . But should that stop you from protecting your privacy or showing others how to prevent unlimited privacy invasions by tech firms?

Family Privacy and Safety

## Reflect

- Does your church have a social media account? Have you ever received an email from the person in charge of social media at your church detailing precautions to take to preserve your privacy?

- Have you ever taken it upon yourself to research news headlines such as the ones I've discussed from *HuffPost*, *Consumer Reports*, or *Forbes*?

## The Point

Some social media platforms state that your privacy is safe with them. That's because they want you to use their services. However, if you catch them violating your privacy, they can conveniently claim there was no expectation of privacy to begin with—scary, isn't it? They are banking on you making *convenience* a priority above your need to preserve your privacy and that of your family.

We've been taught how to safely navigate many dangerous roads of life—whether in the physical realm or in the spiritual realm. But what about cyberspace—the virtual information highway? What about online safety and privacy? Why isn't your church preaching about privacy this Sunday?

It was a great day in my privacy camp when I received a devotional on December 10, 2022, from Pastor Solomon and Apostle Esther Agiri's congregation in Houston. It was titled "Smash Their Cameras." It came with fifteen punchy prayers focused on social media photos, Internet monitoring, pedophiles, privacy settings, and protecting children online, along with five Scriptures to back them up. Of course, *smash* was meant metaphorically, not literally. I love it when a church really gets privacy and preaches responsible

# Church Privacy 101

use of technology. You and your church need to monitor how businesses, tech firms, and your church are handling your privacy.

> *If any of you lacks wisdom, you should ask God, who gives generously to all without finding fault, and it will be given to you.*
> (James 1:5)

# Privacy in Your Relationships

*So in everything, do to others what you would have them do to you, for this sums up the Law and the Prophets.*

(Matthew 7:12)

## Creating Authentic Relationships

How do you find confidants in church? Genuine relationships are becoming much harder to develop these days. I used to think ministers and pastors made friends easily until I met a pastor years ago while helping with a couple of his projects. We got to talking, and I found out I was wrong. Making close friends takes effort, regardless of who you are and what you do. As I mentioned in Chapters 4 and 5, creating authentic friendships requires observation, discretion, patience, and giving of yourself. It doesn't matter how self-sufficient and self-reliant you are—physically, emotionally, or spiritually—navigating life solo is tough. If you are navigating life solo, at a certain point, you'll feel alone in one or more aspects of your life and desire supportive, reliable relationships.

For some clergy, part of their privacy issue is being friends with congregants in their church because of the mixed roles of friend and preacher.

# Church Privacy 101

A conflict of interest could develop when holding members accountable or trying to make an objective decision about them. Some preachers or church leaders find it easier to have close friends outside their congregation; otherwise, they would be constantly on duty. They need to mentally clock out and take off their vestments and robes at the end of the day. Church members must also be intentional about establishing boundaries in order to be comfortable being their authentic self. They have to make a decision about what's important to them in a relationship and what they need. If you're a member of the clergy or leadership, you must also make those decisions. People in leadership as well as members need friends, confidants, and supporters.

Women need reliable women. We play unique roles and face issues only we understand and can offer support and guidance on. Men need reliable men for the same reasons. It's unrealistic to expect someone to be essential to you if you aren't reciprocal. Friendships and solid relationships aren't transactional; they're reciprocal. At times, technology leads us to believe that we have access to all the answers. If we have a question, we ask Google. But that's for surface issues. Google can't guide us through deeper emotional issues, struggles, or decisions. For that, we need relationships—supporters, friends, and confidants. We need people who are honest, trustworthy, loyal, understanding, reliable, sensible, practical, and caring. But we have the responsibility to also be all of those things for others. For an authentic, reciprocal relationship, we have to be for others what we desire others to be for us.

We all have one need in common that glues it all together—privacy. Although we need privacy, paradoxically, transparency is required to build trust. And it's just as important to protect the other person's privacy as our own. Typically, we put our confidence in people who give us the freedom to share openly both the good and the bad and to be ourselves without suffering consequences. It's no different in church. Have you given some thought to what you're looking for in a close relationship in church? Whatever it is, are

## Privacy in Our Relationships

you intentional about creating it for yourself and then giving it to others instead of waiting for someone else to come along and meet your needs? For instance, if you need privacy and understanding from others, are you giving privacy and understanding to others?

*Everything you do to and for others you do to and for yourself.*
(Bruce Van Horn)

*The bond of friendship is held together when there's trust and privacy.*

Deep and supportive relationships develop over time and sometimes through trial and error as we get to know each other and our boundaries. This is where respect for and an understanding of each other's privacy needs is vital. We can be open and vulnerable when we are with people who understand us and who we are confident will protect our need for privacy.

To illustrate my point, I want to use the most talked about best friends on TV and in print, such as Martha Stewart and Snoop Dogg, Jennifer Aniston and Courteney Cox, Taraji P. Henson and Mary J. Blige, and countless other interesting pairs. But none have the same level of historical data as Oprah and Gayle. Yes, Oprah Winfrey and Gayle King are famous, not only in their own rights but also for being best friends. On the cover of the November 9, 2019, *O, The Oprah Magazine*, is a photo of Oprah and Gayle.[1] Just looking at them, you can see that they are very close and comfortable with each other. Their love and devotion to each other shines in their eyes. The issue's theme was friendship, and it was appropriate that Oprah and her bestie graced the cover.

We don't always consider that celebrities and the wealthy are vulnerable when it comes to friendships. A deep friendship requires commitment, transparency, and trust. It's human. And it's an important need. Celebrities do have the added challenge of being wealthy, successful, and well-connected, which attracts many false friends and makes them even more vulnerable to privacy violations. When we consider that Oprah and Gayle have known each other for decades and are privy to each other's deepest thoughts and private lives and have never betrayed them, we have a deep appreciation for these two women and their lasting, supportive relationship. Below are four of Oprah's thoughts on what she's learned about friendship:

1. A true friend cannot be jealous of you or take advantage of you in any way.

2. God put the two of us in each other's path to do exactly what we've been doing since the night in Baltimore when I was 22 and she was 21. Listening. Listening. Talking. Listening. Laughing (a lot) . . . Speaking the truth. Being the truth!

3. We've never lived in the same city, but we share the same values.

4. The trust Gayle and I have cultivated is hard to describe—and hard to find. It's part of what makes our friendship so special.[2]

How do you cultivate trust? Privacy is intimacy—an intimate, nonjudgmental knowledge and understanding of someone over time. These days, most of us have information about people. We look someone up online seconds after meeting them. Now we know more about them based on what we see or a profile we've read. That's information, not knowledge. Yet we think we know the person. We don't have an understanding of them on an emotional or day-to-day level. That takes observation and time rather than research. Understanding them takes into account their private life, values, feelings, circumstances, and emotions that we've observed. It takes some experience with the person over time. In Oprah and Gayle's case, over forty years.

## Privacy in Our Relationships

After reading Oprah's thoughts about friendship, I read another article in the magazine by Molly Sims and Amy Maclin titled "Companion Commandment." Although they didn't mention the word *privacy* in the article, they were talking about privacy (in my opinion). Remember, privacy is also control over access to self. The six commandments they covered were superb. As a privacy expert, two commandments especially stood out to me, numbers one and three.

**Commandment One:** "Thou shall not post a photo in which your friend has a double chin or is holding a margarita in a foot-tall plastic cup with a crazy straw."[3]

Agreed. Especially if you don't first ask their permission. Think about the potential impact and consequences. Shock. Disappointment. Embarrassment. Broken trust. Not only that, but depending on how others perceive the photo, they may lose out on an opportunity to get a job interview, a job offer, or a promotion if their potential or current employer checks social media photos they're tagged in. Their stellar qualifications won't even matter much.

**Commandment Three:** "Thou shall not divulge personal details on a friend's Facebook page, no matter how badly you're wondering, 'how did Gary's vasectomy go?'"[4]

Agreed. The update on the vasectomy can wait until you both talk privately. It must wait.

In the article was a great anecdote about author Lauren Mechling, who visited a close friend and her family in Europe. When she got home, Mechling loaded her Facebook page with photos showing the fantastic time she had. Then she noticed that her friend hadn't posted any photos of their blissful time together. Confused and hurt, she asked her friend why she hadn't posted any photos. To Mechling's surprise, the friend said that it was out of consideration for her father, who didn't like the way he looked in the photos. What a considerate daughter. I don't think her father said she shouldn't post the photos. I believe that when he commented about how he looked, she decided not to post them.

Mechling's friend enjoyed their time together but took into consideration her father's need for privacy. We don't always think twice about how our decisions affect others. We post first and ask questions later—or never. Perhaps her friend was more conscious of privacy because, in Europe, privacy is treated with more sensitivity as a human rights issue.

## Reflect

- Can you resist the temptation of posting a photo out of consideration for someone in that photo who doesn't like how he or she looks?

- Would you contact someone following an event you both attended to say, "Hey, check out this shot of both of us at the event. Are you okay with me posting it on Instagram? If you're not, no big deal"?

- Has someone said lately that they didn't like how they looked in a photo? They didn't say you shouldn't share it, but you figured they wouldn't be happy if you did?

- In how many friendships or relationships have you cultivated trust because you're sensitive to the needs of others?

## The Point

When someone needs privacy or doesn't want to share personal images or information publicly, respect their wishes. Be sensitive. Don't push or try to fix their feelings. Accommodate privacy first. Ask questions later if necessary, and don't be quick to judge. At times, we handle personal information about others casually or carelessly by spreading it, and we never really get to cultivate knowledge of the person we end up hurting.

Privacy is human. It lends respect and garners trust. It applies to you and your relationships both in and out of your church community. Your role models don't have to be featured in magazines, the news, or TV shows. Those close friendships you admire in your church community will suffice. Sensitivity to privacy binds together the love, trust, and respect you observe in those friendships. Imitate them and be the model friend you can be to other folks.

> *It is God alone who judges;*
> *he decides who will rise and who will fall.*
> (Psalm 75:7 NLT)

## When the Bond of Friendship Breaks

Every close relationship is put through trials from time to time. Let's talk about David and King Saul. Though not best friends, they had a bond of shared interests and goals. They made hard decisions and took risks for and with each other.

David was a gifted musician in his day as recorded in 1 Samuel 16:14–23. His music had the power to cause spiritual deliverance from evil oppression. He even got to play at the palace of Israel, what we would consider the White House today, when Saul was commander in chief. His music was soothing and helped calm the king's bouts of rage and depression.

David, the musician, went on to become a warrior. But as a lad, he hadn't filled out enough yet to carry war arms or wear a soldier's uniform. What really set him apart was that he had ten times the confidence of the entire army despite having no military training. And he wouldn't stand for anyone disrespecting God. He was willing to face any giant. And he did.

David was an overnight sensation. The inexperienced warrior defeated one of the nation's worst enemies and captured the fancy of many women. He won several wars after that, which brought Israel much honor. Sounds like David was a gift to the kingdom. King Saul should have been happy, right? He was, and he promoted David, even giving him his daughter, Princess Michal, in marriage. However, Saul was jealous, and he arranged the marriage to use Michal to monitor David's every move. Talk about invasion of privacy.

David wouldn't stop trending. Every battle David won went viral. His following surpassed King Saul's. Bards were dropping hits to celebrate David's wins. The lyrics went something along the lines of "Saul has killed his thousands, and David his ten thousands!" (1 Samuel 18:7 NLT). Saul couldn't handle it. He was so covetous that he forgot everything he was supposed to be in his relationship with David—honest, trustworthy, committed, supportive, compassionate, and reliable. He wanted David dead. He wanted blood.

I'm not saying Saul was David's bestie. But he was his boss, the commander in chief, a fellow soldier in God's army, and his father-in-law. Saul made promises to David in exchange for national security victories. Yet Saul turned around and broke all his promises—not because David wasn't winning wars but because, in light of David's victories, Saul's national approval rating plunged. Unlike Saul, David got all the likes, friend requests, and follows without really focusing on approval ratings. Saul's friendship and support for David were conditional. Conditional friendships are not genuine and rarely last.

# Reflect

- Are you prone to disclosing the private life of someone you're jealous of?

- Have you ever been betrayed by a conditional friendship that broke all the privacy rules in the book?

- Like David, have you ever been in a close relationship with a "Saul" and didn't know it? Are you close to a Saul right now?

- Have you ever been so mad at someone that you shared private details about them to be spiteful?

- Have you ever thrown someone else's privacy under the bus to secure a position or approval by others?

- Are you a Saul in your actions, not realizing you can't stop or reverse God's favor or promotion of another person?

- In your close relationship with others, do you zip your lips and respect privacy only when you're getting along in the relationship?

- Can you keep things private when you don't see eye to eye? Matthew 18:15 says to talk privately.

*By this everyone will know that you are*
*my disciples, if you love one another.*
(John 13:35)

## The Point

Watch out for fellow church members, friends, associates, colleagues, or relatives who are manipulative. I mean, they want things to go their way all the time. They're not happy if they're not in control. They'll connive, conspire, probe, and stage situations just to get to know another person's personal business, which they can use to harm that person directly or indirectly in the present or in the future. They like leaking people's personal information in the most clever ways possible so no one will ever suspect their motive. This type of person is easily intimidated by other people's successes—they constantly compare how they're doing to other people. They negate other people's accomplishments or compliments. If someone says, "I really like the car; it fits his personality." The person might say, "It's a rental. He told me." Another compliment could be, "She looks stunning. I really love her hair!" The person might say, "Those are hair extensions! Can't you tell?" Someone might say, "I'm so happy for her that she passed her board exam!" The person might say, "After failing like a hundred times, I'm glad too."

They bring up your most imperfect past or long-forgotten mistakes and weaknesses just when you're at your peak of joy. If you have a Saul in your life, they've manipulated you not once or twice but multiple times. They've manipulated people you both know. You're an accessory to them. You could be enabling their immaturity and their destructive and privacy-invading behavior knowingly, or unknowingly. They're normal-looking folks who regularly attend and volunteer at church. They're invading privacy for their own gain and hurting others.

# Be a Good Neighbor

Have you read *The World According to Mister Rogers* by Fred Rogers (a.k.a. Mr. Rogers)? In it are many profound reflections about fellowship and what it means to be a good neighbor in the spiritual sense. I fell in love with this quote from the book: "Love isn't a state of perfect caring. It is an active noun like struggle. To love someone is to strive to accept that person exactly the way he or she is, right here and now."[5]

Profound words. And it's not surprising because Fred Rogers was prepped to become a church minister. But God made him a loving neighbor to the world, which is what we all should be—a good neighbor. Love was Fred Rogers' ministry. Loving selflessly meets the needs of others in our lives. Rogers became the role model he wanted to see out in the world. When I interpret Rogers' quote in a privacy context, *accept* means don't neglect to make them comfortable and at peace with you. Don't criticize them to their face or behind their back because they needed or asked for privacy. Lastly, don't judge. Privacy is perfectly healthy. Just respect it even if you don't fully understand the person's need for privacy.

*Random acts of privacy kindness is neighborly.*

Speaking of being a good neighbor, let me tell you the story of how I met Lily. Unless I'm in a hurry, I read just about every piece of paper on the sidewalk. I don't know why I do it. I kick it around to see what it says—just in case it's important. Maybe it's the kid in me. Or maybe it's a rare data protection ailment. I don't really know. But on this particular day, I saw a piece of paper on the ground, and everyone was stepping on it. It looked important. I got a piece of tissue out of my pocket and picked it up by its corners to examine the writing.

It was a page of Lily's medical record. I had no clue who Lily was. It had her full name, age, address, phone number, and medication—*everything*. She may have been returning from a doctor's appointment and accidentally dropped it. I wasn't familiar with the names of the meds on the Rx paper, but given the amounts and other info, I figured she needed them ASAP!

I didn't know her, but I certainly wouldn't want all my information *literally* out on the street. So I called the number listed. When Lily picked up, I introduced myself and told her I had her health information. She screamed with joy. I screamed back in excitement. I asked if she needed help to get her meds. As it turned out, Lily did have a few medical conditions. She lived semi-alone and didn't have a car. Her spirit was still as energetic as a person half her age. During the call, we sorted out which medications she needed so she could get them right away. Lily then prayed God's blessings over me before we hung up. I took the paper home and got her private life off the streets.

Vulnerable people like Lily are often targeted by folks who will use personal health information to obtain medications they can sell on the black market. You're a Lily—we all are. The prescription you take on a regular basis is a hot commodity to someone who is dealing meds on the streets or on the dark web. Lily had already realized this before we talked that day. "Darling, that's why you're my angel," she told me.

That's how Lily and I became friends. That was over three years ago, and we've never met. Lily knows only my first name and phone number, but she adores me. She calls me almost every major holiday. She's consistent. When she leaves a voicemail, I can feel a big smile come through. She has that pure, contagious joy. She takes her time to speak simple words of blessings. She always starts with "God's Grace, I will never forget you. I will never forget

## Privacy in Our Relationships

your kindness to me. I want you to know I'm thinking about you and praying for you wherever you are."

In these messages, I feel her gratitude and appreciation. A random act of privacy kindness can mean the world to someone who is exposed and vulnerable but you come along and cover them. Privacy is a human need. It's protection. I'm thankful that God used me to bless Lily with some neighborly love that day. This is what it means to be a good neighbor. We sometimes forget that behind every piece of personal information we handle, mishandle, discuss, or misuse at church or work, there is a real person we betray, violate, ignore, or neglect—a "Lily."

## Reflect

- Can you recollect a faceless Lily whose information you didn't protect or defend because you felt it was none of your business, and consequently, the information got circulated?

- Which character describes you in Luke 10:25–37?

- How would you like others to treat you if your private life were left vulnerable to danger or exposed for all to see?

## The Point

Be a good neighbor with privacy, even if you don't know the person very well or at all, and even if they can never reward you, as Matthew 6:1 explains.

# Church Privacy 101

Every day, God puts people in your path for you to protect. It's not by accident. Protection means giving confidence and security to another person. When you do a selfless act because it's the right thing to do, you'll be blessed far beyond any physical reward. Are you planting the seed of security, confidence, and dignity in others?

> *Not looking to your own interests but
> each of you to the interests of the others.*
> (Philippians 2:4)

# 15

# Keep Your Private Life Private

> *Whoever guards his mouth preserves his life;*
> *he who opens wide his lips comes to ruin.*
>
> (Proverbs 13:3 ESV)

## Manage Your Inner Circle

Absolute privacy in all areas of your life is impossible. Not even when you're buried six feet under will you have absolute privacy. Remember the flood in Louisiana in 2016 that left coffins floating on the streets?[1] Definitely no privacy there. Just wait until I get into privacy in the afterlife in Chapter 17. Privacy tailors itself to your need or somebody else's need. Here's how it happens: privacy takes into account what personal information about you should be protected, when it should be protected, where it should be protected, how you want it to be protected and from whom, and how much of it should be disclosed. Privacy is a choice you make: to meet your need or someone else's—who may not even be aware they have that need. Lily is a perfect example. She didn't realize her personal health information was lying on the sidewalk. These things happen. That's just real life.

We need each other. That's how God created us—to be relational. We can't avoid interacting with other people. We go grocery shopping, buy gas, buy clothing, and pay bills. We attend church, Bible studies, Torah studies, Mass, and prayer services. We can't avoid people in all those places. While privacy is healthy for all humans, absolute privacy is not healthy. Excessive isolation is a set-up for depression and despair. If that's you, get out and interact with other humans.

You were taught that salads, water, workouts, and righteousness are good for you. Privacy is no different, except that nobody ever told you that privacy is good for you or showed you how to protect it. Privacy is the peace you need to be who you are. It helps you get through the day, and it helps you sleep at night. Sometimes you think you have your privacy under control. Other times you know you don't—you kick yourself for falling victim to a privacy invasion or for carelessly violating somebody else's privacy. Relationships are all over the place because privacy is not managed. You were taught how to manage your finances and do your taxes. So why not manage your privacy, which carries negative consequences if mismanaged?

Speaking of salads, let's talk about onion rings. I introduced them back in Chapter 4. In case you skipped that chapter, onion rings are a privacy model I created to manage privacy in our relationships. You use them to help decide who is a confidant or who is in your privacy circle. You need one onion for each aspect of your private life or information—health, marriage, family, career, mental health, and parenting as examples. Think about the rings in the onion as different folks or groups of people in your life. Let's work from the inner, delicate rings out to the outer rings that are less protected. You should be intentional about your private life and relationships. Get a pen and paper and break it down. You may have to write it down a few times until it sticks. The onion you draw on paper is going to be the image that flashes in your

# Keep Your Private Life Private

mind when you're making a decision to trust someone, even without having your physical onion template in front of you.

Why does it need to stick in your mind?

Because sometimes we get excited, emotional, and forgetful. It's like trying to do math in your head and forgetting there's a calculator in your phone. You need to be calculated about this. If you get it wrong, it'll hurt, and for a long time in some cases. Learn to trust your onion once you've made your rings. That's the problem with some people. They make the onion rings but don't use them. Instead, they react emotionally and betray their own confidence rather than being proactive in protecting their private lives. We make onion rings so that we don't have to decide on the fly whom we can trust with what aspect of our private lives.

So let's prioritize privacy. Write down how you'll handle different levels of your private information and make it clear. That way you won't trust the wrong person in the heat of the moment when you need a confidant.

### Who to tell and what you share should be grouped.

Start by splitting aspects of your life into categories. Let's start with nine categories: health, work, marriage, finances, parenting, single life, social life, education, and spiritual life. You can always add more as needed or skip the ones that don't apply to you. How you prioritize the categories depends on the context. How the loss of privacy will impact you depends on whether personal information is disclosed without your permission or too early or to the wrong person and what that person does with it. Remember, privacy invasion is not only about the loss of . Even more important is the loss of peace and emotional distress.

I find that sometimes couples have a good understanding of what is private in their relationship, but the problem is that they don't think writing down their privacy desires is important enough. Then just one or two mistakes from one person in the relationship, and trust and peace begin to erode. Using an onion is a sure way to write down your privacy needs so they're not violated.

Think about a private thing in your life that you don't want to tell everyone or need to do so by priority. Your onion rings will vary based on how close you are to certain family members or others in your circle. Where someone belongs in the order of onion rings doesn't define them as good or bad. It's about how they can and will handle personal information or privacy to meet your needs in this circumstance.

Also, how relevant someone is in a particular circumstance determines which ring you assign them to. An expert or someone who can give direction may be in your inner ring, depending on your needs. God is an expert in everything, so he's always relevant. A doctor or other professional could bring an objective insight into your situation. Someone who has had the same or similar experience is relevant to a particular ring or onion.

Let's say we're dealing with pregnancy. Mr. and Mrs. Dorsey think they're pregnant, so we can call this a pregnancy onion. Take a look at the illustration below and the timetable the Dorseys used for their rings.

## Keep Your Private Life Private

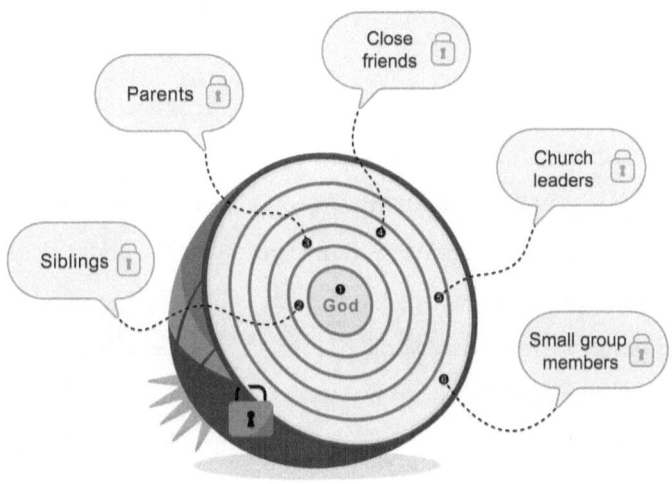

*Figure 4. Onion rings with trust assigned according to individual groups*

After confirming via a pregnancy test, Mrs. Dorsey shared the wonderful news with her husband, of course. God already knew, but they told God anyway—via a victory dance and prayers. They then pulled out an old onion ring drawing they'd scribbled on paper when they were engaged—based on everything they learned in Chapters 11 and 12. They realized they needed to update it—by creating a new onion called a pregnancy onion. God was the first ring, as always. They changed the second ring to include their doctor. They didn't scratch off the siblings. But they decided they should tell their doctor first and their siblings next. Great call. A doctor has a lot to offer in this situation. They may not be related to the couple, but they are trained to give good and objective health advice. The doctor would also respect the Dorseys' privacy while addressing their concerns. Note that some people on your rings are the most important people on that particular ring. I call them ring leaders. Personally, if there's a professional on any of my rings, I see them as the ring leader—I share more with them. Here's an outline of the Dorseys' rings:

After her pregnancy test confirmation, Mrs. Dorsey told her husband.
**First Ring:** they told God.
**Second Ring:** within the first two weeks, the couple told their doctor.

Later, they told Mrs. Dorsey's siblings because she's really close with her siblings—plus, they'd all recently had babies.

**Third Ring:** within weeks three to four, the couple told their parents.
**Fourth Ring:** around four to five weeks, they told their closest friends.
**Fifth Ring:** at around five months (a bump was emerging), they told close members of the clergy—pastor, reverend, minister, bishop, rabbi, or priest.
**Sixth Ring:** at six months (a serious bump was emerging, and at this point, there was no doubt Mrs. Dorsey was pregnant), they told their small group members and/or close church members.

We can stop here.

The rings depend on your need for privacy, the circumstances, the timing, and who you're telling. I've seen parents on the sixth onion ring or farther out, closer to the birth of the grandchild or even after. This order of priority will be different for everyone. You know your circle best. Do what works for you. Don't give in to the press or other people's ideas about who they would tell first, and so on.

Telling an employer, prospective employer, or your coworkers too early can become problematic. If you're employed, look at your work culture. Are expectant mothers typically promoted to leadership positions they qualify for? Keep in mind that another reason privacy and antidiscrimination laws are so important is to prevent employers from discriminating against pregnant women and mothers, people with disabilities, people on leave, and peo-

Keep Your Private Life Private

ple from different racial, ethnic, religious, and political backgrounds. Observe and decide.

Telling family or relatives too early may attract unwelcome attention and unwanted advice. That's not all, though. Let's say you're Mrs. Dorsey, and your very chatty cousin also works for your employer and knows your immediate colleagues. It might be safe to put your cousin on the same onion ring as your coworkers—that is, the people you'll tell last. Odd? Yes. Effective? Certainly.

Once you've disclosed your news to the confidants on your onion rings, expect an avalanche of advice. If you're a parent or grandparent, consider how to give advice tactfully and in a delicate way. Back to you, the expectant mother. Privacy is about choice, peace, and timing. Other factors contribute too. Understand that some questions members of your rings will ask may not be ridiculous, given your relationship and the context. It depends on who is asking, the location, and the audience. It also depends on how you feel at the time. The interesting thing about privacy is that what is private today or in a given environment or moment may not be private another day or in a different environment with different people. When time, place, audience, and environment are appropriate, you feel more comfortable revealing personal pregnancy information. But the control is yours.

# Reflect

- Has anyone ever asked you a perfectly good question at the wrong time, in the wrong place, and around the wrong people?

- Have you ever been a privacy offender?

- Have you figured out yet that the best way to avoid revealing more than you intend to is to not argue about unwanted advice but simply say thanks? What else could you say?

> *Let every person be quick to hear, slow to speak, slow to anger.*
> (James 1:19 ESV)

## The Point

Be sensitive to the fact that sometimes ring members will disappoint you. That's life. I booted a ring leader—a health-care provider who sent me home with a folder of printouts with somebody else's health information and showed no remorse about their mistake. It may be a church member who slips up. Either way, how you respond is important. Two wrongs will definitely not make a right. Should you confront them? You could. It depends on many factors, including the type of person you're confronting. But be tactful and know the risks. Many good people in the world cannot handle being told they were wrong or that they betrayed your confidence. How they respond can hurt you even more than the previous betrayal of confidence. My advice would be to quickly update your onion rings. Shuffle the people on your rings around. Learn from any mistakes on your part. Did the error occur because you based your trust on the number of years you've known that person, their title in church, or other factors?

What did I do about my ring leader? I didn't stop at merely booting them off my ring. I helped the other patient get the Department of Health and Human Services (Office of Civil Rights) involved. That's the correct way the federal government advises you to handle disclosed protected health information. The goal is accountability.

## Keep Your Private Life Private

*When singles become a couple, privacy must be transparent.*

Let's talk about singles—not only single ladies but single guys too. We need a separate onion and a set of rings for this topic, depending on what it is—education, health, emotional needs, spiritual needs, or dating/courting-related information. If you're single, who do you confide in?

There's power in having a plan. If you don't know who to tell your private business to, make some onion rings. If we're talking about dating or courting, the onion rings might be different for you than for others, but the idea is the same.

Once you develop interest in someone, start a conversation with God. Let's break down how that onion might look:

**First Ring:** tell God (pray about it).

**Second Ring:** within week two, tell your closest friends/best friend(s).

**Third Ring:** within three to four months (up to a year depending on your relationship with your family or when you're entering courtship), tell your parents and/or siblings. After five to six months, tell a few relatives.

**Fourth Ring:** if the relationship is noticeable and progressing, tell your church family (starting with your small group) after seven months.

**Fifth Ring:** around the same time, if you're in love and are now a couple, mention it to coworkers. Then mention it to everybody else.

I know what you're thinking. You'd order this differently. You're right. You have many options. Set your privacy thermostat according to what's comfortable. You know your circle better than anyone. Privacy is different for everyone. Don't let anyone define whom you should trust—you have a role to play in the decision. Don't define it for others either.

My prayer is that if you're looking for privacy, peace, and freedom, your first onion ring shouldn't have Mark Zuckerberg (not a bad person, but he shouldn't be on it), or social media in general, on it. For some, social media is on their second ring—sharing photos about their love interests, dating activities, and love life—before it's had a chance to develop privately and peacefully.

If your onion rings are labeled like the one illustrated above, after the second onion ring, you may even wait until the relationship leads to an engagement or marriage before saying anything to anyone else. In some cases, that depends on culture, tradition, or the specific country you live in.

Some areas of your life or situations where you need to preserve your privacy will require you to start a new onion. In terms of privacy, pregnancy is different from dating, engagement, terminal disease, starting a new job, being employed, domestic abuse, a mental crisis, divorce, getting a traffic ticket, and being in a car accident.

Sometimes, when courting, your tight friends in church are even closer than your family. Culture, family dynamics, and traditions all play a role in the choices you make in your onion. If your family is not very close, they may be on the last ring of this particular onion, possibly sharing the same ring as your beloved coworkers and employer.

### *Wedding bells are ringing.*

The moment you get engaged, the battle for privacy is on. You have to set boundaries with family, friends, colleagues, and sometimes complete strangers. As soon as you start a new relationship, everyone is in your business. They're asking questions about concerns you're still deciding on. They mean well, but it can be overwhelming. Moving to a new city, state, or town is a sure way for newlyweds to maintain their privacy.

Privacy also gets dramatic at wedding receptions. Have you ever noticed the newlyweds cringe when a particular person takes the mic at their reception? It could be that loveable but chatterbox uncle. Sometimes it's a church member or friend. Other times, it's the best man or lady of honor who knows the bride's and/or groom's past relationships. I hate when they overshare.

The solution to that is simple: plan, prioritize, and protect your privacy. Make a list of who can toast or give speeches at your reception, and let the MC know their pay depends on keeping the mic from unauthorized relatives or friends. You don't owe the MC any details. Just create a rule that says if they're not on the list, the answer is no. The MC can let them know they're not on the speech list.

Every toast should be okayed by the bride and groom ahead of time—not thirty seconds before the person grabs the mic. Names should be written down and decided on before the speakers are informed. That goes for clergy, ministry members, church members, and other church support roles. Unless you hand over the list of people who can speak, you'll get plenty of surprises and privacy invasions.

Isn't wedding planning about delegation? Delegate. No impromptu speakers, please. Plus, everyone gets three minutes *max*. If they don't know anything about why long speeches are not good, create a "memo of understanding" and quote Proverbs 10:19. Dispatch this to all toasters or speakers. It saves you from trying to explain your needs over and over. Toasters can be hilarious without embarrassing or violating the bride and groom's privacy. Planning and prioritizing are not just for décor and invitations. Planning who speaks will protect your privacy and help you relax and enjoy making special memories with friends and family.

### What if you're not invited to the wedding?

Can you handle it if you're not on the list? If you're not invited, you're still a great person. I'm a believer that one important way to live a contented and considerate Christian life is to manage your expectations of other people.

# Church Privacy 101

Trust me, you'll be happier. With events, it's more helpful to consider what's best for the bride and groom and not why they didn't invite you. It's the same for privacy. Consider what's best for the other person. What will make that day peaceful and happy for the couple? What are their needs? Is it to save ? Or to have a more private gathering that's not overwhelming for them? And consider finances. The cost per person for food and location can be staggering.

Forget yourself. Instead, pray that the event is as happy, joyful, and loving as they envisioned it. Their happiness should be the priority on that day. You'll have many other days to celebrate. Maybe watch the video with them if they choose to share it. Let them know you're genuinely happy for them.

Privacy means loving the people you know beyond being invited to all of their personal special occasions. Send a card or a gift. Be sincere with the words you write on the card. And don't practice retaliation or payback when you have your own special occasion.

I have a collection of great friends whose weddings I didn't attend. I relished looking at the beautiful photos with them. I offered advice, helped with planning, and gave emotional support when it was needed both before the event and after. But I wasn't there. Sometimes it's really not even about the or staying within their budget. They just wanted immediate family—siblings and parents. No big hall. No limo. Just family.

## Reflect

- Actors and public figures are successful and rich because of their fans, teams, supporters, and the media. Yet they close their personal events to

Keep Your Private Life Private

these same people. Why? They need privacy. Then they're back with their friends, fans, and the media. What's wrong with that?

- Do you stop watching your favorite actor or sports star because you don't get an invitation to their wedding or birthday party?

## The Point

It's the same with your church friends and all your friends. Care for someone even if you can't attend their special event of any type. Even with all the public figures have, they can't possibly have every important person in their lives at their wedding and other personal events. They plan, prioritize, budget, and spend on protecting their privacy. Most of the time, media and fan presence are a no-no, even if you're Kate and William or Meghan and Harry.

Kate Middleton and Prince William's wedding cost $34 million. Wedding security and privacy gobbled up a whopping $32 million.[2] About $800,000 was spent on flowers,[3] and the rest was spent on food and champagne. Similarly, "with security costing an eye-watering £30 million [$38,500,000], Meghan and Harry splashed out on a £32m [41,089,600] wedding," and the catering was only £286,000 ($365,659) of that.[4]

The first time I read this, I mused over the rationale behind how Kate's planners divvied up the for food. I'm a foodie. My first question was, *How do you rationalize $800,000 worth of flowers?* I hope they were edible flowers.

Not many people were invited to the wedding. I hope they were happy for the couple nonetheless. That's the point. It's not about being invited. How the couple wanted to handle their private occasion and who they wanted to be present were important.

To preserve privacy on their special day, Justin Timberlake and Jessica Biel booked and locked down an entire Italian hotel for their friends and family to lodge in. They even paid the owners of the surrounding buildings to help them deter even the most determined paparazzi.

## Reflect

- Can you be excited for a friend or church member who doesn't invite you to their occasion?

- Can you be happy for someone if they don't need your participation?

- Do you sometimes feel entitled to invitations—to graduations, baptisms, and weddings?

- How far have you ever gone to create a private moment for just you and your closest ones? Did you fear you might offend someone you didn't invite?

## The Point

Did you notice how much of the budget privacy and security ate up? Privacy is a serious human need for everyone, not only when you're in the public eye. People differ in what they need, when they need it, and where they need it. You can't push your privacy tolerance level on somebody else. Speaking of exceptions, Kim Kardashian (circa 2010) invited just five hundred guests to her wedding. What about privacy? It was on her own terms. The wedding was filmed for a two-part, four-hour reality TV special. Did she care about privacy? You bet. She wanted you to see the wedding after the fact, but she didn't want you there in person.

Again, the dynamics of your culture may be different for weddings, parties, funerals, birthdays, graduations, baby showers, and other events. However, your need for privacy is still important. The consequence of not addressing that need is typically getting hurt.

## Invasive Questions

Have you ever heard couples being asked really invasive questions and you thought, *I'm so glad I'm not the one they're addressing*? I've come across tons of questions to avoid (and what not to do) before and during a wedding. It's so serious that *HuffPost* penned a few unique questions people should not ask a couple as their wedding is fast approaching or just days before their big day.

A few examples are "Will there be liquor?" "Do you mind if I show up a little late?" "Can I pick my table?" "Are there going to be vegan, gluten-free, or keto-friendly options?" "Can I bring the person I'm dating?" "Who else is invited?" "What's the cost per plate?"[5] Unless the bride or groom is a celebrity who doesn't mind making information about expenses public, it's not anyone's business.

I've actually heard worse. Seriously. For instance, "You're not serving liquor? That's not how you do a reception. Never mind. I'll just bring my own." If that's not disrespectful and dishonoring of the couple's beliefs, I don't know what is. Wanting to enjoy wine or alcohol at a celebration is perfectly fine, but questioning why it's not there or insisting on it isn't. Aside from being disrespectful, it's adding stress to what is already a stressful time for the bride and groom.

## Reflect

- Have you ever been asked such questions?

- How did it feel, and how did you respond?

- Have you ever asked a couple these questions? What answers were you expecting, and how did those answers benefit you in any way?

## The Point

These questions are very invasive and put the bridal party in an uncomfortable situation. Choose your questions wisely, and avoid questions that are really none of your business. You risk robbing the bride and groom of their peace. Depending on your relationship with them, these questions are an invasion of their privacy and could erode your relationship with the couple.

### *Do we need to justify our choices?*

Weeks before a wedding, Joey asked his wife, Delia, to ask the bride why he wasn't invited. The worst part was that she did. She didn't know better. Joey was being selfish. His wife got an invitation, but he didn't. He'd rather the bride take on extra pressure and regret on her big day because he was sulking over an invitation. The bride will never forget how Joey made her feel because she didn't invite him. Whatever happened to love being patient and kind? Or what about . . . it is not proud, it does not dishonor others (and their privacy), it protects (privacy), it preserves (privacy), it is not self-seeking, and it is not easily angered? That's my version. But 1 Corinthians 13:4–7 will prove useful if you ever feel like confronting a bride or groom for not inviting you.

WeddingWire published its own taboo wedding-day questions in an article titled "20 Questions You Shouldn't Ask a Couple on Their Wedding Day." Below are a few examples:

- Why did you invite X to your wedding?
- How much did your wedding cost?
- Did your parents pay for it?
- Are you sure this is a good idea?
- Why didn't you ask me to be in the wedding party?
- Can I make a toast?
- When are you planning on having kids?[6]

Before you ask questions like these, ask yourself, "What's the point? How will these questions make them feel?" There's nothing a couple desires like privacy, peace, and the freedom to do what they want on their wedding day. Privacy is peace. They're already under a lot of pressure trying to plan and prepare every detail as it is. They're praying everything works out close to 80 percent as perfect as they've planned. Then a couple like Joey and Delia comes along to make it more stressful.

If you are not invited to the wedding and you find out through the grapevine who made it as guests, it's never nice to interrogate the couple about why such and such is invited and you aren't. The couple shouldn't have to explain anything. Nobody likes to feel excluded. But believe me, if they don't want you there, it's not the end of the world. Look at it this way: you just gave them three precious wedding gifts—peace, freedom, and privacy, even though they didn't put those on their wedding registry. Do it with grace.

## Reflect

- Which questions worked your nerves the most or did you find the most intrusive?

- Have you heard worse questions?

- Do you recall a time you asked someone similar questions but didn't mean any harm?

- How would you answer these questions if you were asked?

*Make it your ambition to lead a quiet life:*
*You should mind your own business.*
(1 Thessalonians 4:11)

## The Point

It's human to be curious. But minding your business shows self-control. Anyone can be an offender; it's not only church people who ask questions like these. But they do. We need reminders that these questions are inappropriate and invasive. I remember I was at a wedding when a wedding planner suggested letting the bride know that the punch ran out. The reception was going well and strong. In this instance, if you're a friend of the bride, run out to the store and grab drinks. Don't tell the world about it. And definitely don't take the bride's peace and joy away. Learn from the wedding at Cana (John 2:1–11). What did Mary do? She took care of it by delegating the task to her son Jesus. His first miracle protected privacy and prevented public shame and the distress that would have resulted from such embarrassment.

**How do you answer privacy-invading questions?**

## Keep Your Private Life Private

It depends on who asks the question. You could gently say, "That doesn't concern you," "It's not your business," or "It's not open for discussion." One that works for many occasions is "I'm really not looking for feedback." What's most important is to respond in a way that the intruding person can learn from it so they're not likely to do that to you again, or to anyone else.

What are things you shouldn't do on the day of the wedding or at the reception?

An article in *Good Housekeeping* had some great suggestions.[7] I'll add my insight to each.

*Don't record the ceremony.* A photographer is hired to do that. If the guests are busy holding up their phones to tape or capture the bride, they're not only missing out on the celebration, but the quality of the photography will suffer—with every professional shot ruined by people standing in the background holding up their phones. Instead, be a guest and enjoy the moment.

*Don't overshare on social media.* I would say don't share at all unless the couple approves it beforehand. If you didn't ask the wedding planner or coordinator previously about how the couple feels about social media sharing, don't ask during the ceremony. If you're close to the couple, ask way before the wedding.

*Don't bring an unexpected plus one.* If your friend, spouse, child, coworker, or fellow church member wasn't invited, don't RSVP with their names or show up unexpectedly with them.

*Don't talk during speeches.* If you're talking on the phone during a speech, it's rude. Your attention is divided, and you're not present in that moment. Let the moment stay in the moment. Don't call someone who wasn't invited to listen in. Relax and enjoy.

I'd also like to add *Don't ask the couple if you can be in their professional shots after the wedding*, especially when family and relatives are queuing, waiting for their turn with the couple. Overfamiliarity can cause you to invade privacy. Be sure to give them space.

If you're not related, just wait. Unless they specifically call for you to join them for the professional photos, go to the reception hall and wait.

You shouldn't expect to be the couple's priority. Be selfless. Let them make choices that don't favor your own desires. It will make your relationship with them better.

## Reflect

- Have you ever been to a wedding where the photographer kept announcing, "Please, family only. If you're not family, wait"? Have you ever tried to insert yourself into the family photos?

- In what ways can you be the best guest while respecting the celebrants' privacy?

## The Point

Giving someone privacy means giving them the freedom and power to make choices. Depending on the church, sometimes it is assumed that all members are invited. The same goes for ministry members who work closely with the couple in church. I've often heard, "What do you mean you want to keep it small? We're your family." I don't buy that. Members may show up anyway, thinking the couple shouldn't mind. Unless the church is catering, there may not be enough food, drinks, and seating. Many cultures differ on this because

## Keep Your Private Life Private

you have many people supplying food and people bringing their own seats. If that's the case, you may not have much to worry about in terms of supplies. But privacy is a need that can't be exchanged for free food, supplies, or .

If you're given a chance to do a spontaneous toast, don't abuse it by disclosing personal or private information about the couple. Nobody needs to know that they share everything with you or how much you know about their private lives. Ask permission first to tell certain stories. Do a dry run with someone else who can help you package the story and keep it respectfully short.

### *Invaders shouldn't say everything they think.*

I thought I'd heard all the privacy-invading questions that people ask couples, including, "Are you guys trying or not?" But this list of select questions and comments directed toward pregnant women reminded me that I haven't even scratched the surface:

1. "Did you get pregnant before or after the wedding?"

2. "Where are you giving birth?"

3. "Are you done yet?"

4. "No baby yet?"

5. "Just wait," or "It's just starting . . ." (regarding pregnancy body changes).

6. "I don't know how you're going to make it through the summer or winter."

7. "You are definitely hormonal right now . . ."

8. "Can I feel your belly?"

9. "Was your pregnancy a surprise or planned?"[8]

Unless someone is pouring out their heart to you (even so), you shouldn't ask these questions. How do you respond to prying, invasive questions like these? You could say, "That's between me and my spouse," or "I don't discuss that with anyone other than my spouse." A few years ago, I ran into a lady—let's call her Dorothy—who knew a couple I was acquainted with. She talked about their beautiful wedding. I didn't attend, but I was ecstatic to hear how blissful it was.

Then Dorothy whispered, "She's pregnant."

"Fantastic!" I screamed.

But by the look on Dorothy's face, that wasn't the response she expected.

"Well, calculating from when I went to that wedding and now, I don't see how she could be this far along after just X number of weeks since the wedding," Dorothy said.

I cut the conversation short and told Dorothy I wasn't interested in her math. I was happy for the couple. Even if the couple conceived before their wedding, it was a shame that she was spreading that information everywhere to people who didn't care about those details. I was just happy to know that the couple wedded, were expecting a baby, and were as diligent in ministry work as when I first met them.

## Reflect

- Have people asked you these types of pregnancy questions or made worse comments?

- How did you feel?

- What did you do?

- Are you comfortable politely letting someone know you don't feel like taking a photo right now?

- Will you state that you're not comfortable with someone touching or rubbing your belly?

- Do you know anyone like this lady who is sort of like a "walking calculator" trying to prove how much she knows—at the expense of someone else's privacy?

- How did you handle the situation?

- Have you ever been that person who's keen on proving someone's flaw?

## The Point

Everyone should be taught to be sensitive to other people's privacy. Don't count on one sermon taking care of privacy awareness in your church. Take it upon yourself to speak up gently but firmly.

*And how can they hear without someone preaching to them?* (Romans 10:14)

## Setting Privacy Boundaries

How you share information with people should reflect the trust and value of the relationship. People in your circle should earn your trust. Don't share emotionally. Use these three *P*s: *plan, prioritize,* and *protect* your privacy. In addition, The Onion Model is useful for controlling when it is necessary to

# Church Privacy 101

share and who you share with. Use your observation and judgment, depending on the circumstances.

Don't succumb to what I call *righteous guilt* with folks at church, no matter how sweetly they come at you. You may worry that if you don't tell Sister Ann, but you tell Sister Donna, it may seem like you don't trust Sister Ann. Or it may seem like you're secretive or that you're not confident in your faith. As a single person, married couple, or family, you need to set and agree on privacy boundaries. You set boundaries every day without realizing it. The problem is that you're not as intentional about it. That's why it doesn't always work for you. That's why, in excitement (good or bad), you may mess up the order of rings and make silly mistakes, disclosing personal information you end up regretting.

Remember, don't announce to anyone which ring they're on. Don't say, "Grace said you belong on ring two of my private life." No, but when you share private information with people on your first couple of rings, you can say, "Keep it to yourself: you're the only person I've told." That's if you don't want them to make the mistake of sharing your business. It depends on the information. In the pregnancy example, your doctor is not going to share it with anyone you know. Your contract with him says so already. But your parents? That depends on the parents you've got. The excitement about a baby often impairs parents' ability to hush. This is where you can say, "You're the first and only people we've told. We're not yet ready to tell anyone else."

Don't be shy. Remind the confidants on your inner rings to keep your information private. People may love you, but they're just not thinking about what you need or want when they're excited. I can't tell you who should be a member of your first, second, or third rings in any given situation. Those members need to earn the ring they're on. Their titles—sibling, parent, pastor, pastor's wife, bishop, preacher, leader, deaconess, reverend, priest, minister—are not qualifiers. Base your ring assignment on wisdom, good judgment, observation, gut feeling, and experience with each person. Trust your instincts. Don't try to make this perfect. According to Valorie Burton, the best-selling author of *Successful Women Think Differently*, perfectionists are less happy than those who have high standards but aren't obsessed with perfection.[9] You've got high privacy standards; now get started and keep it moving. The beauty of your ring is that it doesn't need to be perfect as soon as you create it—you can move folks up and down at any time and for any reason. Some people don't earn their keep on a particular ring. Well, move them. Just don't announce it. Most importantly, don't make them your enemy. Good people make mistakes too. Forgive them, learn from it, talk about it with them privately, and reposition them on a different ring.

# Reflect

- What's the worst privacy mistake you've ever made?

- What's the best privacy decision you've ever made (about family, friends, or church members)?

- Have you ever had a member of your first onion ring spill your beans, and you thought, *I wish I had reminded him that he was the only one I told?*

- What is the most important privacy decision you're facing right now?

- Who do you need to move to a different ring today so you have more peace?

- Who are your closest confidants—with your health, parenting, marriage, spiritual life, and personal growth matters?

# Church Privacy 101

## The Point

What if you don't really want to marry someone, but sweet church people who know your personal business too early begin to pester you? And before you know it, they've pushed you from courtship into marriage.

Have you ever heard folks pry or ask questions like the following?

- "What are you two waiting for?"
- "You two will make a fine couple."
- "I can just see your kids now."
- "Where's the ring?"
- "If you don't make a move, somebody else is going to snatch her up."
- "You're no spring chicken. Hurry up."

You can let pestering and privacy invasion push you, or you can take control. They may mean well, but they must learn that you need your privacy to properly observe and discern God's direction, get to know your prospective spouse, and then decide. When there's too much room in your head for noise or persuasion, it may be difficult to sort through all the advice and opinions. You don't need opinions; you need onions.

### *Be held accountable.*

I'm not saying you and your special someone should keep your courtship a secret. No. It helps to have spiritual mentors in the equation from the beginning. These people will hold you accountable. You need a couple of knowledgeable, trusted confidants who are objective, recognize risks when they see them, want to see you succeed, and are great judges of character.

These are not individuals who will ask questions that completely derail your priorities, such as the ones I just listed. When my brother married a woman from a different city, someone asked my mom why he chose to marry a woman from out of town.

That's like asking Moses' father, "Why a Midianite?"

Or asking Joseph's father, "Why a high-born Egyptian aristocrat?"

Or asking Boaz's mother, "Why a poor-as-dirt Moabite?"

Or asking Esther, "Why a filthy rich Persian King?"

The answer to all of these questions is, "That's God's choice." Everyone's opinion isn't relevant.

Proverbs 31:10 states, "A wife of noble character who can find?" It emphasizes character, not a certain race, ethnicity, nationality, or zip code. It applies to guys too. Acts 1:15–26 says that a male leader in church must be selected based on his character and how he manages his wife and kids at home. This means there's no way you can be better than someone else if your character is faulty.

People still ask this extremely invasive question about other people's spouses in creative ways: Why did you choose an Ethiopian, why an African-American, why a Caucasian, why a Hispanic? International speaker Jo Saxton has a great response to this question. A London-born Nigerian, she is married to a white British man a couple of years younger than she is. She simply responds, "Why not?" Respecting another person's privacy is not dependent on you understanding why they need privacy or why they've made certain choices in their lives. The only thing you need to understand is that privacy is theirs to control.

Before you reflect on this, remember, we're human. We're all flawed. We ask invasive questions because we're curious and don't give much thought to the negative impact. I'm guilty myself. We all make mistakes. But we can learn to ask better questions and know when not to ask questions at all. Also, when our privacy is invaded, we can learn to respond or to not answer at all. Proverbs 26:4 says that if you answer a bad question, well, both you and the asker are no different. To answer or to not answer? Ask God which option to take before answering (or not).

## Reflect

- Have you ever asked questions you now realize made another person uncomfortable?

- Can you think of some questions people ask that not only violate privacy but also cast doubt on and steal peace from the person being asked the question?

- What conscientious steps can you take to ask better, less insensitive questions? Will you consider the necessity of the question? Or the negative impact on the other person?

> *The one who has knowledge uses words with restraint,*
> *and whoever has understanding is even-tempered.*
> (Proverbs 17:27)

## The Point

Think before you ask questions. Even if it sounds like a sensible question to you, assess how the person you're questioning may process it. In a Listening Communications course back in my undergraduate days, my professor tirelessly reminded us, "Under the circumstances, think about how the other person decodes your message or communication." Yes, how will they unravel your question?

## Our Confidants

Sometimes we find comfort in venting to or sharing a story with a complete stranger on our flight or at a restaurant, barbershop, bus stop, or grocery store. It allows us to get a heavy burden off our chest with no strings attached. It's likely we'll never see them again, so it's like private therapy. We all need it. These are spontaneous confidants, as long as the stranger doesn't know your full name and is not recording or posting your conversation online.

Doctors, financial advisors, therapists/counselors, and pharmacists are paid confidants. By virtue of their services to you, they're bound by law to protect your confidence—your privacy—from public disclosure, depending on the circumstances. They are typically on the second ring of your health onion, depending on what you're protecting. You may have more confidence in them than in people you've known for much longer. The people you know don't always think of the legal effects or consequences, but those professionals do.

People you know personally might decide to disclose your business at any time and might not feel they owe you the protection you desire. This is why it's important to be more intentional about your privacy. There's nothing wrong with setting expectations for others and letting them know you have boundaries. There's also nothing wrong with having professionals, spontaneous confidants, and personal confidants at the same time. It's healthy. Either way, it's important to pray about all of them. You might feel that setting expectations or boundaries hampers relationships in the church community; however, the absence of expectations and boundaries is what destroys relationships.

The problem with privacy invasion or violation is that you can stop or minimize it, but you can't undo it. Once it's out there, it's out there forever. That's why it wounds so deeply and sometimes irrevocably.

Trust and confide in someone based on what you've expressly outlined and agreed to. Managing privacy is healthy, like watching what you eat. Healthy privacy boundaries are intentional, well-thought-out, and communicated. Clear communication—letting people know what you need and what works or doesn't work for you—helps others protect your privacy better.

## Reflect

- Do you find yourself trusting certain professionals outside of church more than within the church? Why?

- Have you become the type of person someone can entrust with their deepest personal information? If not, how could you create that person in you?

- Do you carry past privacy violation scars? How has that affected your ability to freely enjoy your circle?

- What can you do to avoid inflicting the same scars on others?

- Do you know people struggling with those scars from church? How can you help?

## The Point

Establishing boundaries and communicating your wants and needs is healthy. If you've been hurt a few times, you probably tend to withdraw. But you have options: Look outside your circle. Confide in professionals. Within your circle, it takes a little bit of onion ring planning on your part to prioritize your privacy to make sharing more controlled and beneficial to you. Realize the risks of not planning. Do they outweigh the benefits—peace, security, and freedom?

*Transparency is a choice.*

Have you ever listened to someone being very open and transparent about their life or their past? A speaker giving a TED Talk is a good example. She shares life challenges you can relate to. Her openness and honesty make you want to be transparent too. She makes transparency cool and invigorating. But keep in mind that, although it flows like she is speaking spontaneously, she may have prayed about her transparency and felt peace, direction, and the freedom to be transparent. She's organized and intentional about every word. She's not speaking off the cuff. It's a prepared talk after all. Although she may seem completely transparent, there's plenty she doesn't tell you. And that's healthy, normal, and expected. She planned this talk perhaps for days or months ahead of time. She edited and revised it. It's healthy for her not to tell you everything. She is intentional about it. Be intentional about your story before you open up.

Transparency is a part of privacy, but it's a choice. Spontaneous disclosure or sharing might be what you need to release pressure. That's healthy and important. What you don't want to do for the sake of privacy is hold anything in until your nerves burst or break down. If you don't feel ready, listen to your instincts before you share. Maybe you're not ready to share. If other people are sharing, that's probably because they feel ready. It's not so much about your mistrust of others, but it's about trusting God that "there is a time for everything" (Ecclesiastes 3:1–8). Don't feel pressured to be spontaneous about your testimony, gory hurts, disappointments, failures, or challenges in a church setting without praying about it and being organized about it.

Not everyone can handle your transparency or your truth—good or bad. Give different audiences different levels of transparency. Whether the truth is, "I only have a dime to my name, but I trust Jesus," or "I won a lawsuit and was paid ten million dollars in damages the very day HSBC Bank sent me an alert that my account balance was below one hundred dollars." That's just my wild imagination, but you get the point.

## Reflect

- Can you handle the fact that everyone can't handle your transparency?

- Do you have reasons for being transparent other than using your story to reach others and help them?

- Does transparency help you get things off your chest, or do you worry after the fact?

- What do you worry about privately but you're ready to be transparent about? If it involves others, are you prepared to avoid violating their privacy in the process?

## The Point

Share as long as you can handle it, and understand that others may not react or accept it the way you expected. That's the key. If you have specific expectations, you might be disappointed. Know your goal and focus. There's a time and a place for everything. Don't feel obligated when someone says, "It's just us; loosen up," or "Let's all be transparent." Privacy and transparency are about timing. No peer pressure should drive them. Your timing and readiness are not that person's, and theirs are not yours.

Loosening up should happen when you can do it fearlessly, freely, and confidently without remorse. It should bring peace rather than anxiety. Transparency has personal benefits. A well-managed, controlled, and prioritized level of transparency is healthy and beneficial.

*Needing space is okay.*

Have you ever moved away or thought about moving for privacy's sake? I'm sure you didn't tell your family and friends that was the reason you moved. If you did, you would have heard people ask, "Privacy? From whom in particular?" Who really says they need privacy and space? Maybe space. Maybe you said you needed a new environment. But what you really wanted to say was, "I love you guys, but privacy is the reason I'm moving." Of course, you don't want to hurt the feelings of your family or your church family. I get it.

We often judge people who are courageous enough to say they need privacy. We leave them to craft an excuse so they aren't stigmatized or misunderstood. However, if you need privacy because you're having difficulty dealing with a privacy issue related to your household, it should be discussed. Not so much with extended family.

Dana, who has a big extended family, told me that she moved far away from her relatives because she didn't want any surprises. Here's what she meant. When she lived nearby, they would show up unannounced all the time and at all hours—resulting in issues and conflicts. Dana moved not because she didn't love her family but because she wanted to *continue* to love them. Distance gave her the privacy she needed to do that.

For my friend Tim, distance wasn't enough. He and his wife opted for a gated, secured community. In these complexes, when a visitor arrives at the gate, the security guard calls the resident and asks if they are expecting the visitor. If the answer is "no," the guard will tell the visitor that there's been no response. This doesn't mean that Tim missed major holidays or events with his family. No. He and his wife visited his family often. Outside of those visits, Tim wanted to be let alone—to live. He wanted privacy, meaning the ability to control when he saw his relatives and for how long.

## Reflect

- Have you ever felt like moving for privacy's sake?

- Why do you need distance from extended family or certain friends?

- What do you think about limiting certain people's access to you? Have you ever done it, even for a day or a week? Did it feel peaceful? Did it help the situation you were in? Or did you feel guilty?

# The Point

It's all about privacy and freedom. It's a human need you can't get rid of, even if you try. You were born like this—to need privacy and freedom to be who you were made to be. Privacy and freedom go hand in hand like guacamole and nachos. Every time I say "privacy and freedom," it reminds me of the book *Privacy and Freedom*, written in 1967 by Alan Westin, a young law professor. It was given to me years ago as an appreciation gift from the largest global privacy community. The book offers a foundation on views about privacy and personal freedom. It is not a book about church or faith, but it consistently describes privacy as a spiritual need. I couldn't agree more. Westin explains one's inner circle as sheltering your "hopes, fears, and prayers" that are beyond sharing with anyone unless the pressure is just too intense, so you "pour" it out because you need relief.[10]

This is why privacy in our relationships is vital. We need good people in our lives to talk to, to identify with and pray with, and to celebrate and rejoice with. We need to manage our privacy so we can maintain the relationships in our lives in a way that feels safe for us. Privacy is not about getting your needs met and distancing people. It's about managing and prioritizing your needs, like Dana and Tim, in whatever way that works for you so you can love others better.

*Realize that if you have time to whine and complain about something, then you have time to do something about it.*
(Anthony J. D'Angelo)

# 16

# Privacy in the Workplace

*Whatever you do, work heartily, as for the Lord and
not for men, knowing that from the Lord you will
receive the inheritance as your reward.
You are serving the Lord Christ.*

(Colossians 3:23–24 ESV)

## The Best of Both Worlds

Most of us will never know what it's like to be an employee of a church. The rest of us will never know what it's like to have a good corporate or government job, a factory job, or a farm job. Some of us have the best of both worlds. We hold jobs outside the church but are also employees of churches. Perhaps, like me, you're a volunteer at church. Although it's not quite the same as being an employee, it allows you access to other people's personal information. Yes, personal information. Wherever we work, our attitude and practices toward privacy can be very telling.

Most churches don't know how to sufficiently protect and handle personal information. You probably already knew that. But did you know that they don't know how to start a conversation about privacy with their staff so that each person in the church's workforce understands the human need behind protecting private information that the church takes, gives out, and uses daily? Even if some of this information is provided to the church via technology like email, given verbally, or handwritten, it needs special protection.

We're human; we make mistakes. Privacy mistakes have consequences no matter who makes them—clergy, employees, or volunteers. By the way, volunteers, vendors, and contract workers can break church privacy just as paid employees can. But always remember that no matter who you work for, you're on one of your employer's onion rings. If you were your employer, how would you like people on your onion rings to act? To be careless and spill information? Or to be committed to you and your rules? Let's unpack privacy at the workplace—both as a church employee or volunteer and as an employee outside the church community.

### *Working for God means caring for needs and obeying authority.*

When you work for the church, what really goes on behind the scenes? Do you clock in, do your job, pray, and leave? Are there rules? Or is everyone super obedient and independent? Is it an environment where anything goes? How do you conduct yourself when it comes to protecting information—whether it is written, spoken, recorded, or digital?

You may wonder, *Grace, how should I conduct myself at work when it comes to protecting my privacy, the privacy of church members, and that of other church workers?* My answer to this is simple. But I'll answer your question with a question. Actually, two questions:

1. If God hired you, how would you handle the responsibility of protecting, prioritizing, and preserving other people's private information and private lives?

2. Whatever your expertise, what does God say in general about your job responsibilities and duties?

# Church Privacy 101

I'm not sure if you know it, but God is your boss and the president of HR at every job. Simply following rules and guidelines at work earns you loyalty points toward your obedience to God. I'm talking about how well you follow policies and how you handle customers', members', and other employees' information. You've been briefed on all these from day one. But by day thirty, you relax. You begin to do things your way or your coworkers' way. Have you ever skipped a step you should have followed, and a coworker enabled your behavior with "That's fine; it's the procedure, but nobody really checks that stuff anyway"?

Colossians 3:22 says you shouldn't relax thirty days or sixty days after you made it past your probation period. It doesn't use the word *probation*, but it states, "Obey your earthly masters [bosses] in everything you do. Try to please them all the time, not just when they are watching you. Serve them sincerely because of your reverent fear of the Lord" (NLT). Same thing.

Employees tend to relax a lot when handling information and computer use. We've all done this to some degree. If you're in an environment where everyone has five windows open on their work computer, but four of those windows belong to J.Crew, Pinterest, Amazon, Macy's, or Home Depot, chances are you will do the same if you're not a committed and focused employee. It's only a matter of time. Work rules or policies typically state that employees must avoid using work computers and electronic devices for personal reasons. There's a purpose for that. To do so might expose the church or employer to risks.

Don't utilize your employer's equipment for personal use. That goes for fax machines, copiers, phones, laptops, and email accounts. The Internet is a minefield. Every click is a dangerous step. You don't know what risks in the form of viruses, hackers, or malware are waiting for you at a particular website that you visit. If your computer becomes infected, you might compromise the computer network it's connected to. You don't know the enemy

## Privacy in the Workplace

is behind the scenes, watching and waiting for an opportunity to hack your clicks, slip into other church computers, and steal precious personal and financial information.

You browse the Internet all day, and along the way you accept cookies. Anyone who browses the Web has run into cookies. Remember when you visit a website and notice a banner on the page or a window that pops up and states, "Accept cookies"? Most times you respond by clicking "Accept All" so the banner will go away and you can enter the site. Do you know what it means to accept all cookies? Imagine walking to an office building, and a stranger hands you a cookie and says that before you can enter, you must accept and eat the cookie. You accept and eat it, even though you know you should never accept cookies or candies from strangers. But you do it anyway to get in. That's a risk. It's from a stranger—you don't know what's in the cookie.

Of course, you don't eat a web cookie. They're files created by websites you visit. Those files are then stored on your web browser (for example, Apple Safari, Microsoft Edge, or Google Chrome). The cookies then monitor how you use the website you're visiting. They also track how you use other websites. How? They can track your browsing history, spending habits, and behavior. It's like being in someone's house, and the owner follows you around to every room you enter and records every object that fascinates you, anything that you pick up and examine, and what you do with it. That actually describes my niece. But I won't digress. On the Internet, that could mean items you click on and view closely, what you buy or almost buy, which web pages you visit, and other online behavior.

Cookies also remember you when you return to that particular site, and they keep creating records of your activities on that site and reminding you of items you previously seemed interested in. That's not a bad thing. But some cookies can be programmed to last for many years, which means they're not

# Church Privacy 101

intended to help you. Rather, they will violate your privacy for a long period of time. They can follow you to other websites that don't have cookies and monitor your activities. Cookies can view your browsing history and, depending on the cookie, may get access to your credit card information. Imagine if hackers got a hold of these cookies. This can lead hackers to further violate your privacy and steal your identity.

You should treat all websites as strangers. When you're offered web cookies and you accept, it's similar to throwing a party at your house when your parents are away. You asked everyone to bring all their friends. It was fun. But when the guests leave, you notice that things are missing, stolen, or compromised because of your carelessness. Someone went into your parents' room and rifled through the drawers and the medicine cabinet. You can't figure out who took what. What are you going to tell your parents? If that were personal information from your church that you were in charge of but is now missing or stolen, what are you going to tell the church?

Perhaps you're not thinking of these risks. You may have forgotten everything you learned and agreed to during the new employee orientation or after you accepted the job. But everyone else is breaking the rules, so you follow suit. It's worse in church. We tend to do a better job of holding other people accountable against fornication, covetousness, idolatry, extortion, and drunkenness (1 Corinthians 5:11) than we do of holding ourselves and others accountable for not abiding by privacy principles, which are just as important.

You hardly see much accountability for the use of church computers or people's personal information. We're dangerously accommodating when it comes to handling personal information. We don't ask questions. We assume Sister Abby is really good with kids in the nursery. You've never found a kinder and gentler soul. True. But nobody dares question her about her use of the church laptop or her handling of children's and parents' personal infor-

## Privacy in the Workplace

mation. Nobody thinks about risks. Or maybe they do, but they just look the other way. They avoid offending anyone. You may think, *She's harmless. She won't do anything to hurt the church. She's been here for thirty years.*

Think again.

What you should be thinking is, *Does she know how to properly handle privacy?* For example, when she takes church forms home—forms that have people's full names, physical addresses, phone numbers, email addresses, dates of birth, and who knows what else—does she leave them on the back seat of her car? Does she leave them on her dining table for any person who visits her house to read?

Let's start with you right now. Yes, you too. Where is the laptop that you use to help the church process people's personal information? Is it encrypted? Where do you keep church papers with other people's personal information? Are they on your coffee table or dining table? Are they at work—on your desk? Are they visible where the cleaning crew can see and read them?

Ignorance happens to good people. But we can learn. The number of years you've been doing your job is one thing. Whether you're doing it right is another. Whether you understand why you're doing it right or not is yet another concern. We need to be taught. It's better to do a task the right way than to just get it done. It's equally important to know why you're required to do things a certain way. This way, you can better understand the positive and negative impacts of your actions and have accountability.

Just because you've made the same mistake for a long time doesn't mean not correcting it makes it right. I worked as an intern at a renowned corporation while keeping a side job at a taco shop—I'm a hopeless foodie; I admit there's no cure. Between serving customers, my supervisor, Ann, used to watch me wash the pans and trays in the kitchen. I thought my dishwashing was fascinating until one day when Ann briskly walked up to me at the sink and said, "Step aside." I realized her watching me was not a compliment.

# Church Privacy 101

"You wash these pans as if you're washing your own dishes at home." I drew a blank, wondering how else I was supposed to wash dishes and pans.

"You work too hard," Ann whispered sternly.

"But that's how we're supposed to wash," I explained, pointing to the kitchen manual.

"Watch me!"

Ann rattled through the pans to demonstrate her point. I looked on.

"Okay, I see what you're saying. You got more dishes washed faster," I said.

"You bet." Ann nodded.

"But you skipped some steps about sanitizing," I added.

"How many restaurants have you worked in? Take it from me: I've worked in restaurants longer than you've been alive."

I knew that was an exaggeration. But I didn't argue.

"Nobody pays attention to the steps you're worried about," Ann scoffed, walking back to her office.

As a newbie, I didn't have much else to say. So when Ann was around, I did the dishes her way.

When you're dishonest in little things, you're more likely to be dishonest in bigger things (Luke 16:10–15). I was serving two masters, Ann and God. The manual represented the authority that God put in place to guide me. Ann had years on the job. I had two weeks on the job. Ann's actions, rather than mine, could have potentially caused health inspectors to shut down the restaurant. Do you see what I'm saying? Over time, as I observed my other colleagues, I noticed they all did the dishes Ann's way.

I didn't want to stick out like a sore thumb. If I did it my way, even if Ann was off duty, someone would tell on me. I'd be alienated. So I trained myself to do the minimum.

## Privacy in the Workplace

It's the same scenario when it comes to how much care we give other people's personal information. We do the minimum, unaware that regulators will penalize churches in the same manner they do businesses. People who want to protect the privacy of others are sometimes alienated and told they're making a mountain out of a molehill. This is the truth if the person in the lead role doesn't share the same privacy concerns or values. Just like a good practical sermon, privacy principles that are practiced by church leadership are most effective in creating a culture of respect, dignity, and peace. Most times, people treat other people's privacy the same way they treat their own. If they don't see or know the value of protecting theirs, they're less likely to protect others', even if the policy at work says they should protect privacy.

Fast-forward to many years later. I was working in Spain and relaxing with a dozen or so business colleagues after work. One gentleman in particular was being very vocal about his private life. Let's call him Gerardo. It was the first time we'd all met him. We didn't need to meet him a second time to know everything about his love life, his counseling sessions, and his wild side. We knew where he lived, where he used to live, where he was moving, and his familial decisions. A few of us found this laughable. And it was enjoyable until he realized he was the only one talking and sharing his private life. He started asking each individual in the group personal questions and was surprised when we all declined to answer. Every church has a Gerardo pressing other people to share at his level of openness.

Privacy shouldn't depend on your preferences but on the preferences of the person whose information you seek to obtain or process. Gerardo wanted to handle our private lives in the same way he handled his. We desperately need to protect how personal information is processed in churches because the church is loaded with information about people. This information is in people's heads, notepads, computers, and phones. The law mandates the protection of privacy, and as such, this is a civic duty of the church. What's important is that the information is personal to someone, and that person may protest if their personal information is inappropriately handled, disclosed to the wrong person, lost, or stolen. The problem with that is, depending on what actually happens in a given incident, it may drag the church into a legal mess, which can be costly and damaging to the church's credibility.

## Reflect

- Can you recall sharing information in church that you should have been more careful about (e.g., leaving a form or notes with someone's personal information out in the open, in your car, or at home)?

- Do you know folks in your church who think that privacy rules are nonsense?

- How often is someone in your church held accountable for inappropriately handling private information?

- What about being held accountable for the use of church-provided computer equipment to run personal business or the use of church information to do the same?

- Do you discuss the personal information people put on church forms with other people who do not have any business knowing that information?

## The Point

If there's anything the church does well, it's meeting the needs of people—both members and the public. In my church, we fulfill a long list of basic needs in our community. For the majority of members and visitors, the es-

Privacy in the Workplace

sential need is the Word of God for edification and direction. For others, the need includes shelter, food, clothing, skill building, empowerment, and encouragement. Rich or poor, everyone has a common need: the need for *dignity*. That's why it's important to respect privacy when handling personal information. The church benefits from having employees who respect privacy because it's the right thing to do—all the time. For example, if a piece of paper has personal information on it, don't toss it in the recycle bin. That may be convenient for you, but it's not secure. Find a paper shredder. If you're in a hurry, lock it up away from prying eyes until you have time. If church employees are attuned to privacy rules, they'll hold church volunteers accountable too, especially as volunteers typically outnumber paid church workers.

*So whatever you wish that others would do to you, do also to them, for this is the Law and the Prophets.*
(Matthew 7:12 ESV)

## Consistency Inside and Outside of the Church

The same privacy issues exist outside of the church. You're one person, one body, and one spirit. There's not one version of you when you're in church and a different one when you drive off the church parking lot. Christianity is not a hat you hang up or heels you kick off your feet when you get home.

Your behavior and values should be consistent. They should be your identifier. You should be recognizable. If you're a grape, you should be found at all times of the day being a grape, not a nectarine. That's what Matthew 7:16 is talking about. The difference between church and business workplaces is that people often fear other environments over churches because they'll face harsher penalties if they don't comply with rules. Churches are more forgiving and relaxed about privacy education, training, and awareness.

# Church Privacy 101

Most folks have had some sort of privacy training and awareness at work. You were taught all the privacy policies, standards, guidelines, and rules of behavior before you were allowed to touch any of your employer's work. You've done this for years and aren't breaking the rules. Why aren't you transferring those routines and practices to church? Are you lax because you feel the church is different? Don't forget, a church is a person. It's you, me, and other members. So why aren't you consistent? Why aren't you complying?

## Reflect

- As a church member volunteering and observing things all the time, why do you think you don't speak up when you notice that the church's privacy practices are lax?

- Why do you think God blessed you with corporate opportunities to expose you to business practices that could benefit the church?

- Will you speak up in church to the right person at the right time and say, "I see some risks in who we let handle XYZ. We need a policy and procedure to help handle that process. I'll look for a template we can use"?

## The Point

Like your job, the church is about adding value. The church fulfills many spiritual needs. But we, as the body of the church, must contribute. We must add value. And if we're not adding value, we must certainly not take value away as a result of our indiscretions. Even if you're not an expert in a particular field, all the church needs is an awareness that a certain practice in church is a risk or can be improved. Then someone can be assigned who can

Privacy in the Workplace

be dedicated to the task. Have you ever seen or read about any good change that happened without someone exposing a problem? I haven't. You have a role to play in making the needed difference.

To cross the Red Sea, a believer had to step up and do their part, regardless of being afraid. They preserved hope by walking between two gigantic walls of water in the middle of the Red Sea (Exodus 14:29). A believer added value by taking his long overdue vacation days to work on rebuilding the ruined walls of Jerusalem despite opposition so there'd be security from adversaries for the present and future generations (Nehemiah 2:17). Similarly, you add value. In church, you can roll up your sleeves and contribute for the greater good.

***Strive for excellence.***

These days, it's not unusual to work outside the church building and still be on the church payroll. But be respectful of both environments. Don't save confidential and private documents for the church on the same flash drive you use for work outside of church. Keep them separate. The beauty of working in both places is transferrable wisdom and skills, not documents. That works for the betterment of both workplaces.

When David was a boy, he tended sheep. When his flock took a nap, David killed time by composing music and writing the psalms we meditate on today. It was a thankless gig. No applause. Nothing. David's reason for playing was not to be noticed. He was simply worshipping God with the gift of music. He kept perfecting his gift. One day, his dad told him that the king needed his services. To do what? David was a shepherd. King Saul tasked David with playing music at the palace to soothe him. Someone among the king's employees had once heard David play the harp and thought it was miraculous. David was hired before he arrived at the palace (1 Samuel

16:14–23). So here's David reporting to work to do what he did well privately. King Saul was so impressed that he asked David to live at the palace. Regardless of which shift you work or role you play, you need excellence both in the field and in the palace. You can do it—for sheep and king.

## Reflect

- How many years has God blessed you with jobs outside the church? How much of that experience do you use to improve administrative practices at church?

- What poor information-handling practices have you observed at church?

- How does your employer handle those practices? What do they expect of you? Do you comply, or do you wait for somebody else to step up?

- At church, do you ignore inappropriate and illegal practices because it's not your role to question or change things or because the church provides no consequences for ignoring them?

- Does the idea of speaking up make you choke? Are you afraid others at church may judge you if you speak up and say that a certain privacy practice is against the law? I understand that, but remember that Nehemiah pressed through criticism, mockery, and attacks.

## The Point

You might think, *The church is different. We can't possibly run it like a corporation.* Why not? It's an organization—it processes financial transactions and people's personal information. That data has equal market value. If you believe

Privacy in the Workplace

that the corporate world and the church follow different business principles, you are mistaken. Many business principles are documented in the Bible, but the Bible doesn't get credit. I laugh when I hear a church leader say that the corporate world dictates privacy to the church. How is that even possible? The church has always been about respecting human dignity. Privacy principles are about that. Whatever we do, "there is nothing better for people than to be happy and to do good while they live" (Ecclesiastes 3:12). We should not exclude one extra good thing. "You shall have just balances, just weights" (Leviticus 19:36 ESV). That means churches shouldn't give the impression that their practices are fair when they're not, even if nobody is complaining or thinks they should be changed. The Bible says not to take advantage because the other person has no clue that what you're doing is unjust—or might even feel powerless about confronting you. That's Leviticus 19:14. Isn't this why laws, privacy policies, and privacy notices exist?

*Do unto others . . .*

The Bible teaches us to treat others fairly and honestly, protect others, maintain integrity and a high standard of care, and not take advantage of others. The UN took that same truth and ran with it. The organization penned and signed the Universal Declaration of Human Rights a couple of weeks before Christmas 1948. Twenty plus years later, in 1973, the US federal government published the Fair Information Practices to stop personal information abuses and the mishandling of personal information in the government. Same principles. It went viral immediately and hasn't stopped trending. Almost every country in the world came up with its own version of the Fair Information Practices plus its own unique caravan of privacy laws to make sure every person and organization complies. Because of this, almost every corporation in the world has privacy policies, notices, you name it. The government and businesses get Leviticus 19:14 and Leviticus 19:36. But what's your church doing? Let me ask that differently. What are *you* doing? With all the exposure you've got, what could you do?

Being careful and diligent is wise. We're all employees of God in different ways. Some of us are on church payroll, and some are not. But payroll or not, the risks of how we mishandle personal information given to and used by the church are the same. Proverbs 27:12 specifically talks about diligence. It essentially states that the prudent anticipates and avoids risks, but a fool walks right into risks and suffers.

## *Be an influencer.*

You may be a church employee who handles food preparation, curriculum or outreach planning, or other activities that don't require the handling of personal information. I may be a volunteer who registers conference attendees, and I process their credit cards. Unlike you, I have more access to the crown jewels of the church: personal information. My role poses more risks than yours, even though you're a full-time employee and I'm only volunteering for one Saturday. This brings up many privacy implications for the church. If I know what I'm doing, have good intentions, and follow the rules that I know, that'll be good for the church. If not, I'll be a risk waiting to manifest. You should do *something*. Speak up. Be proactive to avoid privacy violations that could be detrimental for the church and impact members' lives. Help your church avoid giving personal information handling roles to employees or volunteers who have no privacy training. What if nobody listens to you? Your mission is still accomplished! You've done the right thing. There's a Scripture for that. "Whoever loves discipline loves knowledge, but he who hates reproof is stupid" (Proverbs 12:1 ESV). Don't give up though.

## Privacy in the Workplace

Find another approach and someone who will listen. Think about what's at stake: the church breaking the law and church members getting hurt.

*Ignorance is not bliss.*

Sometimes we can get out of trouble by claiming ignorance. But it doesn't work that way with privacy. As an employee anywhere, if you have read and signed a policy, you have accepted the consequences should anything go wrong. The same goes for the church as a body. The church cannot claim ignorance either. No, not before a judge. You'll face consequences for ignorance and for breaking the law.

*What could possibly go wrong?*

COVID-19 has caused a lot of people to reconsider their long-lost dream of being their own boss. Folks are getting creative. I've supported several people who've dared to start their own business during the pandemic. Entrepreneurship can be empowering. I wish I'd started sooner. But when you're your own boss, there's a lot of temptation to cut corners at the expense of others. There's also the temptation to steal information to help your business get off the ground by downloading client lists from your employer to expand your network or taking supplies from your office to use at home. You're building your business at your employer's expense.

In a church environment, that could be copying members' personal information—emails, phone numbers, and home addresses—to advertise and market your business to them. You're taking an unfair advantage. It's like working as a teller in a bank and withdrawing from customers' accounts to fund your new business. Not only are you implicating your employer, but you've defrauded customers of their . You've broken the law. You're running your business on stolen goods. You've taken advantage of and abused the access entrusted to you. Your church is like that bank, and the victims will likely sue when they find out.

### *Who will the law make an example of next?*

In 2004, David Nosal, a former Korn/Ferry recruiter, fell into a similar temptation.[1] With a dream to build the best recruiting firm in the world, he resigned from his $300,000 a year job to start a business to compete against his employer. He got three of his former work buddies to help him out. He needed to download confidential customer details, including the names of the executives in the clients' companies. His buddies sent the information to Nosal. What followed was a painful criminal prosecution, prison time, and a hefty $60,000 worth of fines. What was his crime? Nosal was convicted of "conspiring to gain unauthorized access to the computer system of his former employer . . . to illegally obtain trade secrets."[2] Technically, he violated CFAA, the Computer Fraud and Abuse Act. CFAA is a US federal law that covers thefts having to do with improper access to computers.

Many employees and former employees have run afoul of CFAA for either accessing an organization's computers they were not given authorization to access or going beyond the level of access granted them in order to steal information for personal use. Nosal didn't have direct access, so he conspired and got the support of his three former coworkers, which is also a violation of CFAA.

## Reflect

- Is your personal business competing with God?

Privacy in the Workplace

- Have you been a "Nosal" at some point in your employment history? What about at church as a church volunteer or employee?

- Would you stop a Nosal at work or at church, or are you typically like one of the three former coworkers?

- Have you helped yourself to church members' personal information because nobody held you accountable for not taking it? Did you use it for personal gain?

- Have you thought about what would happen if their personal information got stolen while it was with you? Would you report it to the police or the church if it did? Or would you be comfortable with doing nothing because you'd be exposed?

- Are you chasing success by any means necessary?

## The Point

The church is no different from a corporation when it comes to stealing. The same privacy rules at Trader Joe's, Target, Wells Fargo, law firms, and other for-profit companies apply to the church. When you leave an organization, don't go back to log in and check out files or paperwork you'd like to have. Don't do it. It doesn't matter if it's before midnight on your last day of employment. You could be in violation of CFAA and other laws and incur criminal and civil charges. Be careful with former coworkers who make bizarre requests of you. If you're the requestor, even if your buddies are willing to help you out, your request and their help could be illegal.

Understand that when your employer or church collects personal information, by law your employer is accountable for what happens to it. If it gets disclosed to the wrong person or gets lost or stolen, they're held responsible. Why implicate your employer or your church? Why violate people's privacy? Because of 2 Timothy 3:2—"People will be lovers of themselves, lovers of, boastful, proud, abusive"? It's not all about your success; it's about fulfillment. Fulfilling your purpose doesn't require forcing success. If you still have passwords to the network of the church you left, don't take advantage. Call the church and remind them to delete your access and accounts.

*Litigation awaits church workers who steal.*

Whether you win or lose in court, is it worth disrespecting another person's privacy and bringing civil and criminal charges on yourself, even if it happens in a friendly church environment? Assistant US Attorney Kyle Waldinger said this about Nosal's case: "At the end of the day, stealing is stealing, whether you use a crowbar or a computer."[3]

Like David Nosal, because you are trusted, you might raid church records and stash them away. One day, you want to start your own ministry or business, and you think that, after all, ministry and your personal business are God's work anyway. Wrong. Familiarity with the church can make you feel like you're not breaking any law, but you are. God knows your destiny and the resources you'll need today and months from now to get there. Take into account the words I heard preached in church: "Are you chasing just success, or fulfillment and destiny too?" I'd say honor God, respect others, and take all three.

# Privacy in the Workplace

*The peril of payback is that you end up losing more.*

People who violate privacy do not always do it for financial gain. They can do it out of spite. In 2003, Huping Zhou, a research assistant at the University of California Health System, was criminally charged. He accessed thousands of patients' health records after he received notice of his employer's plan to terminate his employment.[4] He accessed patients' records 323 times for no job-related reason. After he got caught, Zhou said he didn't know that what he did was illegal. The government wasn't having it. The FBI investigated UCLA's School of Medicine and confirmed that Zhou had violated HIPAA (Health Insurance Portability and Accountability Act), a federal health information privacy law. Zhou committed a federal crime. The judge, Magistrate Andrew J. Wistrich, didn't just blast Zhou for his lack of respect for privacy but slammed him with a prison sentence.

For the most part, Zhou was perusing the medical records for personal gratification, starting with the folks he was really mad at. He perused his immediate boss' medical records first and then his coworkers'. Three weeks into binge-viewing everyone's health records, Zhou took it up a notch. He dug into celebrities' health files. *CBS News* named a few of the high-profile celebrities affected, including Tom Hanks, Drew Barrymore, and Arnold Schwarzenegger. The list also included Sharon Osbourne, Barbara Walters, Elizabeth Banks, Leonardo DiCaprio, and Anne Rice.[5] That's unacceptable, no matter whose records they are. Celebs are humans and value their privacy too.

## Reflect

- Even if you didn't lose any , would it hurt you to know that an employee of an organization you entrusted with information was viewing your health and other personal information for personal gratification or out of spite?

- Even if you didn't lose any , how would you feel if your coworkers with access to your employment records were reading your personal information?

- How would you feel knowing someone who was upset with you was going after your confidential information and private life in your employment files? Sounds far-fetched? Unfortunately not.

- How would you feel knowing this happens more often than you think, including in church?

- Would you like others to respect your privacy? Why?

## The Point

Be neither a Nosal nor a Zhou at your place of employment—in the church or outside the church. Don't excuse your law-breaking actions with "This is church. It's different. We're family." No, it isn't different. Take proper care of personal information people give to the church, especially if you're the recipient or recorder of that information. Don't neglect it. And don't share a mailing list with another church member who needs it for unrelated business. If that information gets out, you'll be held responsible. The law says to respect the privacy of others. The Bible's golden rule says to love, show respect, and be fair to others—the way you'd like to be treated. Remember Matthew 7:12: "In everything, do to others what you would have them do to you."

## *Be a catalyst for change.*

When it comes to the law, the Bible requires everyone to comply with the governing authority (Romans 13:1–7). That includes privacy authorities, regulations, and laws, whether it's the United States' HIPAA or CFAA, the European Union's GDPR, California's CPRA/CCPA, Canada's PIPEDA, or other local, state, and international privacy laws and regulations. The laws or rules you break are the same rules put in place to protect you. If you're not helping your employer or church keep its promise of protecting customers' or members' personal information, realize that your own personal information is at the mercy of an employee or church member who may choose to break the rules concerning your privacy. *Do unto others . . .*

Don't forget Mrs. Bodil Lindqvist. Sister Bodil was one of the first people to be sued for privacy violations based on the European data protection rules. She did what many of us do now or have thought about doing. She published group photos of fellow church workers on her personal website. She then tagged them and included hobbies, phone numbers, and family statuses. She even mentioned that someone in the group was on medical leave. People in the photo took issue with that, and the matter ended up in court. Bodil pulled down the information from her website. She apologized vehemently, but the government wasn't having it. She violated the privacy rights of others. She disrespected other church members' needs by not asking permission before publishing their personal information on her webpage. Sister Bodil faced harsh consequences. That was in 1998. Things have changed since then. These days, privacy laws are even more unforgiving, and the number of laws has more than doubled. This means that *all* workers are vulnerable to privacy breaches. Because they're vulnerable, employers are vulnerable.

It's clear that the church work environment is not immune to privacy drama. From experience, a lot of workplaces are like church workplaces, and vice versa. Productivity can suffer, and privacy risks can get out of control in both environments if people don't know what's acceptable or if they're not held accountable.

What should you do? Be the catalyst for change. If you're uncomfortable speaking up in public, get a copy of this book for one member of the church leadership who can help you champion the change. Be the person you want others to be for you. Be accountable. Be a person of integrity—respect others' needs and obey the rules, not just when leaders are watching you. If nothing else, think about the source of your blessings—that's who's always watching. What is it you want? Do you want only success in life? Or do you want success, fulfillment, and your God-given destiny? Then show respect and fairness to others.

*Remember the* Lord *your God, for it is he who gives you the ability to produce wealth.*
(Deuteronomy 8:18)

# 17

# Privacy in the Afterlife

*For the living know that they will die,
but the dead know nothing.*

(Ecclesiastes 9:5)

## Privacy Is for the Living

Privacy is for a living, breathing person. At least that's how the law treats it. However, the dearly departed still have a right to privacy—typically exercised by their successors—to protect themselves. Organizations such as the military may protect privacy or refuse to release records of deceased members, even under federal information access rights and even if the person was convicted of crimes. Sometimes families try to protect their deceased loved ones from ID theft, also known as *ghosting*. You could be dead and in heaven, but on paper you're buying homes, applying for credit cards, and signing up for an unlimited calling plan. Disturbing, yes. Impossible, no. Unfortunately, it happens to about 2.5 million dead Americans yearly.[1] In the first quarter of 2023, "the IRS identified nearly 1.1 million tax returns as potentially fraudulent as of March 2 [2023]. . . . The associated refunds were worth about $6.3 billion."[2] Clearly, the devil is at work.

# Church Privacy 101

*The pain of the past controls the present.*

Families arrive at funerals of their loved ones with "a wide range of emotions: pain, sadness, anger, denial, and guilt."[3] If the devil goes to prayer meetings, bachelor and bachelorette parties, weddings, and birthday parties, he also pencils in time for funerals. He's the grinch of anything related to family unity. Funerals are a form of reunion on a sad note, but they can be full of peace. If the deceased was well advanced in their golden years, it can also be a celebration of their life.

Depending on your culture, a lot of privacy palaver may go down during a funeral. In some cultures, funerals are an all-day event. No matter your relationship with the family, always be in the moment. Nothing says you're not there like your obsession with selfies. I'm not just talking about taking photos of yourself but also of the very private and personal moments during the funeral. People might be so overwhelmed with grief that they have to be restrained from accompanying the casket into the grave. That's not all. Big reveals happen at funerals—illegitimate children, jilted lovers, and estranged spouses could show up and give a dramatic performance. Their presence must not be mistaken for support. At times they show up to shame the dead—who, ten out of ten times, don't care—but the family must endure the embarrassment. Estranged children of the deceased make their presence known to publicly inform mourners that they have a share in the inheritance. Why do you need videos or photos of these?

*Honoring the dearly departed means being in the moment.*

Taking and posting photos is not the reason you've been invited to a funeral. You are there to pay your respects and support the family of the deceased. Not everything is edifying to post or share. Some events are sacred and are meant to be experienced in the moment. It's never a good time to take photos when the pallbearers are ceremoniously escorting the coffin to its resting place. Actually, you won't find any good time for taking photos at a funeral—unless the family specifically requests it. It's already a sad occasion, and inconsiderate behavior does not provide consolation. Granted, some funerals can be very public by virtue of who is deceased or the circumstances surrounding the death. It may be a politician, celebrity, religious leader, or a victim of injustice. Regardless, privacy boundaries still exist. Ask permission rather than seek forgiveness for your invasion of the family's privacy.

*Family feuds can be avoided.*

Believe it or not, people have threatened to break a family member's leg if they were to show up at a funeral. Other times, they block their access to viewing the deceased family member. Don't go to a funeral if you've been asked by the family to stay away. Don't go if your presence will likely result in tumult or upset the family. It's best to stay home—even if you think you haven't done anything wrong. Some family members excuse their threat as the wishes of the deceased. Should they honor mischief in a will? Dysfunctional families do. The deceased no longer has a say, but you do—protect your own peace. Ask yourself, "How would God prefer I handle this?"

Quite often, generational pain and conflicts stem from privacy violations. People just don't describe them as such. If you show up, you're making it easier for your privacy to be violated (mentally, emotionally, and publicly)—just stay home. Families openly feud and fight over a family member, shedding light on an aspect of the private life of the deceased when given a chance to take the mic and say a few words. Some families anticipate the troublemakers and hire security. Sometimes resting in peace is easier said than done.

## Reflect

- Have you ever withheld information about a loved one's death from a relative or delivered the news to them carelessly because you had estranged the person? Or have you ever made a scene to express your disapproval when they showed up at the funeral?

- Would you ever attend the funeral of someone you felt bitter toward? Would you reveal their dark side when it was your turn to give a speech?

- What would you do if you knew a family member was planning to stump the funeral—even if their message was the truth? Would you stop them ahead of time?

- Have you ever taken funeral photos and posted them online without the permission of the family?

- Do you have unapproved funeral photos that would have a serious privacy impact on the members of a family who invited you to attend the funeral? Have you considered deleting those photos so they don't surface?

## The Point

Respect the family. Families are not perfect, regardless of their appearance. If you have a chance to give a speech at a funeral, do that with grace. I don't believe it's mandatory to talk at all. I'm sure you've heard the saying "If you don't have anything good to say, don't say anything at all."

Ephesians 4:29 is clear in this context. A funeral is an occasion where people come to be encouraged and support others. If you plan to repurpose this occasion to hurt mourners—by violating their privacy—you should read

## Privacy in the Afterlife

Proverbs 17:28 and reflect before you head out to a funeral. My mom encountered such a person when my brother died.

My brother transitioned while he was trying to save someone's life. My mom confided in me that someone asked her at his funeral, "What was he thinking?" A funeral is not a press conference for the bereaved to answer your burning questions. Respecting privacy is key. Being respectfully present and in the moment with the bereaved is ideal.

Also, please don't distribute your business cards to attendees during a funeral service. It doesn't matter if you're a member of that church—it's just plain wrong. Repurposing someone else's personal occasion is an invasion of their privacy.

> *Let no corrupting talk come out of your mouths, but only such as is good for building up, as fits the occasion, that it may give grace to those who hear.*
> (Ephesians 4:29 ESV)

### *Take a stand for privacy and peace.*

The most hilarious and memorable funeral service I've ever attended was that of a family friend's relative. It was like watching a show at the Apollo. No, it was like watching its audience, best known as "the world's toughest audience." It was what you'd expect at the funeral of a barber famous for his ardent consumption of fashion trends and his love for luxury cars. All his customers in attendance had their turn to share their remarks. This funeral gave me the feeling of a hair show (I discreetly loved it!). Did I hear some of the most interesting stories or what! It was all cherry until one gentleman, a close buddy of the deceased, went over the five minutes allowed. In the most entertaining way, the attendees went from cheering to booing—motioning with their hands for him to get off the pulpit. He should've walked away at that point. He gleefully added, "There are some things I know about Robert that will shock all of you. I probably shouldn't share . . ." Then he spilled. That's when the crowd went wild, chanting, "Don't share! Don't share!" Rightfully so. I mean, a little "vulnerability hangover" is healthy but not at a grieving family's expense. I was impressed at their sincere love and respect for the privacy of Robert's widow and the entire grieving family. Remarkable! The world needs funeral attendees like that. Yes, I was at a funeral, but it was a happy moment in a privacy expert's day.

At some funerals, only immediate family members are granted a few minutes to make remarks. Other funerals allow more people—family and friends combined. Respect the program and stick to great memories and funny stories that can be told in three minutes max. Don't say anything eyebrow-raising or make any public statements you'll later have to apologize for—even if you're the presiding church leader at the occasion. The bottom line is, be slow to speak.

> *When words are many, transgression is not lacking,*
> *but whoever restrains his lips is prudent.*
> (Proverbs 10:19 ESV)

**Do not disturb.**

Mute your phone as soon as you arrive at the funeral. If you have tons of deadlines, stay in your car and work. Tell folks you're attending a funeral so they don't expect you to be available. Don't sit in the church foyer with your laptop. That's disrespectful. I see this a lot.

## Privacy in the Afterlife

Approach the grieving family only when necessary—even if you attend church there. They probably have enough people already attending to them. Observe so you know when they need you, but don't overwhelm them. You can't go wrong with giving them a little space. They'll understand. When you don't know what to say, "I love you" or "I'm praying for you and your family" is enough. Then move aside so other mourners or supporters can engage with the family members.

Privacy is not only about ID cards, passwords, and passports; it's also a human need—a desire to be left alone. Funerals are a place of reflection and vulnerability. Allow people to exist in that moment—even if they're not crying. Do not record attendees as they're sobbing and stricken by grief. You should be pre-approved before the funeral service to play that role. Even if the program does not state that the grieving family requests privacy, don't assume privacy is unimportant. They're counting on you to apply a little consideration and godly wisdom without them having to ask.

Because violations of funeral privacy can happen on church grounds or in church facilities, it doesn't mean church members are the only privacy violators. Funerals attract people who are not church members. But the church can help control privacy violations. That means you have a role to play. You're the church. Let your church leaders know about any issues you notice. If you're on the church leadership team and a funeral is taking place at your church, you're responsible if someone gets hurt—not just physically but emotionally as well.

The deceased may no longer need protection, but the living do. If a member of your church is always saying that their family is wild and violent, believe them. You might have heard enough clues over time to help anticipate what could happen at that family's funeral. Have able-bodied men around, hire security to protect your church members, or step in if there's a conflict by informing the leaders.

*Choose who should deliver the sad news.*

Sometimes families fuss at funerals because someone shared the news of the death of a loved one outside the desired order of announcement. This happened to Aubrey. Her family members were upset with her because she told her grandpa that her cousin had passed away.

"He's in a nursing home. He deserved to know. Besides, nobody said I couldn't tell him," Aubrey rationalized.

She had a point there—no one said she couldn't tell her grandfather the news. Aubrey's aunt and uncle also had a point for being upset. This was their child. And they may have had a time period in mind for disclosing the heartbreaking news themselves to their father. Some family members went to the funeral feeling resentful. This was the devil interfering with family unity. But we all have responsibilities too.

# Reflect

- Have you ever been in Aubrey's shoes? Can you relate?

- Can you relate to her aunt and uncle? Have you assumed people know when you plan to disclose information—without you making known your wishes?

- Bad news travels fast. Have you ever spread news about the death of someone's family member without permission?

- Have you ever been the victim of a privacy violation related to the loss of a loved one? What happened?

Privacy in the Afterlife

## The Point

Losing a loved one is tough! You should be intentional and proactive about who to tell, what to tell, and when to tell it. Don't assume everyone will do what makes you feel peaceful. Speak up and make your expectations known as soon as possible. Onion rings work—you get to plan ahead how you want to share sad news. Make it clear who you won't tell until much later. Let everyone in your onion know. Perhaps Aubrey's aunt and uncle should've made it clear to the family right away not to disclose the news of their son's death (to certain people) until a particular time. But I understand how overwhelming the news of the passing of a loved one can be.

## Death of Privacy—Wills and Probate

I know you're tempted to skip this section because you think you're too young to worry about writing a will. First consider these two things: nobody is too young to die, and you don't need to be rich with lots of assets to need a will. Many items you own have monetary or sentimental value, or both. You might have a family member, a friend, or an organization you'd like to bequeath specific belongings or possessions to when you die. If you don't have a will, your personal effects will probably still go to your relatives, friends, or church members, or they will be donated or end up in a dumpster. Without a will, you won't know for sure where your things will go. Why not be intentional about it?

If you own a car, condo, house, boat, or apartment, consider creating a will after you read this quote from a *Business Insider* article written by Angie Chatman: "My mother purchased her home on the south side of Chicago for $55,000 in 1986, the equivalent of $123,000 today. When she died without a will, court fees and fines left our family with just $40,500—a loss of over $80,000 on the purchase price of her house."[4]

There's always chaos and confusion after a death. I don't wish it on anyone. Heaven is the perfect place to be, but it's tough to think about death and the end. One of the best happy endings you can have is an organized ending done in a way that doesn't disturb your privacy while you're still here. But even I dreaded the soul-searching and house-rummaging aspects of preparing a will and doing estate planning.

The difficult part of getting organized is that your mind roams. Once I started thinking about it, I reflected on all the people who will miss me and how long it will take them to heal. It was one of the hardest exercises of my life. But once I started a list, I got excited about it. I thought of all my loved ones—both born and unborn. What will make them smile, empower them, show them what I was really like, and give them a glimpse of my cherished moments and conversations with God?

I dug up paperwork for my various account information. Then I called The Hartford to check my employee retirement balance. I was put on hold for forty minutes, only to realize that my accounts were actually with Vanguard. Oops. Good thing I wasn't dead! My family would have fought The Hartford for a hundred years while Vanguard pocketed the . I was glad I called. I then updated beneficiary information on all my accounts. By the time it was all over, I felt so organized. Not everyone has a chance to get organized. Death catches many people off guard. God forbid you get sick and you're unable to get organized. Death comes for you when he's ready. Only God knows when. A will allows you to get organized before death comes unexpectedly.

Preparing your will requires privacy.

Keep it hush. Revealing too much may create the temptation for someone to expedite your death in their favor. You don't want to arrive in heaven earlier than scheduled. Don't tempt a relative or anyone else to murder you so

## Privacy in the Afterlife

they can spend your sooner. I recently read Kim Bryan's article "5 Children Who Murdered Their Parents for the Inheritance." Sometimes relatives who feel entitled get help from the devil. On Bryan's list was James D. "Jimmy" Robertson, who had been cut off financially by his parents after they learned he'd been expelled from Georgia Tech for failing to complete his classes. Andrew Wamsley had a similar story. He was cut off financially. All the people mentioned in the article had drug use in common. Most were in college.[5] It's never a good idea to threaten anyone with the idea that you'll pull them from your will as punishment. You'll be provoking a bull in a china shop. Watch out.

Not all parts of a will are private. Your best friend, a parent, or your spouse can be significantly trusted—hopefully they've earned it. Don't trust people by their title or role in your life. I'm talking about real gut trust. Let those you trust know who your estate planner or probate lawyer is. Give the probate company the names of those you trust. Actually, they will likely be the ones to sign as witnesses to make your last will official. You might as well let them know you've prepared a will. Make onion rings for your will.

Just because you tell the significant people (who will sign your will) that you have a will, that doesn't mean they have any business knowing the content of your will. What should you share? Funeral arrangements, your final resting place, whether you prefer the velvet-lined box or cremation, an open casket or closed casket, where you want your ashes scattered, or if you just want loved ones to decide that part. Someone needs to know if you want to depart in style with a specific color scheme and if you have a special account to pay for it all. The good thing about being transparent about this aspect is that if people in your family forget, your friends will remind them. End of discussion. No family brawl.

A trusted person, possibly one of the signatories, should know where you'll keep the original will—in the bottom drawer of your dining room

# Church Privacy 101

cabinet, under your mattress, or wherever. The probate lawyer can include more details, such as gathering the family at the appropriate time to read your wishes—where they'll find details on who gets an antique vase versus who gets the house. No one knows your family like you do. Give detailed instructions, even for the reading of the will. For instance, "Make sure Amber doesn't sit next to Jared during the reading of the will" is a clear instruction. If they didn't get along while you were alive, it's not happening at the reading of your will. One of your trusted friends or family members you select ahead of time can also coordinate other wishes you have expressed, including details such as your final outfit, makeup tones and hair style, the funeral program, the person to deliver the eulogy, whether you opted for burial or cremation, the site to deposit ashes, and other logistics.

It feels great to leave things in an orderly fashion. After going through this preparation, I can attest that it's not just a good feeling; it's the right thing to do. Not everyone will agree with your decisions, but that's okay. You did what you saw fit and in the best way you knew how—unless you were the discreet lady that *ABC News* reported left $13 million to her cat Tommaso.[6]

You can never run out of options for what to do to better others' lives—while you're still alive and after you've relocated to heaven. Even if humans don't treat you well, don't leave everything to your cat, dog, or fish. Don't drag your family's private life into court fighting a pet or trying to prove your undocumented decisions. Anticipate what may transpire because of your decisions, and respect their privacy accordingly before you sign off.

*A good man leaves an inheritance to his children's children.*
(Proverbs 13:22 ESV)

## Privacy in the Afterlife

If you don't know what to do with your personal effects, possessions, or belongings, consider nieces or nephews, grandkids, churches, local schools, local shelters, and orphanages. If you have a surplus, do what billionaire Robert F. Smith did. He is still alive, but he pledged that he and his family would pay off the student loans for the entire graduating class of 2019 at Morehouse College.

You're probably not Mr. Smith, but you may have an item or an object that could be the miracle someone is praying for. The best gift is the type of gift the receiver cannot thank you for. Your will is a great way to do that. The person cannot pay you back or acknowledge you with a thank-you (Matthew 5:47–48). God calls this "perfection."

Some people carry their will in their heads. It's just an idea they've mulled over. They think they have it down and that it's private. But they're not intentional about it. It's the same thing they do with privacy. Please don't be that person who doesn't write down your will. According to probate lawyer Marcia, "Even if you have not written a will, you have a will written by the state" (quotation used with permission).

Do what I did. Create a Word document and plug the information in. If you have a template from a probate lawyer, fine. They can help answer some questions you may run into. Start making a list of the following:

- bank accounts (savings, checking, and market)

- retirement accounts (of any type)

- investments (of any type)

- real estate (any property you own or rent-to-own—condo, duplex, single-family, cottage, or mansion)

- vehicles (all your Bentleys, Toyotas, Volkswagens, Nissans, bicycles, and scooters)

- jewelry (fine jewelry or faux)

- list of debts (student, mortgage, and credit cards)

Next, take it one room at a time. Think. If your house was on fire, what would you grab first, second, and third based on their value . . . until everything is accounted for? I'm asking you to prioritize the value. Of course, if there's a real fire and you have children and a spouse, you should save them first.

## Reflect

- Did you know that you don't need to discuss your will with relatives until you're ready to involve them? And if you're married, you should both think about it first without getting others involved.

- If you're concerned about handing your sensitive and personal information to a probate lawyer while planning, you could ask your probate lawyer what measures they take to protect your information against cyberattacks.

- Would you rather not think about death and how you want to leave things for your loved ones?

- Did you know you could request a template from a probate lawyer and start an inventory of your assets?

## The Point

Don't let the state call the shots with your earthly possessions. The state will take a big piece of the inheritance to cover fees. Remember Angie Chatman's story about how the state left her family with just $40,500 instead of the $123,000 that her mother's home was worth.[7] Your family will end up spending their to get a fraction of your hard-earned —if you don't have a will.

Probate lawyer Marcia shared the following suggestions:

A last will and testament is an opportunity to state in a legal document those whom you want to receive the assets of your estate, and to select the Personal Representative (commonly known as an Executor) to manage the administration of your estate. Here are other considerations:

- If you have minor children, a will may provide who'll be their guardian to oversee their daily care and/or who'll be the trustee to manage their finances should you meet an untimely death.

- You must be (1) at least 18 years old in both the District of Columbia and the state of Maryland, (2) competent to make a will, and (3) the will must be properly executed (quotation used with permission).

If you die without a will, the state in which you were domiciled upon your death legally prescribes how much and to whom your assets will be distributed. You definitely don't want the state involved in your asset distribution.

### Who gets the kids?

It's prudent to decide who will take care of your children after your passing, not just physically but also emotionally and spiritually. Suppose the funds you left for the caretakers run out. Will they stand by your child or children? Or will they put them out? Will they care for your children beyond the provisions you left? Some churches or Christian denominations have the tradition of choosing godparents. I think it sets the stage for planning for your children's well-being and development in the event of your death. It protects your children's privacy. You may not have godparents for your children, but you get the idea. Use that logic. Select folks based on character, integrity, and reliability. For privacy's sake, prematurely sharing too much about who you selected could invite the pestering of relatives or friends you didn't select for that role.

### What if death is not quick?

That's a possibility to consider. God forbid you're sick or in a serious condition. An advance health-care directive is when you get to choose ahead which life-sustaining treatments you'd like and what you don't want to happen to you if you slip into a coma or if your body is breaking down. This means you have already selected an agent to make decisions for you based on prearranged preferences. It's very personal and private, definitely not a decision you make when a room is filled with family members. You need privacy. Of course, they'll eventually know your wishes. Some decisions are emotionally tough for families to have to make, so by setting up an advance health-care directive, you're paying it forward for your family so they don't live with the regret or guilt of whether or not they made the right decisions for you. They can heal better, even if they disagree with your decision—but at the end of the day, they'll know it was what you wanted.

## The Cost of Saying Goodbye

The first time I calculated what I would be giving away to my loved ones, it would be whatever I had left minus debt. My pure excitement at seeing the total made me forget that people get buried after they die. So, what am I saying? Add funeral expenses and how much should be spent, along with which account it should be paid from. Whether you're one of those who want to exit this world in style or without much fanfare, it still costs. Don't announce it to your family and risk losing your peace. Only people who'll execute your will must know—in writing.

## *Beneficiaries—who's getting what?*

Name the person who will execute the will—an attorney, your spouse, or a very good friend. You can have more than one executor as a backup. These are serious private decisions we're talking about here. Manage your privacy well. Be intentional. Don't assume. Should you tell your beneficiaries who is getting what? Should you keep that private? Some probate lawyers may say no, tell them. Every family is different. It depends on who's in it and how functional or dysfunctional they are. Only you would know.

## *Protect your progress.*

Have a shredder at home to destroy the different versions of your inventory, list of beneficiaries, and assets they'll receive. For privacy's sake, don't leave it on your dining or coffee table where a visitor can glance over it. This should be a document you create a password for in your folders. Give the file a unique name that's not suggestive of the content. I know of a rich elderly man in my region who left his draft will on his dining table and wondered why he was experiencing resentment from his relatives. One person peeked at his will and saw that he was leaving a six-figure payout to his nurse. His private decision leaked to other relatives. They stopped visiting or helping.

So if you share your personal computer with your loved ones or kids, prevent anyone from peeking at your will. Use this opportunity to create a guest account on your computer. If someone other than you needs your computer, they can use it as a guest with zero access to your files.

**Online forms and templates can help, but protect your privacy.**

The Internet is raining an abundance of free forms made available by different sources. Don't go to any website and enter your personal and bank account information. Think privacy. It is best to print out the form or create the same headings in your own document and fill them out. Notice I didn't say download the forms. You need to be careful. You can mistakenly download forms that can introduce malicious software into your computer—possibly resulting in personal information being compromised. Chat with a probate lawyer and ask them to point you to a safe template or email you one.

Start looking up probates in your area. Read their website and call them to ask questions. They may ask you to come in—ask if that will cost. If you haven't yet found someone, keep researching. If you hear a friend talk about a will, ask them for the name of the probate attorney who helped them. Meet with a probate lawyer who will answer questions without charging a fee. By the time you're ready to pay for them to go to work for you, you should have all your homework done.

Hold up. Remember, you'll be giving a probate lawyer tons of sensitive information about you and your family. If a cyber thief gets ahold of that information, your finances can be wiped clean. Treat your probate lawyer as your tax person or a bank. Don't give all your information away without asking empowering privacy questions. For example, does your firm periodically assess cybersecurity risks? How? How secure will my files be? Ask questions about the probate's website privacy notice—read it ahead of time. And read

## Privacy in the Afterlife

their other privacy and confidentiality notices. Get copies. Read and save them. Because of the sensitivity of the personal information that law firms handle, they are attractive targets for cybercriminals. Some law firms have been hacked without even realizing they've been attacked.[8] These attacks are increasing. It makes sense to choose your probate firm with privacy and security in mind. If your probate lawyer is a member of your church, don't let down your guard. Ask questions. Be informed, but keep it private. Let them know your expectation of privacy. Wills are such an empowering document, but your entire church or circle doesn't need the details.

### *Exclude people, but don't announce it.*

You can divvy up your belongings any way your heart desires—as God directs. You might have good reasons for excluding people, especially anyone showing a significant level of recklessness—like wasting on substance abuse and wild living. Nobody wants to feel responsible for giving hard-earned to a loved one who might waste it or hurt themselves and others.

Let's say you exclude a relative because of a long-standing misunderstanding or grudge. Giving can mark your forgiveness of a family member. Suppose in your will you leave an antique clock to a relative you've had disagreements with for as long as you can remember. You leave him a note saying that he should get it appraised because you're sure it's worth more than $5,000. The next thing he knows, he's on *Antiques Roadshow* and finds out it's worth $10,000. You didn't give him $10,000; you gave him a baton of forgiveness to pass on. Even if he rejects the gift, at least you showed that you let go of any malice. Hopefully, he will pay it forward by dropping the bitterness so the next generation won't catch it.

For privacy reasons, again, if you choose to exclude someone from your will, keep it to yourself or risk being murdered. That's no exaggeration.

# Church Privacy 101

Whether you exclude or include them, don't rub it in their faces. If you think that's unrealistic, consider Luke 6:45: "A good person produces good things from the treasury of a good heart, and an evil person produces evil things from the treasury of an evil heart. What you say flows from what is in your heart" (NLT).

### *Don't get ghosted.*

Again, ID theft of the dead is called *ghosting*. Just how do crooks get your information posthumously? They troll hospice facility records, hospitals, social media posts, newspapers, funeral homes, and anything with obituaries. How do you prepare for this? The Holy Bible states, "There is a time for everything" (Ecclesiastes 3:1). Allow family members some time to grieve you, but leave extra instructions for them so you aren't ghosted.

Sid Kirchheimer, the author of *Scam-Proof Your Life* and columnist for AARP, has some great suggestions about how to protect yourself. I've paraphrased them below. You could leave his recommendations in your instructions.

1. Have your loved ones give minimal information upon your death. This means that, as you plan your will, you should leave instructions for your loved ones to publicize minimal information. This is for funeral programs and other published items. For example, they can list your age and transition date rather than your birthdate. Make it easy. They should follow your template, assuming you created one. Do what I'd do. Drop a watermark that says, "No deviations allowed."

2. Leave your mother out of this! I mean her maiden name. In America, a mother's maiden name and a Social Security number are critical pieces

of identification to protect. Also, calling the Social Security office to report the death is an important step the family should take.

3. If you wisely don't post home addresses and your location information on Facebook, Instagram, WhatsApp, and Twitter, treat funerals in the same way. Criminals can search for physical addresses mentioned on a funeral program, flyer, or related post. Knowing those families are going to be at the funeral at a particular time gives them an opportunity to rob those homes. I'm not talking about them stealing furniture. You should be more concerned about thieves getting away with Social Security information, computers, phones, documents, credit cards, and more before you get home. Don't put personal address information on flyers, obituaries, or related announcements. It doesn't matter whose it is.

4. The family of the deceased should mail a copy of the death certificate to the Social Security office, DMV, major credit bureaus, banks, and other financial institutions to close all accounts. Even so, Sid says, "Several weeks following the death, use this service—at www.annualcreditreport.com—to run a credit report on the deceased to ensure there's no suspicious activity."

5. And don't forget to close or cancel any services, memberships, and accounts such as utilities, cell phones, cable, insurance accounts, outstanding memberships, and social media profiles if you're able.[9]

# Reflect

- Do you want your family to spend years fighting to clear your name? Or make your family members responsible for paying back debt incurred by crooks? If not, then what Sid suggests makes sense.

- Do you want your family members or the executor of your will to think that an important detail you had shared isn't a big deal? If not, then my suggestion is to pen it as part of your last will and testament. If you don't, you leave your family or spouse fighting an unending battle.

## The Point

I agree with Sid that you should protect yourself when a family member dies. I also think you should protect loved ones before *you* die. Save them from themselves, and provide wisdom along the way. Family members often forget important steps or wait until it's too late, so write it down as part of your will. If I were you, I'd make sure. No, I take that back. You can't really make sure—not when you're dead. At least ask the executor of your will to ensure that your family does this part first before they get any or whatever you left them. Yep, you read that right. They should finish this step before getting anything you left for them.

I'm a big believer in creating and using incentives to do what you need them to do. Come up with conditions.

> *But if anyone does not provide for his relatives, and especially for members of his household, he has denied the faith and is worse than an unbeliever.*
> (1 Timothy 5:8 ESV)

# 18

# People Who Leave the Church

*Surely there is a future,
and your hope will not be cut off.*

(Proverbs 23:18 ESV)

## God Is Calling Me Elsewhere

Have you ever left your church? We've all switched but maybe for different reasons. Why do people leave their church? It depends on who you ask. You'll get many reasons. Below are just a few.

- distance—save gasoline and time (because the next day is a work day)

- work—transferred to another job location and moved

- growth—need more challenging material and spiritual growth

- connection—need more opportunity to engage or contribute

- models—need more truth and fewer double standards

- representation—need a place where they see people like them: their age, ethnicity, and socioeconomic background

- worship—style of worship service (presentation, emotionalism, expression such as dancing, singing, and praising, ambience, and culture)

Privacy reasons hardly ever make the list. Sometimes folks leave the church because they're ashamed of themselves. They leave suddenly after being caught living an immoral double life in any shape or form. Other times, people just need privacy. Like doctors say, "You just need rest." Privacy is rest. It helps you recharge. It can help you cut down on church activities for a while so you can revive and come back refreshed. A friend of mine left her church and worshipped at another church for about a year. She then went right back to her home church revitalized and renewed. They were excited to have her back.

Have you ever told your church community, "God is calling me elsewhere," but what you meant was that you needed some privacy and peace? We're all leaving or joining churches like we switch mobile plans. The reason and the timing are different for everyone. I've noticed that people leave a location, a denomination, or a group, but not God. When they do leave, there's no need to judge them harshly or snub them.

> *"Do not stop him," Jesus said,*
> *"for whoever is not against you is for you."*
> (Luke 9:50)

A preacher I know put it this way: people are basically "changing parking lots." Churches are more similar than they are different. Even people who don't go to church anymore stream or listen to services from the privacy of their own homes without anyone knowing. I've concluded that people have found God to be reliable. Each other? Not so much at times.

*Truth is exposed, not discovered.*

Now, let's continue with the not-so-positive reasons why people leave—because of privacy violations. Members often leave their church because they shared something personal with someone who later betrayed their trust. It brought them unwanted attention, misjudgment, and discrimination. If they reacted, they were called secretive or told that they were overreacting, immature, selfish, or of little faith. Has a situation or person ever hurt you deeply? And a church member said something like "Ignore it. You're dwelling too much on it"? But, in fact, you weren't. It just hurt. And it's your subjective hurt. You're entitled to feel hurt. What hurts you may not hurt another person. It doesn't mean your hurt is invalid or should be ignored or ridiculed—it's your feeling and your trauma. That's how privacy invasions or violations sometimes play out. Your trust or confidence is betrayed, and nobody understands the hurt but you.

The problem then becomes magnified beyond the one or two people who hurt you. That person tells one person, then another. It spreads. It's even tougher for folks who end up leaving their church because this is tough to handle. They're having to start all over again to build trust. They are often

- so deeply wounded by what happened,
- not feeling heard, defended, or supported by their church family,
- feeling their needs are disrespected,
- invalidated, and
- dismissed.

Why is this more complex or worse than other reasons a person may leave a church? A sting like this robs you of your peace, trust, and the sanctity of the church community. It can also interfere with fellowshipping with church members, even when you know they're instrumental in your spiritual growth.

When you're in that situation, you don't look forward to going to church. You drag your feet to shower and get dressed. You habitually arrive late. You dread church fellowships—hugs, smiles, picnics, Bible studies, fish fries, even someone asking you, "Hey, what's going on?" Yours is the first car to speed out of the parking lot before the church even says the final "Amen!" Sound familiar?

People who have left the church because their privacy was violated can be of any age. I've talked to people serving in leadership positions who have faced these moments at some point in their ministry service.

This is real. I want you to meet these folks. You might be able to identify with some more than others. It might even take you back in time. Or maybe you're going through church privacy issues right now. If so, you're reading the right book.

Many people who left their churches mainly because of privacy issues are reluctant to talk about it because it still hurts. They don't think anything good can come out of trying to resolve their issues in church as long as privacy is not perceived as a real need that should be respected. This attitude of treating privacy as taboo needs to change.

A dear pastor friend once said to me, "Grace, truth is exposed, not discovered. You have to tell it." I soon realized that healing ourselves and helping others grow come when we talk about things that are uncomfortable. If that doesn't resonate with you, how about "tell the truth and shame the devil"? I found three people willing to do just that. Below, they tell the real truth about why they left their churches. Let's hear them out.

# People Who Leave the Church

## *Jana's story*

I was invited to have dinner at the church treasurer's home. The fellowship and conversations were lively and warm. It was just the right place to be. We prayed in depth before dinner was ready. My hosts had one male guest whom I didn't know. Also attending was a male guest I had seen in church (and who had asked to get to know me better in the months before the dinner). It was great to see him.

During dinner, the treasurer's wife said to me, "I'm so proud of you with all the you've given the church for all these years. You're one of the biggest givers."

"She's *the* biggest giver," her husband corrected her.

She laughed and pinched me. "Girl, if you add it all up, that's enough for a big business or a house."

They meant well, but I wasn't flattered. Everyone grinned as if they'd already had this discussion before I'd gotten there. I was shocked.

The guy who had asked me out said, "Wow, that's really great. I've heard good things about you."

I gave him the "Who asked you?" look. I pushed my chair back from the table. I couldn't pretend all was fine. Yet I didn't know what to say or how to start, you know, without making the situation worse. My appetite was gone. I struggled to compose the words to say, but I finally did. "I don't want to discuss my tithes and offerings—it's between me and God."

The man asked, "So what do you do for a living again?" He wasn't getting my point and wasn't going to drop the topic. On that note, I excused myself and left.

I don't talk about things like that. I could never give God enough of what I have that would be worth talking about. It's personal. When my fingers drop into that offering basket or I click a button to give online, it's personal.

That's it, *personal*. I love and respect our treasurer. Yes, his job as treasurer is to manage the giving. But there's a line between that job and a dinner conversation. I expected them to know better. Oh well. That was it for me. I never confronted them about how they made me feel. It was obvious. At least I think it was obvious. I didn't want this to get any worse than it was. Thinking back now, I should have said something later. I forgave them, but I was hurt and looked for another church.

## Reflect

- Have you ever heard a "Jana" complain about a church worker? Did you discourage her by responding, "What's the big deal? That's just the devil"? Or did you identify with her or show empathy?

- Have you ever been a Jana? How did it happen, and what decisions did you make because of it?

- Do you identify more with the other people in the story than you do with Jana? Who and why?

- What could each person have done to avoid the breach or at least stop it?

## The Point

Author and TV host Dave Ramsey says this about tithing: "We don't give to get, but God often blesses us with more if we're good managers of what we already have. Tithing recognizes that God is our provider and that we will prosper with more than just if we rely on Him."[1]

## People Who Leave the Church

Some churches call it *collection*, *giving*, *tithing*, or *offering*. My church goes with all four. Whether you have an envelope with a special number designated to you, mail it to church ahead of Sunday service, drop it in the collection plate, lay it on the altar, or submit it online, it's the same thing. But we don't give to get attention, compliments, conversations, or rewards. We give to honor God in a personal and private way.

> *Honor the* L*ord* *with your wealth,*
> *with the firstfruits of all your crops.*
> (Proverbs 3:9)

### *Be careful of your reaction.*

I'm sure the couple figured something was wrong when Jana left. Arguing with them may not have solved anything then. Some people stigmatize anyone who is concerned about their privacy. They will even call you paranoid—to your face. Of course, that helps the offender get off the hook of never taking responsibility, which reminds me of Proverbs 18:2: "A fool takes no pleasure in understanding, but only in expressing his opinion" (ESV). You don't need to talk in the heat of the moment. They didn't mean to hurt you. But it hurts. I think the offender should learn from the situation, but withholding your full vent of rage, like Proverbs 29:11 says shows, you're wise and understanding. Another thing to consider is that speaking up would have meant fully exposing the couple's fault in the presence of their dinner guests rather than doing that privately according to the conflict resolution guidelines of Matthew 18:15.

That's why privacy is an issue here. Whether you give a dollar or a thousand dollars, it's a private and very personal act of faith and worship between you and God. To bring this up during a dinner conversation in front of guests would be hard for anyone who really honors God with their giving.

> *Be careful not to practice your righteousness*
> *in front of others to be seen by them.*
> (Matthew 6:1)

Is it clear why Jana felt her privacy was violated? Like Randy Alcorn, the author of *Managing God's*, you may argue that Matthew 6:1 doesn't apply to Jana, as her motive for giving was right. Therefore, she shouldn't worry that others know at this point. It's not her fault. Alcorn says, "The body of Christ can benefit from seeing open models of generous giving such as Barnabas'."[2] That is, as long as you, the giver, "don't cough loudly just as you're giving. Don't slam-dunk your offering in the plate."[3] Alcorn also sees privacy as temptation, anti-accountability, and a cover for those who are disobedient in their giving. While I see his point, Jana is still not comfortable that someone other than the treasurer knows how much she gives. Yes, the Bible models examples of open giving, but those tend to be exceptions rather than the norm. Jana's privacy and peace meant not being put on a pedestal. Should she have left the church? That's a different argument altogether. Regardless, privacy was the cause. That's why we should not look at the violation alone but also at how to correct such situations and salvage relationships.

### *Louann's story*

I went outside the church to get counseling. I felt I needed professional counseling because I was seeking answers on whether to continue with my marriage or dissolve it.

Privacy didn't enter my mind, but subconsciously, it was there. I've had church counseling over the years and have had a positive experience with it. I don't believe I was cheating by going outside of the church. Since my spouse is not a member of the church, he wouldn't have participated anyway if I had chosen church counseling. He needed a neutral party more than I did. I also wanted to protect my relationships in my church community.

The counselor explained the psychology of how childhood affects adulthood and how just knowing better doesn't always mean we'll do better. Also, if we don't acknowledge there's an issue, nothing will be resolved. So you can keep praying for the other person, but you need to do what you need to do to function in the relationship. In my case, I had to reframe it to live with the circumstances. I definitely recommend outside counseling.

## Reflect

- Do you feel like you have to explain that you're not cheating on your church when you get help, such as counseling, outside of church?

- Do you or would you get counseling or professional services outside of your church for privacy's sake? Have you made someone feel like they made a mistake because they made that choice?

- Has anyone in church ever estranged you because you sought help outside your church? (If that happened to Louann, she would not have stayed with her church.)

- Do you identify with Louann and with seeking the most objective and privacy-preserving help for your husband and marriage?

- How would you encourage a "Louann" in your church to seek help?

# Church Privacy 101

## The Point

For Louann, going outside the church for counseling wasn't for privacy's sake, or so she thought. And it wasn't even for her as much as it was for her husband. Privacy protects us and those we love from biases, discrimination, and misjudgment. Louann was applying important privacy principles without even realizing it. Spiritually, Louann was the stronger spiritual partner in the marriage relationship. Her husband wasn't a churchgoer. She didn't want this to get in the way of getting the help they needed for their marriage. She knew her husband might find it difficult to apply Christian principles in the middle of heated conflicts. She was also more familiar with her church leaders and counselors than her spouse was. She sought fairness over actual or perceived favoritism. She didn't want him to feel like he was taking the blame for everything based on the fact that he wasn't a Christian or a member of her church. She wanted him to experience balance in the resolution. It worked.

If you go outside your church for professional counseling, it's not cheating. Do it for privacy or if your church does not have qualified counselors. Don't feel guilty. Although you have a home church, look for wellness solutions where God leads you. Not all churches are equipped to handle certain problems. Let's be honest: churches can make situations worse if they don't admit they can't handle them. Some churches are very flexible in this aspect and point their members to outside resources available to them. Yes, really. Privacy-centric churches recognize that a bishop, priest, minister, reverend, pastor, evangelist, or apostle is not a marriage counselor unless they have been trained in counseling.

God answers prayers, but he expects us to move and act. He works through unbelieving professionals also.

## People Who Leave the Church

Going outside is not cheating at all. If it works for you, it's healthy. When you go outside and it works well for you, share it if you'd like. Another church member may be trying to make the same decision. You never know. People don't talk to each other often enough about privacy. And they don't know their options. Someone out there needs a Louann to say, "I went outside the church for help and it worked. You should try it." Church folks don't like to admit they need and want privacy. That's why people would rather leave a church than speak up about privacy violations or concerns. Louann sought help outside the church, which allowed her to resolve her issues. She didn't leave her church, but she kept her marriage and the help she sought for it to herself.

### *Pam's story*

I was going through a bitter marital season in my life. My spouse was rebellious at home, at work, in church, and everywhere. He'd argue everyone down. He was bitter and didn't accept any help. He quit jobs and was financially irresponsible. He neglected his responsibilities at home and his ministry duties at church. Plus, he cursed people out—yeah, in church. Adultery became his new hobby, and we spoke about it with our pastor. However, after each session, my spouse took one step forward and ten steps backward. The hardest part was when he acted out his hostility in front of both adults and children. I was hopeful for a turnaround, although I didn't know when it would happen. I asked the pastor for privacy for my marriage's sake.

At my church, we always had visiting clergy from other church communities. Some were friends with our pastor. My spouse and I were not close to any of them. We didn't know them well enough to confide in them about our marriage the way we did with our pastor. We never spent time socially with those pastors either. We saw them in the sanctuary once in a while. Some of them started asking my spouse things about our marriage that neither of us had shared with them. It was difficult to handle that. My husband became even more irrational. He accused me of telling everyone his business. He used this as a reason to abort every effort I'd already made to restore our marriage.

When you have a spouse who is not cooperating to make the marriage work and blames you for everything, you end up feeling like you shouldn't talk to anyone or get help. I did my best to respect my husband's privacy and the confidentiality of our marriage concerns. This was why we had gone to our pastor in the first place. As soon as the other pastors knew, their spouses knew, and their congregations knew. Soon, it spread like wildfire, and folks from other churches wanted to confirm what they had heard. It was hard to endure different opinions and to suddenly have everyone in our business. And it wasn't helping the situation.

I asked the pastor why he divulged our personal business. He said that preachers work together to solve problems in churches and that my concern for privacy was wrong.

I didn't even bother to ask why he didn't hide the details to protect us or why he wasn't discreet. I wondered if he realized that he had made matters worse, but I didn't bother to ask this either. Why? Because there was nothing to say. I wasn't going to get a good answer. He had already told me that privacy was wrong, that I lacked faith, and that those concerns were interfering with what God was doing to restore my marriage. It was hard to take that. My husband was blaming me for something I didn't do, and the pastor was blaming me for needing privacy.

I shut down. The only relief came when I stopped sharing anything. I took the pain and trusted God. We decided to leave the church.

## Reflect

- Can you identify with Pam or someone who is in Pam's shoes?

- Do you identify more with others in the story than with Pam? Who and why?

- What could each person have done to avoid what happened or to make it better?

- Do you remember a time when your privacy was violated in church by a member, worker, or member of leadership? How did the violator/offender handle it? How did the church handle it? What decision did you make because of it?

- Have you seen somebody else's privacy violated in this way? Did you say anything, or were you afraid of criticism?

## The Point

While we can never explain exactly why a particular marriage ends despite all efforts to restore it, Pam is right. The lack of privacy can interfere with conflict resolution. She made a decision. She did what most of us don't do: "If another believer sins against you, go privately and point out the offense. If the other person listens and confesses it, you have won that person back" (Matthew 18:15 NLT). In this case, the pastor neither listened nor apologized. Pam was shocked that the pastor didn't understand her need for privacy. She didn't want to start anything that might lead to more gossip or slander in church. Maybe she was too ashamed to tell fellow church members or leaders that the unwanted attention hurt. Pam was hurt not only by a cheating spouse but also by church leadership who mishandled the conflict.

She gave up pursuing the issue because she felt powerless against the pastor's influence. Nobody would have admitted that the pastor was wrong.

Pam's privacy was violated by members of the clergy. They were insensitive to her needs, but escalating the privacy issue would have been a difficult fight for Pam, given the wounds and suffering her husband caused. When the devil attacks a marriage, he is attacking the church and every relationship associated with that marriage. I'm not suggesting she go back and trust, but that she forgive them and pray for them like Job did (Job 42:10). Don't hold yourself hostage. If they knew better, they would not have done what they did. Pray for God to train them on privacy by leading them to this book. Maybe this is your contribution to the church—privacy awareness.

### *Pray for your friends and move forward.*

Always remember this simple math: one wrong + one wrong = two wrongs. You may be the offended party, but how is your heart handling the offense? If you're holding a grudge, you're the second wrong. You may appear right, but you're not. Job prayed for his friends—that God would forgive them of their foolish talk and perspective. God gave Job the strength to forgive them, and Job's heart was willing to do the unthinkable—forgive. If he hadn't, his story could have ended differently. Ask for strength to forgive, but don't compromise on your privacy or healthy boundaries.

> *If they will not listen, take one or two others along,*
> *so that "every matter may be established by*
> *the testimony of two or three witnesses."*
> (Matthew 18:16)

## People Who Leave the Church

### *Privacy is not paranoia.*

You're neither faithless nor paranoid. You need privacy—inside and outside of church. Privacy is the ability to control what you wish to share, including when, where, with whom, and with what level of detail. Once you understand what privacy is, you won't beat yourself up about needing it and will create healthy boundaries to ensure you get it.

There's no commandment that says you need to trust an offender again (the same way that you used to trust them) if they haven't earned back that trust. Use onion rings. A privacy violation injures even more deeply when it comes from a relative, friend, or clergyperson. Even the faithful are fallible. Churches are made up of people—people who need to know different ways of caring for each other's privacy needs. You can keep switching churches until you're left without churches to switch to. But realize the offender doesn't know any better and will do this again. Churches need to be taught. You're reading this book, which means you're a great catalyst for change in your church.

> *Remember, it is sin to know what you ought to do*
> *and then not do it.*
> (James 4:17 NLT)

### *Privacy Conflict Resolution in the Church*

For those of you wondering where God was when Sister Bodil got slammed in court, God was there. But where was the church? The church didn't see it coming. We've seen it now that an example was made of Sister Bodil. The church needs to think ahead and set up conflict resolution resources for members' privacy concerns before these sorts of issues end up in court. Other organizations do. Laws and regulations require processes.

Who should you go to when your privacy is violated? Ask your church. It doesn't matter how privacy is violated. It could be someone within or outside the church who is offended by what a church leader or member does. Some cases may be similar, and some may be very unique. In my work with privacy laws, frameworks, and regulations around the globe, one of a few important things needs to happen without undue delay: conflict resolution. Both parties need to have a conversation. They both need a complaint process that looks at what really happened and comes up with a timely resolution.

Does your church have a way to start a dialogue or receive a privacy complaint from individuals? Doing the right thing because it's the right thing to do and doing it because you might get in legal trouble are two separate things. Both the Bible and regulators respect organizations that do the right thing. Regulations specify that if you don't have a complaint process for your members and customers, that's huge noncompliance and could incur fines or penalties for you or your church. In privacy practices, ignoring an individual's privacy rights or complaints is an absolute legal no-no. You can argue, but you won't win.

Privacy regulators are not out to issue hefty fines or penalize organizations for noncompliance. It may seem like it, but that's not what they do at work all day. They also take lunch breaks and check personal emails. Most importantly, they want to see organizations making efforts to prevent or correct situations before privacy issues escalate to the courts. The Bible warns against being quick to take matters to court. The law has given privacy rights to individuals. The church needs to create a process to honor those rights so people don't need to turn to the courts. Churches cannot count on the offended individual to live by the scriptural principle that advises, "When one of you has a grievance against another, does he dare go to law before the unrighteous instead of the saints?" (1 Corinthians 6:1 ESV). I'm not sure many

## People Who Leave the Church

churchgoers will read that passage the morning before filing a lawsuit. These days it appears everyone goes straight to court since churches are either slow to respond or don't have privacy complaint processes at all. What happened to Mrs. Bodil Lindqvist is a prime example.

> *Whoever restrains his words has knowledge,*
> *and he who has a cool spirit is a man of understanding.*
> (Proverbs 17:27 ESV)

# Conclusion

*Then the righteous will shine like the sun in the kingdom of their Father. Whoever has ears, let them hear.*

(Matthew 13:43)

## Our Privacy Journey

It has been exciting taking you on this journey with me. Although we've discussed many privacy issues, it really boils down to one thing: privacy is a human need. We need it on a physical, mental, spiritual, and emotional level. When we are denied privacy in any way, it is emotionally draining and abusive. We need privacy, even if we don't know it. We may not have the words, but we know what it feels like when our privacy is invaded and violated. Privacy is not about secrets; it is about protection. It's not a crutch to help people nurse secret sins or unhealthy habits. Don't be tempted to use privacy as an excuse to do or cover up anything physically or spiritually destructive or harmful.

When you're in doubt about who to tell your business to, make some onion rings. It will help you clear your head. Be intentional, and plan your privacy. The benefits are sweet. There's accountability in privacy. Someone on your onion ring can get you back on track when you're living dangerously—or using privacy as a cover-up for unhealthy choices. The consequences of not managing your onion rings are disappointments, lost relationships, excessive drama, and regrets.

# Conclusion

Use your onion rings to manage your privacy expectations of others. Not all of your good friends should become your confidants. If you force them, you set them up to fail. Be careful not to snub friends who are not confidant material. They're in your life for a reason. Everyone in your life has a role to play in a particular *season* and for a particular *purpose* of your life (Ecclesiastes 3:1).

The government doesn't make onion rings—it makes privacy laws. Privacy laws are standardized personal boundaries the government designed to protect us—from ourselves and from others. For this reason, the government manages laws—while you manage your onion rings. It makes, interprets, and enforces privacy laws to keep individuals, the government, businesses, and organizations accountable—and from violating your privacy. Think about it. If you didn't first have privacy rights or the right *to be let alone* (which is your fundamental human right), you wouldn't have the many civil liberties and freedoms you enjoy today. Civil liberties protect your phone conversations, opinions, thoughts, and freedom of speech as well as your right to vote, protest, practice your religion, marry whomever you choose, reproduce, and have a fair trial, among many other rights. These liberties also provide protection from being oppressed by any individual or business more powerful, influential, or dominant than you. And your liberties protect you from oppression from your country or state authorities through wrongful arrests and privacy violations, including illegal searches and seizures, surveillance, entry into your home, and interference in your personal documents, belongings, and activities. But civil liberties are limited to your country or state. Your privacy rights are broader than your civil liberties. It's a human right and—with minor variations—extends universally beyond your state or country. If you ignore privacy needs or take them away, you strip away a person's spiritual, mental, emotional, and physical well-being—their dignity, trust, sense of safety, relationship, reputation, and honor—although it may not look like you are.

If you don't respect your own privacy and that of your close personal relationships, it's tough to see why it's important. If you don't respect privacy at work, you might be setting yourself up to become a statistic—as the employee, volunteer, or manager who led the organization to ruinous lawsuits. I believe that a great steward of his or her own privacy makes an outstanding steward of personal information in church and out of church. It all starts with you.

You don't need to have it all figured out; just start. Are you a good confidant to people close to you? What about people at church? Are you in the children, senior, nursing home/hospital visitation, or other ministries? Start with one group. Make a big deal of privacy. Hold each other accountable and demonstrate your accountability. Trust me, the church will catch on—one ministry at a time. Before you know it, your church will be inspiring other churches in the community. God sees his church as one church. If one church fails, all churches have failed. The church is a community, a family. We're all in the same boat, calling on the same name when the storm rages.

> *Your adversary the devil prowls around like a roaring lion, seeking someone to devour.*
> (1 Peter 5:8 ESV)

The church cares about people. If the church wasn't about people, there'd be no church. Jesus said each person is the church. You're called to care. I'm called to care. Together, we care collectively for people's needs. If the church turns a blind eye to privacy concerns, is it truly caring for the people? You may not know where to start with privacy laws, but you're not powerless. Refer to *Church Privacy Team*. That's your manual. Help the church make its own rules. Start where you are—right here and right now. Create an environment that'll meet people's need for privacy. Then make sure you align those needs with regulatory and legal requirements.

Okay, let me slow down a bit. How does this look in reality? Set up a complaint process to give the church a chance to resolve issues first so the person violated won't feel they're not being heard—this takes care of their initial emotional and psychological needs. Then solve the problem with guidance from regulations so the person won't resort to filing a lawsuit as their first recourse. Listen to people more and handle their complaints with understanding. That's what corporations do. Some complaints may sound unrelated to privacy. But if you read between the lines, you may find that a privacy need wasn't met or, worse, was violated.

Sister Bodil took the hit, but we're all guilty. Her case has forever changed her church and surrounding churches. I'd like to see it change you and your church community. The General Data Protection Regulation (GDPR) and the California Consumer Privacy Act (CCPA) are some of the strictest laws in the history of privacy (at the time I wrote this book). Their enforcement went into effect in 2018 and 2020, respectively. Since 2016, many states and countries have updated their privacy laws. Their privacy laws are now more stringent. As with Sister Bodil in 1998, I believe that history will repeat itself in the church, especially with more churches now online and processing more of their members' personal information than ever. With privacy laws mushrooming everywhere, privacy lawsuits might be coming for your church or one near you. Relaxing about privacy is risky. Individual church members having a brush with the law reflects badly on the church as a body. That's not good publicity. It's time we decided that we, as the church, will not get dinged again and end up going through destructive cycles.

What do you want for yourself when it comes to privacy? Are you ready for a change? What can you do to be saved or to save someone else from

# Church Privacy 101

privacy violations? I suggest you revisit some of your favorite topics in this book and then recommend it to your church family.

Erastus was the director of public works. Paul was a tentmaker. Dorcas was a seamstress and designer. Deborah was a judge. Esther was a queen. Joseph and Daniel were like governors or VPs, if you will. They used what they had where they were planted at a particular time in history to serve. I'm a privacy expert and a reader-proclaimed privacy prophet. Hilarious! I'm using what I have—I'm an avid observer of the workings of churches and how they handle information. I want to see churches succeed in their calling and purpose as well as in managing privacy requirements and people's needs. Now that you've read this book, what's next? And what would you like to achieve? A better-managed private life for you and others? What would you like your church to achieve? Equipping you to give people more assurance of privacy?

Technology is not the only area where privacy issues exist. I typically save any mention of technology for last; otherwise, a church leader will quickly advise me to talk to their IT team. You can achieve privacy in the digital and cyber realms. Use apps or platforms that respect privacy, and do not give tech firms or their third-party companies uncontrolled access to personal information, which, if disclosed or stolen, could negatively impact the lives of your members. Learn how to customize your privacy and cookie settings. Don't blithely accept all cookie settings; tailor the settings to your needs, or don't use the site if you can't adjust the settings. You have a choice. You should use your choices to protect yourself, your loved ones, and those whose personal information is in your care.

Laws and regulations exist to protect our dignity, rights, freedoms, and liberties. Help people and your church leadership make better decisions about privacy. Church leaders and congregants may not immediately receive your efforts with open arms—don't worry about being misunderstood. Love

Conclusion

them and let God handle how they react. Just be obedient, do your part with humility, and wait for another opportunity.

> *Obedience is better than sacrifice.*
> (1 Samuel 15:22 NLT)

## The Evolution of Privacy Laws

The IRS penned the "Tax Guide for Churches and Religious Organizations."[1] It's all spelled out. No guessing there. Privacy regulators do the same for private citizens. They'll hold the church responsible if it violates privacy. Remember, your church can't plead ignorance.

Laws and regulators won't always win. Even the IRS doesn't always win. But you shouldn't relax. As privacy laws evolve, they're becoming similar to tax laws in terms of stringency and enforcement. Like privacy laws, tax laws don't differ in enforcement whether the violator is an individual tax preparer, an accounting firm, or a mini, mega, or gigachurch. Like tax laws, privacy laws should strike fear in your heart. Unlike taxes, however, you don't get to split up your compliance responsibilities quarterly or, in some cases, wait until spring. Privacy rules are enforced 365 days a year. Privacy needs attention 24/7 because a breach or violation of privacy can happen at any time.

The law made an example of Sister Bodil Lindqvist. That's an experience that would test anyone's faith. But I'm glad that, although hard-pressed, she wasn't crushed (2 Corinthians 4:9). I pray the same for those who brought the suit. Sister Bodil is thriving and living a fulfilling life as a volunteer in her church and community. As an individual, you have a duty to honor, respect, and preserve the privacy of others. It's not only the church as a body that has a duty. As a worker or volunteer at church, you have responsibilities to meet people's needs—just like in the song "Love God Love People" by Danny Gokey.

> *No one hates his own body but feeds and cares for it,*
> *just as Christ cares for the church.*
> (Ephesians 5:29 NLT)

A scribe asked Jesus, out of the Ten Commandments, which one he should most focus on.

He was asking, "Which commandment is the most important of all?" (Mark 12:28 ESV)

Jesus said, "And you must love the LORD your God with all your heart, all your soul, all your mind, and all your strength. The second is equally important: 'Love your neighbor as yourself.' No other commandment is greater than these" (Mark 12:30–31 NLT).

On being a good neighbor to others, Jesus concluded the story of the good Samaritan with the question, "Which of these three do you think was a neighbor to the man who fell into the hands of robbers?" (Luke 10:36)

Unsure if this was one of Jesus' trick questions, someone slowly put up his hand. "The expert in the law replied, 'The one who had mercy on him.' Jesus told him, 'Go and do likewise'" (Luke 10:37).

I hope you'll join me in protecting privacy and spreading love. Be a good privacy neighbor to others and show privacy mercy. *Go and do likewise.*

If you need more guidance on church privacy, the companion course and the book *Church Privacy Team* are great for teaching individuals and church groups. You can find out more in the Connect with Grace Beyond the Page section. And check out the excerpt from *Church Privacy Team* at the back of this book. After the Privacy Prayer in the next section, you can find out how to reach me. Please stay in touch. I have so much to share. And I'm excited to share it with you. I look forward to hearing from you soon.

# Conclusion

*Charity begins at home, and justice begins next door.*
(Charles Dickens)

# PRIVACY Prayer

*Grace g*

> This is the confidence we have in approaching God: that if we ask anything according to his will, he hears us. (1 John 5:14)

**Help me understand that sometimes it's a blessing not to know somebody else's business.**

Dear God,

As I volunteer in the church, work for the church, or serve in leadership roles in church, help me look for little blocks of time to be still before you so I don't overload and crash.

Help me be intentional about my privacy (including my alone time) so that I make better choices.

Remind me that privacy is what allows me to reflect, regroup, reenergize, and spend quality time with you.

Help me use my privacy thermostat the right way with people—not on low or high all the time, which is ineffective.

Teach me how to manage my relationships with the use of onion rings. My friendships will be healthier and last longer, and I'll be less likely to cause hurt with the decisions I make.

Dear God, help me to not try to control other people's onion rings by wanting to be on theirs.

Help me realize that even if someone didn't make the cut in my onion, it's not a sign that they are unfit as a friend. They are simply not who you led me to put on my onion rings.

Help me remember that asking for privacy doesn't mean I shouldn't share or that I'll never confide in others under other circumstances. Give me the courage to discuss my concerns with a confidant. Help me be a confidant to someone in need, and show me who is a great confidant for me.

Scan Here for More Information

© GRACE BUCKLER 2023 | ALL RIGHTS RESERVED.

ChurchPrivacyBookSeries.com | GraceBuckler.com | NadPublishing.com

Help me remember that social media, public ambitions, or events are not more important than protecting people's private lives or needs. After all, caring for people is our mission. Respecting privacy is a gift we can give to others. I pray that all the organizations that have my personal information are doing what I would do for others, protecting and respecting my personal information. Guide me to be a change agent by giving me the strength to defend the rights of the poor and needy and those who need privacy (Proverbs 31:8).

Lord, help me treat other folks' privacy and personal information like the valued possessions that they are. Without this precious information, our church cannot carry out all its missions. Help us as the church to understand that the personal information we've been given belongs to the person who entrusted it to us and should be handled with the utmost care. Help me do what is just and right (Jeremiah 22:3) to meet the needs of others, even when nobody is watching, and even when folks don't know or understand their privacy rights.

I want to be a friend and an encourager to someone in need from my heart, not out of selfish ambition (Philippians 2:3). You said, "Mind your own business" (1 Thessalonians 4:11). I will not gossip about others' personal information. Forgive me for looking the other way when someone was mishandling somebody else's personal information and privacy.

Forgive me for trying to extract salacious details before I extended help to a person who was terribly hurt due to bad news or a traumatic situation. Help me not to ask why and make someone feel worse when they say they need privacy.

Forgive my hurt pride when somebody was conscious enough about what they needed to say, "I need privacy." Even if they didn't say it, forgive me for ignoring the signals just because I wanted things my way.

Forgive me for being insensitive when someone was still healing and the time was not right for them to share their struggles with me.

> I understand that I am your church. Help me to be a solution to the privacy concerns that people have. Help me be obedient to the governing privacy authorities (Romans 13:1–7). Forgive me of the sin of negligence with personal information.

© GRACE BUCKLER 2023 | ALL RIGHTS RESERVED.

ChurchPrivacyBookSeries.com | GraceBuckler.com | NadPublishing.com

> Forgive me if I've boasted that my life is an open book or that I had nothing to hide to make the point that other people shouldn't need privacy.

Forgive me for prying and not praying for them.

Forgive me for not sending a card or text to let someone know they were loved because they turned down my request to visit them. Forgive me for being stuck on wanting to talk or visit. Clearly, I did not do to others what I wanted others to do to me (Matthew 7:12).

Teach me that flowers, a helium balloon, a card, and my warm thoughts left at someone's door or at a hospital lobby can ignite a smile, healing, and hope—even if I'm not allowed to see it in person (Proverbs 3:27). Heal my frustration when people I've tried to help didn't cooperate with how, when, and why I wanted to help them. They may have just needed privacy.

Give me the wisdom and courage to express my frustration without tearing the person down or divulging things about their life because I'm upset.

Help me understand that Romans 14 is simply saying I should pursue peace and things that build up, not things that tear down. Also help me understand that I shouldn't let my good choices cause spiritual harm to others but walk in love.

Be with all my friends and family members who are enduring their pains and hurts in private. Help me bear their burdens with them. Remind them they have people they can speak with (not necessarily me).

Provide what they need to feel safe or protected, to heal, to feel whole again. Let my prayers for them be out of love as I practice gentleness and self-control with joy and peace. I'm filled with kindness and goodness (Galatians 5:22–23), not for appreciation or gratitude or praise, but according to your guidance, not mine. I pray that you, Lord, who sees my heart and what I do in private, will respond accordingly (Matthew 6:4).

Help me and the church plan ahead, be educated on privacy, and be diligent about privacy and information protection—doing whatever our responsibilities are so you'll add to our talents (Matthew 25:27–29). Help us hire professionals who are competent and ethical and who respect you, God—who won't cut corners to get us glitzy results that you're not pleased with.

*In Jesus' name I pray. Amen!*

More on this topic in Grace's book *Church Privacy 101*. Sign up for more freebies, news, and alerts at ChurchPrivacyBookSeries.com.

© GRACE BUCKLER 2023 | ALL RIGHTS RESERVED.

ChurchPrivacyBookSeries.com | GraceBuckler.com | NadPublishing.com

# Church Privacy Team Introduction

*To one who has faith, no explanation is necessary.*
*To one without faith, no explanation is possible.*

—Thomas Aquinas

## Protect Your Privacy

In 2019, St. Ambrose Catholic Parish Church in Ohio hired Marous Brothers Construction to do work at the parish. Every month, the church paid the company an installment via wire transfer and received confirmation from the bank. Two months later, St. Ambrose received a troubling call. According to Father Bob Stec, Marous Brothers wanted to know why the church had not paid the installment for the last two months, totaling approximately $1,750,000. Father Stec was confused. "This was shocking news to us, as we have been very prompt on our payments every month and have received all the appropriate confirmations from the bank that the wire transfers of to Marous were executed/confirmed."[1]

The church called the FBI to help figure out why the contractor had not received the payments the church had wired to the company's account. After an investigation, the FBI found that there was nothing wrong at Marous Brothers Construction; the issue was with St. Ambrose. Two St. Ambrose email accounts had been hacked.[2] According to news sources, it appeared that St. Ambrose workers may have clicked on emails or attachments that looked legitimate but were in fact designed to give identity thieves access to the parish network. Unnoticed, the hackers monitored private emails within St. Ambrose and stole enough personal information about Marous Brothers to open a bogus bank account in the company's name. By impersonating the owners of the two email addresses, they convinced other members of St. Ambrose that Marous Brothers had changed the bank account St. Ambrose should use to wire the payments. The thieves then made a phone call to St. Ambrose to inquire about a purported late payment. An unsuspecting worker who answered the call remitted the $1.75 million to the forged account without first verifying it with other contacts at Marous Brothers Construction. Father Stec painfully concluded the story of what happened: "The was then swept out by the perpetrators before anyone knew what had happened."[3]

Situations such as these are common. Churches are frequent victims of cyberattacks, and church members are subject to theft and fraud. But if you think a cyber thief is only after your church's , you're mistaken. Not only does vanish from virtual collection plates, but criminals also monetize the personal information they steal. For example, church members' passwords, names, credit card numbers, and other financial and personal information are illegally collected and sold.[4] Identity thieves don't waste any information. They steal but also violate privacy.

Long before cybercriminals steal , they first violate the privacy of their victims. How? Hackers violate privacy by compromising passwords and accessing and reading personal emails of the email account owner to find out about the business affairs of the church, including employees, roles, vendors, and people with authority and access to . Besides stealing identities, reading personal conversations, and stealing financial account passwords, some hackers' objective is to expose churches by leaking confidential documents, clergy's emails, and other personal information that could embarrass the leadership and disrupt church services. These are all privacy issues. Our personal infor-

Church Privacy Team: Introduction

mation is now widely accessible electronically. These days, thieves can steal more personal information with a computer than with a weapon. Keyboards can do more damage than bombs. And what's scary is, your church could be next.

> *If you are working on something that you really care about,*
> *you don't have to be pushed. The vision pulls you.*
> (Steve Jobs)

## Should Your Church Take Privacy Seriously?

Protecting and preserving the privacy of your church members is imperative. But doing so goes beyond faith; it takes planning, strategy, information, and special tools and techniques. If you think your church has more important issues to worry about or that privacy protection isn't an issue your church needs to consider, you may think differently after what happened at St. Ambrose and after you read the rest of this book.

St. Ambrose was not an isolated incident. For hackers to gain access to a computer, all they have to do is persuade or deceive the account owner into giving them personal information. Once they have that, they can access the account or impersonate the user, stealing what church folks often shrug off as unimportant but is even more important than —personal information. Control of personal information allows for a myriad of crimes to be committed, as the following examples illustrate:

1. Human error led the Southern Baptist International Mission Board to lose control over the personal information of thousands of its current and former employees in a massive privacy breach. Stolen information included names, contact information, and even some health information.[5]

# Church Privacy 101

2. At the First Presbyterian Church of Birmingham, malicious email attachments were opened by unsuspecting church workers, allowing hackers to take over the church computer system with CryptoLocker ransomware. The church was locked out of its records and was asked to pay a ransom in order to regain access.[6]

3. At the St. Pius X Catholic Church in Greensboro, North Carolina, criminals impersonated the email address of the priest in order to solicit church members and the public to buy iTunes gift cards.[7]

4. The Michigan Catholic Conference was robbed of personal information from its human resources and employee wage reporting system. Sensitive, personal information that could be quickly monetized by criminals included Social Security numbers, dates of birth, and addresses.[8]

5. At a cathedral in Des Moines, Iowa, $680,000 raised to support homeless and abused women vanished from the electronic collection plate.[9]

This list goes on and on, with *CBS News* reporting that the FBI has over four hundred active investigations into account takeover fraud and is opening new cases every week.

The information collected by churches is attractive to criminals because it's so lucrative. Personal information has more value than the actual equipment it's stored in, such as church monitors, cameras, and other electronics. Thieves can use or sell the personal information they obtain as is, or they can create or clone multiple accounts from one person's financial information.

On the dark web (the Internet's black market), personal information sells just like illegal substances. The going rate in 2021 for personal information is eye-opening:

## Church Privacy Team: Introduction

- cloned credit or debit card information: $25–$35

- credit card with account balance up to $5,000: $250+

- online payment gateways (i.e., Stripe, PayPal, and others): $50–$1,000, depending on account balance

- US Driver's License/ID: $100–$185, depending on the state

- passport: $1,500–$6,500, depending on the country

- health/medical record: up to $1,000 per record, depending on the health record details[10]

You simply don't know when a hacker is waiting for just one vulnerable church worker or a weakness in your church computer system. Any church worker who accidentally sends an email (with personal information) to the wrong person could be the cause of your church's data breach. But there's good news: identity theft is preventable, and churches can take concrete steps to protect their confidential data and the privacy of their church members. Because most data breaches are the result of human error, the best way to avoid identity theft is to train church employees, volunteers, and contract workers about information privacy.

Education, training, compliance, and best practices are not only the right thing to do, they also help prevent lawsuits and regulatory penalties and fines. Church members in the US have sued churches over privacy breaches and won. And even when members don't have the courage or legal right to sue, regulators in the state where your church is located can still sue on behalf of their residents who are impacted by the breach your church caused.

In Duncan v. Peterson, a minister, Richard Duncan, and Moody Church sued Erwin Lutzer, the senior pastor of the church, and Bervin Peterson, the chairman of the board of elders, for false light invasion of privacy. Snyder v.

## Church Privacy 101

Evangelical Orthodox Church involved the public dissemination of private information to a congregation despite a church official's promise not to do so.

Beyond this, your church's insurance company can decline coverage or file a lawsuit against the church depending on the situation. This can happen if the insurance company investigates and discovers the church could have prevented the breach or reported it sooner. Failure to protect against privacy breaches can be enormously expensive to your church. You don't have to become a privacy expert, but every minute you delay managing privacy could cost you thousands or—like St. Ambrose—even millions of dollars.

Besides the growing number of technology-related data breaches, *people* violate other people the worst: violations of privacy happen in non-technological church settings more frequently than you might think. Ministers, pastors, bishops, deacons, priests, and other members of the clergy who disclose personal information gleaned during private counseling sessions, for example, can face legal repercussions. Lawsuits by church members against other members and church leadership are becoming more prevalent, with *The Wartburg Watch* noting that "people have brought an increasing number of lawsuits against pastors for invasion of privacy and other tort claims arising out of the disclosure of confidential information by a pastor or other church official. The result of these suits has brought recognition that the obligation to maintain confidentiality is not only a moral obligation, but also often a legal one."[11]

The increase in lawsuits is partly related to the fact that privacy laws are mushrooming now more than ever. Many states now treat invasion of privacy as grounds for liability. But the concept of an invasion of privacy covers a lot of ground and can involve one or more of the following:

- intruding into someone's solitude or peace and quiet

- publicly exposing private facts about another person

- using another person's image, name, or resemblance without permission

- publicly misrepresenting someone or putting the person in a false light

Knowing the many different ways that a church can accidentally cross the line is increasingly difficult to grasp without the proper information, insight, or training. But once a lawsuit is filed against your church, it becomes part of the online public record. It doesn't matter if the plaintiff wins or loses the case—the church bears the most losses in the long run. Negative publicity is not good for any church, especially if it can be avoided. In a famous case from the 1980s, a single mom sued the Church of Christ for invasion of privacy, intentional infliction of emotional distress, and other causes. The story gained national attention and made the *New York Times* and *The Phil Donahue Show*.[12]

> *Even if you are on the right track,*
> *you'll get run over if you just sit there.*
> (Will Rogers)

## Who Is Responsible for Church Privacy?

Whether it's a hacker breaking into church systems due to weak security and inadequate privacy training or a preacher violating the confidentiality of members, a church should be more concerned about trust than almost any other organization. And as an organization, all of its members are responsible for privacy. But it should have one person who is solely accountable for privacy. Churches must take an organizational-wide approach to privacy.

No matter who encounters personal information, the church is ultimately responsible for the privacy protection of that information and anyone who works with it.

Privacy requirements extend to church members, workers, vendors, contractors, and volunteers collecting personal information on behalf of the church to support its operation. To be clear, this is not just about entering data into a church computer or collecting it online via a website. This also happens when people working on behalf of the church interact with someone one-on-one, ask for personal information, and write it down. For example, an EU court ruled that the Jehovah's Witnesses were illegally collecting personal information obtained from the people they spoke to during their door-to-door preaching because they didn't obtain consent before doing so.[13]

You may not be the Jehovah's Witnesses, but does your church organize community outreach? Do you evangelize on the streets? Do you engage in door-knocking or in other forms of community engagement? Do you obtain consent or permission before you take people's names, addresses, phone numbers, emails, ages, or personal information about them or their family members?

Do you know the rules regarding privacy that apply in the situations above? How would it make you feel to discover your church is guilty of privacy transgressions similar to those that have plagued larger corporations? Odds are your church is making similar mistakes. More than two-thirds of all countries (137) currently have privacy laws, and states are rapidly following suit.[14]

California enacted one of the most stringent privacy laws in the world, the California Consumer Privacy Act (CCPA). These strict laws are motivated by people's increased use of the Internet and increased adoption of new technology products and services. Prevalent use of technology presents opportunities for businesses to over-collect, overuse, over-retain, and over-

## Church Privacy Team: Introduction

expose personal information with little limitation. This applies not just to businesses but churches as well.

The scary trend of some laws and regulations is that they now apply to organizations regardless of where they're located. Your church doesn't have to be in California or the European Union to be subject to their laws—if you have members or people who are residents in those jurisdictions interacting with your church online, their laws could apply to you. Have you noticed that with the rise of virtual worship, several activities spanning membership, donations, tithes, baptisms, and confessions require personal information to be processed? With some churches inviting participants from all over the world, you should be concerned about how privacy laws and regulations in other jurisdictions may apply to you. With churches now processing personal information of members in different states and countries, there may be more laws or regulations that apply to your church now than ever before.

This might sound like an expensive proposition. It's not. I will outline a bootstrap approach that shows how all churches can get started the right way regardless of budget constraints. Managing privacy is not all about big budgets or hyped projects aimed at making a handful of people title rich. It's about instilling a compassionate culture and influence, communication, and good practices that are consistent with the beliefs and values within the church. How? Your church's privacy mission is helping others walk in physical, mental, emotional, and spiritual freedom—by respectfully and empathetically walking a mile in their shoes when responding to their need for privacy.

Of course, church culture can make privacy challenging. Your church may never make the list of "100 Best Places to Work," but it may be the best place to work. You work together, pray together, worship together, and make a difference in the world together. Team relationships are sturdier because people rarely quit those jobs. This is good! The downside is, churches don't want to hurt people's feelings, so they don't hold them accountable enough (even major corporations have a hard time with holding business partners, vendors, employees, and others accountable). But risks and growth require you to show responsible love. You can't achieve privacy in your church without accountability: it's ingrained in privacy principles.

For instance, imagine a worker has turned in her resignation or no longer wants to volunteer at your church. What happens to the loads of personal information she's processed? Do you have an exit interview conducted to see what data she may have at work or at home or what she needs to delete, shred, or return? This is not just a consideration for commercial businesses. You need established processes for departing employees and volunteers. To comply with your privacy obligations, you need to make accountability your policy.

> *The Bible tells us to love our neighbors, and also to love our enemies; probably because generally they are the same people.*
> (G. K. Chesterton)

## What Can You Do about Church Privacy?

Despite the profusion of stories about the serious threat info-thirsty hackers pose, many churchgoers remain oblivious and indifferent to the need for privacy protection. They are like the bystanders in the days of Noah who saw a man building an ark but, rather than preparing for the rain, continued eating and drinking (Matthew 24:38). Don't make the mistake of assuming that thieves are only targeting the big churches or companies like Equifax or Home Depot. Scammers on the hunt for personal information will not respect the size or innocence of your church. They are on the lookout for per-

## Church Privacy Team: Introduction

sonal information and will glean it from any source that is careless enough to divulge it. And if anything goes awry, a church faces the same liabilities as a corporation—this includes lawsuits, hefty fines, regulatory penalties, imprisonment, a wrecked reputation, and loss of trust, members, and partners.

Your church is ripe for criminals to prey upon the personal information in your charge. Some hackers belong to international consortiums like Evil Corp., a Russian hacking group that locates and attacks weak Wi-Fi connection spots. But more likely than not, your data breach will occur closer to home. Some data thieves are in your church neighborhood. Some have volunteered or worked at your church, visited your church, hugged you, or shaken your hand. And when church employees work from home, it requires even more care and diligence because human error is the cause of most data breaches. Technology is not the problem most of the time. The errors that insiders make can lead to legal battles that can drain your treasury or threaten projects and your overall mission. Awareness and training are crucial.

What can you do? Get to know your privacy obligations. Formulate a good strategy and gather expert advice. Think of the technology and processes your members' personal information goes through like doors. Each piece of personal information your church collects, even if it's stored for later use, creates an opening for many threats. And just like a door, it won't lock itself. A door needs additional security for restricting access—bolts, locks, or alarms—so be sure to check your church's privacy doors. Are they locked? Do the people you assign to handle personal information know about best privacy practices? Are they trained? To restrict access to personal information and protect the members you serve, you must act *now*.

*Church Privacy Team* is designed to help you identify the types of privacy you must preserve, give you protective measures to implement, and teach you how to manage the personal information with which you've been entrusted. Every step you take and every set of activities you apply from this book will help you secure many vulnerable doors that threaten valuable personal information. This book will help your congregation or ministry, whether it is a small prayer circle or a large gathering. You'll be able to assess the ways in which you're vulnerable to privacy breaches or violations and learn how to prevent them.

It is time for all churches to recognize the importance of protecting privacy. Doing the right thing before it's required is the best policy and the best privacy practice. I realize that privacy can be a difficult conversation to have, especially in church circles and even among individuals. People can be disinterested, nonchalant, and dismissive. They may even accuse the prudent of being unreasonably paranoid or self-centered.

But even beyond their legal obligations, churches have a theological imperative to respond to privacy concerns. As the parable of the lost sheep (Luke 15:4) suggests, if even one sheep out of a hundred complains that his privacy has been violated, a caring shepherd seeks to help resolve his concerns. The shepherd goes after the sheep. The individual privacy needs of every member of the flock are important; it doesn't matter if the other ninety-nine sheep do not feel that their privacy is violated. A good shepherd does not judge the one that exercises their right to speak up. (Indeed, 1 Corinthians 6:5–7 says you should appoint the right people to handle complaints and put processes in place so concerns don't end up in court.) Still, a shepherd is not able to control what the sheep do. What you can control is first understanding what privacy is about, then doing what laws and regulations say is best to do. In this way, you can ensure you're equipped to go after and rescue the sheep that has lost their privacy.

Church Privacy Team: Introduction

> *Who is wise and understanding among you?*
> *Let them show it by their good life, by deeds*
> *done in the humility that comes from wisdom.*
> (James 3:13)

# How to Use This Book

*Church Privacy Team* is an actionable companion book to *Church Privacy 101* that will allow you to get relevant information and make the hard decisions about privacy. It's a step-by-step guide designed to offer you practical solutions, let you enjoy significant privacy improvements, and help you understand diverse privacy matters so your church can retain the trust of its members and community. Each chapter explores and breaks down a privacy topic and includes actionable steps you and your church can take. Starting with a narrative of a particular privacy concern or topic, each chapter also contains activities that offer you opportunities to reflect on where you stand on action items, allow you to record questions as they come up in your assessment and implementation, and help you plan your next move. After reading about each topic, you'll have a checklist to help you assess what your church has already done about that specific topic and what you could be working on next to reduce or control privacy risks. You'll grow used to planning, execution, accountability, and documentation in order to implement these concepts.

Together, *Church Privacy 101*, *Church Privacy Team*, and the companion privacy course will give you and your church all the information, skills, and guidelines needed to better protect privacy. You can find information about the privacy course on my website: www.LearnChurchPrivacy.com.

This book is for small, medium, large, mega, and gigachurches. It's for all churches regardless of how members meet, their location, or the extent of their online activity. It's for churches and ministry managers, ministry leaders, chief ministry officers, chief financial officers, chief operations officers, and church staff, including other clergy, leadership, administrative staff, missionaries, and counselors. It's also ideal for volunteers, freelancers, contractors, vendors, and other church workers. Regardless of their title, those in church who process people's personal information digitally, physically, verbally, and otherwise need this book.

As Matthew 6:34 suggests, responding to the need for privacy today is better and easier than solving a breach tomorrow. Don't put it off. This doesn't mean you have to do everything all at once—as the saying goes, "Don't try to boil the ocean." When applying this to good privacy practices, you're better off dividing up the seemingly overwhelming privacy ocean into one cupful at a time with the limited resources you've got than trying to deal with the entire ocean of requirements and problems all at once. If you follow this book one step at a time, applying privacy in your church will become simpler and rewarding. It will help you see what's important and assess where you are currently, and it will show you how prepared or unprepared you are to face your members and regulators should they come knocking with privacy concerns. It's also designed to help you prioritize and focus on a few critical tasks so you can start achieving them today. I'm right here for you! With that said, grab some coffee or whatever beverage you drink at this time of the day, and let's get started!

*We are what we repeatedly do.*
*Excellence, then, is not an act, but a habit.*
(Will Durant, *The Story of Philosophy*)

# Further Reading

1. Focus on The Family, "Social Media: Signs of Negative Impact on Marriage," https://www.focusonthefamily.com/family-qa/social-media-signs-of-negative-impact-on-marriage/.

2. Family Life, "4 Ways to Avoid Being a Social Media Marriage Casualty," https://www.familylife.com/articles/topics/life-issues/challenges/media-and-entertainment/4-ways-to-avoid-being-a-social-media-marriage-casualty/.

3. Perspectives of Troy, "Is Social Media Ruining Your Marriage? (Signs to Watch Out For)," https://www.perspectivesoftroy.com/2020/10/06/is-social-media-ruining-your-marriage-signs-to-watch-out-for.

4. McKinley Irvin, "Effects of Social Media Use (and Misuse) on Marriages & Relationships," https://www.mckinleyirvin.com/resources/digital-divorce-a-guide-for-social-media-digital/how-social-media-affects-marriage/.

5. Only You Forever, "Social Media Is Destroying Your Marriage," https://www.onlyyouforever.com/social-media-is-destroying-your-marriage/.

6. Robert P. Chappell Jr., *Child Identity Theft: What Every Parent Needs to Know* (Lanham, Maryland: Rowman & Littlefield, 2012).

# Connect with Grace beyond the Page

While Grace partners with organizations to achieve legal and regulatory compliance, train employees, and develop content, she is also available for the following favorites:

*Keynotes, Talks, and Workshops*

Grace delivers targeted content for groups and breakout workshop sessions that speak to church members, employees, and anyone in a ministry facilitator or other leadership role. Perfect for conferences, retreats, conventions, and meetings.

*Leadership Privacy Development Training*

In this lecture, Grace uncovers the potential of leaders and teaches them how to recognize and minimize privacy risks. She unravels the key principles that align their vision and mission to help leaders grow in how they care for people.

# Connect with Grace beyond the Page

## *Organizational Privacy Consulting*

Grace gives churches and ministries the tools, strategic direction, and tailored and customized solutions to help them reach their full privacy potential.

## *Divinity Schools, Colleges, Universities, Seminaries, and Associations*

Grace gives talks under different types of budgets and programs including Training and Development, Learning Materials, Continuing Education, and Speaker Budgets.

## *Privacy Concierge Coaching*

Grace maintains a select portfolio for leaders who need one-on-one coaching to maintain their own privacy balance while leading their church organizations.

## *See What Grace Is Up To*

Request Grace to speak at your next event or for a media interview. Visit GraceBuckler.com/Speaking.

"Absolutely wonderful. I didn't realize how much I didn't know about privacy in the church! It's amazing as well as warm, educational, empowering, and relatable. Her humor keeps it interesting."

"She's practical, candid, affirming, and on point with biblical and life applications. Where was Grace when I was in seminary? It's never too late to unlearn the harmful practices I've learned for many years. I definitely wouldn't have thought about privacy in this way."

"Brilliant illustrations and thought-provoking real-world examples. I felt closer to our mission as a church thanks to her passion for fostering more trust, lasting relationships, and genuine fellowship in the church."

Scan this QR code for more information on courses.

# About Grace

Grace Buckler is a recognized privacy, data protection, cybersecurity, and in-demand global privacy author, advisor, expert, and speaker. She has presented numerous topics on privacy for corporations, associations, business groups, colleges, universities, governments, and youth organizations worldwide. Grace is the founder of The Privacy Advocate, a data privacy consulting firm. Her fifteen-year career budded in the federal market where she served as a consultant and subject-matter expert both in the US and overseas. As an award-winning consultant for the United States Secret Service, Grace also served numerous federal entities with acknowledged excellence, including the Department of Health and Human Services (HHS), the Transportation Security Administration (TSA), the Defense Information Security Agency (DISA), the Department of Justice (DOJ), the Department of Homeland Security (DHS), the Department of Defense (DoD), and the Defense Counterintelligence and Security Agency (DCSA). Seven years of

# Church Privacy 101

her career have been spent serving diverse markets, including Fortune 500 companies, startups, and nonprofits. She has authored articles for industry journals, functioned as an expert reviewer for US and European books in her industry, and served as faculty and an advisory board member for the largest global privacy association, the International Association of Privacy Professionals. Grace speaks regularly as a privacy subject matter expert for Startup Law 101 Series.

Grace is a go-to privacy advisor, coach, and instructor for many leading organizations, law firms, churches, educational institutions, religious organizations, and clergy who desire to improve or master privacy risk management, gain members' trust, and achieve legal and regulatory compliance. In addition to her experience in cybersecurity, data privacy, and technical communication, Grace graduated summa cum laude from Albany Law School and holds a wealth of industry certifications including the Certified Information Systems Security Professional (CISSP), Certified Information Systems Auditor (CISA), Certification in Risk and Information Systems Control (CRISC), Project Management Professional (PMP), Certified Information Privacy Professional (European Data Protection Law & Practice), Certified Information Privacy Professional (US Corporate Privacy Law), Certified Information Privacy Professional (Government), Certified Information Privacy Manager (CIPM), and Certified Data Privacy Solutions Engineer (CDPSE).

When not wrangling privacy issues, Grace is a foodie! Some of her favorite street foods include Puerto Rican elote, West African boiled peanuts and roasted maize with plums, and Belgian waffles with strawberries and cream. She enjoys theater, traveling, discovering quaint towns, and trying new recipes from all parts of the world.

# Ways You Can Engage with Grace throughout the Year

## Speaking and Consulting Programs

7 Distorted Privacy Beliefs

Take Grace to Work Day

Take Grace to Church Day

Leadership Privacy Makeover

Grace, Teach My Parents Privacy

Single and Private

Privacy and Purity

Married and Private

Privacy with Kids and Teens

Senior and Private

Privacy That Heals

Startup and Small Business Privacy

Beyond Privacy

Tough Questions, Tough Conversations

For information, visit GraceBuckler.com/Speaking.

# Church Privacy 101

**Stay in the Loop:** Subscribe to Grace's emails for more spicy church privacy musings and for a chance to receive a free virtual privacy course ($699 value). Visit ChurchPrivacyBookSeries.com.

When you sign up, you'll also receive

- up-to-date info on her latest releases,

- downloads and other freebies when available (e.g., the world's first Privacy Prayer Poster), and

- information about when she's at a conference or church near you discussing privacy matters.

**Get a Free 15-Minute Live Privacy Breakfast with Grace:** This is a custom offer with a Q&A session ($499 value). It's for your church, your leadership, or individual ministry groups (singles, couples, teens, men, women, and seniors). This free gift is subject to availability. Send us your request via GraceBuckler.com/Speaking.

**Take Grace to Church Day:** You can take Grace to your church any day of the week. There's no place she'd rather be. Grace is available for your church's

- business meetings,

- employee retreats,

- organizational and operational consulting,

- leadership coaching,

- privacy courses, and

- privacy orientation for new employees.

## Ways You Can Engage with Grace throughout the Year

Book Grace at GraceBuckler.com/Speaking.

**Tough Questions, Tough Conversations:** Got embarrassing, burning, frustrating, and tough privacy questions? We can relate. Send questions to grace@gracebuckler.com with the subject "Tough Questions." Limited to two questions per person and also subject to availability.

# Available Anywhere Books and E-books Are Sold

**Bulk Orders:** You can purchase *Church Privacy: Who Cares? You!*; *Church Privacy 101*; and *Church Privacy Team* for church leadership and for different ministries in your church. Let your church and church bookstore know you need copies. You'll receive a discounted rate for bulk orders of 10 or more if you order at NADPublishing.com. You can also scan this QR code to save 30–40% on our books.

## Available Anywhere Books and E-books Are Sold

**Thoughts:** Did you enjoy this book? Was it helpful? Great, let's hear about it. One of your first steps in making a privacy difference starts here. That is, helping other people enjoy and learn from this content. Grace would appreciate you taking just a few minutes of your precious time to leave a review of this book—let Grace and other readers know what you enjoyed most, how it helped, and how you're applying or planning to apply your newfound knowledge. Imagine how many people you'd help by leaving a review on Amazon (even if you bought your book elsewhere).

**Your Bright Ideas:** Did you know you could email Grace and let her know your thoughts and the bright privacy ideas you've come up with that have helped you personally and at church? Also, if you'd like for Grace to feature your thoughts, experiences, and ideas in her next release or post, let us know, and we'll consider them based on availability.

Send emails to grace@gracebuckler.com.

# Special FREE Bonus Gift for You

To help you achieve more success, there are extra **BONUS GIFTS** for you at **ChurchPrivacyBookSeries.com**.

## Bonus Gifts:

Privacy Prayer

Onion Rings Privacy Template

7 Responses to Privacy Invaders

## Secure your spot for a free virtual course.

Scan the QR code below.

# Additional Training Resources

## Privacy Success for Church Volunteers and Employees

This resource provides secrets to turning volunteers into privacy allies who can protect your church and ministry from privacy violations and regulatory and legal issues. To access these quarterly tips, subscribe to the newsletter at ChurchPrivacyBookSeries.com.

*Photo Credit: The Climate Reality Project*

## NEW Church Privacy Team Course

Planning on reading *Church Privacy Team* next? Cool beans! Congrats! After you do, you will have a ton of questions and tough church privacy decisions to make, and you'll love to have Grace on your side for your church's privacy journey. Don't wait, friend. This course is the best news since *Church Privacy*

# Church Privacy 101

*Team* was penned. Join Grace in this fun and simple course. Let yourself be a beginner. Let Grace show you how to get it done every step of the way. Secure your spot at LearnChurchPrivacy.com or scan the QR code.

## NEW Expert Resources

Attend Grace's Church Privacy On Demand live privacy coaching. Wrangle privacy in church like a pro. And if your church would love to hack her caravan of phenomenal privacy experts, data protection specialists, and privacy lawyers in your area (including proven and trusted cybersecurity and insurance gurus), we'll provide suggestions to attendees.

Additional Training Resources

## Connect with Grace Online

Find Grace online and on social media. Help her protect privacy and spread love. Visit ChurchPrivacyBookSeries.com and GraceBuckler.com. Better yet, scan this QR code so you don't need to type. Get there quicker!

# Church Privacy Team

## *Introduction Notes*

1. Sam Bocetta, "How Hackers Emptied Church Coffers with a Simple Phishing Scam," *Dark Reading*, June 19, 2019, https://www.darkreading.com/network-and-perimeter-security/how-hackers-emptied-church-coffers-with-a-simple-phishing-scam/a/d-id/1334971.

2. Lindsey O'Donnell, "BEC Hack Cons Catholic Church Out of $1.75 Million," *Threatpost*, April 30, 2019, https://threatpost.com/bec-hack-cons-catholic-church/144212.

3. Bocetta, "How Hackers Emptied Church Coffers with a Simple Phishing Scam."

4. Armen Keteyian, "Hackers Hit Church's Collection Plate," *CBS News*, June 30, 2011, https://www.cbsnews.com/news/hackers-hit-churchs-collection-plate/.

5. Bob Allen, "Southern Baptist Mission Board Reports Data Breach," *Baptist News Global*, August 1, 2018, https://baptistnews.com/article/southern-baptist-mission-board-reports-data-breach/.

6. Mark Huffman, "Hackers Increasingly Target the Church Collection Plate," *Consumer Affairs*, January 26, 2015, https://www.consumeraffairs.com/news/hackers-increasingly-target-the-church-collection-plate-012615.html.

7. Adaure Achumba, "Triad Church Warns of Phishing Scam Asking for Gift Card Purchase," *WFMY News 2*, August 2, 2018, https://www.wfmynews2.com/article/news/local/triad-church-warns-of-phishing-scam-asking-for-gift-card-purchase/83-579667892.

8. "Information About Recent Cyber Attack and Data Breach," *Michigan Catholic Conference*, accessed April 27, 2023, https://www.micatholic.org/benefits/data-breach/.

9. Keteyian, "Hackers Hit Church's Collection Plate."

10. Zachary Ignoffo, "Dark Web Price Index 2021." *Privacy Affairs*, August 8, 2022, https://www.privacyaffairs.com/dark-web-price-index-2021/.

11. Dee Parsons, "Pastors Ignoring Confidentiality: Having Gospel Gossip Authority?" *The Wartburg Watch*, February 27, 2012, http://thewartburgwatch.com/2012/02/27/pastors-ignoring-confidentiality-having-gospel-gossip-authority/.

12. Steve Gardner, "Church of Christ on Trial and Donahue: Fornication Publicly Disclosed in the Disfellowship Process," *Authentic Theology*, January 8, 2020, https://authentictheology.com/2020/01/08/church-of-christ-on-trial-and-donahue-fornication-publicly-disclosed-in-the-disfellowship-process/.

13. Yun Chee Foo, "EU Court Says Jehovah's Witnesses Must Comply with Data Privacy Laws in Door-to-Door Preaching," *Reuters*, July 8, 2018, https://www.reuters.com/article/us-eu-data-jehovahwitnesses-idUSKBN1K01LJ.

14. "Data Protection and Privacy Legislation Worldwide," *UCTAD*, December 14, 2021, https://unctad.org/page/data-protection-and-privacy-legislation-worldwide.

# Notes

## Introduction

1. Melina, "Church Giving Statistics," BalancingEverything, updated May 20, 2023, https://balancingeverything.com/church-giving-statistics/.

2. Thomas Costello, "25 Church Statistics You Need to Know for 2021," *REACHRIGHT*, January 27, 2021, https://reachrightstudios.com/25-church-statistics-for-2021/.

3. Aaron Earls, "Americans Aren't Sure They Can Trust Pastors," Lifeway Research, November 11, 2019, https://research.lifeway.com/2019/11/11/americans-arent-sure-they-can-trust-pastors/.

4. Richard J. Krejcir, "Statistics on Why Churches Fail," Church Leadership, 2007, http://www.churchleadership.org/apps/articles/default.asp?articleid=42338.

5. Denis Kelleher, "After Safe Harbor: Is It Time to Close the Lindqvist Loophole?" IAPP, accessed July 17, 2023, https://iapp.org/news/a/after-safe-harbor-is-it-time-to-close-the-lindqvist-loophole/.

6. Maya Angelou, "Maya Angelou Quotes," Goodreads, accessed June 27, 2023, https://www.goodreads.com/quotes/7273813-do-the-best-you-can-until-you-know-better-then.

7. Ben Wolford, "What Is GDPR, the EU's New Data Protection Law?" GDPR.EU, accessed July 17, 2023, https://gdpr.eu/what-is-gdpr/.

## 1. A Church Lady Gets Sued Over Privacy

1. Wikipedia, s.v. "Catholic Catechesis," last modified July 15, 2023, https://en.wikipedia.org/wiki/Catholic_catechesis.

2. Criminal Proceedings against Bodil Lindqvist, Case C-101/01 (Court of Sweden, 2002), https://eur-lex.europa.eu/legal-content/EN/TXT/?uri=CELEX:62001CJ0101.

3. *Criminal Proceedings against Bodil Lindqvist*.

# Notes

4. *Criminal Proceedings against Bodil Lindqvist.*

5. Flora J. Garcia, "Bodil Lindqvist: A Swedish Churchgoer's Violation of the European Union's Data Protection Directive Should Be a Warning to U.S. Legislators," *Fordham Intellectual Property, Media and Entertainment Law Journal*, Vol. 15, No. 4 (2005), https://ir.lawnet.fordham.edu/cgi/viewcontent.cgi?article=1335&context=iplj.

6. *Criminal Proceedings against Bodil Lindqvist.*

7. European Court of Justice, 6 November 2003, Lindqvist (2003), http://www.ippt.eu/sites/ippt/files/2003/IPPT20031106_ECJ_Lindqvist.pdf.

8. European Commission, "What Constitutes Data Processing?" accessed February 2, 2024, https://commission.europa.eu/law/law-topic/data-protection/reform/what-constitutes-data-processing_en.

9. University of Michigan, "Case C-101/01: Criminal Proceedings against Bodil Lindqvist," accessed July 3, 2023, http://www-personal.umich.edu/~jdlitman/classes/cyber/cases/Lindqvist.pdf.

10. *Criminal Proceedings against Bodil Lindqvist.*

11. Robert Orben, "Robert Orben Quotes," Goodreads, accessed July 3, 2023, https://www.goodreads.com/quotes/76033-if-you-think-education-is-expensive-try-ignorance.

## 2. What Is Privacy?

1. Alan F. Westin, *Privacy and Freedom* (New York: Athaneum, 1967), 53.

2. Westin, *Privacy and Freedom* 35, 34.

3. *Merriam-Webster Dictionary*, s.v. "privacy," accessed June 28, 2023, https://www.merriam-webster.com/dictionary/privacy.

4. Daniel Solove, "Why Privacy Matters Even if You Have 'Nothing to Hide,'" *The Chronicles of Higher Education*, May 15, 2011, https://www.chronicle.com/article/why-privacy-matters-even-if-you-have-nothing-to-hide/.

5. William Shakespeare, *As You Like It*, eds. Barbara A. Mowat and Paul Werstine (New York: Simon and Schuster Paperbacks, 2019), 2.7.139.

6. Brian Stack, "Here's How Much Your Personal Information Is Selling for on the Dark Web," Experian, December 6, 2017, https://www.experian.com/blogs/ask-experian/heres-how-much-your-personal-information-is-selling-for-on-the-dark-web/.

7. Stack, "Here's How Much Your Personal Information Is Selling for on the Dark Web."

### *3. Five Things the Bible Says to Hush About*

1. Aaron Shust, interviewed by Kevin Krueger, "Going Deeper," WGTS, August 22, 2014, https://www.wgts919.com/podcast-breakaway/aaron-shust.

### *4. Managing Your Circle*

1. Idil Ahmed (@idillionaire), "Just because you don't share it on social media doesn't mean you're not up to big things. Live it and stay low key. Privacy is everything," Twitter, November 5, 2016, https://twitter.com/idillionaire/status/795016449915879424.

### *6. Confession Privacy Sacred Confidence*

1. Ellen K. Boegel, "The Seal of Confession and Mandatory Reporting: A Survey of State Laws," *America*, July 1, 2019, https://www.americamagazine.org/2019/07/01/mandatory-reporting-seal-confession-state-laws.

2. *TMZ*, "Catholic Church Cuts Confessions Amid Pandemic . . . Sacraments for Dying Only," April 12, 2020, https://www.tmz.com/2020/04/12/catholic-church-cancelling-confessionals-sacraments-dying-last-rites/.

3. Dorothy Cummings McLean, "Law Passes in Australia Requiring Priests to Break Seal of Confession, Bishop Protests," *LifeSiteNews*, June 12, 2018, https://www.lifesitenews.com/news/australia-passes-law-requiring-priests-to-break-seal-of-confession-bishop-p.

# Notes

## 7. Financial Privacy: Money Matters

1. ABC 13 *Eyewitness News*, "Houston Megachurch Pastor Kirbyjon Caldwell Sentenced to Prison for Investment Scheme," January 13, 2021, https://abc13.com/kirbyjon-caldwell-houston-indictment-megachurch/9631555/.

2. Kate Shellnutt, "Houston Pastor Pleads Guilty in $3.5M Bond Fraud Scheme Targeting Elderly," *Christianity Today*, March 17, 2020, https://www.christianitytoday.com/news/2020/march/houston-pastor-kirbyjon-caldwell-guilty-plea-bond-fraud-umc.html.

3. Chris Allen, "A Smart Person Learns from Their Mistakes. A Wise Person Learns from the Mistakes of Others," Simple Secrets, accessed July 17, 2023, https://simplesecrets.com/a-smart-person-learns-from-their-mistakes-a-wise-person-learns-from-the-mistakes-of-others/.

## 8. Personal Privacy: Emotional and Physical Well-Being

1. Tobias Kohler, "Erectile Dysfunction," Mayo Clinic, March 29, 2022, https://www.mayoclinic.org/diseases-conditions/erectile-dysfunction/diagnosis-treatment/drc-20355782.

## 9. Mental Health Privacy: The Illusion of Perfection

1. Mental Health First Aid USA, "Why Mental Health First Aid?" January 22, 2020, https://www.mentalhealthfirstaid.org/2020/01/why-mental-health-first-aid/.

2. Hannah Smothers, "18 Things You Should Never Say to Someone with Divorced Parents," *Cosmopolitan*, April 7, 2016, https://www.cosmopolitan.com/sex-love/news/a56502/things-you-should-never-say-to-someone-with-divorced-parents/.

3. Rachel Moss, "20 Things You Should Never Say to Someone Who's Just Lost Their Job," *HuffPost*, updated September 22, 2020, https://www.huffingtonpost.co.uk/entry/20-things-you-should-never-say-to-someone-whos-just-lost-their-job_uk_5f632481c5b6184558671167.

Church Privacy 101

## *10. Medical Privacy: Your Body Is the Temple*

1. PBS, *Finding Your Roots*, "About the Series," Accessed June 23, 2023, https://www.pbs.org/weta/finding-your-roots/about/about-series.

2. Adele Peters, "DNA Testing Is Being Used to Keep Families Apart–Not Reunify Them," *Fast Company*, July 11, 2018, https://www.fastcompany.com/90200992/dna-testing-is-being-used-to-keep-families-apart-not-reunify-them.

3. Heather Murphy and Mihir Zaveri, "Pentagon Warns Military Personnel Against At-Home DNA Tests," *New York Times*, December 24, 2019, https://www.nytimes.com/2019/12/24/us/military-dna-tests.html.

4. Jocelyn Kaiser, "A Judge Said Police Can Search the DNA of 1 Million Americans without Their Consent. What's Next?" *Science*, November 7, 2019, https://www.science.org/content/article/judge-said-police-can-search-dna-millions-americans-without-their-consent-what-s-next.

5. Peter Aldhous, "This Genealogy Database Helped Solve Dozens of Crimes. But Its New Privacy Rules Will Restrict Access by Cops," *BuzzFeed News*, May 19, 2019, https://www.buzzfeednews.com/article/peteraldhous/this-genealogy-database-helped-solve-dozens-of-crimes-but.

6. Dianne Small-Jordan, "Organ Harvesting, Human Trafficking, and the Black Market," *The Millennium Report*, November 28, 2017, https://themillenniumreport.com/2017/11/organ-harvesting-human-trafficking-and-the-black-market/.

7. Scott Carney, "Inside the Business of Selling Human Body Parts," *Wired*, January 31, 2011, https://www.wired.com/2011/01/ff_redmarkets/.

## *11. Privacy in Marriage and Courtship*

1. Maya Angelou, "Maya Angelou Quotes," BrainyQuote.com, accessed July 6, 2023, https://www.brainyquote.com/quotes/maya_angelou_383371.

2. Wikipedia, s.v. "Spokeo, Inc. v. Robins," last modified January 29, 2023, https://en.wikipedia.org/wiki/Spokeo, Inc. v. Robins.

# Notes

3. HG Legal Resources, "Facebook Has Become a Leading Cause in Divorce Cases," accessed July 6, 2023, https://www.hg.org/legal-articles/facebook-has-become-a-leading-cause-in-divorce-cases-27803.

4. HG Legal Resources, "Facebook Has Become a Leading Cause in Divorce Cases."

5. HG Legal Resources, "Facebook Has Become a Leading Cause in Divorce Cases."

6. HG Legal Resources, "Facebook Has Become a Leading Cause in Divorce Cases."

7. HG Legal Resources, "Facebook Has Become a Leading Cause in Divorce Cases."

8. The People of the State of Illinois, Appellant, v. Bethany Austin, Appellee, 2019 IL 123910 (2019), https://law.justia.com/cases/illinois/supreme-court/2019/123910.html.

9. *First Amendment Watch*, "Illinois Supreme Court Rules That Revenge Porn Is Not Protected by the First Amendment," May 21, 2019, https://firstamendmentwatch.org/is-revenge-porn-protected-by-the-first-amendment/.

10. *Austin*, 2019 IL 123910.

11. SWGfL, "Research Reveals Gendered Trends in Revenge Porn Crimes," August 23, 2019, https://swgfl.org.uk/magazine/revenge-porn-research-2019/.

12. Katie Smith, "Illinois Supreme Court Reverses Ruling in 'Revenge Porn' Case," *Northwest Herald*, October 30, 2019, https://www.nwherald.com/2019/10/29/illinois-supreme-court-reverses-ruling-in-revenge-porn-case/afathon/.

13. Joshua Espinoza, "Woman Awarded $3.2 Million in Revenge Porn Case Against Her Ex-Husband and His New Girlfriend," *Complex*, August 27, 2019, https://www.complex.com/life/a/cmplxjoshua-espinoza/north-carolina-woman-receives-over-3-million-dollars-in-revenge-porn-case.

14. Paul Larkin, "Fighting Back Against 'Revenge Porn,'" The Heritage Foundation, February 23, 2017, https://www.heritage.org/crime-and-justice/report/fighting-back-against-revenge-porn.

15. Larkin, "Fighting Back Against 'Revenge Porn.'"

## 12. Parenting and Privacy at Home

1. Stacia Tauscher, "Stacia Tauscher Quotes," Goodreads, accessed July 7, 2023, https://www.goodreads.com/quotes/7572812-we-worry-about-what-a-child-will-become-tomorrow-yet.

## 13. Family Privacy and Safety

1. *Merriam-Webster Dictionary*, s.v. "dirty laundry," accessed May 31, 2023, https://www.merriam-webster.com/dictionary/dirty%20laundry.

2. Tom Porter, "How FDR Kept His Partial Paralysis a Secret from the American Public—Even While He Was on the Campaign Trail," *Insider*, May 10, 2019, https://www.businessinsider.com.au/how-fdr-hid-his-paralysis-from-american-public-even-while-campaigning-2019-4.

3. Jonathan H. Levy, "Can I Record a Phone Call without Telling the Other Person?" Avvo, May 18, 2009, https://www.avvo.com/legal-guides/ugc/can-i-record-a-phone-call-without-telling-the-other-person.

4. *Associated Press*, "Rise in Teen Suicide Connected to Social Media Popularity: Study," *New York Post*, November 14, 2017, https://nypost.com/2017/11/14/rise-in-teen-suicide-connected-to-social-media-popularity-study/.

5. Jeremy Redmon, "CDC: Suicide Is Second Leading Cause of Death for People 10 to 34," EMS1, December 29, 2022, https://www.ems1.com/suicide/articles/cdc-suicide-is-second-leading-cause-of-death-for-people-10-to-34-ozEOelXE9iKJymc7/.

6. SAVE, "Suicide Statistics: 2021 USA General Statistics," January 12, 2023, https://save.org/about-suicide/suicide-statistics/.

# Notes

7. Jacqueline Howard, "Suicide Rates among America's Young People Continue to Soar, Study Shows," *CNN Health*, June 18, 2019, https://www.cnn.com/2019/06/18/health/suicide-rates-teens-young-adults-us-study/index.html.

8. CDC, "The Relationship Between Bullying and Suicide: What We Know and What It Means for Schools," National Center for Injury Prevention and Control, 2014, https://www.cdc.gov/violenceprevention/pdf/bullying-suicide-translation-final-a.pdf.

9. Rob Gabriele, "5 Child Identity Theft Statistics Every Parent Should Know," SafeHome.org, June 11, 2023, https://www.safehome.org/news/child-identity-theft-protection/.

10. Gerry Smith, "Family Secrets: Parents Prey on Children's Identities as Victims Stay Silent," *HuffPost*, updated December 6, 2017, https://www.huffpost.com/entry/child-identity-theft-parents-credit-fraud-debt_n_1010093.

11. State of Minnesota, Respondent, v. Daniel Joseph Decker, Appellant, No. A16-0830 Minnesota Ct. App. (August 8, 2018), https://law.justia.com/cases/minnesota/supreme-court/2018/a16-0830.html.

12. Bill Chappell, "'Playboy' Model Sentenced Over Body-Shaming Woman at Gym," *The Two-Way*, May 25, 2017, https://www.npr.org/sections/thetwo-way/2017/05/25/529999618/playboy-model-sentenced-over-body-shaming-woman-at-gym.

13. Got Questions, "What Does It Mean to Uncover Nakedness in the Bible," accessed July 10, 2023, https://www.gotquestions.org/uncover-nakedness.html.

14. *Harvard Law Review*, "Packingham v. North Carolina," vol. 131, no. 1 (November 2017), https://harvardlawreview.org/2017/11/packingham-v-north-carolina/.

15. *Harvard Law Review*, "Packingham v. North Carolina."

16. Lester Gerard Packingham, Petitioner v. North Carolina, 137 S. Ct. 1730 (2017), https://casetext.com/case/packingham-v-north-carolina-1.

17. Eliana Dockterman, "Can Bad Men Change? What It's Like inside Sex Offender Therapy," *Time*, updated May 14, 2018, https://time.com/5272337/sex-offenders-therapy-treatment/.

18. Dockterman, "Can Bad Men Change?"

19. Sam Benson Smith, "SBCSD: Man Who Met 13-Year-Old Victim at Church Arrested for 29 Palms Child Pornography," *KESQ News*, February 3, 2020, https://kesq.com/news/2020/02/03/sbcsd-man-who-met-13-year-old-victim-at-church-arrested-for-29-palms-child-pornography/.

20. Kate Cox, "Unredacted Suit Shows Google's Own Engineers Confused by Privacy Settings," *Ars Technica*, August 25, 2020, https://arstechnica.com/tech-policy/2020/08/unredacted-suit-shows-googles-own-engineers-confused-by-privacy-settings/.

21. Howard Steven Friedman, "You Are Responsible for Your Own (Facebook) Privacy," *Huffington Post*, updated May 25, 2011, https://www.huffpost.com/entry/you-are-responsible-for-y_b_830652.

22. Allen St. John, "How Facebook Tracks You, Even When You're Not on Facebook," *Consumer Reports*, April 11, 2018, https://www.consumerreports.org/privacy/how-facebook-tracks-you-even-when-youre-not-on-facebook/.

23. Thomas Brewster, "Facebook Is Playing Games with Your Privacy and There's Nothing You Can Do about It," *Forbes*, June 29, 2016, https://www.forbes.com/sites/thomasbrewster/2016/06/29/facebook-location-tracking-friend-games/?sh=5793a92735f9.

24. Brewster, "Facebook Is Playing Games."

## *14. Privacy in Your Relationships*

1. "Cover Photo," *O, The Oprah Magazine*, September 2019.

2. Oprah Winfrey, "The Keys to Lasting Friendship," *O The Oprah Magazine*, September 2019, 128.

3. Molly Sims and Amy Maclin, "Companion Commandment," *O The Oprah Magazine*, September 2019, 95.

4. Sims and Maclin, "Companion Commandment."

# Notes

5. Fred Rogers, "Fred Rogers Quotes," Goodreads, accessed August 7, 2023, https://www.goodreads.com/quotes/180952-love-isn-t-a-state-of-perfect-caring-it-is-an.

## 15. Keep Your Private Life Private

1. Lydia O'Connor, "Even the Dead Have Been Displaced by Louisiana Flooding," *Huffington Post*, August 18, 2016, https://www.huffpost.com/entry/louisiana-flooding-caskets_n_57b5e6d7e4b034dc73262ee2.

2. Moyena Parikh, "Throwback to 10 of the Most Expensive Royal Weddings of All Time," *Lifestyle Asia*, February 26, 2022, https://www.lifestyleasia.com/ind/weddings/biggest-most-expensive-royal-weddings-in-history/.

3. Jack Slate, "The Duchess of Cambridge's Wedding Bouquet Featured a Flower Called Sweet William and Hinted at the Couple They Were to Become Years Later," *Woman&Home*, April 29, 2023, https://www.womanandhome.com/life/royal-news/the-duchess-of-cambridges-wedding-bouquet-featured-a-flower-called-sweet-william-and-hinted-at-the-couple-they-were-to-become-years-later/.

4. Amy Duncan, "How Much Did the Royal Wedding Cost and Who Paid for It?" *Metro*, May 22, 2018, https://metro.co.uk/2018/05/22/much-royal-wedding-cost-paid-7567772/.

5. Brittany Wong, "12 Questions You Should Never Ask a Bride or Groom before a Wedding," *HuffPost*, May 17, 2019, https://www.huffpost.com/entry/wedding-questionshouldnt-ask-bride-or-groom_1_5cdd8b06e4b09648227c953f.

6. Sarah Title, "20 Questions You Shouldn't Ask a Couple on Their Wedding Day," WeddingWire, February 7, 2017, https://www.weddingwire.com/wedding-ideas/20-questions-you-shouldnt-ask-a-couple-on-their-wedding-day.

7. Amanda Garrity and Charlotte Chilton, "The Absolute Rudest Things You Can Do at a Wedding," *Good Housekeeping*, updated August 21, 2020, https://www.goodhousekeeping.com/life/g20651278/bad-wedding-etiquette/.

8. *Pregnancy Corner*, "20 Things You Should Never Say to a Pregnant Woman," updated June 2017, https://www.pregnancycorner.com/blog/things-you-should-never-say.html.

9. Valorie Burton, *Successful Women Think Differently* (Eugene, Oregon: Harvest House Publishers, 2012), 168.

10. Westin, *Privacy and Freedom*, 32.

## 16. Privacy in the Workplace

1. United States of America, Plaintiff–Appellant, v. David Nosal, Defendant–Appellee, 676 F.3d 854 (9th Cir. 2012), https://casetext.com/case/united-states-v-nosal-2.

2. *JD Supra*, "Breaking: David Nosal Sentenced to Prison on CFAA Computer Intrusion and Trade Secret Charges," January 9, 2014, https://www.jdsupra.com/legalnews/breaking-david-nosal-sentenced-to-priso-81789/.

3. *JD Supra*, "Breaking: David Nosal Sentenced to Prison."

4. FBI: Los Angeles Division, "Ex-UCLA Healthcare Employee Sentenced to Federal Prison for Illegally Peeking at Patient Records," April 27, 2010, https://archives.fbi.gov/archives/losangeles/press-releases/2010/la042710a.htm.

5. Caroline Black, "Hanks, Barrymore, Schwarzenegger: Medical Files Breached at UCLA, Researcher Convicted," *CBS News*, April 29, 2010, https://www.cbsnews.com/news/hanks-barrymore-schwarzenegger-medical-files-breached-at-ucla-reseacher-convicted/.

## 17. Privacy in the Afterlife

1. Empathy's Estate Specialists, "Identity Theft after Death: A Widespread Problem," *Empathy*, accessed February 15, 2024, https://www.empathy.com/identity-theft-prevention/identity-theft-after-death-a-widespread-problem.

2. Greg Iacurci, "IRS Flagged More than 1 Million Tax Returns for Identity Fraud in 2023," CNBC, May 17, 2023, https://www.cnbc.com/2023/05/17/irs-flagged-more-than-1-million-tax-returns-for-identity-fraud-in-2023.html.

# Notes

3. Funeralocity, "How to Manage Family Conflict When Planning a Funeral," November 29, 2023, https://www.funeralocity.com/blog/2018/09/27/avoiding-family-fights-at-funerals/.

4. Angie Chatman, "When My Mother Died without a Will, I Learned a Big Lesson about Management as an African American," *Business Insider*, September 9, 2019, https://www.businessinsider.com/what-mothers-death-taught-me-about--as-african-american-2019-9.

5. Kim Bryan, "5 Kids Who Killed Their Parents for the Insurance," *The Crime Wire*, January 10, 2023, https://thecrimewire.com/true-crime/children-who-murdered-parents-.

6. Kevin Dolak, "Woman Leaves $13M Fortune to Pet Cat," *ABC News*, December 12, 2011, https://abcnews.go.com/blogs/headlines/2011/12/woman-leaves-13m-fortune-to-pet-cat.

7. Chatman, "When My Mother Died without a Will."

8. Cyfor Secure, "Cyber-Attacks against Law Firms Are Increasing. Is Your Firm Secure?" accessed July 12, 2023, https://cyfor.co.uk/cyber-attacks-law-firms-increasing-firm-secure/.

9. Sid Kirchheimer, "Grave Robbery: Stop Identity Theft of the Dead," *Today*, May 8, 2007, https://www.today.com/news/grave-robbery-stop-identity-theft-dead-wbna18495531.

## 18. People Who Leave the Church

1. Dave Ramsey, "Tithes and Offerings: Your Questions, Answered," Ramsey.com, May 31, 2023 (quoted in Enon Baptist Church, "Give," accessed July 21, 2023, https://www.ebcjayess.org/donate).

2. Randy Alcorn, "Should Giving Always Be Kept Secret?" Eternal Perspective Ministries, March 11, 2010, https://www.epm.org/resources/2010/Mar/11/should-giving-always-be-kept-secret/.

3. Alcorn, "Should Giving Always Be Kept Secret?"

## Conclusion

1. IRS, "Tax Guide for Churches and Religious Organizations," accessed June 20, 2023, https://www.irs.gov/pub/irs-pdf/p1828.pdf.

www.ingramcontent.com/pod-product-compliance
Lightning Source LLC
Chambersburg PA
CBHW030538080526
44585CB00012B/191